PATTERNS OF INFIDELITY AND THEIR TREATMENT

PATTERNS OF INFIDELITY AND THEIR TREATMENT

Second Edition

Emily M. Brown, MSW, LCSW

BRUNNER-ROUTLEDGE
ALERE FLAMMAM
Taylor & Francis Group

USA	Publishing Office:	BRUNNER-ROUTLEDGE
		A member of the Taylor & Francis Group
		325 Chestnut Street
		Philadelphia, PA 19106
		Tel: (215) 625-8900
		Fax: (215) 625-2940
	Distribution Center:	BRUNNER-ROUTLEDGE
		A member of the Taylor & Francis Group
		7625 Empire Drive
		Florence, KY 41042
		Tel: 1-800-634-7064
		Fax: 1-800-248-4724
UK		BRUNNER-ROUTLEDGE
		A member of the Taylor & Francis Group
		27 Church Road
		Hove
		E. Sussex, BN3 2FA
		Tel: +44 (0) 1273 207411
		Fax: +44 (0) 1273 205612

PATTERNS OF INFIDELITY AND THEIR TREATMENT, 2/E

1 2 3 4 5 6 7 8 9 0

Printed by Edwards Brothers, Ann Arbor, MI, 2001.
Cover design by Curt Tow.

A CIP catalog record for this book is available from the British Library.
∞ The paper in this publication meets the requirements of the ANSI Standard Z39.48-1984 (Permanence of Paper)

Library of Congress Cataloging-in-Publication Data

Brown, Emily M.
    Patterns of infidelity and their treatment / Emily M. Brown.—2nd ed.
        p. cm.
    Includes bibliographical references and index.
    ISBN 1-58391-369-6 (alk. paper)
    1. Marital psychotherapy. 2. Adultery. I. Title.

    RC488.5.B75 2001
    616.89'156—dc21

                                                                    2001018084

ISBN 1-58391-369-6 (case)

CONTENTS

126068

ACKNOWLEDGMENTS

I felt sustained, embraced, and energized by the sharing and support I received while writing this second edition. Whenever I needed information, feedback, encouragement, or distraction, it was there. The process of writing was made easier by this community of support.

My thanks go especially to those clients, workshop participants, friends, and strangers who lived with an affair and told me how it was. You shared with me your stories, your pain, and your ways of coming to a resolution, and although I cannot use your names, your words and experiences are present here. Some of you critiqued the manuscript as well. You have been most generous, and I continue to learn from you.

My appreciation goes as well to the many workshop participants who challenged me, who offered their insights, and otherwise sharpened my thinking about affairs and their treatment.

To those friends and colleagues who read, supported, critiqued, and offered ideas about the manuscript, I am especially appreciative. They include: Venus Masselam, Ph.D.; Betsy Mandel-Carly, M.S.W.; Isolina Ricci, Ph.D.; Diane Wiltjer; Marcia Lebowitz, M.S.W.; Dick Anderson; Linda Girdner, Ph.D.; Peter Maida, Ph.D., J.D.; and Karen Smith, Ph.D.

And finally, my thanks to Lansing Hays, Tim Julet, Katherine Mortimer, and all the others at Brunner-Routledge who have contributed to making the second edition a reality.

PREFACE

Affairs are an issue that we as therapists have all struggled with. They are emotionally loaded, and there has not been much guidance in how to help our clients address an affair. It is easy to get tangled up in the emotions that are generated by affairs.

My interest in affairs began with annoyance—annoyance that divorce was so often equated with affairs, and affairs with divorce. It just is not so. However, an affair at the end of the marriage muddies the waters, obscuring the real issues and making the divorce more difficult. I also found that some affairs are relatively easy to treat, which surprised me because that is not the way it's supposed to be. Other affairs were tremendously difficult. I began to realize that affairs differ greatly in meaning, and that treatment needs to vary accordingly. My fascination with the dynamics of love and betrayal as they are played out in affairs, began to grow.

I have learned from my mistakes as well as my successes. When I colluded in keeping the secret, we all got trapped in a dysfunctional triangle. When I permitted obsessing about the affair to continue, the process got stuck. I did not understand the importance of closure in the way I do now. I learned that helping people who have cared about each other be honest about an affair is painful, but the alternative is paralyzing.

My goal is to provide a framework for therapists to use in evaluating and treating clients when there is an affair. I assume that you already have many techniques that you find effective in working with couples. Therefore, I focus on the unique aspects of treating affairs, and not on couples treatment in general. The issues that I believe are the most important or the most difficult are emphasized. My approach is primarily systemic, an approach I find useful whether the client is the individual, the couple, the family, or the child. To avoid the awkwardness of he/she pronouns, a single pronoun is sometimes used. This does not reflect a gender bias, nor does it necessarily mean that the role under discussion is usually taken by that gender. Gender differences, when they exist, are clearly stated.

The approach described here is not to be applied to the population at large, but only to those who seek our professional help. For example, I believe it is essential for couples in marital therapy to reveal a hidden affair (subject to the caveats in Chapter 3). However to apply this standard to couples not in therapy is inappropriate. These couples may be choosing to live their lives in a different, possibly less intimate, manner but that is their choice.

This framework for understanding and treating affairs is based on my experience in helping hundreds of individuals and couples in their struggle with an affair, discussions with my professional colleagues, and conversations with others who have been willing to share their own experiences. These people have been instrumental in helping me develop and refine this framework. I have listened to the words and tried to understand their meaning.

Although I have drawn on real people and real situations, details have been changed to protect identities. As Morton Hunt (1969) said, "Any resemblance to real persons is strictly intentional; any identification with real persons is, I trust, impossible" (p. xv).

The interest I have in affairs began with annoyance, shifted to fascination with the dynamics of love and betrayal, and has been sustained by opportunities for healing. I hope that you will take what I offer, see how it works for you, and expand on it.

I

PATTERNS OF INFIDELITY

Love and betrayal, those powerful and human themes, are most dramatic in the extramarital affair. Affairs and the emotions they arouse have been described over the centuries in literature, history, and religion. Works of art depict scenes of the unfaithful. Modern tales are told in movies, song, and other media. Both old and new tales recount great passions and deadly secrets, deep love and idyllic illusions, pain and punishment, and in some cases redemption and healing. With such great drama, it is no wonder that now, as in the past, affairs capture everyone's interest.

Our interest in affairs is not just dramatic appreciation. Our personal stake runs high. Family is where we have a feeling of belonging, whether we like our family members or not. Anything that disrupts the family threatens our sense of belonging. Affairs threaten the structure of the family and thus our very basis of belonging. An affair arouses and fuels our fear of abandonment, a feeling so basic and primitive it goes to the core of our being.

Pointing a finger at those who have an affair seems at times to be a way of saying "It can't happen to me."

Simmel (1950) asserts: "Existence rests on a thousand premises which the single individual cannot trace and verify . . . but must take on faith. Our modern life is based . . . upon the faith in the honesty of the other. . . . If the few persons closest to us lie, life becomes unbearable" (p. 313).

For the spouse, the betrayal seems unbearable. But for the unfaithful partner, the affair is an aphrodisiac. The aura of romance and intrigue is compelling, especially when reality feels barren or boring. Affairs promise so much: an opportunity to pursue dreams that have been dormant, a chance to come alive again and the hope of connecting with someone who truly understands. Their hidden promise is pain.

☐ Our Society and Affairs: The Attraction and the Threat

Despite the prevalence of affairs, as a society we remain both intrigued and threatened. The idea of an affair conjures up romantic fantasies and dreams of forbidden sexual desires, along with fears of betrayal and emotional devastation. As a society we have developed various methods for minimizing these threatening feelings. Our laws are a method of inducing people to stay within accepted boundaries of behavior. The heavy punishment exacted, until recently, of adulterers in our divorce courts was intended to reduce the number of affairs, thus lessening the threat. Religion inveighs against the sin of adultery. Again this is a dual thrust. Religion attempts to prevent adultery and, failing that, to place the offenders outside the social boundaries; to distance "them" from "us." When the adulterer is a minister and thus charged with keeping moral order, our righteous outrage at the betrayal of that charge is even stronger.

The approach to affairs presented in this book is specific to our culture and to those cultures that are most like ours. Culture shapes the particular ways in which personal issues are expressed. Of most importance however, is the meaning of the affair within the particular marriage. The culture provides the context, but specific meanings are learned in the family of origin.

Double Messages

Ours is a society that values marriage, but that has a mixed heritage and great ambivalence regarding sexuality. On one hand, adultery continues to be used in our legal system as a tool for administering blame and punishment. At the same time the entertainment world creates a continual stream of movies and television shows that use an affair as the major story line. Pornography is hated, yet it is big business. Arguments abound over the line between art and pornography. One branch of the federal government designs a National Survey of Health and Sexual Behavior, but "politicians, federal health officials and bureaucrats at the Office of Management and Budget . . . have frozen the study in committees, conferences and councils" (Specter, 1990, p. B1). American families constantly receive and transmit mixed messages about sexuality and about affairs.

The movies too, convey dual messages about affairs. They invite us into the fantasy then help us control our anxiety about the affair. Movies that have an affair as part of the story line tend to be either comedies or murder mysteries. In the murder mysteries, the bad guy gets punished, getting the message across once more that it is the outsider, the bad guy, not us, who has an affair. Comedies, such as "Hannah and Her Sisters" make light of the threat: if we can laugh at the affair, it is not so threatening.

Double Standards

In addition to the duality within our culture about affairs, the double standard pertains as well. In "Fatal Attraction" (Lyne, 1987), Alex, the unmarried lover, dies, while Dan, the straying partner, ends up in a warm embrace with his wife. (Of course therapists know that this miracle cure for the Conflict Avoidance Affair will be short lived. If Dan and his wife are smart they will call for a therapy appointment soon.) If the straying partner was a woman and the unmarried lover was male, we would see a different ending. The husband would be a hero of sorts, and his cheating wife would be out in the cold.

Ellen Goodman (1998) contrasted the public's response to Hillary Clinton's efforts at health care reform and her public humiliation by the Bill and Monica scandal. Goodman speculates that perhaps Americans, "prefer a betrayed woman to an uppity woman" (p. A19).

The double standard also is alive in books such as *The Rules* (Fein & Schneider, 1996) which suggests it is the woman's responsibility to keep her husband from straying. If he has an affair, she must somehow be at fault. Unfortunately, many women believe this, as do many of their husbands. TV talk shows hammer home the same message. Even when the host and the guests do not assume the man's affair is the wife's fault, many in the audience do. And if the woman has an affair, that's her fault too.

☐ Affairs in Other Cultures

Some societies view affairs quite differently than does ours. In a highly publicized trial in 1989 in New York, a man who had murdered his wife because she was having an affair, was sentenced to five years probation. He had recently immigrated from China, and testimony provided by an anthropologist indicated that "the Chinese hold marriage to be sacred and that a Chinese man could 'reasonably be expected to become enraged' upon learning of his wife's Infidelity" (Yen, 1989, p. A3).

For years the Irish ruefully referred to affairs as the Irish divorce. It has been only since 1997 that divorce is an option in Ireland. Before then the Irish developed the alternative of long serious affairs, much like what we would call serial monogamy, but without the benefit of divorce or remarriage. (Of course the Irish were not strangers to other types of affairs.)

Melina Mercouri describes the Greek man as "A good friend and a good husband because, although he has Infidelity in his blood, he has his wife above all, and he always goes back to her" (Shearer, 1987, p. 19). In cultures where marriages are arranged, the union is based on political and economic factors, rather than the personal or emotional. Affairs then are a way to construct space for the personal within one's life.

An Iranian man observed that in present day Iran, "Married people who commit adultery are generally given a chance to stop the affair. If they don't, in some cases they are executed." (Heavey, 1998, p. E10). In Pakistan, honor killings—women killed by a relative when they are judged to have shamed the family—occur at the approximate rate of 500 per year (Beattie, 1999).

The mistress system still continues in parts of the world. The wife and the children of the marriage have the husband's name and whatever perks come with his name. The husband is entitled to have as many additional women and children as he can afford, provided they don't usurp the wife's status. Married women in these cultures who have an affair, or are even suspected of doing so, may pay with their lives. This is especially true in rural areas. In Africa, an important contributing factor to the out-of-control AIDS epidemic are the cultural mores that encourage men to have several wives.

In Japan only rich men could afford mistresses until recently because of the high cost of maintaining them (they were usually longterm.) Nowadays, many young girls are looking for easy money and are willing to accept brief liaisons in exchange for luxurious presents or money. Men's affairs, especially those of high ranking officials, are viewed as normal. When Clinton's affair with Monica surfaced, the talk among the Japanese was that Americans were overreacting and that all men in power are the same. "It's no big deal," so why not just accept it and forget about it? However an acclaimed Japanese film-maker committed suicide after learning that a magazine was going to publish a story alleging he was having an affair (Sullivan, 1997). Maybe the most significant point is that affairs engender stronger feelings when they are close to home.

In times past, "Adultery was punished in many North American Indian tribes by cutting off the hair, amputating the ears, the lips, or the nose, and sometimes by beatings. In the Carolines [Caroline Islands], by contrast, the matter was settled with small gifts" (Mantegazza, 1935, p. 200). Other cultures had their own methods for dealing with sexual infidelity, many of which were physically punitive. Today's spouses often fantasize about similar punishment for their straying partner.

☐ Who Has an Affair?

As you might imagine, accurate statistics on affairs are hard to come by. The secrecy that is intrinsic to an affair inhibits research as does the emotional freight carried by the topic. Judging from the available statistics, the incidence of affairs appears to be increasing, particularly among younger women who are now participating in affairs at a higher rate than their husbands (Lawson, 1988). However, there is a difference between early intent and later behavior. Using a British sample, Lawson also found that "over 90 percent of women and over 80 percent of men intended to remain sexually faithful at the point of their first marriage" (p. 69), and expected the same of their spouse. This decreased during marriage, so that about 53% of those still married to a first spouse at the time of the study believed in fidelity. However, 88% of remarried women strongly believed in fidelity. Only 57% of remarried men shared that belief.

Estimates of the incidence of affairs range from 16.3% of ever-married adults (Laumann, Gagnon, Michael, & Michaels, 1994) to 70% of all women (Hite, 1987). A large national study (Laumann, Gagnon, Michael, & Michaels, 1994) found that only 21% of the men and 12.8% of the women had participated in an affair. However, it is likely that many of the respondents have not yet had an affair but will have one in the future. And it's certain that some others are not telling. Hite's data, at the other end of the continuum, raises questions about reliability (Streitfeld, 1987).

A review of research on infidelity by Maggie Scarf (1987) indicates that about 55% of married men have affairs, and 45% of married women have affairs. Looking at these statistics in terms of the couple suggests that about 70% of marriages experience an affair at some point during the marriage. In a therapy practice, especially one focusing on issues of marriage and divorce, a very high rate of affairs is to be expected.

Buss (2000) seems to have the most believable estimates. Based on a number of studies, he states that, "Approximately 20 to 40 percent of American women and 30 to 50 percent of American men have at least one affair over the course of the marriage." This is the rate for individuals. The number of marriages that experience an affair is higher. Thompson (1983) suggests it may be as high as 76%.

Salovey and Rodin (1985) found that 45% of the respondents to a survey on jealousy and envy admitted to an affair, although 72% considered monogamy very important and another 20% considered it important. This gap between behavior and belief is common for issues that carry a high emotional charge.

On an irreverent note, Jonathan Yardley (1988) notes that "The average American newsroom makes a rabbit hutch seem a model of monogamous placidity. To say this is not to endorse such behavior but to acknowledge its universality. Rabbits stray, and so do people; this is unfortunate and can have unhappy effects on the lives of those touched by it, but it is a manifestation not of malignity but of human fallibility" (p. D2).

For the most part, surveys provide conservative figures, based on what people are willing to reveal. Many people will not admit to an affair for fear of disapproval or negative repercussions, or because they have not fully acknowledged it to themselves, let alone their spouse. Some research designs work against honesty about infidelity, as when the possibility of a follow-up interview arouses fears that the spouse will learn of one's affair in the process. In other studies many of those surveyed have not yet had an affair, but will at some future time, and thus the findings do not reflect lifetime rates. Reliability of the study also is affected by the number of participants who refuse to answer questions about affairs or drop out of the study.

Maybe the most accurate comment of all is that of social researcher Tom Smith of the University of Chicago: "There are probably more scientifically worthless 'facts' on extra-marital relations than on any other facet of human behavior" (Morin, 1994, p. A17).

☐ Differences Between Men and Women

Gender differences appear repeatedly in studies on infidelity. The participation, justifications, reactions, and outcomes for each type of affair are influenced by different expectations of men and women. Gender differences also mean that certain types of affairs are more common for men and others for women. Further complexity is added by the social changes of the last few decades in which expectations about life, love, and work, as a man or as a woman, have changed dramatically. Data from the 60s and 70s needs to be examined in the context of the sex role expectations for men and women which were prevalent at that time. Women coming of age in the 80s, 90s, and 2000s grew up with very different messages than those in earlier generations.

Until recently, married men were much more likely to have an affair than were their wives. (Kinsey, Pomeroy, & Martin, 1948; Kinsey, Pomeroy, Martin, & Gebbhard, 1953; Thompson, 1983). Now the overall rate of participation is similar for men and women. However young married women are more likely to participate in an affair than are their husbands. Part of the change has to do with women's sweeping move into the workplace and the resulting increase in their opportunities for an affair. Women however, differ from men in their use of such opportunities. Women who are happy in their marriages are unaware of opportunities for an affair. For men, opportunity and prior justification are predictive of an affair. (Glass & Wright, 1989). Not surprisingly, men still have more lovers than do women (Lawson, 1988).

Affairs come sooner in marriage than in the past according to Lawson's (1988) study. Almost two thirds of the women and nearly half the men marrying for the first time in the 70s had an affair within the first five years of marriage. This was true for only one fourth of those who married before 1960. Younger women have affairs sooner than their husbands, while just the reverse is true for those married before 1960. Thus the younger marriages occurred in the context of the sexual freedom of the 60s and 70s.

Johnson's 1970 study indicated that twice as many husbands as wives had an affair. However, only 29% of the women reported having an opportunity as compared to 72% of the men. When viewed in this manner, women in the study participated in affairs at a greater rate than did their husbands, and look rather similar to young wives today. Possibly opportunity is a more important variable for women than has been realized in the past.

The growing similarities between younger men and women contrast with the significant differences found between men and women at older ages as to the decision whether to have an affair and the choice of a partner. Lawson (1988) found that women married after 1970 waited only four years (one year less than did men) to have their first affair, whereas women married before 1960 waited 14.6 years (four years longer than did the men). Among the younger generation "Men have begun (statistically speaking) to 'look like' women, and vice versa" (Lawson, 1988, p. 78). Even so, "There remain striking differences because for women the experience of adultery and divorce is different and much more serious than for men" (Lawson, 1988, p. 288).

Type of Involvement

Involvement in an affair can be sexual, emotional, or both. Women are more likely than men to be emotionally involved in an affair, while men's involvement more often emphasizes the sexual (Glass & Wright, 1985; Thompson, 1984). The combination of sexual and emotional involvement presents a greater threat to the marriage than either sexual or emotional involvement alone. Marital dissatisfaction is greater, when both sexual and emotional involvement are present (Glass & Wright, 1985). This dissatisfaction, coupled with women's greater likelihood of emotional involvement, would suggest that women are more likely than men to leave their marriage to pursue the affair. On the other hand, economic factors and parental responsibilities often work in the opposite direction, holding women in the marriage.

Glass and Wright (1985) postulate a double code in which men and women approach extramarital relationships in ways that parallel their sex-role behaviors in premarital and marital relationships. The female "code" of extramarital behavior permits women to be emotionally but not sexually involved with another man. The male "code" prohibits emotional, although not sexual, involvement with other women.

Marital Dissatisfaction and Affairs

A variety of studies report that married women, much more than married men, become involved in an affair because of their dissatisfaction with the emotional content of their marriage or their desire for an emotionally satisfying relationship (Buss, 1989; Glass & Wright, 1985; Lawson, 1988; Spring, 1996). "Women see sex as following from emotional intimacy, while men see sex itself as a road to intimacy" (Gottman & Krokoff, 1989). Thus it is not surprising that women's marital dissatisfaction centers on emotional issues, while men's dissatisfaction focuses on the lack of sex.

Even in the 2000s many young women still hold traditional sex role expectations: In puzzling over why she had an affair 18 months into her marriage Lucy declared, "He gave me everything I ever wanted." A few weeks later she insisted, "If something's wrong it's not anything about him. I'm to blame." It was only some time later that Lucy acknowledged that she had been very disappointed with her husband's frequent moodiness. She had felt it was somehow her fault, and had not said anything to her husband, instead turning to someone else.

For men, sexual dissatisfaction in the marriage is a major complaint and is correlated with extramarital sex (Buss, 2000; Glass & Wright, 1992; Johnson, 1970). Given this complaint, it is not surprising then that men's affairs most often begin with sexual involvement, and emotional involvement comes later, if at all. For women just the opposite is true, with emotional involvement preceding sexual involvement. (Glass & Wright, 1989).

Clinical experience matches research findings indicating that a woman's affair is more likely to threaten the marriage (Glass & Wright, 1989; Lawson, 1988). Women who have affairs tend to be more dissatisfied with their marriage than are men, and are more likely to be emotionally involved with the third party, both factors increasing the likelihood of divorce.

☐ Reasons for the Increased Participation in Affairs

Why the current increase in affairs? A common response is that the increase is due to a moral breakdown in our society. Others point to birth control which allows for much greater sexual freedom. Women's increased participation in the workplace certainly provides many more opportunities for women to have affairs. Some suggest that people are focusing on the personal whereas in the past they were more concerned with family and community. Some say there is no increase in the number of affairs.

Murstein (1974) contends "The transitory nature of employment patterns and of interpersonal relations has weakened the supportive role once given by peers, parents, and community. Monogamy is now asked to bear alone a rather overwhelming burden. In addition, all the educational media stress the search for self-actualization" (p. 544).

Hunt (1969) claims that extramarital love is "Everyman's answer to the impersonality, the disconnectedness, the gigantism of modern society." . . . "Love is a way to remain human in an inhuman society; it is therefore more prized, in every form, than ever" (pp. 283–284).

The most likely explanation for the increase in affairs is a confluence of factors: our greater expectations for emotional satisfaction in marriage, the tremendous deficiency in communication and relationship skills, the sexual revolution, and the changing structure of daily life. For example, communication about feelings becomes more important when emotional satisfaction is the goal of marriage, yet as a society we do little to help children learn these skills. Women are feeling more entitled than ever before to emotional satisfaction, and seek it in the workplace as well as at home. Our economic structure has changed in recent decades, bringing drastic changes to daily life, so that couples who only a few generations ago would have worked together on the farm, now see little of each other during their waking hours. Instead they spend most of their working hours away from home, involved, sometimes intimately, with others. And the internet has added the search option for finding new partners.

The decades of the 60s and 70s were the first time in history when sex has been relatively risk free. STDs could be cured, and "the pill" had arrived. This coincided with an era in which personal growth and feeling good were emphasized. It is no wonder that the number of affairs increased! In the 80s AIDS became very visible but the widespread disbelief that AIDS posed a serious threat to heterosexuals meant sexual behavior among heterosexuals changed little. The 90s and 2000s have seen an increased interest in nesting, but no letup in the search to have it all. It seems likely that the current emphasis on children's performance and achievement will result in a bumper crop of Split Self Affairs in the future.

☐ The Mental Health Profession, Anxiety, and Affairs

The mental health profession has some catching up to do. In the past we have carefully declined to discuss affairs, and have helped our clients do likewise. Whether it is due to our lack of knowledge about how to proceed, or our own discomforts and fears, our abdication is striking, particularly when seen against a backdrop of increasing popularity of marital therapy.

The mental health field is concerned with shaping behavior, and sometimes allies with law and religion for that purpose. The traditional morality regarding infidelity is a product of such an alliance. "The traditional code justifies the imposition of fidelity not only on religious and moral grounds, but on the ground that it is a *sine qua non* of successful marriage and the happy life" (Hunt, 1969, p. 282).

In other instances law and religion are ignored or rejected by mental health. Ellen Goodman's (1988) analysis of the Bakker-Gorman-Swaggart sex scandals revealed a deep "split between those who analyze human failings in terms of psychology and those who analyze them in terms of scripture. . . . The Swaggart story is the essence of a larger melodrama played before two cultures, one that thinks the preacher has been led astray and another that thinks he's a neurotic mess" (p. A19). Yet for some people financial betrayal is a greater sin than sexual betrayal. At James Bakker's trial on charges of fraud and conspiracy, one witness testified that "I do forgive them for the . . . sexual thing, but I have a hard time dealing with the misuse of money" (*The Washington Post*, 1989, p. C11).

Much like the general public, mental health professionals have mixed emotions and varying experiences with affairs, both their own and those of their clients. We need to understand how our own feelings and experiences with affairs can spill over into our work with clients. When we can separate our own issues from those of our clients, we can engage in the process of therapy in an honest, compassionate, and therapeutic manner.

An Affair is a Family Issue

Affairs have little to do with sex. They are about fear and disappointment, anger and emptiness. They are also about the hope for love and acceptance. When combined with secrecy and betrayal, affairs generate a volatile situation for many couples. The context in which to examine the affair is the family—both the current family and the family of origin.

What does an affair mean for the participants? For the marital partner? For friends and relatives? In what ways is the affair a reenactment of family patterns? And what is to be done when they come to therapy? Thinking systemically is the clearest guide when sorting out the complexities of an affair.

☐ The Marriage

True intimacy depends on talking to each other about joys and sorrows, the mundane and the profound, and the pain and the pleasures, likes and dislikes of life together. It means standing up to each other and confronting differences until they are satisfactorily resolved. Intimacy means sharing who one really is, rather than who one would like to be, and accepting the other for who he or she is. It means caring and comforting, taking and giving. Above all, intimacy means being honest with each other, knowing that each other's word is good. Any false word casts doubts about all the rest.

Marriage is a complex creation, and every marriage has its convolutions. Couples marry for love, fear, money, and an assortment of other reasons, both sound and unsound. Their hopes and intentions for the marriage are colored by what they have learned in their families of origin, by their dreams for something better, and by their sense of self. Each partner does what he or she is able to do to steer the marriage in the desired direction. Couples with emotionally stable backgrounds and some maturity are able to work out a relationship that is more satisfying than not. Couples who do not have the skills or the knowledge to talk about or resolve problems, struggle with the issues as best they know how. For many of them, extramarital affairs are part of the journey in their search for a good relationship.

The Marriage Contract

Couples marry with conscious and unconscious expectations and desires. These are tied to patterns and experiences in the family of origin, as much as to current reality. The spouses agree, or agree to disagree, on matters relating to work and money, children and in-laws, religion and recreation. Sexual fidelity is almost always part of the commitment, whether it is verbalized or assumed (Lawson, 1988; Westfall, 1989).

For many couples, part of the unwritten marital contract is that the spouse will remedy those negative self-perceptions and feelings dating back to childhood. Societal changes in recent years have reinforced this expectation. As Mace and Mace (1959) state, "Dreams of bliss in heaven hereafter have been replaced by dreams of bliss in marriage here and now" (p. 325). Husbands and wives often confuse dependency with intimacy, and are bewildered at why their spouse is not making them feel better about themselves. When such expectations are not met, disappointments not shared, comfort not given or received, the terms of the original contract come under pressure. Or as one young wife described it, "We each had a movie in mind, but it wasn't the same movie."

> After five years of marriage the initial expectations of Ted and Judy are bumping up against reality. Ted was attracted to Judy because he saw her as loving, outgoing, and smart. When she is depressed he does not like it, and is only dimly aware of his expectation that she should be attentive to him when he needs her. Just outside consciousness is Ted's fear of being abandoned which stems from his mother's preference for his older sister. Judy was drawn to Ted because, "He made me feel important."

Ted feels loveable as long as Judy is loving. When she is not, he feels panicky. He attributes his discomfort to Judy's bad mood and nudges her to snap out of it. Underneath he fears that if she finds him unlovable she will abandon him. Judy is upbeat most of the time, but she gets tired of having to work so hard to please Ted. When Ted is not approving, Judy feels unworthy and becomes depressed. She then works harder to gain Ted's approval.

Ted and Judy have made an unconscious contract which enables each to avoid their own issues. Reciprocal behaviors are at the heart of such contracts. Judy for example, devotes herself to Ted's career. Before they were married she helped him get through school, and now she helps him organize himself and his work. Ted is disorganized, losing important papers periodically, and running late most of the time. The bargain they have unconsciously arranged is that Judy will pick up the slack for Ted so that he never feels abandoned, and in return Ted will provide Judy with enough work so that she does not have to risk deciding what she wants to do with her own life.

Judy and Ted committed to a monogamous relationship at the time they became engaged. So far they have both kept their commitment.

The Family of Origin

Affairs are intricately tied to family patterns, particularly in those areas where we have unfinished business. Patterns of avoidance, seduction, secrecy, or betrayal in our families of origin lay the groundwork for turning to an affair when there is a problem. An affair is more likely among those whose parents had an affair (Carnes, 1983; Gerson, 1989). Not only is the parent's affair a model, but so is the pattern of avoidance. If the issues underlying the parent's affair are not addressed, as seems most often to be the case, family members are left on their own to make sense and cope with the affair and its aftermath, sometimes without even knowing it is an affair that is at the heart of their unease. When the family history includes a pattern of affairs, the current affair is clearly a repetition of family of origin issues. In many cases the affair is a dynamic rather than a literal replication of problematic triangles in the family of origin.

☐ Motivations and Precipitants of an Affair

Marriage is a process: a process of learning about one's self and one's spouse, about sharing, about growing up, about being individuals within a family, and about being a member of the family team. The reality of marriage differs from premarital expectations. Neither spouse gets everything she or he hoped for, and both encounter the unexpected. After the honeymoon phase is over, couples have to decide how they will adapt to the gaps between their dreams and the reality of their marriage. Possible adaptations include attempting to change one's partner or one's self, changing patterns of interacting with each other such as improving communication, finding other ways to meet some needs, or accepting the status quo.

An affair is another possible adaptation, with many potential outcomes. An affair indicates that an important emotional element is missing, such as the ability to sustain intimacy or to resolve conflicts without losing self-esteem. Many couples do not talk about the gaps in their marriage. An affair, when used to fill the gap, may enable the marriage to continue as it is, or it may rock the boat enough to stimulate change. In some cases the affair is destructive, either for the spouses, for the marriage, or for both. Whatever the outcome, and however misguided the effort, an affair is an attempt at problem solving.

Setting the Stage

What sets the stage for whether an affair is chosen as a means of adaptation? In part, it depends on the couple's communication and decision making patterns. Jointly made decisions, by spouses who are able to act upon their decisions, usually result in a workable arrangement for both partners. When spouses are unable to communicate honestly with each other about what is happening in their relationship, decisions begin to be made separately. These decisions are made without input from the partner and are often based on erroneous assumptions and misinterpretations. When such a decision is hidden or contradicts the spouses' commitment to each other it creates a situation which is conducive to an affair.

> Ted assumed that Judy didn't really care about him when she began spending more time growing her orchids and violets than helping him. Instead of telling her that, he tried to pick a fight with her, just as his father used to do with his mother. Judy believed it was best not to go looking for trouble (her alcoholic father had provided plenty of it), so she backed away from Ted and turned to her friends. Ted in turn was furious at Judy for not responding to him emotionally, but he kept it all inside. He began to fantasize about an old girlfriend who had recently called, and decided to get together with her, "since Judy doesn't ever want to do anything together."

Research confirms that poor communication and unresolved marital problems are linked to affairs. In the major studies of extramarital sex, marital dissatisfaction emerges as a common motivator, especially for women (Buss, 2000; Glass & Wright, 1985; Scarf, 1987). For example, the women that Atwater (1982) interviewed described their husbands as "inexpressive" and repeatedly mentioned their need for intimacy as the reason for their affairs.

Says Scarf,

> The phase of disillusionment and disenchantment—when disappoint-ment and restlessness are prominent—is one during which sexual acting out is much likelier to happen. Not only is infidelity more probable during this period, but the betrayal of the bond will feel most justified. For it is at this point in their relationship that the husband who has married the 'girl of his dreams' is being forced to come to terms with her fundamental *otherness*. He must, now, recognize the dream for what a dream is. . . . But he may instead, blame her for being different from the person he'd thought he'd married. . . . During the midlife period—when feelings about what has been given up in order to remain with *this* partner, in *this* relationship intensify—the likelihood of an extramarital affair will rise sharply" (1987, p. 21).

Readiness for an Affair

Readiness for an affair is not a static quality but is related to feeling fed up, restless, ready for change. The perception of the marriage shifts, and events are interpreted differently than in the past. The latest rep-etition of an old fight results this time in feeling "This is not where I belong!" The primary identity shifts almost imperceptibly to an indi-vidual identity, with a greater focus on personal growth and indi-vidual responsibility.

The most significant predictor of an affair for women is marital dis-satisfaction. For men, affairs are more related to attitudes, beliefs, and values than to marital dissatisfaction (Glass & Wright, 1985). Premari-tal sexual experience also has been shown to correlate with extra-marital sex (Atwater, 1982; Lawson, 1988).

Clinicians are aware that a common step in the build-up to an affair is commiserating with a friend of the opposite sex about marital prob-lems. The friends become allied against their spouses, thus creating an atmosphere that serves to justify an affair. Atwater's (1982) research with women indicates a link between talking about affairs with some-one who has been a participant in an affair, and personal readiness. It seems likely that such discussions are the bridge between the fantasy and the actuality of the affair, at least for women. As such, they are probably one of the final steps in becoming ready for an affair.

An affair is most likely to develop at several points in the marriage:

- Early in the marriage when the partners are struggling with issues of commitment and intimacy.
- When the first or second child arrives and motherhood becomes a major focus for the wife.
- When the children leave home.
- When it becomes clear that no matter what the straying partner does, the spouse is not going to fit the idealized image.

Opportunities

Affairs have always been with us and always will be. Only the details change. Technology is one of those details. Almost a century ago, the invention of automobiles and telephones provided new and less visible ways to meet potential affair partners and to carry on an affair. In recent decades, the migration of women into the work force provided new opportunities for affairs. Today the internet is becoming the technology of choice for many people in finding an affair partner. It's not that they set out to find an affair partner, but that the technology provides many opportunities for the person who is ready. The inner dialogue of the about-to-stray spouse is probably not much changed from that of the past, with one exception. The internet, with its anonymity and its chat rooms, encourages intimate revelations about the self and fantasies about the perfect partner. The internet is a significant meeting room for online and offline affairs.

The old means of finding an affair partner have not gone away, however. Work situations are still one of the most common meeting grounds for affair partners. Close working relationships that encompass trust and respect can easily ripen into friendships with intimate discussions of personal problems. Unless boundaries are clearly maintained, it's not too far from there to an affair. The affairs that develop from a strong work friendship tend to be serious affairs. Other work situations also provide affair opportunities: interactions with people elsewhere in the office, or with vendors, clients, and others encountered in the workplace.

Actually, any place two people can get acquainted, minimally or in depth, provides an opportunity for an affair. Short of being a hermit, any real protection from an affair has to come from inside. When someone is ready for an affair, even if they're not looking for one, the many available opportunities mean it's likely an affair will occur.

☐ The Affair

Tales abound of affairs where no one gets hurt, or where the marriage improves as a result of the affair. This is true in a sense. An affair takes pressure off the marital relationship. Less is expected from one's spouse, one's own needs are met, and disappointment is lessened. It is much easier to negotiate distance in an affair than in a marriage. Sometimes the emotional potential of the marriage is already limited and that is why the affair is sought. In other cases, the potential for the marriage is limited by the investment of emotional energy in the affair. Morton Hunt (1969) comments "I have not yet seen any evidence that the loving, satisfying, and close marriage can be improved—or even that it can remain unthreatened—by affairs" (p. 157).

The focus here is on affairs that are painful and destructive for one or both spouses; not on arrangements that couples sometimes work out, verbally or nonverbally, to lead separate lives. In the latter case the partners indicate they don't want to know if there is an affair, and the secret affair stays secret. Generally, these are not the people who come for marital therapy. For individuals and couples in therapy, the existence of an affair, their own or their spouse's, is a problem. Peck (1975) comments, "Marital infidelity . . . is not a harbinger of impending divorce, but rather is an inefficient, joint venture by a couple to transfuse life into the marriage" (p. 52).

Definitions

An affair is a sexual involvement with someone other than the spouse, which is hidden from the spouse. The key elements are extramarital, sexual, and secret. This definition excludes open marriages and other consensual, if nonverbal, arrangements between spouses. Affairs also occur among unmarried couples and among gay and lesbian couples who are committed to sexual exclusivity. Affairs of the heart (often called emotional affairs) that do not include sexual contact are often not seen as affairs. Although the dynamics are similar, the lack of an overt sexual component means that the volatility and the sense of betrayal are substantially less. Often, however, affairs of the heart are sexual affairs in the making.

The affair is a symptom of problems in the marital relationship. The discovery of the affair precipitates a crisis in the marriage. The most threatening aspect is not the affair itself, but the dishonesty that casts doubt on the entire relationship. The affair is a giant wake-up call for those willing to hear the alarm. Those who do not hear the alarm are already in deep trouble—they are unable to pay attention to their own feelings.

The Stages of an Affair

The life of an affair has six stages. First is a period of creating a climate in which an affair can germinate. Dissatisfactions, hurts, differences, and other issues go undiscussed and unresolved. The spouses begin to feel they are in a rut. Next is the betrayal itself, when the more dissatisfied partner slides into an affair. During this stage the straying partner denies the affair and the spouse colludes by ignoring the signs of the affair. The third stage is the revelation of the affair. This is a major turning point because the couple's picture of themselves and their marriage will never again be the same. This revelation precipitates the fourth stage, which is the crisis in the marriage. The spouse is obsessed with the affair, sure that the affair is the problem. It is at this critical point that the decision is made to address the underlying issues or to bury them. For those who choose to address the issues, either separately or together, a lengthy stage of rebuilding ensues. After a long journey into new territory, the final stage of the process is possible: forgiveness.

The Participants

Existing terminology for talking about affairs tends to be negative and moralistic. For lack of a better option, the term "straying partner" is used here for the married person who has an affair, and "betrayed spouse" or "spouse" is used for the other partner in the marriage or committed relationship. In some marriages where there are dual affairs, each spouse is both the straying partner and the betrayed spouse. The third party in the affair is referred to as the "third party," or if unmarried, the "unmarried third party." For that person the meaning of the affair needs to be examined in the context of his or her marriage or relationship patterns.

Straying partners, except for the Sexual Addict, most often choose a sexual partner who is known and therefore "safe," especially for the first affair. (For the sexual addict, safety may mean someone who is not known). The third party may be a work associate, a family friend, or a neighbor. Often the spouse knows or has heard about the third party. One of the most painful situations occurs when the third party is a relative or the best friend of the spouse. The affair partner is less likely to be an acquaintance if the affair occurs at an out of town conference or while on travel.

The Meaning of an Affair

Affairs can make or break a marriage. They're sexy, but they have little to do with sex—and a lot to do with keeping anger, fear, and emptiness at bay. Even passionate affairs are complex dances played out against the backdrop of the marriage. Understanding the meaning of the affair makes it possible to get to the heart of the real issues.

The meaning of the affair is related to the nature of the message hidden within each affair. The message has to do with the straying partner's way of relating to other people, particularly the spouse. In keeping with systems thinking, the two spouses have a reciprocal set of behaviors. Each of the following messages reflects a particular type of affair:

- I'll make you pay attention to me! (Conflict Avoidance Affair)
- I don't want to need you so much (so I'll get some of my needs met elsewhere). (Intimacy Avoidance Affair)
- Fill me up (I'm running on empty). (Sexual Addiction Affair)
- I love my family but I'm in love with my affair partner. (Split Self Affair)
- Help me make it out the door. (Exit Affair)

Other therapists view affairs differently. Pittman (1989) assigns total responsibility for an affair to the straying partner, and views the betrayed spouse as a victim. He categorizes affairs as accidental, philandering, marital arrangements, or romantic, and regards infidelity as "the primary disrupter of families" (p. 33). He too believes that the secrecy and dishonesty, not the sex, are the real problems with infidelity.

Carnes (1985) focuses on the sexual addiction that underlies some affairs. "Sexual experience has become the driving force of people's lives to the point of sacrificing their health, family, friends, values, and work. They are people who have lost the power to choose when, where, and with whom they wish to be sexual. The irony is that sexual pleasure is not rewarding for them. It is a source of despair and shame" (p. ii).

Strean (1980) examines affairs from a classic psychodynamic perspective. "The husband or wife in a sustained extramarital affair must be distinguished from one who from time to time engages in extramarital sex . . . . Whenever the idea of ending the affair presents itself, the individual begins to feel an underlying depression, latent homo-sexual fantasies, or repressed sadism or masochism. An occasional 'one night stand' can be a fairly harmless regression, but a sustained extra-marital affair is a form of neurotic compulsion in a person who is too immature to cope with the emotional and interpersonal tasks of marriage" (p. 19). He goes on to say that "Only a minority of individu-als can engage in a devoted, intimate sexual relationship where they freely admire the loved one and where the attachment is not threaten-ing" (p. 43).

Buss (2000) views affairs from the perspective of evolutionary psy-chology. Men's biological mission is to reproduce and in so doing, men want to put their investment in their own children. Women are genetically predisposed to seek "mate insurance" so that they are not abandoned during child rearing. Buss believes jealousy represents, "a form of ancestral wisdom that can have useful as well as destructive consequences." . . . The view of jealousy as pathological ignores a profound fact about an important defense designed to combat a real threat. . . . Moderate jealousy . . . signals commitment" (2000, pp. 8–9).

Lawson, (1988) sees adultery as paradoxical. "A way in which the world is actually *reordered* according to strongly held beliefs about the proper relationship between women and men. The marriage comes to be seen as where the chaos is; the alternative relationship one where sense and meaning are rediscovered or perhaps discovered for the first time (p. 276).

Becoming Involved in an Affair

Since most married people never expect to have an affair at the time they marry, nor do they seek out an affair, how does it happen that over 50% of married people in this country become involved in an affair? Some claim "It just happened." While it may feel like "it just happened," an affair is not an accident. Most people gradually slide into an affair through a series of small choices. (The exception is the addict who actively seeks sexual partners.) Some choices have to do with lost opportunities, as when Sheila once again rationalizes away her annoyance with Fred when he tunes her out. Other choices are about exploring new possibilities, as when Sheila stays late at the office to have a stimulating conversation with Eric, the first man who really listens to her.

All affairs embody an element of fantasy, of making a dream come true. Of course fantasies are fragile and need protection to survive. This may account for the straying partner's single-mindedness in pursuing the affair while being oblivious to the risks. Even when others spot an affair in the making, the potential betrayer often denies any such intent and may believe his or her own denial.

A sense of powerlessness within the marriage permeates the struggle over whether to have an affair. The most commonly heard justifications for an affair are pain and emptiness in the marriage and anger at the spouse's lack of sexual or emotional responsiveness. As one straying partner said sadly, "She has expectations of what I should be and I'm not it."

Reasons for resisting involvement in an affair, such as guilt, anticipation of the spouse's pain and fury, or fear of AIDS are often pushed aside by the force of other motivations. As therapists often hear, remarkably little protection is used against the risk of various sexually transmitted diseases, or even pregnancy. It is as if the magic of the affair (and the magical thinking) will offer sufficient protection: "It feels right, so it must be love, and if it's love then it's okay." In some ways, little has changed over the course of history when it comes to affairs: incurable venereal diseases or even the threat of burning at the stake did not prevent affairs in the past.

> Ted called his old girlfriend, Betts, the next day and arranged to have a drink with her after work a few days later. He said nothing to Judy other than he would be home late. He told himself he was just going to catch up on the news with an old friend. On seeing Betts, Ted was struck by how attractive she was. And she was just as easy to talk to as she used to be. A bottle of wine and a bite to eat later, Ted offered Betts a ride home. Betts invited Ted in to see her new condo. As soon as the door closed Ted grabbed Betts and began kissing her passionately. Within a few minutes they were in bed. Two hours and a lifetime later Ted left to go home to Judy.

How the Affair Is Lived

Affairs are most alike in their early moments: exciting, compelling, with the thrill of the forbidden. With the typical one-night stand, the excitement is present but there is little in the way of a relationship and the outcome may be guilt or simply relief at getting one's fix. When emotional attachment to the person is part of the affair, its durability usually exceeds one night. Feelings that have been dormant spring to life. The affair is "our secret" and little else seems as important. Risks are ignored or rationalized. The intoxication is so heady that the straying partner is blinded.

> Much later, Ted described the early days of his affair, "The fantasy is powerful—it's exciting! I really didn't believe I was doing anything wrong. Hidden moments—that's exciting. I couldn't let myself know the truth because I'd have to give up the fantasy."

At the same time, lovers in their first affair know that life has changed significantly. No longer can they define themselves in the old ways; no longer are they honest innocents, trying to work things out at home. There will be consequences—but in the distant future. For now, let's enjoy what we have. The lovers talk voraciously, eagerly, passionately, trying to cram years into a short period of time.

> Ted felt excited and scared. He wanted to hide the affair from Judy, but his guilt did not stop him from finding time to be with Betts. "Working late" became his theme. When he was home, he went out of his way to do "good deeds," attempting to compensate for his absences. (He was not naive enough to think good deeds would compensate for the affair.)
> Betts made Ted feel good about himself. She was attentive and affectionate, and he didn't have to work so hard to get her attention. They talked somewhat about their dissatisfactions but mostly they concentrated on having fun.

The affair is a protected relationship. It does not have the everyday worries and chores of marriage nor the pressures of living intimately with another person over time. It is a hidden relationship, shared only with one or two confidantes who are chosen for their ability to be supportive and keep the secret. The secrecy provides a shield against outside pressures. Despite the shield, the marriage impinges on the affair that is ongoing. The spouse still comes first in many matters: finances, family crisis and celebrations, and in public. The straying partner is pulled between the demands of the spouse and the third party in deciding how to allocate free time. Always hovering in the background is the marriage. Even the shared secret is a reference to the spouse. When the affair is an enduring one, it also is affected by changes that occur over time: a job change, illness, a move, a parent dying, a child leaving home.

The End of the Affair

The affair contrasts ever more sharply with the situation at home. Dissatisfactions have a harder edge than before. Nevertheless, the straying partner attempts, usually rather poorly, to hide the affair. Those with a greater degree of guilt about the affair, more ambivalence about the marriage, or both, usually provide their spouses with many clues. The spouse may discover the affair, or may choose not to see or acknowledge the affair.

The life of an affair can be exceedingly brief, or may endure until the death of one of the lovers. The briefest affairs are one-night stands—they may not even last the night out. Some affairs end when they are discovered by the spouse, and some continue even then. Probably the greatest number of affairs last anywhere from a few months to a year or two. Beyond that, the marriage ends, or in some cases the affair becomes an accepted arrangement that parallels the marriage.

Occasionally the guilt is so great that the straying partner confesses. Sometimes a friend learns about the affair and tells the spouse. Most often the spouse finds evidence that is unmistakable, such as hotel receipts or long distance charges, and the cat is out of the bag.

> It was a long time since Ted had felt appreciated. He rationalized to himself that he deserved Bett's attention. He bought shirts and ties in new colors and went on a diet. He also charged two dinners with Betts on his Visa card.
>
> Judy knew something was wrong, and asked Ted whether he was having an affair. Ted said, "Of course not!" Judy, hearing what she wanted to hear, felt relieved and dropped the issue for the time being. This impasse escalated, with Ted leaving more clues and Judy expressing greater dissatisfaction with Ted's late nights at work. Ted wanted to be found out, although he was not consciously aware of it at the time.
>
> For Judy, the moment of recognition came with the Visa bill. When Ted came home late that night, Judy was waiting. This time she knew, and she told Ted so. Ted again denied having an affair but this time Judy persisted: "It's right here on the Visa bill! What do you mean you're not having an affair! I should have known! And to think I believed you! All this time you've been lying to me! Well I don't believe you now!" Finally Ted said, "I didn't want to hurt you," and went on to admit the truth.

Discovery of the affair often turns out to be validation rather than new information. Classically the spouse responds, "I knew something was wrong but I didn't think you'd ever do anything like that." Lawson's (1988) study indicates that about two thirds of spouses were told of the affair by their own husbands or wives, often after the spouse discovered evidence. Ten percent of the spouses who were told professed not to have suspected anything. Yet clinical experience suggests that the spouse has subliminal knowledge of the affair, often being able to name the third party when the affair is revealed, even though prior to revelation that knowledge was not conscious.

The Aftermath

Our societal emphasis on adultery encourages spouses to think of legalistic remedies for an affair, as do many of the spouses' friends and relatives. Lawyers, when consulted about an affair, all too often promote the use of a detective or recommend proceeding toward divorce. The legal arena is always an inappropriate place to deal with affairs. Emotional issues—an affair is nothing if not an emotional issue—deserve to be dealt with in a setting that understands emotions.

When the affair is disclosed the betrayed spouse moves from shock to anger to rumination about the betrayal, asking over and over again for details but not believing anything. This obsession, which is a function of the rational self rather than the emotional self, is a way of avoiding pain and fear. When the betrayed spouse is able to shift from obsessing to experiencing the underlying emotions, the couple is ready to begin rebuilding. Problems that arise during this period include the recurrence of an affair, the persistence of obsession, attempts to resolve the issues by making premature decisions about the marriage, continued avoidance of the underlying issues, and the spouse's erroneous impression that the significant issues belong only to the straying partner.

> After tears, threats, and recriminations, Ted and Judy decided to see a therapist together. They began to understand that their "niceness" was not so nice and had in fact precipitated Ted's affair. Gradually they began to rebuild their relationship and this time they included honesty with each other. Ted began incorporating the playful self he had discovered with Betts into the marriage.

If all goes well (just the normal ups and downs of treatment), the couple reaches the stage of forgiving each other for their mutual betrayals. Even when all does not go well, forgiveness and closure are still possible at a much later date. What happens after the affair is discovered holds great significance for the eventual outcome for the individuals and for the marriage.

☐ Role of the Therapist

When our clients are involved in an affair they are hurting, even though the affair itself may be deeply satisfying. The affair indicates they want something better in their marriage and in their life, but that they do not know how to pursue it honestly. Often they are not clear about what they do want, knowing best what they do not want. It is their pain that has brought them to therapy, and they know at some level that pain also will be a part of changing how they handle their intimate relationships.

As therapists, we can be most helpful if we take a systemic approach. What does the affair mean? What is the message to the spouse? What issues are being avoided? Is the affair holding the marriage together, keeping the marriage in a rut, or providing a way out of the marriage? Our role is to help the client address and sort through these issues. The process of therapy must be an honest one. Issues of betrayal can not be addressed through secrecy and further betrayal.

Our reactions to clients' affairs stem from attitudes we learned as children and from our own experience with betrayal and abandonment. We may want to dismiss the straying partner as a callous lout, or swoop in to protect the wounded spouse. Or we may be frightened at the prospect of revealing an affair, and want to collude with the secret instead. We may have our own secrets that we want to protect. Or we may want the affair revealed, but without anyone feeling hurt (our clients would like that too). Do we really believe that trust can be rebuilt? And once the straying partner apologizes, isn't that enough? When we can stay open to hearing our clients, separating our fears from theirs, and refraining from moral judgments or attitudes that separate "us" from "them," we can offer our clients an opportunity that does not turn out to be another betrayal.

Infidelity is not the greatest sin.

Types of Affairs
and Their Messages

Craig's affair with a woman he met on a business trip was never that involved. He saw Karen a total of three times before his wife discovered the affair. Although he liked Karen a lot, he doesn't miss her. His wife will never forget Karen, and does not like her, but now that she and Craig can air their differences, and even have a good fight, she is grateful to Karen.

Charlie's wife feels differently. Charlie left Jane after 31 years of marriage to live with Sally, with whom he'd been having an affair for four years. Jane hasn't recovered, even though Charlie left two years ago. She feels humiliated and blames herself for not having done more to make Charlie happy, although she doesn't know what else she could have done. She can taste the bile when she thinks of Sally, and hates herself for being so bitter. Charlie avoids his guilt and Jane's outbursts by avoiding all contact with her—not that they had much contact before he left. Right now he has his hands full making Sally happy.

John's righteous indignation about his wife's affair surfaces whenever he talks about the end of his marriage. "Yes, we had problems, but if Arnie, that double-crossing bastard she works with, had left her alone, we could have worked things out. What's more, he even pretended to be my friend." John and Lisa have never yet discussed their separation with each other, though their friends have heard about it in detail. Both prefer to engage in the fiction that Arnie stole her away: for John it means that he is blameless—Lisa didn't leave him because of anything he did; it is all Arnie's fault. For Lisa it means she is also blameless—after all one can't deny true love; true love conquers all.

Each of these affairs is different, and each is a classic type. In each is a hidden message. The nature of the hidden message is related to the underlying emotional reasons for the affair. Altogether I have identified five types of affairs, each conveying a different message. The typology is based on the underlying issues and patterns of interaction between the marital partners, not on those of the straying partner alone.

In Craig's case, the intent of his Conflict Avoidance Affair was to get his wife's attention. At the other extreme, Lisa's Exit Affair was intended to get validation for leaving the marriage, while attempting to avoid the pain of doing so. In between are the couples who fear intimacy, the womanizers and temptresses, and the passionless marriages such as Charlie and Jane's that are based on "doing things right." The patterns of unmarried third parties are different yet, ranging from sexual addiction to a desire for intimacy coupled with the fear of being dependent.

This typology is not about morality or pathology. The type of affair has to do with the interaction pattern between the two spouses and the issues underlying the affair. Consider the marital partners as a matched set, playing reciprocal roles in the same dance. Each of the five types of affairs has a characteristic pattern, marked by differences in feelings, behavior, age, gender, and outcome (see Figure 2.1). By identifying the message embedded in the affair, the therapist can begin to formulate a plan for treatment. The typology is based on the behavior patterns and emotional dynamics of the couple, and is meant to be a guide to understanding the underlying emotional dynamics between the spouses. There is a wide range of functioning within each category.

☐ Conflict Avoidance Affairs

The Conflict Avoidance Affair screams to the spouse, "I'll make you pay attention to me." Couples who cannot talk about their differences and disappointments may use an affair to get out from under a blanket of controlled amiability. The straying partner is the more dissatisfied spouse, whether that is the husband or the wife. The partner having the affair always manages to be discovered, and the discovery blasts loose the covers and makes it clear that there are serious problems in the marriage. This kind of an affair usually occurs relatively early in

	CONFLICT AVOIDANCE	INTIMACY AVOIDANCE	SEXUAL ADDICTION	SPLIT SELF	EXIT
Gender of straying partner	male or female	male and female	male	male	female or male
Age of straying partner	20s and 30s	20s and 30s	any	40 and up	any
Length of marriage before affair	less than 12 years	less than 6 years	0 years	20 or more years	less than 15 years
Theme of affair	avoid conflict	avoid intimacy	individual feels empty	family and shoulds vs wants	avoid facing ending of marriage
Duration of affair	brief	brief	brief	2 or more years	6 months to 2 years
Level of emotional involvement in affair	minimal	minimal	none	great	some
Presenting affect of straying partner	guilty	angry and chaotic	grandiose and/or seductive	depressed	uninvolved
Presenting affect of spouse	angry but extra-nice	angry and chaotic	denial	depressed	angry

FIGURE 2.1. Typical characteristics by type of affair.

(continues)

	CONFLICT AVOIDANCE	INTIMACY AVOIDANCE	SEXUAL ADDICTION	SPLIT SELF	EXIT
Interaction pattern of couple	conflict is deflected	continual conflict	separate lives	troubled communication	straying partner uninvolved, spouse angry
Who presents for therapy	straying partner or couple	couple	straying partner or spouse	couple, straying partner, or spouse	couple or spouse
Primary treatment mode initially	couple	couple	individual	individual	couple
Prognosis for resolving issues	very good	very good	poor	good	good
Probability of divorce	low	low	low	above average	extremely high
Best outcome	solid marriage	solid marriage	family in recovery	revived marriage or divorce	resolves issues of ending marriage
Worst outcome	other affairs or divorce	other affairs or divorce	damaged family and public humiliation	empty shell marriage or divorce	unresolved loss

FIGURE 2.1. (*Continued*) Typical characteristics by type of affair. © 1990 Emily M. Brown.

the marriage, with couples in their twenties or thirties who have never learned how to resolve conflicts. It also may occur in subsequent marriages. The timing of the affair is tied to increased frustration combined with opportunity. Sometimes the frustration is obvious, such as the spouse's preoccupation with a new baby. In other cases it is a matter of the final straw, such as being told for the fifty-seventh time, "You don't need to get upset dear, it's not anything important."

These are the couples who try to make their marriage work, who attempt to please, who are self-sacrificing, and who can be somewhat perfectionistic. They often are regarded as model couples. Communication is limited by the efforts to avoid conflict, and also by the couple's collusive focus on idealistic goals instead of on reality. Underneath the surface is a tendency towards depression.

Those who were taught as a child that anger was bad, who were instructed to "look at the positive side of things," or were punished for disagreeing, are likely to have a hard time expressing dissatisfactions. They also find it difficult to discuss problems. Sometimes they are not even aware of how dissatisfied they are.

> Craig learned early to suppress his anger because his mother cried every time he got angry, and he hated feeling guilty. With his father, it was important to rise above any pain and do the manly thing. In his marriage, Craig continued to suppress any pain or anger, and took pride in how rationally he handled problems. It's no wonder his wife, Ruth, found it hard to talk to him about problems, but she took pride in his even disposition. She too felt it was best to put aside minor annoyances.
>
> With their differences unattended, resentment crept in quietly. Craig didn't intend to get involved with Karen, but his pattern of overlooking differences and resentments made him vulnerable. Hidden away, his anger at Ruth grew, and in suppressing it, he suppressed his own internal warning signals. When Karen came along, Craig wasn't consciously aware of all the feelings that were propelling him forward. Later he said that his sexual involvement with Karen "just happened." Once it did, guilt added to the pressure on Craig. One day he got "careless:" he left receipts for the hotel sauna for two in his jacket, and then asked Ruth to take the jacket to the cleaners. Ruth discovered the receipts, confronted Craig, and the affair was out in the open. Ruth was devastated, and cried uncontrollably. Craig felt tremendous guilt, but was surprised to experience a sense of relief—the hiding was over.

Craig and Ruth are typical. In Conflict Avoidance Affairs, differences get put aside, and resentments begin to pile up. The pressure builds, and without verbal means to resolve the issues, they explode into an affair which is discovered. The affair itself is rarely a serious relationship since the real purpose is to get the spouse's attention.

The threat to the marriage is not the affair, but the avoidance of conflict. The affair becomes a threat only when its message is misinterpreted or ignored. Considering the affair an aberration, or forgiving prematurely is the equivalent of doing nothing. The result is more affairs (send the message again and again until it is heard!). Getting even by ending the marriage is like throwing the baby out with the bath water. Ending the marriage abruptly shortchanges both spouses— neither learns how to handle the normal give and take of a marriage. There is a very good prognosis for the marriage when the affair serves as the catalyst for facing problems and learning how to resolve differences. If the marriage should end, it will end with understanding and closure if the spouses have addressed their issues with each other.

Discovery of an affair is a common reason for seeking therapy. Sometimes it is the straying partner who comes individually for help, having been sent by the spouse to find out what's wrong with him and to fix it. The straying partner's guilt, plus his tendency to be over-responsible, may make him willing to accept full responsibility for the situation. In other cases, the spouse comes to the initial appointment individually, to inform or check out the therapist before bringing in the straying partner. If they present initially as a couple, the spouse is likely to be extremely obsessive about the affair, and will probably attempt to hand the therapist the responsibility for blaming, punishing, or fixing the straying partner.

This is the only type of affair in which the straying partner expresses much guilt. He is also bewildered by his behavior, commenting "I don't know why I got involved. It goes against what I believe in. I know what I did was wrong, but. . . ." The latter comment reflects a mix of anger and guilt. The spouse, though angry, tries to respond in a controlled manner, even being extra nice on occasion. If the spouse lashes out a bit, the straying partner will try to deflect the anger with an apology or with reason. It's not that there's never any conflict, but that conflict goes nowhere. If one lobs a shot at the other, the other is reluctant to return the volley. Both collude in their attempts to make things go back to the way they used to be.

Conflict Avoiders may also begin therapy with the affair still hidden away. The next chapter discusses how to handle the situation when the affair is a secret.

☐ Intimacy Avoidance Affairs

Problems with intimacy are present in all types of affairs, but in the Intimacy Avoidance Affair, intimacy is *the* issue. This affair protects against hurt and disappointment. It is saying "I don't want to need you so much (so I'll get some of my needs met elsewhere)." Both spouses fear letting down the barriers and becoming emotionally vulnerable. It feels safer to keep things stirred up a bit. Arguments about anything and everything protect against exposing too much of oneself and one's insecurities. Arguments are especially useful to prevent undue relaxation when things are going well. Of course nothing ever gets settled, so that becomes an excuse for turning to someone else. The affair, which is soon revealed, becomes the newest weapon in the armament. Frequently it is countered with another affair. The emotional intensity between the partners increases, but is spent fighting about the affair.

Intimacy Avoidance Affairs are most likely to occur after several years of marriage, when the honeymoon period is over and the partners know each other fairly well, and the potential for developing real intimacy looms fearfully close. Couples are likely to be in their twenties or thirties, and as with the Conflict Avoiders, the spouses still care about each other. It is likely that the marital partners grew up in rather chaotic households, for example, an alcoholic or abusive family, or in a family that is roiling beneath a placid surface. Since unpredictability is the only thing that is predictable, successful coping means always being on guard, and keeping enough distance to make rejection less painful. Among Intimacy Avoiders the level of functioning varies greatly from couple to couple, ranging from high-functioning professionally successful couples to those with a borderline personality disorder.

One of the clearest indicators of an Intimacy Avoidance Affair is that both spouses are involved in affairs. The affairs bring new players into the conflict, establishing the triangular interactions so well known to therapists. This couple will involve whoever is handy in their fights, in whatever way the other person is willing to be involved. Obviously therapists are fair game. Intimacy Avoiders are very good at fighting. The battles may be heated or icy, but the partners' emotional connection with each other is through fighting. Their sexual relationship is almost always a part of the conflict, and their verbal interchange is filled with criticism, sarcasm, and blame. Expressions of guilt are not part of the picture. Under the surface however is a great deal of pain and fear. It is as if they are doing a dance where each wants the other to say "I really want to be with you," but both fear that saying so would leave them exposed and vulnerable. Instead, both of them equivocate, back off, and then threaten with someone or something else. Yet they remain connected by the push-pull.

Ed and Nancy's marriage improved after her affair, which occurred four years into the marriage. Nancy had always found it hard to talk about her lack of sexual pleasure with Ed. After they'd been married a couple of years she began the "too tired" routine. Ed didn't want to share his hurt feelings—after all, he wasn't supposed to feel hurt and he certainly didn't want to give Nancy an excuse to jump all over him the way his father did. Instead he criticized Nancy's housekeeping, her family, her friends, and even the way she fed the dog. Nancy countered with similar attacks, always ending with "Men are all like that anyway—you just want a woman to take care of you, in bed and out of bed."

As their dissatisfaction grew, each was sure the other was at fault, but their complaints always ended up leading to another go-nowhere fight. When Peter came along, Nancy was vulnerable—she was emotionally needy and simmered with resentment toward Ed. "Ed just won't give me what I need—he doesn't understand, he just wants it his way. Peter always wants me to have what I need," she told herself. Ed was furious and humiliated when he discovered pictures of Peter in her desk. Nancy was incensed by Ed's righteousness. Ed reacted by having a one-night stand with a woman he met in a bar, and made sure that Nancy knew about it by coming in at 3 am with makeup on his shirt.

This escalating spiral of anger between the spouses is central to the Intimacy Avoidance Affair. It is used to explain and justify the affair. The spouse is portrayed as totally uncaring, in contrast to the lover who "cares a lot about me, and he's not even married to me." The lover takes on the role of knight-on-the-white-horse, adding the illusion of true love, as it did for Nancy. Not burdened with the dailiness of everyday life, this affair provides double indemnity against intimacy: the cloak of romantic fantasy prevents real intimacy in the affair, and there is little incentive to attempt intimacy with a spouse who is "not as giving" as the lover. The pursuit of true love is more fun and guards against having to reveal one's real self. Intimacy Avoidance Affairs are paradoxical—they embody the pursuit of the romantic fantasy while providing the means to avoid intimacy. The paradox serves nicely to justify the affair while remaining oblivious to one's own difficulties with intimacy.

In some ways the Intimacy Avoidance Affair is a mirror image of the Conflict Avoidance Affair: The former feeds on conflict and minimizes cooperation, and the latter avoids conflict and feeds on accommodation. In a way, Ed and Nancy are just the opposite of Craig and Ruth: Ed and Nancy welcome conflict, and use it to keep from getting too close. Craig and Ruth avoid conflict for fear it will push them too far apart. Both couples are struggling with the duality of being separate individuals and yet interdependent, but each has embraced only one side of the duality.

The revelation of an Intimacy Avoidance Affair—or Affairs—can lead to a new round of fighting, and it is often the fighting, rather than the affair, that induces couples to seek help. They usually present as a couple, and each knows about the other's affair(s). They have a lot of energy, which has been used for fighting, and the therapist who taps into their energy can direct it towards positive change. The outlook for the marriage is very favorable provided both learn to risk expressing their real feelings to each other. Only by doing so can their emotional needs be met. If the issues around vulnerability and dependency are not dealt with, distancing with affairs or other maneuvers may become a way of life.

Open marriages might be considered a variation of this type of affair, with both spouses agreeing not to "put all their eggs in one basket." However, the characteristic lying and fighting that accompany an affair are lacking. With some couples this arrangement breaks down when their emotional self responds more strongly and more traditionally than anticipated.

☐ Sexual Addiction Affairs

Fill Me Up (I'm Running on Empty) is the theme of the womanizer or the temptress. These affairs are the province of those who deal with their emotional neediness by winning battles and making conquests in the hope of gaining love. Emotionally deprived, overwhelmed, or abused as children, they haven't finished growing up. They often seek power in arenas where public acclaim is possible, such as politics, and in private life through sexual conquests.

In this type of affair, it matters little who the sexual partner is, although it may matter that they have looks, power, or other surface attributes. There are likely to be many sexual partners over time, since no one ever succeeds in filling the emptiness. A particular sexual encounter may soothe the pain or fill the emptiness briefly, but as with other addictions, there is never enough. These affairs occur at any age and at any point in the marriage. Husbands are more likely than wives to be Sexual Addicts, probably because this use of sex and power is more acceptable for men. In addition, husbands are less willing to put up with a sexually addicted mate than are wives. The temptress is more often an unmarried third party.

These are the affairs that people love to hate. When played out in public, as they often are, they elicit feelings of fear and fascination. The participants feign innocence while flaunting behavior that is outside the rules. There is an element of daring, or not caring, a defiance—"catch me if you can." When these affairs blow up, they usually do so with great furor, and if the participants are well known, it is front-page news. Bystanders, while fascinated by the drama and its trappings, defend themselves against fears of betrayal and humiliation by assessing blame and invoking suitable retribution. (Many of our divorce laws were designed with those functions in mind, rather than to establish procedures for divorce.) It is not so much the affair that draws the fire, but the lying and the flaunting of being above the rules, an especially dangerous position for rule-makers, such as politicians.

Bill Clinton epitomizes this pattern, as did Gary Hart and many others before him. Pat Schroeder, the former Democratic Congresswoman, was stunned by Clinton's behavior: "I just can't connect the dots. It was no great secret that people were looking at everything he was doing under a microscope. . . . Who would do this kind of insane thing right under the nose of the special prosecutor who is out to hang him?" (Mann, 1998, p. D14). Jim Hoagland (1999), a *Washington Post* columnist, questioned the security risks in Clinton's behavior: "To create a shared secret in which the risks of discovery are so wildly disproportionate—as the president did in romancing a careerless, unmarried, talkative intern half his age—is the height of recklessness for a national leader."

The spouse of someone who is a Sexual Addict will probably overlook it, especially if the marriage has been a long one. The marriage may be little but a shell, but that shell provides some comfort. However if the philandering spouse leaves the marriage, or if the philandering comes to public attention, facing the situation is unavoidable. It is also extremely humiliating and painful, and the shell is likely to be damaged beyond repair. Those who know the couple view the spouse as heroically loyal, or as stupid. Neither is true. The spouse is motivated by other matters. She is concerned with maintaining a positive image before the world.

Hillary Clinton's response is classic among political wives whose husbands' affair(s) explode in public. Her comments in *Talk* magazine indicate that despite great pain and anger she is still very deeply connected to her husband. She defends his behavior, "I have been with him half my life and he is a very, very good man. . . . He couldn't protect me, and so he lied" (Frank, 1999, p. 174). Gail Sheehy attributes Hillary's need for accomplishment to her narcissistic and withholding father, and suggests that in Bill, she found someone who respected and admired her. Sheehy notes that, "Hillary has the most incredible ability to separate her personal hurts, her personal indignity, from a bigger picture and a bigger goal and a bigger love for him" (Sheehy, 1999, p. 6).

Sexual addiction occurs out of the spotlight as well. Alan and Marcia's situation is also classic:

Alan and Marcia had been married for 15 years when her best friend told her that Alan was involved with another woman. When Marcia confronted Alan, he promised to end the affair, claiming "It felt right at the moment, but I can see I made a mistake." Earlier in their marriage, Marcia had many clues that Alan was having sex elsewhere but wasn't ready to look at the truth, so she explained them away. A few months after Alan's admission of the one affair, indications surfaced periodically that Alan continued to have affairs but Marcia still chose to keep her blinders on. Marcia's tunnel vision was focused on presenting a good face to their relatives and in their community.

Alan had his own set of problems. Attractive and successful, he had never felt completely comfortable with Marcia—or for that matter, with any woman. He was an only child, and his mother leaned on him for companionship and affection during his father's frequent travels. She also had him sleep in her bed until he was 11, thus protecting her from having to have sex with her husband. She wanted Alan to "be the man his father wasn't." Alan liked being special, but it was a very mixed blessing: "I sometimes felt I was going to be gobbled up by her."

Intense relationships like this with the parent of the opposite sex can set a child up to engage in this type of affair as an adult. Being "Daddy's Girl," or "Mama's Big Boy" often means that not only is the child favored over the other parent, but also that the relationship between parent and child is sexualized. For a child, the promise of being better or more loveable than the other parent is an aphrodisiac, but fraught with danger. Such a relationship with a parent sexualizes the child, blocks normal emotional development, diminishes self-esteem, and interferes with the ability to relate appropriately to others as an adult. It also may set the stage for incestuous behavior.

Many Sexual Addicts have experienced sexual abuse in childhood, with all the pain and emptiness that entails. Others felt neglected or unloved as children, also creating a feeling of emptiness. The compulsive sexual behavior is an attempt to numb the pain and fill the emptiness. Seeking someone who will fulfill the fantasy of total love is often part of the picture. If this person doesn't fit the dream (and they won't) then maybe the next person will. In the meantime, the marriage provides structure and some comfort, which is also important. As with other addictions the spouse must be viewed as a codependent with her own set of issues stemming from childhood wounds.

Among the different types of affairs, Sexual Addicts are least likely to seek help, but when they do, they are very recognizable. Several presentations are possible. The straying partner may come in alone, often at the spouse's behest, sometimes because of a court order or another situation where it is "therapy or else." Some Sexual Addicts appear to be bragging about their many affairs, others are struggling to hide the truth about their behavior and their shame. In many of these cases the straying partner comes in only a few times because of his tremendous denial or if he has little at risk. Therapists without training in addictions may be confused about how to work with the Addict and prone to overlook the signs of addiction. Occasionally the Addict's spouse comes in alone, to find out what's wrong with the marriage. If they present as a couple, it's usually at the spouse's insistence—a positive indicator for treatment.

Doris Kearns Goodwin's (1987) description of Joe Kennedy's relationship with Gloria Swanson is a perfect description of this type of affair. For Kennedy, who had a reputation as a ladies' man "the affair with Gloria was a relentless pursuit of more, a quest to have it all, to live beyond the rules in a world of his own making" (pp. 454–455). Goodwin speculates that the marriage satisfied Rose Kennedy's desire for sexual distance while providing her with what really mattered: wealth, children, and privilege. "Better perhaps . . . to suffer in silence rather than take the enormous risk of shattering the entire family and bringing public disgrace upon herself and her husband. So long as she felt secure about remaining Mrs. Joseph Kennedy, what did the rest really matter?" (p. 460).

These marriages tend to continue as they are for many years. The male Sexual Addict is not likely to leave the marriage because it provides him with a desired image as well as personal services. As long as his wife overlooks the affairs and continues to focus on meeting her husband's needs, there is no impetus toward change. If the spouse steps back from the codependent role, it precipitates a crisis in the marriage. Stepping back usually results from changes made in response to a personal crisis such as the death of a parent, and not to the pain and indignity of the partner's affairs unless there is significant cost or humiliation.

Some Sexual Addicts settle down later in life after having confronted a serious personal issue. Others continue with Sexual Addiction as long as life allows. In order for there to be any significant change in the marriage, both spouses must examine and resolve their reciprocal issues. Most choose however, to look the other way, and pretend that all is well.

☐ Split Self Affairs

The Split Self Affair is an attempt to experience the emotional self that has been denied for a lifetime in the service of doing things right. Typically, this has been a middle aged man's affair—someone who has been married for twenty or more years, and who regards himself as a family man. These men may never have had a strong emotional bond with their wives, and married to gain security or status, to get away from home, to legitimize a child already on the way, or because it seemed to be what they should do. They say now that they didn't love their spouse, or that they had doubts about the marriage but went ahead anyway—they would make it work. Personal needs were sublimated as they tried to make their family be what they believed a family should be. This often meant focusing the family resources, financial and emotional, on the children.

Split Selves, both the straying partner and the spouse, are people who learned early in life that they were supposed to do the right thing, rather than pay attention to their own needs and feelings. They have used their rational selves to survive and succeed. They are often quite accomplished professionally. Because they have had to sacrifice their emotional selves in order to survive, they are about five years old emotionally.

The family they know best—the one they grew up in—provided a negative model. Split Selves have worked at being just the opposite of their original family. If Mother was smothering, they create some distance. If Dad was angry, they are nice. Their intent is to do family right—to build the perfect family. Doing the right thing at home usually means caretaking and accommodating. When it becomes apparent that the formula isn't producing satisfaction, these people are puzzled and frustrated. It often becomes apparent in mid-life, when the kids leave home. When the kids have been the only significant mutual interest and they're gone, there is even less to talk about. Lacking an emotional partnership at home, husbands—and increasingly wives— look elsewhere for relief and satisfaction.

Close work friendships often provide some of the emotional satisfaction that is missing at home. Such a friendship may gradually evolve into a Split Self Affair. In the traditional Split Self Affair the third party is an unmarried woman a generation younger who has some unresolved issues with her father that she plays out in the affair. The younger woman is attentive, understanding, and accommodating. The affair is invigorating, it kindles fantasies of excitement and romance— its name is *passion*. It is the kind of affair that is viewed as part of the male mid-life crisis, although the situation is much more complex than that.

In the Split Self Affair, the marriage feels empty, as opposed to Sexual Addiction where the individual feels empty. The partners may or may not share a bedroom, any sexual relationship is likely to be pro forma, and they lead very separate lives. Communication is limited to practical matters like taking the garbage out or social necessities.

The affair itself is a serious relationship, with a history of one, two, five, ten years, or longer. Straying partners in Split Self Affairs don't flaunt their involvement, as do Sexual Addicts. They are troubled by their inability to act appropriately, whether they think that means ending the marriage or ending the affair and they flip-flop repeatedly on which relationship should be ended. These affairs can inflict mortal wounds on marriages that are not already dead.

Until recently, married women were rarely the straying partners in Split Self Affairs. Though still few in number, their participation appears to be a growing phenomenon. As a group, they tend to be younger, usually in their thirties or early forties, in contrast to their male counterparts who are in their forties, fifties, and sixties. (At older ages women have fewer opportunities for an affair.) Their affair partners are likely to be closer to their own age and may or may not be married. Since she is younger than her male counterpart, the children may still be at home, but their presence is not sufficient to get a dull marriage off the rocks. Once involved sexually, she intends that the affair remain hidden. In contrast to her male counterparts, she is more successful in keeping it a secret. Our society still deals harshly with married women who have affairs, and she is very aware that she could risk losing her children and her financial security if her affair is discovered. It is also possible that she is more afraid of her spouse's retaliation—physically, financially, and as a parent—than a man would be.

Patterns for males are beginning to change too—younger married men are increasingly involved as the straying partner in Split Self Affairs, although the total numbers are still small.

Initial Presentation

Split Selves present themselves for therapy in several different ways. One of the most common is the straying partner who comes in individually. When he comes to a therapist, it is usually to get help in leaving the marriage. He has been trying to sort things out rationally and it has not worked. He feels troubled, unentitled, and stuck. He is chronically depressed, although he often functions very well in his career. He wonders whether he will ever be able to resolve the situation. He flip-flops, one day deciding to stay in the marriage, and the next day deciding to leave for the other woman. He lives a dual life, spending as little time at home as possible, and providing thinly veiled reasons for his frequent overnight absences. His wife makes barbed comments every so often, but puts up with the situation. The woman friend, who is 25 years younger and unmarried, is getting tired of being patient while he gets up the courage to leave. Yet for him the fear of facing a void, of not having Family, is also deadly. He wants the therapist to help him decide which is the right woman. The real issue is that his rational self is over-developed and his emotional self is underdeveloped, and these two parts of himself are mutually exclusive.

> George, who is 58, decided years ago that he wanted to leave Vivian, but he can't quite do it. It's not affection for Vivian; what little there was is long gone, although he acknowledges Vivian is a good person. He's had an affair for eight years now with Caroline. He drops by Caroline's apartment almost every day after work, sometimes spending the night, and occasionally taking a weekend trip or vacation with her. He'd like to live with her and feels frustrated by his inability to say a word to Vivian about leaving the marriage. The ghost of George's mother hovers over the marriage. Never satisfied, Mother attempted to assuage her emptiness with alcohol. George tried to be a good son, to please her, and as he got older he tried to save her from herself. Nothing worked, and Mother ended up destitute and drunk. George moved away at the age of 17 and, over the years married, had children, and became successful professionally.
>
> He wanted a real family, one that offered stability, and he married Vivian because she came from a family with status. To George that meant she would know how to create a stable family. In his desire for something better, George ignored his need for love and acceptance, telling himself that he could learn from Vivian's criticisms. She was different than his Mother and he would be able to make her happy. Now he hates Vivian's constant nit-picking and nattering, but quietly puts up with it. With Vivian he is still the little boy, trying to please Mother, and attempting to save her from her unhappiness. He can't leave until he saves her, or gives up his fantasy of saving her (and of saving Mother). Since his self-esteem is based on saving her, this is a tall order. He ruminates, "Even with Caroline, the idea of leaving my family terrorizes me."

Another presentation is that of the couple. Here the straying partner's nonverbal message is, "Please take care of her so that I can leave." His wife's very verbal message is, "You've got to make him stay." We are not going to be able to meet the agenda of either, and unless they become interested in working at a deeper level, they will probably drop out of therapy after a few sessions.

> Charlie decided to leave his marriage, and hesitantly began to tell his wife, Jane, of his plans. He also mentioned to her that his relationship with Sally has continued. He brought Jane to a therapist because she is upset about the impending separation. His nonverbal message to the

therapist is that he doesn't know what to do about Jane's upset and wants the therapist to take over. Although she was hurting, Jane didn't want help from someone she perceived as helping Charlie dump her and ended therapy after the third joint session. Charlie moved out, planning to marry Sally, but after he was gone a week, his fear became so immense that he told Sally he had made a mistake and was moving back in with Jane. Jane took him back, but a week later Charlie was despondent and depressed, regretting the move home and trying to decide what to do next. Jane felt hurt, angry, and obsessed with the affair but was also trying to take better care of Charlie so he wouldn't leave again.

The Split Self Betrayed Spouse

The female spouse in the Split Self Affair believes that if there is a problem in the marriage it is due to something she has or hasn't done. She too, is caught up in trying to make her family fit her image of what family should be. (The wife of the Sexual Addict is more concerned with maintaining the public image than with her own image of family.) She sees her role as the key one in guiding the family, and if her husband doesn't share in that endeavor, she tries to compensate for his absence. Although she would prefer that her husband be involved, her focus is on creating the right kind of family for the children. She sees herself as the primary parent and the major caretaker for family matters. Earlier in the marriage, he may have had an affair or so, probably of the Conflict Avoidance type. If she discovered an affair, she overlooked it in order to preserve the structure of family, although she let him know she was deeply hurt. The issues behind the affair were never examined.

> Margaret married Tom for his humor, his brains, because it was time she should be getting married, and because he was safe. Safe meant she wasn't in love, wasn't even attracted to him sexually. (To her mother, men were not people—they were there to take care of you). Margaret would make the marriage work by giving Tom what he needed. If she treated him with care, and didn't get angry or confront him, it would show him what it was like to have someone really care about him. Then he would like her and would give her the attention she wanted. She worked at this for 30 years, raising their four children almost single-handedly, entertaining his business associates, and changing those things he criticized. "I spent a lot of time bridging gaps and trying to make it whole, make it what I wanted."
> Twelve years into the marriage, Margaret found out Tom was having an affair. Though devastated, she continued to function as the bridge

between Tom and the kids, and handled the family rituals and responsibilities as she always had. "I wanted to believe him, to believe that the
affair was over, that things were going to get better. . . . If they didn't it
would be my fault. It would mean I wasn't good enough."

They went to counseling for several months but never actually explored Tom's affair and its meaning. However she did begin to confront
Tom about his unwillingness to give to her emotionally. She thinks he
had other affairs after that, but she tried to ignore any clues because it
was too painful otherwise. She was shocked when Tom announced he
was leaving for another woman whom he'd been seeing for five years.
A year after the separation she admitted, "I stayed in the marriage because I wasn't enough by myself; I don't feel complete when I'm with
other people, without a man."

The Split Self spouse who comes alone for therapy often comes some
time after her husband has left for good. By the time she gives up the
idea that her husband "will come to his senses" and return to the
marriage she is extremely depressed. She alternates between blaming
herself, avoiding her husband's rejection of her, and feeling devastated. She may express the belief that her life is ending. Certainly life
as she knew it is ending, and the role of divorced older woman in our
society is not an easy one.

In a Split Self Affair the outlook for the marriage is poor. Frequently
it is too late to create a satisfying emotional partnership between the
spouses. The husband may leave to marry the other woman, or may
stay in the marriage but be emotionally committed to the affair. Women
usually choose the latter option. These affairs can continue until death.
It seems likely from reports of Franklin D. Roosevelt's relationship
with Lucy Mercer, that it was a Split Self Affair.

☐ Exit Affairs

"Help Me Make It Out The Door" is the message conveyed by the Exit
Affair. Either spouse may slide into this type of affair as they think
about ending the marriage. These affairs are somewhat like trial
balloons. They ask "Can I make it on my own?" "Is the world really
the way I think it is?" "Am I still a desirable person?" and most importantly, "Can I get you to kick me out?"

The purpose is two-fold: at the surface is the quest for self-valida-
tion, while much deeper lies the desire to avoid taking responsibility
for ending the marriage. An affair, if discovered, might provoke the
spouse into ending the marriage. For some people this seems infi-
nitely easier than facing the spouse's pain and recriminations. At the

very least, the affair is a distraction from the difficulties and the pain of ending the marriage.

The third party, often referred to as "my friend" is someone to talk to about feelings, about dissatisfactions, about hopes for the future. It's someone who "understands." This affair confirms that indeed, the marriage is unsatisfactory, and justifies moving ahead with the decision to separate. Because these affairs occur right before separation, they are often perceived as the cause of the split, although this is not the case. These affairs are the route used to end the marriage after a decision has been made to do so.

Although many participants in Exit Affairs claim they don't want their spouse to discover their affair, it seldom works out that way. When the primary purpose of the affair is to get the other spouse to take responsibility for ending the marriage, the unfaithful spouse ensures (unconsciously on purpose) that the affair is discovered. Many straying partners have been disappointed to discover that even with an affair, their spouse won't end the marriage. The emotional intensity of a disintegrating marriage and both partners' desire for an external reason for an impending separation also contribute to making secrecy impossible.

Although the relationship style of the marital partners tends to be conflict avoidant, these affairs tend to have a lot of sound and fury attached—it makes for good camouflage. Most of the sound and fury comes from the spouse. The straying partner remains relatively uninvolved, claiming "I didn't want to hurt you," but backing off as far as possible. This further infuriates the spouse. The partners become more polarized as they battle over which one is the "bad guy."

For many spouses, the idea of the third party as the bad guy is protective: "She left because he stole her away, not because of anything I did." Even so, the affair is a painful betrayal. The unfaithful spouse may attempt to validate the affair by marrying the third party, thus still avoiding the real issues. When this occurs, there is a high likelihood that this marriage too will end, and in much the same way that the first marriage ended. Most often, this affair ends some months after its purpose has been served.

> Lisa didn't consciously plan to have an affair. "John and I were having a rough time in our marriage, and I needed somebody to talk to. So I started talking to Gary, my office mate. He's such a good listener. I never thought I'd have an affair, but it just happened. When John found out, I moved out. I know he's really upset with me, but I didn't mean to hurt him. Besides, it's better for him too, not to have a wife there who doesn't really want to be there."

Those who leave the marriage through an affair in order to avoid responsibility and pain, find that they carry the pain and guilt into the future until they face themselves.

Differentiating Between Types of Affairs

Observation of the behavior patterns being played out in front of you helps in distinguishing between the different types of affairs. Some clients make it easy to identify the type of affair by providing a detailed picture of their relationship issues. Couples are sometimes less forthcoming than individuals about their situation initially, but with both partners present, observation of their communication patterns provides information about the type of affair. Figure 2.2 depicts the differing communication patterns of Conflict Avoiders, Intimacy Avoiders, and Exiters.

The dominant affect with Conflict Avoiders is a controlled amicability. Both spouses are fully engaged with each other, but they continue to avoid open conflict. It's not that there's never any conflict—it's that any conflict expressed by one spouse is dropped by the other. Even the spouse's obsession with the affair has an element of control. If the spouse "gets too emotional," the straying partner deflects the charge with a rational response, and vice versa. They try to move as little as possible from an invisible centerline. Conflict goes nowhere.

The Intimacy Avoiders are also fully engaged with each other, but the affect is chaotic. Communication is frequent and highly emotional as charges are tossed back and forth. The primary form of emotional connection is through conflict. Any moments of closeness are invariably followed by renewed fighting. These spouses try to achieve balance through wide swings in opposite directions from the invisible centerline. George and Martha, the battling couple in the movie *Who's Afraid of Virginia Wolf* (1966), are Intimacy Avoiders.

The most striking aspect of the Exit Affair is the straying partner's lack of involvement with the spouse. The straying partner is present physically, but not emotionally. He or she wants to avoid being the bad guy, and while claiming not to want to hurt the partner, sets the spouse up to be the bad guy. When the spouse responds with anger, it's viewed as confirmation that the spouse is the bad guy. For the straying partner, therapy is about leaving, not about connecting with the spouse.

Split Selves generally present a straight story when they come in individually. Their affect is the heaviness of chronic depression. When

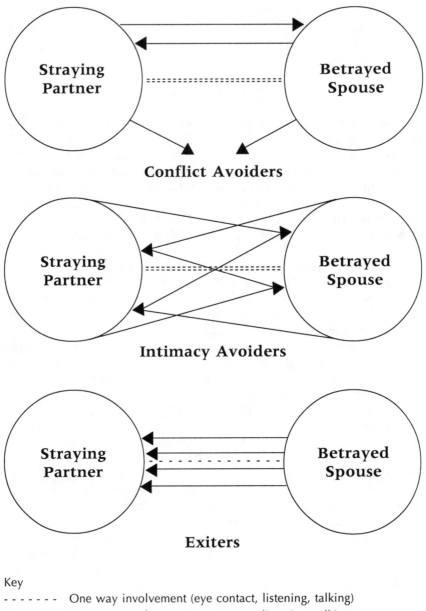

Conflict Avoiders

Intimacy Avoiders

Exiters

Key

- - - - - - One way involvement (eye contact, listening, talking)
========== Two way involvement (eye contact, listening, talking)
————————— Conflict
——————▶ Direction of conflict

FIGURE 2.2. Couples communication patterns in three types of affairs.

they arrive as a couple they are not quite so direct. The straying partner's inner split that is being played out with the spouse and the third party makes for ambiguous communication about the straying partner's intentions. Even if the straying partner indicates today that he wants to leave the marriage, by tomorrow he may be planning to stay.

Sexual Addicts avoid coming to therapists, but when they do the story usually comes out fairly soon, especially when they come because they know they need and want help. More information is likely to emerge if the spouse joins the Addict in coming for therapy. Others come because they've been court-ordered or because they are at risk in some significant way.

In most affairs, whether the third party is married or not makes no difference. The exception is the Split Self Affair, where the male straying partner usually picks a separated, divorced, or never married woman. The straying partner wants someone who is available for a relationship. The marital status of the third party is irrelevant for Conflict and Intimacy Avoiders. These affairs are not about having a relationship; therefore it doesn't matter whether the third party is available. The Sexual Addicts depersonalize their relationships, so anybody is a potential conquest. Some prefer a person who will lend status and others do not care. The marital status of the third party is similarly inconsequential for the Exit types, although that person also is considering separation in many cases.

While the prognosis for the marriage gets steadily worse as we move from the Conflict Avoiders to the Exit Affairs, the outlook for the individuals is different. Those individuals with the worst prognosis are the Sexual Addicts because of their extensive denial and their chaotic and often abusive childhood. The best prognosis is for those who heed the warning of the affair, and examine their real issues.

II

CRITICAL ISSUES IN TREATMENT

Treatment of individuals and couples who are struggling with an extramarital affair is challenging work. Our clients are, in turn, ambivalent, hurt, blinded by love, guilty, angry, fearful, and hopeful. Some seek our help in emerging unscathed, while others look to us for help in making sense out of the mess. A few are set on righteous vengeance, while many sweep it under the rug as soon as the crisis is past. Treatment goals and formats are related to the type of affair and to the stage of treatment.

The crisis of discovery brings many couples to therapy. Others come, either individually or together, prior to revelation of the affair in hopes of resolving their painful situations. During therapy the spouses face many decision points. Will the affair be revealed? If so, will it be concluded or will the marriage end? Is each spouse willing to work on the marriage?

On their own issues? Can they be honest with each other on a daily basis? Can they learn to resolve their differences? Can they forgive each other for the many betrayals in the past? Or if the marriage is ending, can they reach closure with each other? From the beginning we are working to take the affair off center stage so that the underlying issues can be addressed.

The pain associated with the revelation of the affair can be draining for the therapist as well as the couple. For the spouse who discovers the partner's affair, it feels like the end of the world. The therapist's reassurance that they can come to understand what has happened, and that major decisions can be deferred until then, gives hope where otherwise there may be despair.

The spouse's obsession when the affair is revealed is one of the more difficult aspects of therapy. However the affair is not the only betrayal between the spouses. Together they created a situation in which the affair could occur. The therapist needs to help the couple develop a shared definition of their underlying marital problems.

Some couples who want to avoid the pain and the hard work of rebuilding, mouth a hollow forgiveness that they hope will allow them to move directly to "Go," thus bypassing (briefly) "Jail." The therapist must not collude with them, but rather question how their approach will work, and help them talk about their fear that they will be unable to handle the pain. Even then, some couples do not have enough faith in themselves to face their situation.

Rebuilding takes a long time, whether it is focused on the marriage or on the individuals. Without the anchor of the old marital patterns, both spouses feel adrift. They alternate between desperately trying to find the old anchorage and cautious attempts to master new territory. Identifying patterns and issues in the family of origin makes the current situation more understandable. After learning to be honest with themselves as well as with their partner, the spouses are able to make decisions about the viability of their marriage.

As a rule, rebuilding takes longer for Sexual Addicts and Split Selves than for Conflict and Intimacy Avoiders because the issues go deeper and the problematic behavior patterns are longer standing. The ex-spouses in Exit Affairs also require a lengthy period of rebuilding because the issues of the affair are meshed and overlaid with issues of separation and divorce.

Forgiveness is the final phase and brings closure to the affair. Forgiveness goes in both directions, and is important for couples whose marriage ends as well for those who resolve their issues and move ahead together.

☐ Cautions for the Therapist

For the therapist, the field is mined. The unwary therapist can easily be the newest casualty in a field already littered with bodies. Addressing the issues of an affair requires skill on the part of the therapist, and the work can be demanding and emotionally draining. It also can be very satisfying.

Helping couples and individuals rebuild their lives after an affair is emotionally charged work. The therapist's responsibility is for the process, and the clients get to make the decisions about the outcome. The most difficult matters for the therapist are issues around the hidden affair and the spouse's obsession.

Traps for the therapist come from both external and internal sources. Clients often attempt to influence the therapist to take their side, to ignore certain facts, or to assess fault. Therapists themselves bring to the process their own issues, such as their own marital problems, an investment in "success," or a particular moral stance. Additionally, few therapists have training or a cohesive framework for addressing client's affairs. External and internal issues often come together to create confusion about how and whether to address the secret affair. Lack of clarity on the therapist's part guarantees falling into a trap.

A desire to ease the obsessive spouse's pain may reinforce the obsession to the degree that the therapist becomes exasperated and reverses direction, now protecting the betraying partner from the obsessive spouse. For example, one frustrated therapist said to the Betrayed spouse, "It's been two months now. You need to get over it and move on." They moved on—to another therapist. The therapist's role is not to protect but to help both partners explore and understand how they arrived at this painful point. Allowing the spouse's obsession to continue unchecked is destructive to what remains of the relationship. It also makes for a therapist who feels (and is) out of control.

Throughout the process of working with an affair, questions about pacing and timing arise. Each spouse needs sufficient time to sort through and express a wide range of feelings. Pain, in particular, needs to be attended to before moving on. If in doubt, pause. Taking enough time to deal with the difficult issues is essential. Other common traps for the therapist are pushing too hard to support one spouse or to promote a particular solution, avoiding pain or other intense emotions, encouraging discussion of all the details of the affair, judging the morality of the situation, doing the client's work, or attempting to compensate for the client's pain.

The following chapters describe a systemic approach to treatment, and specific techniques for each stage of the process. My process is a sequential one that calls for moving ahead one step at a time, as shown in Figure P2.1.

Clients find structure helpful during this painful and difficult period of their lives. Going step by step keeps the focus on accomplishing one task at a time and curbs the tendency to go off in all directions at once. Within the structure, ample space is provided for experiencing one's emotions, for thinking and talking through, and for examining one's own and one's family's patterns. The therapist needs to stay focused, leading the client through each of these steps while simultaneously being with the client emotionally.

An openness to working with issues of love and betrayal, as well as knowledge about affairs and their treatment, contribute to a successful therapeutic process for both the client and the therapist.

- **Unresolved Individual and Couple Problems**

- **Affair Occurs and is Hidden**

- **Disclosure**

   Therapist suspects or learns of affair
   Therapist confronts the straying partner
   4 Square Analysis—A process for deciding whether to tell
   Preparation for telling
   Telling

- **Crisis**

   Decrease obsession
   Develop a shared definition of the marital problem
   Affair ends?

- **Rebuilding Individually or Together**

   Resolve underlying issues
   Make decision about marriage

- **Forgiveness**

   Spouse
   Self

FIGURE P2.1. Sequence of steps in treating affairs. © 2000 Emily M. Brown.

CHAPTER

Hiding, Telling, or Getting Caught: Issues in Revealing an Affair

What is this dance that couples perform around the secret affair? Who is hiding what from whom? What is the stake of each spouse in keeping the affair a secret? Are the couples that resist exposing the secret different from those who disclose the affair?

☐ Therapists' Perspectives on Disclosure

Whether and how to reveal a hidden affair when working with a couple is the trickiest and most complicated issue facing the marital therapist. Disagreement among therapists is greater on this issue than on any other issue related to affairs. Some therapists strongly believe that it is destructive to take an active role in surfacing a secret that has the power to shatter trust, or even precipitate the end of the marriage. Theirs is more of a problem-solving or skill-based approach that addresses communication problems or other issues with the couple in the hope that this work will eliminate the affair, allowing the couple to move on. (It is possible to resolve some of the peripheral issues, at least at a mechanical level, despite the existence of an affair.) Affairs in the past, or even affairs that have recently ended, are addressed with a "let sleeping dogs lie" attitude. A similar stance is taken by other therapists who think disclosure of this potent a secret is cruel, and want to protect a spouse who will be devastated upon learning of the affair.

The opposite philosophy is held by therapists who believe it is impossible to do marital work with an elephant sized secret in the middle of the room. Generally these therapists are more systemically oriented, and believe that effective marital therapy is based on honesty between spouses and the need to address reality. They regard secrets as crazy-making and information as empowering. They also regard withholding one spouse's secret from the other as a betrayal of trust. Rosemarie Welter-Enderlin, a Swiss therapist, comments: Many secrets in peoples lives have to do not so much with tragedies but with the messes caused by lies or denial (1993, p. 53). In *Dance of Deception* (1993), Harriet Lerner states, "No matter what the potential for intimacy in a marriage, it is impossible to feel close to a person one is hiding from, confusing, throwing off track, deceiving" (p. 159). These therapists are aware that buried secrets often come back to haunt people.

A great many hidden affairs, probably most, do surface sooner or later. What would it mean to the betrayed spouse to learn that you colluded with the straying partner in keeping the affair a secret? Would this not be experienced as another betrayal? Should this happen it would probably mean the end of couples therapy, not only with you but also with any therapist because of the damaged trust.

The therapist's beliefs about disclosing an affair also are influenced by personal experience. Unfinished business about one's own or one's spouse's affair can cut either way, towards disclosure or secrecy, but in this instance, the approach is contaminated since it is not based on clinical theory and experience, nor on the client's situation. A parent's affair too, can unduly influence the therapist's beliefs about disclosure. Resolution of one's own issues about affairs can lead to a more considered stance, based on clinical theory and experience, while also drawing on the lessons of personal experience.

Welter-Enderlin (1993) reflects,

> In my early work with couples, I tended to be so eager not to fall in love with tragedy that I would bravely avoid the topic of secrets and lies. As a result of the emphasis on optimism and quick problem-solving, I acquired what I now call a "fear of darkness.". . . Many of the secrets in couples and couples' therapy are related to issues of sexuality, shame, and violence. If we as therapists try to "fix" things simply by offering positive connotations or behavioral prescriptions as I did early in my practice, we may offer relief from immediate pressure. However if this is all we do, we tend to conspire with a prohibition to put experience into words which often is part of the problem already" (pp. 53–54).

My work is grounded in a systemic approach to couples therapy, and also in the belief that honesty, empathy, and reality are the corner-stones of effective therapy. I regard disclosure as a critical step in treatment, one that precipitates a marital crisis, and thus, an opportunity for change. It also holds various traps for the unwary therapist. Revealing an affair is best viewed in the context of marital therapy, whether your client is a couple or an individual. Before discussing how to reveal an affair, it is important to understand why it is usually essential to do so and to recognize the factors which, in a few cases, indicate that revelation may be destructive.

☐ Secrecy

Secrecy in families is destructive at best. Karpel (1980) describes it thusly: "The unaware are likely to experience anxiety in relation to seemingly inexplicable tension that develops when areas relevant to the secret are discussed with the secret holders. They may also experience confusion and a variety of negative feelings in relation to the 'explanations' they formulate in an attempt to understand this anxiety . . . (Secrets) may contribute to a vague but tenacious sense of shame or guilt in the unaware" (p. 300). Sharon's reaction to secrecy and disclosure illustrates Karpel's point.

> Sharon, a 39-year-old attorney, learned at a young age not to ask her father anything because he exploded, occasionally becoming physically abusive. Sharon's mother made excuses for him, saying "He really loves you. He didn't meant to hurt you." No one ever talked about what family skeletons lay buried underneath the abuse and the cover up.
>
> Sharon chose a husband, Max, whom she knew would not be physically abusive. Max worked long hours, sometimes coming home at 2 a.m., but Sharon never questioned him. Instead she complained about problems with her secretary, or with a colleague. About ten years into the marriage, she began feeling vaguely dissatisfied, which she countered with efforts to be more understanding of Max. It didn't work, and her self-doubt grew. After all, they had everything, why was she so unhappy?
>
> On their twelfth anniversary Max confessed to a series of affairs. A few weeks later Sharon described her reaction. "What a tremendous relief! I thought I was going crazy. Everything I felt makes sense now."

In Sharon's case, the secrecy in her family of origin taught her not to pay attention to her feelings. Without this ability, she could not validate her own experience, making it impossible for her to talk to Max about her dissatisfaction. It is this dynamic which leads to a denial of self, and lays the groundwork for emotional disturbances.

Another perspective on secrecy, that of insiders and outsiders, is germane here. In the family, the one who doesn't know the secret becomes the outsider. This person commonly reacts by searching within for what is wrong, and then attempts to correct it by trying even harder to please. As these efforts fail, resentment grows underneath the surface. Before long, the attempt to gain (or regain) insider status becomes an indiscriminate scramble, as the outsider's efforts fail and self-esteem diminishes. Alternatively, the outsider may cope through denial, until the eventual crisis burns through the denial.

Those in the addictions field believe that family secrets create the shame that underlies addiction. Bradshaw (1988) asserts, "*Families are as sick as their secrets*. The secrets are what they are ashamed of. Family secrets go back for generations. . . . All the secrets get acted out. . . . The pain and suffering of shame generate automatic and unconscious defenses. . . . Because they are unconscious, we lose touch with the shame, hurt and pain they cover up. *We cannot heal what we cannot feel*" (p. 32).

Pittman (1989) comments, "Couples need not tell each other every detail of their activity and every thought that goes through their heads, but they do have to tell each other the bad news. . . . The things people must be sure to talk about are those things that are unsettling, guilt-producing, or controversial" (p. 281).

Monogamous Marriage and the Secret Affair

When the marital contract includes monogamy, and it usually does, a hidden affair is not just a betrayal, but a time-bomb. Not only is information about the affair hidden, but the process of secrecy results in additional layers of secrecy that are necessary to hide the original secret. With a secret affair, communication about other matters is gradually impaired. The person not in on the secret feels left out and wonders, "What's the matter with me?" Attempts to "fix things" fail because the true nature of the problem is not known. Growth is impossible, and the intimacy that once existed erodes. The effect of the secret affair is described by Lawson (1988): "The weight of this secret may then come to control life, shut down activity, and impose unbearable limits to living comfortably" (p. 203).

Traditional gender differences persist when it comes to affairs. Lawson (1988) notes that "Marriage has denoted quite different roles to husbands and to wives: in particular men have held the power and women have been required to serve and nurture them" (p. 53). Women "suffer more acutely from deceit" (1988, p. 233) when the marital contract calls for fidelity. Although men believe that their disclosure of an affair will have little impact on the marriage, "To tell a husband about an affair . . . is really to court the end of the marriage" (pp. 233–234).

My clinical experience corroborates Lawson's findings: betraying females are more reluctant to reveal an affair than are males. Women are more afraid of the anticipated repercussions, whether it is guilt over the spouse's pain, fear of the spouse's retaliation, or apprehension that the marriage will end. When a woman reveals an affair, her marriage is more likely to end, whereas that is not true for the betraying male who reveals his affair (Lawson, 1988, p. 79). Women also choose more often than men to leave the marriage rather than reveal the affair. This may mean that the marriage has deteriorated further by the time the woman has the affair, or that women's affairs tend more often to be Exit Affairs. Possibly leaving is related to the tendency of married women, more than married men, to become emotionally involved in an affair (Glass & Wright, 1985). It may also mean that women leave in order to justify the affair or to avoid repercussions should the spouse find out.

Considerations for the straying partner, and for the therapist as well, initially focus on what disclosure will mean for each spouse and for their relationship. For some therapists, the possible repercussions of disclosures that extend beyond the immediate family are confusing. What are the larger implications of revealing an affair? Will extended family or friends be impacted and in what ways? If the affair becomes known at work will it wreck one's career? What impact will disclosure have on the third party and that individual's personal and professional network? What are the consequences of disclosure or nondisclosure for an employer, as when an individual could be subject to blackmail? Does it make a difference when the straying partner is someone who is highly visible? Might denial of an affair lead to more difficulty than would disclosure, as with President Clinton? How does the ethical therapist view and respond to these considerations?

Fallout may occur whether or not disclosure is made to the spouse, because the affair couple's behavior has usually been quite overt. The danger for the therapist is being so distracted by possible fallout that the central issue, disclosure of the affair, is put aside. A more useful approach is to think through who needs to know what, and how this information can best be shared. The hidden affair is first and foremost a problem between the two spouses, and the immediate and primary focus needs to center on disclosing the affair to the spouse. Beyond that, only those who are directly impacted are entitled to know. Children, for example, usually need to have age-appropriate information (see Chapter 13). If the affair is with a family member, the family is already being impacted, and disclosure takes that reality out from under the rug and puts it on the table. The employer probably does not need to know, depending on whether the affair is directly relevant to the job. With those for whom the affair is relevant, information helps in addressing what is happening in their lives.

☐ Revelation and Couples: When and When Not to Reveal an Affair

Couples who come for help come because they are hurting. When the affair is part of that hurt, it needs to be addressed in order to stop the pain. I believe that the integrity of the therapeutic process with couples depends on open and honest communication. Nowhere is this truer than with affairs. The therapist can not be effective while colluding with one spouse to hide the truth from the other.

In couples therapy, those with the secret affair are most often Conflict Avoiders. The Intimacy Avoiders know about the affair(s)—it has to be known to serve its purpose. The Sexual Addicts seldom come for couples therapy, but when they do, the addictive pattern is usually what brings them and it is known to the spouse. With Split Selves who come as a couple, the affair is generally known because it has impacted the marriage for a considerable time. When the spouse doesn't know, it is because she has put blinders on so as to protect her tremendous investment. Recognizing his affair will bring the whole structure crashing down. Moreover, she believes that if there is something wrong, it is her fault.

The Exit Affair is usually known because it is serving as the getaway vehicle in ending the marriage. Sometimes however, the straying partner is stymied by the spouse who won't look at the affair. The spouse's denial may be an attempt to maintain the marriage, or to prevent being dumped or assigned the blame for ending the marriage. The Intimacy Avoiders are the quickest to recognize an affair, because they search for ammunition to use against each other.

In order to effectively address the hidden affair, the therapist needs to have developed rapport with the couple. This usually takes several sessions. Be cautious about meeting individually with spouses during the first month or so of therapy as you may be given information about an affair which you do not yet have sufficient rapport to use effectively.

Another issue that sometimes arises in an individual session is when the straying spouse shares the secret of the affair, and then says, "But you can't tell my spouse." These mixed messages indicate extreme ambivalence on the part of the betrayer, who offers the secret with one hand and takes it away with the other. Yet at some level, our clients know that the marital therapist is supposed to be an agent of honesty and reality. The straying spouse did not have to disclose the affair, but chose to do so. Therefore I interpret the message as one of asking for help in revealing the secret.

When Not to Reveal an Affair

In a few situations, however, it is best not to reveal an affair. For example, when there is the potential for physical violence or for destructive litigation in divorce courts (violence of another sort), issues of safety and security take precedence. Then there are the situations in which the straying partner remains in the marriage to care for a permanently incapacitated spouse; revelation of the affair serves no good purpose and, in fact, may be harmful. In some cases, your role with the couple will preclude you from working toward disclosure, as when the number of sessions is extremely limited. And sometimes couples choose not to confront the truth. They have the right to make that choice, although that choice effectively ends marital therapy. Most people however, prefer to know the truth and find it easier to handle than lies and secrecy.

Physical Violence

When there is the potential for physical violence, revelation is contra-indicated. Before deciding against disclosure, find out what violence means to your client. For some people "He'll get violent" means "He'll yell," which does not preclude revealing the affair. For others it means "He will beat me," a very different matter. The straying partner's concern about the potential for violence needs to be explored carefully, noting the history of angry outbursts, acting out behavior, previous threats, or destructive behavior. Any history of physical violence that has not been resolved is enough to rule out disclosure. Resolved means that issues regarding power, control, and powerlessness have been dealt with and the individual has developed new skills that replace becoming physical when feeling angry or powerless.

Most spouses who have never lost control are unlikely to do so, even when faced with their partner's affair. However, affair-specific and divorce-specific violence can occur without any prior history of abuse. Violence related to an affair stems primarily from issues of power and powerlessness, rather than sex. Lying and secrecy, which are always present in an affair, are power plays. Disclosure clarifies the truth, not just of the affair, but of the dishonesty. Many betrayed spouses feel powerless upon learning of their partner's affair, and their fury is a defense against feeling so powerless. Most have the skills to restrain their behavior but some don't. For a profile of those who are potentially violent in this situation, see Chapter 14.

Women who have affairs are more likely to be afraid of violence than their male counterparts for several reasons. Women often feel helpless in the face of physical violence, in part because they lack the strength of men. Moreover, in some parts of our society, physical violence is an accepted reaction of a man whose wife has an affair.

The Exit Affair

In the midst of the legal proceedings, initiating revelation of an affair can be counterproductive or even dangerous. Even in the days of "no-fault divorce," the affair can easily be used to confuse more important issues, which leads to violence of another sort: the destructive legal contest. The emotional costs of a legal contest are so great that the therapeutic benefits of disclosure are outweighed. Even when adultery is not used as grounds for divorce, it may influence a judge in making decisions about parenting arrangements and financial matters. These are decisions that should be based on the needs and resources of the family members and not on the basis of "adultery."

If, however, the spouse suspects an affair, and wants to know, the therapist should not be a party to hiding reality. But when the spouse does not know and is not asking, the focus is more appropriately placed on the fact that the marriage is ending, the feelings about reaching this point, and on the practical aspects of separating.

Couples Who Avoid the Truth

The couple may not want to handle the truth immediately. The straying partner has mixed feelings about revealing the affair. On one hand is guilt, and on the other is the desire for integrity. The betrayed spouse is equally ambivalent. Hearing the truth means having to face problems that so far have been avoided. Self-esteem is also involved—an affair means "I have not been what he wanted." Couples who are not ready to face the reality of an affair will collude to end therapy quickly.

Colin and Mary Sue came for marriage counseling because they were dissatisfied with the way their marriage was going. Mary Sue didn't like the time Colin spent away from home on photography, and Colin was uncomfortable with Mary Sue's demands for more time. Neither one was clear about what he or she was feeling. Their goals for therapy were nebulous: essentially to "improve the marriage." The sessions never quite got going.

Colin's pattern of absences from home, combined with my inability to pinpoint the marital problems led me to think that Colin was having an affair. I confronted him individually. He didn't actually admit to the affair, but neither did he deny it, and at that point he knew that I knew. Just before the next session, I received a message from Mary Sue canceling the appointment, and saying, "We can't afford therapy any longer." I interpreted the message to mean that Colin and Mary Sue are still hoping that they won't have to deal with anything as difficult and unpleasant as an affair. Neither of them is sufficiently uncomfortable to be willing to face the truth yet, but by the time they are, it may be too late for the marriage.

Disclosure and the Therapist's Role

Another consideration in whether to work toward revelation of an affair is your role with the couple. If you don't have an ongoing relationship with the couple (as, for example, in Employee Assistance Programs where treatment is limited to a few sessions), and you come across a hidden affair, refer the couple to someone who can help them surface the affair and address its meaning. Take the same approach when the couple's agenda with you is not the marriage, but brief therapy around an issue such as care of an elderly parent. In other words, do not open the issue of an affair unless you will be available to then help resolve the issue, which takes time.

When the symptom is an acting-out child, surfacing the affair and the related marital and family issues may be the key factor in providing appropriate treatment for the child. If you are the child's therapist, it may or may not be appropriate for you to address the affair with the parents, depending on the child's needs. When it is not, refer this piece of the work to an experienced couples therapist, with whom you can work closely. If your role is family therapist, the mandate is different and these issues are yours to address. If you're the marital therapist and the agenda is their relationship, it is essential that you help them uncover the affair.

It is crucial that the couple have enough time to address the issues that are surfaced by disclosure of the affair, time to experience the shock and the fury, time to sort through what has happened and what it means, and time to resolve the underlying issues. This is work that cannot be rushed, for when it is, it leaves in its wake a cracked foundation that will trouble the relationship. Lawson suggests that the disclosure of an affair is not unlike the revelation of past sexual abuse in its impact on the marriage, and needs to be treated as carefully (personal communication, December, 1989).

In the days of managed care, having adequate time to resolve the issues underlying the affair means that clients will have to pay for most or all of their treatment themselves. Many can not afford to do so. Limiting treatment to that approved by managed care means ignoring the underlying issues. As a result, we can expect to see greater negative fallout from affairs including a greater incidence of depression and of physical manifestations of untreated emotional problems, increased severity of marital problems, and negative effects for children that will be carried into the next generation. Family well-being and managed care are diametrically opposed.

Issues in the Disclosure of Ancient Affairs

With ancient affairs (three, five, ten, or more years in the past), whether to reveal an affair is more of a judgment call. In some families, an ancient affair is the next piece of the puzzle and nothing else will fall into place until that piece is surfaced. Therapeutic progress is at a standstill until the affair is revealed. In this situation the therapist clearly needs to help the straying spouse reveal the affair in a responsible and sensitive manner.

Yet some couples appear to be functioning well together despite an ancient and hidden affair. This is where the therapist's judgment comes in. Questions to consider include:

- Can the couple continue their good relationship, or will unresolved problems surface at some future point?
- Was the affair a relationship or a one night stand?
- What will the costs be of revealing the affair now, and what will the costs be if it is discovered later?
- How do these costs compare with the likely costs of not revealing the affair?
- What is the likelihood that the affair will be discovered anyway?

Some therapists believe that the ancient affair is a sleeping dog, best left to sleep. The thinking is that it's over, it's in the past, and doesn't have relevance for the present. My bias is toward revealing ancient affairs when they are discovered in the course of marital therapy. My rationale is that marital therapy is sought out only when other efforts have failed to resolve marital problems. Couples who are willing to invest their time and energy in marital therapy are those who want improvement in the quality of their relationship. Even if the affair was brief and in the past, hiding it means holding back a piece of one's self. Holding one secret leads to hiding other things. The fact that I have learned about the hidden affair suggests it is not a closed issue. Disclosure of an ancient affair is not for the purpose of dumping and getting rid of it, but rather to examine why it happened, what it meant, and how it affected and continues to affect the marriage. Then the affair can be put to rest.

Unless an affair is disclosed, the potential lingers that the spouse will find out.

> The affair burst into Linda's consciousness as she sat reading a woman's magazine article on STDs while waiting for her car to be repaired. Her doctor had never informed her that crabs were sexually transmitted, and her husband had suggested she'd probably gotten crabs when she took the kids camping. Now she knew otherwise. For her it was as if the affair had just occurred, but with 12 years of dishonesty to boot.

Other therapists believe that disclosure of ancient affairs is not always necessary in marital therapy. Westfall (1989) suggests that the therapist can leave disclosure to the client's discretion if the affair ended some time ago and does not appear to have had a lasting impact on the marriage, or if the affair was an isolated instance with no emotional attachment. She cautions however, that the therapist cannot always accurately assess the impact of previous affairs on the present marital relationship, and may need at some point to insist on disclosure.

☐ Disclosure and Individual Clients

The issues about revealing a secret affair are somewhat different when your client is the straying partner rather than the couple. You are not in the position of working with the spouse while keeping the secret. Therefore you have much more time to work with the straying partner toward surfacing the hidden affair. Some straying partners are only able to disclose their affair after they understand its meaning. Welter-Enderlin (1993) finds that

> *temporary secretiveness* nearly always precedes a new balance of power and intimacy with a new regulation of who determines closeness and

distance and how. . . . An extramarital affair, which is kept secret, at first seems to fulfill the not yet conscious need of one or the other to demarcate a 'room of one's own.' If things turn out positively, the secret is disclosed and, eventually, a new balance between the 'I' and the 'we' in the relationship is achieved, with both partners experiencing bonding as well as individual freedom at a new level of differentiation (p. 57).

Other issues are important here as well. Why has the individual come for help? What are the individual's goals? It may be that the presenting problem pertains to the loss of a parent, to dealing with the emotional aspects of physical problems, or other issues. While these are bound to impact the marital relationship, the relationship may not be what the person wants help with. When your client is the straying partner, he or she will probably share the affair with you. If the affair is a Conflict Avoidance affair, timely disclosure can serve as a wake-up call that prevents further deterioration of the marriage. The therapy may shift from individual to marital work once the affair is known.

With Split Self straying partners, the affair is usually known by the spouse at the time the individual first comes in. If not, considerable work may be needed to get it into the open, because Split Selves are deeply invested in being nice so as to avoid emotional pain. Because you will be working with the person individually for a while, you can work on disclosure over time.

Sexual Addicts sometimes present as individuals. Although their reason for coming in may be to pacify a spouse or a lover, underneath the surface is a great deal of shame and a fragment of hope for real help. At the same time the denial and resistance are tremendous. Because of this facade, many therapists assume that the Addict does not want help or cannot be helped, and thus do not attempt to get beneath the denial. Hard confrontation by the therapist about the sexual addiction is in order. This confrontation must be supportive as opposed to judgmental, for the latter leads to increased shame and denial. Look for ways to tap into the addict's dislike of his own behavior and his desire for something better, but be clear that coming out of hiding is essential to change.

The Spouse: Confronting the Hidden Affair

Perhaps your client is a spouse who is bewildered by various marital problems, or who is unhappy and wonders what is wrong with him or herself. If the dissatisfaction seems to stem from the marital relationship, yet the specifics are vague, the problem may be an affair. Asking whether he or she has wondered about an affair will clarify the feelings just below the surface. If the answer is "yes," help your client talk more about his or her suspicions.

Your client may have already asked the partner whether he or she is having an affair and been told "no." Since most straying partners deny an affair when first asked, and many deny for some time, a "no" is not conclusive. If your client is generally a trusting person, but continues to be suspicious, help your client prepare to confront the partner. The client can take essentially the same approach a therapist would take, stating clearly and firmly, "I think you're having an affair," and then wait for a response. Notice that this is not a yes-or-no question. Deciding on optimum timing and a suitable location is part of the planning.

For your client to effectively confront the partner, your client must be ready to accept the truth, whatever that turns out to be. In the movie *Heartburn*, Rachel ignores numerous clues that her husband Mark is having an affair. When she is finally able to confront the truth, she takes an active role in compiling the evidence and confronting Mark.

The oversuspicious spouse is a different matter. This spouse is obsessed, in fact almost paranoid, with the idea that the partner is having an affair, yet the partner continues to deny it. Your knowledge of the partner leads you to believe that there is no affair. It may be that the partner's pattern of secrecy about other matters has been misinterpreted, or the spouse's obsession may represent that person's difficulty in facing their own issues (see Chapter 5 for a discussion of obsession and its treatment).

When to Disclose the Affair

For the great majority of couples in couples therapy, contraindications to disclosure do not apply, and the revelation of the affair needs to be handled promptly and carefully. Karpel (1980) suggests using the standard of "accountability with discretion," which considers the relevance of the information, the likely perspective of the other person, and the timing and consequences of disclosure for that person. He notes that "A current secret extra-marital affair by one spouse is, in most cases, highly relevant to the other spouse, because it involves major issues of trust and trustworthiness, deception, and a violation of reciprocity" (Karpel, 1980, p. 298).

Not all therapists share this view. Humphrey (1987) refuses to take a stance in regard to revealing a current affair, claiming ethical neutrality. He will not insist that the secret affair be revealed, and keeps to himself the confidences revealed in the individual sessions which parallel couples therapy. His rationale is that clients hold exclusive rights to decisions about revealing an affair, and he cautions that revelation means extensive work will be needed to rebuild trust. Glass and Wright (1988) believe "It is inappropriate to conduct conjoint marital therapy when there is a secret alliance between one spouse and an extramarital partner that is being supported by another secret alliance between the involved spouse and the therapist" (p. 327). They however, will see the couple without addressing the affair, if the affair is first terminated.

With marital therapy, once rapport has been established between the couple and the therapist, the earlier the disclosure of an affair, the better. Otherwise, any work that has been done is jeopardized as is the therapy itself, by the fact that it occurred under false pretenses. The spouse's sense of betrayal and outrage is greater and trust is much more difficult to rebuild, than when the affair is revealed early in marital therapy.

☐ Determining Whether There Is an Affair

Although the Conflict Avoidance affair is unconsciously intended to get the partner's attention, the betrayer has great ambivalence about making the affair known. At the same time, the spouse knows at some level about the affair, though denies it consciously (Charny, 1992; Lawson, 1988). The reasons the spouse does not see the affair are closely related to the motivations for the affair in the first place, and to the couple's established patterns of relating to each other.

Sometimes the cues presented by clients clearly suggest an affair. In other cases the situation is not obvious. What is clear is that there is a secret. With couples, nine times out of ten, the secret is an affair. The rest of the time it is something equally significant for the course of therapy.

Therapists are often puzzled that the spouse doesn't tune in to the affair sooner. It is almost as if the spouse is blind to the obvious. The truth is that the spouse doesn't want to know about the affair. Magical thinking at a semi-conscious level is a common defense: "John wouldn't have an affair—I'm just feeling upset these days. I won't think about it, and then it won't be true." A more extreme case of denial occurred with Marty, who rationalized that intercourse six weeks prior to the date of conception might account for his wife's pregnancy: "I don't know, maybe sometimes it takes that long for the sperm to find the egg."

Cues for the Therapist

As the therapist for the couple, you will be picking up the same cues that the betrayer is giving the spouse. Among other things, you'll hear about frequent delays in coming home, sudden changes in grooming, more and more time spent with a colleague, a sudden increase or decrease in sexual activity between the spouses, hours spent chatting on the internet, testiness on the part of the straying partner, and unexplained and recurrent absences from home. There may be a family history of affairs. Once you start to think there may be an affair, consider asking the spouse during a couples session if he or she has wondered if the partner is having an affair. The usual answer is "Yes, I've asked, and she says she's not having an affair," and the issue is dropped immediately. The intent in asking is not to get the straying partner to admit the affair, but to find out whether the spouse suspects an affair. If the spouse has wondered about an affair, this reinforces my suspicions.

Most telling is the sense of a missing piece in the therapy; an elusive quality in defining the marital problem. It seems that I have my hands on the problem, and in the next session it is clear that I don't. This is always an indicator that something is hidden. Usually that something is an affair. If it is not an affair, it is another secret, and will be significant in the therapy. Anything that drains that much energy from the marriage is relevant.

Substantiating an Affair

To substantiate an affair, the therapist needs to confront the suspected betrayer individually. Before this, you need to have established good rapport with the couple, and have a clear sense of their patterns. The straying partner will not reveal an affair in a couple's session, and if confronted in that setting, will probably lie—and has probably lied to the spouse already. Set up the situation, in so far as possible, to prevent the betrayer from lying to you. Arrange separate sessions with each spouse, without explaining why you are doing so. Clients will generally assume that this is what you normally do.

You will want to address issues of confidentiality before you meet with clients separately. Is information that comes up in an individual session confidential, or is it to be brought to the couples session? If the latter, when and by whom? My belief is that anything that is significant for the marriage needs to be brought to the couples work. Some therapists state at the beginning of therapy that they do not keep secrets between spouses. I tell my clients that I will not share one spouse's confidences with the other spouse, but that I will flag anything that they must bring back to the couples' work, and I will help them prepare to do so. You may want to establish as part of your contract with couples that, should they end up separating, they will not request your participation or your records for any legal proceedings.

Some therapists suggest a disclaimer at the beginning of marital therapy to the effect that if one spouse keeps a secret from the other, the therapist will not work with them. This is intended to prevent leading the spouses down a path where they believe what they say to the therapist is confidential—in particular, that it will remain hidden from the spouse—only to find later that unless they share the secret with their spouse, therapy will end. The problems here are that a client may respond by not telling the therapist of an affair, the disclaimer may scare the couple away from therapy, and most important, the clients don't get a chance to process their own decision about whether to tell. Part of the rationale for the disclaimer approach is to be totally up front from the beginning, and partly it is to prevent litigation against the therapist. (Not only do we have managed care driving some treatment decisions, but also a fear of litigation that drives others.)

When issues of confidentiality have been addressed, you can proceed with a few individual sessions. Tell, rather than ask, the straying partner that you think he or she is having an affair. A yes or no question provides an easy way for the straying partner to say "no." State firmly, "I think you are having an affair." Be assertive without being accusatory. This will be a difficult confrontation for you as well as your client. Don't let your anxiety push you to clutter up your statement with a prefix or a postscript. Clutter gives your client ways to avoid your statement. Instead, wait for the straying partner's response. One of four things will happen: The straying partner will admit the affair, the straying partner will admit a different secret, the straying partner will change the subject, or the straying partner will deny an affair and will terminate therapy within a few weeks. If the straying partner changes the subject, make your statement again. The straying partner is very ambivalent about revealing the affair to you, because it is the first step toward revealing it to the spouse. Be supportive but persistent. Stay in touch with your own perception of the situation, keeping in mind your sense of the secrecy that is creating problems in the marriage. Any answer other than a genuine "no," means yes, as the straying partner knows. When the straying partner admits to an affair, respond with, "Okay, let's talk about telling your partner."

When Paula admitted to me that she was having an affair with a man at work, she also confessed, "I've been waiting for you to figure it out, but I wasn't going to help you." Her feelings pro and con were so evenly balanced that she needed my help to get the affair out into the open. Once I knew, she talked at length about her fear and her relief, her ambivalence about telling her husband, and she began to expand her consideration of what she needed to do next. She also divulged, "If you hadn't figured it out, I wouldn't have stayed much longer. That's why I didn't stay with the other therapists." Her intent was not to test therapists; her behavior was a very real reflection of her ambivalence. As therapists, we need to remember that if we don't help our clients get to the issues they need to get to, there's no reason for them to continue in therapy.

If the straying partner really wanted the affair to be a secret, he or she wouldn't have told the therapist. Telling the therapist is a request for help in revealing the situation to the spouse. The mixed message speaks to the person's ambivalence about hiding the affair. When your client is the couple you can not agree to keep an affair secret from the other spouse. To do so creates an alliance with one spouse against the other, so that the process of therapy itself becomes dishonest.

☐ Deciding Whether to Disclose

Once the therapist is in on the secret, it is time to help the straying partner decide whether to get the affair out in the open. Therapy becomes a dysfunctional triangle if you are in on the secret and the spouse is not. Even at this point the straying partner will probably express some resistance to telling the spouse. There is a struggle between "not wanting to hurt the spouse" (which is really a fear of the spouse's pain and rage), and wanting to stop hiding and lying. Conflict Avoiders are prone to feel out of control when they consider letting the cat out of the bag. They may contend, "Well, I've stopped it and I'm not doing it any more, so why should I bring it up now?"

Go with both sides of the ambivalence, helping the straying partner play out the likely consequences of either decision, the pros and cons of each, and the costs of each. Use the four-square technique to ask, "What is the worst possible outcome if you don't reveal the affair?" And, "What is the best possible outcome in that situation?" "What is the worst possible outcome if you reveal the affair?" And, "What is the best possible outcome?" Have the straying partner answer each of the four questions, and then play back what you have heard. Cycle through this as many times as necessary, getting more detail about possible outcomes each time.

You can insert information (but not a decision) into the process with questions. You might wonder aloud whether some aspect of the spouse's behavior about which the betrayer has complained is a reaction to the secrecy, or you might ask whether the outcome would be worse if the spouse found out about the affair from someone other than the betrayer. The process is back and forth, and back and forth again. The straying partner begins to clarify, anticipate, and plan for the disclosure.

After the second or third cycle, ask the person where they think their best chances lie. If they don't know, ask them what they need to know to make a decision. They may try to get some sort of guarantee from you. Resist giving any guarantees, and acknowledge their realization of the risks of telling. Almost everyone who engages in this process arrives at a decision to tell. As the individual realizes the hiding is over, he will experience some relief. Those who will not tell, usually won't even engage in this process.

This preparation process may require several individual sessions over the course of a few weeks. Individual sessions with one spouse present an issue for the therapist when the other spouse does not know about them. If you anticipate the need for individual sessions, tell both spouses in a joint session that you will see each of them separately for a few sessions. In some cases this is not possible, as when the straying partner reveals the secret to you while the spouse is home sick and requests another session before the next joint meeting. Limit such individual sessions to a brief period, and keep them focused on preparing to reveal the affair. Any such sessions must be made known at the time the affair is revealed.

> Evan admitted he was having an affair when I confronted him in a split session. He agreed to tell his wife at the next session. However the next day he called me: "I need to come in and talk with you about this." He had tremendous ambivalence and fear about disclosing his affair, and we went back and forth, exploring each side of his struggle. A growing awareness that he needed to tell Rita if he was to have any chance for the kind of marriage he wanted, led to planning how he would tell her. Evan called me again the day before the next joint session, declaring, "I'm not so sure this is a good idea." I suggested he come in, and once more we explored his ambivalence and his readiness to reveal his secret. This session was more last minute jitters than any real change in direction. The next day he opened the session by turning to Rita and quietly saying, "Rita, there is something I need to tell you. I've been having an affair."
>
> Evan's ambivalence and fear were so great that these individual sessions were essential, although Rita did not know of them at the time. Without this preparation, Evan would not have made the disclosure. His

wife's reaction on being told of the secret sessions, was to inquire how long I had known and how had I figured it out.

Individual sessions in the context of couples therapy that are not known to the spouse can only occur for a brief period of time (weeks, not months), and only if the straying partner is actively working toward revealing the affair. These individual sessions must be disclosed at the time the affair is revealed. Otherwise the individual relationship with the therapist begins to take on attributes of an affair itself. Similarly, once the couples' therapist is in on the secret, the focus needs to be on whether the affair will be disclosed, and if so, planning for the disclosure. Lengthy delays here put the therapist in the position of withholding very relevant information from the spouse, and have the potential to sabotage therapy, or even to be the focus of litigation.

Therapists who continue to work with a couple after learning of an affair without taking any steps toward surfacing the secret may be setting themselves up for malpractice charges, or even a lawsuit filed by the betrayed spouse.

Refusal to Reveal

Sometimes the straying partner refuses to tell the spouse. What does that mean for marital therapy? A refusal to address this big a secret means that marital therapy cannot continue. Once you know about the affair, nothing else can be done until the affair is out in the open. Sometimes the straying partner will persuade the spouse to drop out of treatment at this point to make sure the affair stays hidden, and an insecure spouse will agree in an attempt to gain approval. In other cases you will need to terminate the couple's work. In terminating, leave the secret of the affair for the couple to address. You can state simply that you will not be able to continue seeing them. The spouse will probably inquire why you are terminating therapy. You can simply say, You're not ready for marital therapy," or "Ask your partner," or, "Your partner has made a decision that makes it impossible for me to continue seeing you." Resist the temptation to explain further, because there is nothing you can say without exposing or hiding the secret. If you are tempted to see either or both of them individually, consider the impact on the therapeutic relationship of doing so. Working with both keeps you in the role of secret-keeper, working with the spouse puts therapy in jeopardy when the secret does come out, and working with the straying partner can be seen by both as colluding with the secret. Provide referrals for each to separate therapists.

You may ask, "Shouldn't you let clients know before they decide whether to tell that you won't be able to continue seeing them if they don't tell?" This question implies an unfairness on the therapist's part. The opposite question is: Isn't it unfair to leverage the client's decision-making about disclosure with this consideration. Schlossberger and Hecker (1996) caution that "Therapists who have knowledge of the adultery but remain silent may be in the ethically questionable position of continuing treatment they know to be futile" (p. 36). They suggest several items for inclusion in a disclosure statement that helps address the inherent conflict here.

My decision not to continue seeing the couple is a consequence of one spouse's decision, and should not be a factor in the decision itself. Making it a factor would be biasing a decision that is best made for other reasons. Stating this position prior to helping clients go through their own decision-making process could be construed as saying, "If you don't do it my way, I won't work with you." At the very least it would insert a factor into the client's decision that has more to do with the therapist's concerns than with the client's internal process of weighing the personal pros and cons of telling.

I also believe that it sets an important standard for therapy: Therapy is about reality and honesty. To broach whether therapy with me can continue, prior to the decision, sets the situation up to be one of bargaining with me for guarantees or advantages: "Why won't you continue to see us?" "If I tell, will you continue to see us?" "If I don't tell, can I come in by myself to see you?" This is a real trap for the therapist, and a distraction from the real issue: to tell or not to tell. And, as in the rest of life, whatever decision the straying partner makes, it will have consequences.

Are the couples that resist exposing the secret any different from those who disclose the affair themselves? There is little research to answer this question. Lawson's (1988) study of adultery indicates that "In general, the more guilty people felt, the *less* they spoke at all" (p. 233). Guilt was in part a function of whether the straying partners believed they had a pact to be faithful. Men with such a pact were more likely to reveal an affair, believing that they would be forgiven, while women more often hid their affairs for fear it would mean the end of the marriage. For female betrayers, this is a realistic fear, because their marriages are more likely to end than are those of their male counterparts. It also may be that women who have affairs are closer to ending their marriages than are men.

In my experience, greater resistance is related to greater ambivalence within oneself. The ambivalence is not just about the marriage, but is based on one's self-esteem, personal history with honesty, and general sense of hope. My experience indicates that those with higher self-esteem, who value and practice honesty, and who tend to be optimistic, are more likely to get beyond their resistance and ambivalence.

☐ Issues for the Therapist

Therapists often find it difficult to actively promote revelation of an affair. We want to protect the "innocent" spouse; we want to help them avoid the pain of their situation; we hope that maybe the affair doesn't have to be addressed; we are not sure we can handle the intense emotions; or we are afraid the situation will get out of control. We can easily get tangled up in these issues.

Underestimating the couple's ability to face tough issues can get in the way of the process the couple needs to engage in to arrive at their own decisions. If we avoid the issue of disclosing the secret affair, we will be as stuck as they are, and so will the therapy process. A useful distinction pertains to the therapist's responsibility for the process rather than for the couple's decisions. The therapist is responsible for conducting a process that is based on sharing all relevant information, that holds each spouse accountable for their own behavior, and that offers emotional support. The decisions about behavior and about the marriage belong to the couple.

It is important that we don't collude with the couple's avoidant selves. An honest process is essential to the therapeutic process, especially when the issue is dishonesty and betrayal. Surfacing the secret affair requires courage of both spouses. As therapists we need to have enough courage to share some with our clients at this difficult time. We also need to keep in mind that protection from the truth is not protective; it is another betrayal.

Maybe the most apt comment is this revision of the old adage: The truth will set you free, but first it will make you miserable.

Disclosing the Affair

Disclosure of an affair is a momentous event in a marriage, especially if it's the first such disclosure. Once out, the secret can't be rescinded. Life changes for each spouse. The unwanted or denied information indicates a major problem and will probably forever change aspects of the marriage. The old marriage is over. For better or worse, the relationship will be different in the future.

The first element in rebuilding is telling the betrayed spouse the truth. A well-planned disclosure opens the door to a process of growing and resolution. Our work as therapists is to help the straying partner disclose the secret in the best possible way. The process of disclosure encompasses preparation, disclosure, the betrayed spouse's response, and development of a plan for getting through the next few days.

☐ Therapists' Difficulties with Disclosure

While therapists generally agree that if there is to be disclosure, it needs to be done carefully, they often have difficulty moving ahead with it. They know that disclosure will be wounding, and for the betrayed spouse it may echo wounds of the past.

This discussion among therapists captures some of the mixed feelings about facilitating disclosure. Mary remarked, "I became a therapist to help people, not to hurt them." Angela responded, "I know it needs to be done, but I cringe. I hate seeing my client so hurt." Tom pondered aloud, "I wonder whether they'll make it, and what responsibility I have if they don't." Rhonda observed, "I have a lot of feelings

about this part of the work, but the damage has already been done—
one of them has gone outside the bounds. It's not fair that the other
one not know it." Jerry added, "Not knowing means they can't get to
work on whatever the issues are. But I always get anxious when I
know that's what's coming in the next session—you don't know if it's
going to be tears or fireworks."

In thinking through the ethical issues about facilitating disclosure,
the primary issue facing the couples therapist is whether it is ethical to
continue working with the couple and withhold the secret from the
other spouse when you know that one spouse is having or has had an
affair. Many say, "No, I don't keep secrets between spouses." Some
however say, "Yes, I'll help them rebuild their relationship first and
then the affair can be disclosed later and the betrayed spouse will
be better able to handle it." Others say, "We'll work on rebuilding
their relationship and the affair may never need to be disclosed." Still
others say, "Revealing the affair could destroy their relationship."

In the latter two instances, it is important to look at issues of protection and responsibility. Should we be protecting one spouse from real
but painful information that has relevance for the marriage? Should
we be carrying the responsibility for whether the marriage ends or
not? I think not. The couple created the situation that provided enough
space for an affair. One spouse chose to enter into an affair for whatever reasons. Although it is a painful way to learn, our clients need to
experience the consequences of their choices. Rescuing our clients is
much like being the overindulgent parent who protects a child from
the consequences of the child's behavior, with the result that the child
doesn't learn important lessons about boundaries and consequences.
What we can do is help the partners resolve the underlying issues that
led to the affair.

Think also about your professional code of ethics and what the implications are for this situation. Does the code mean that you must
keep confidential any secrets between spouses who are involved in
couples therapy? The AAMFT Code of Ethics addresses the issue of
confidentiality when multiple family members receive therapy: "Marriage and family therapists may not disclose client confidences except:
. . . (I)f there is a waiver previously obtained in writing, and then such
information may be revealed only in accordance with the terms of the
waiver. . . . [E]ach such family member who is legally competent to
execute a waiver must agree to the waiver." If you were to reveal the
affair to the spouse (or to anyone else) without such a waiver you
would be breaking confidentiality. You are not breaking a confidence
when the straying partner has made a decision to reveal the affair and
does so. However the issue of confidentiality makes it all the more

important that your client has come to an informed decision to tell, after considering the ramifications of doing so.

☐ Preparing for Disclosure

Once the straying partner decides to disclose the secret affair to the spouse, preparation is in order. This work needs to be done in a subsequent individual session. At best, disclosing the affair will be a very painful experience. Doing it poorly adds unnecessary pain. The therapist can be pivotal in helping the client think through what information needs to be disclosed and in what manner. The straying partner, and not the therapist, needs to be the one to tell the spouse about the affair. Considerations include timing, content, phrasing, where the disclosure will take place, and the spouse's response.

You can begin the preparation by asking the straying partner what she plans to say. If she begins by blaming, with statements such as, "You were always too busy," insist that this is not the time to take the offensive position. This is the time to take responsibility for the choices made and the actions taken.

> Jeanie's "first draft" is a good illustration of what not to say: "Roger, I'm scared to talk to you right now. I don't know how to say this without you being angry. I really didn't mean to hurt you. I've sort of become friends with someone you don't know. Please don't be upset with me."

Help your client keep the disclosure short and simple. It can be as simple as, "I need to tell you I'm having an affair." Make sure that the disclosure is not cluttered up with comments such as, "Honey, I don't want to hurt you," "I don't know how to tell you this," or "Dear, I'm so sorry, and I really do love you, and I don't want to upset you." This type of comment is designed to lessen the spouse's pain and anger at the straying partner, not to help the betrayed spouse. Instead, comments such as these will enrage the betrayed spouse.

> I asked Jeanie how she would react if Roger was saying those words to her. She began to see the problem and refined her statement until she had pared it down to, "Roger, there's something I need to tell you. I've been having an affair." As we worked on what Jeanie would say, I stayed in my role as therapist rather than take the role of Roger. Disclosing the hidden affair is so scary that even in rehearsal your client may need you to be there as therapist. Use a technique such as the empty chair instead.

Inquire whether there are other secrets that need to come out. For example, if there is more than one affair, this is the time to make sure the true situation is fully revealed. Additional secrets that dribble out over time increase distrust and make it impossible for either spouse to work on rebuilding the relationship. The spouse experiences each subsequent disclosure as an additional betrayal and any trust that has been rebuilt in the interim comes crashing down when the foundation is discovered to have additional cracks.

Where and when will the disclosure occur? Once a firm decision to tell has been made, the straying partner is usually anxious to get it over with. Occasionally someone wants to delay telling. This may mean that the decision wasn't really firm, in which case go back to the Four-Square technique described in Chapter 3. Sometimes it's just a matter of last minute jitters, and the person needs the therapist to nudge them along.

The straying partner may choose to reveal the secret at home, although those in therapy often prefer to do so with the safety and structure of the therapy session. In either case talk about timing. There is no good time, but just before an out of town trip, a big event, or family occasion is not desirable. Help your client develop a specific plan such as in the next couples therapy session, or this Friday morning when the spouse is home and the children are in school. Most people realize that a restaurant or other public place is not a suitable location.

If the straying partner decides to tell in a therapy session, instruct that person to share the secret at the beginning of the session, because the entire session will be needed to handle the disclosure. When possible, schedule the session when you can run overtime because you may find it necessary.

Another element of preparation is anticipating the betrayed spouse's reaction. Ask your client about how the spouse is likely to react to the disclosure. You can tell your client that most spouses are initially in shock, then are hurt and angry and have numerous questions. Tell your client that the questions that will need to be answered are who the affair is with, how long it has lasted, whether it has ended, who else knows about it, whether it occurred on "marital turf," and whether sexual protection was used. Make sure that your client does not lump in all this information with the disclosure of the affair itself. It is enough at first just to tell the reality of the affair. This additional information is to be provided when the spouse asks, which will be when the spouse is ready for the answers.

☐ The Disclosure

The therapist must be ready for a painful and exhausting session as the marital partners begin to share their pain. It is important that the revelation be made at the very beginning of the session. If the therapist's anxiety results in delays, the straying partner will lose the necessary courage to disclose the secret. After greeting the couple, wait for the straying partner to begin. The spouse, sensing that something big is coming, may talk to alleviate anxiety or to delay the bombshell. If the spouse starts a discussion, comment that there are other issues to deal with today, and pause again. Do not try to set the stage for what is coming, but instead clear the stage and let it come.

The Betrayed Spouse's Response

The revelation itself is a simple statement, but one that forever changes the marital relationship. The straying partner turns to the spouse and says, "I need to tell you that I've been having an affair." Typically the spouse reacts with a mixture of shock and recognition. The spouse may name the third party as all those fragmented pieces fall into place. Relief and rage are next; relief at knowing the truth, and rage at the betrayal. The straying partner may apologize, but forgiveness is out of the question at this time.

> Evan's wife Rita knew, although she hadn't admitted it to herself. When Evan divulged his affair, Rita said, "It's Carolyn, isn't it?" Evan acknowledged that it was Carolyn, and Rita began to cry. She tried to get angry, but the best she could do was to ask Evan through her tears how he could do this to her. Evan was subdued and visibly guilty, and apologized weakly to Rita for hurting her. Rita refused his apologies. She did admit she was relieved: "I thought you were going to tell me you were going to leave me."

It is one thing to suspect an affair, and quite another to face the reality of an affair. As long as the secret is not put into words, it isn't real. The spouse's initial reaction to the disclosure is usually shock, followed by tears. Yelling and screaming and some hysteria are not uncommon. Fears that the marriage is ending are mixed with threats of divorce.

As the therapist, you will need to provide strong emotional support to both spouses as they struggle with the difficult emotions generated by disclosure of the affair. The betrayed spouse may be numb or in shock. Alternatively, the spouse may express pain and rage. She will be unable to move until her anger has been heard, if not by her partner, at least by you. Provide the opportunity for this within the session. A few betrayed spouses are able to express their pain, but for most the pain is so overwhelming that at first they stay with their numbness or their rage. You will need to focus most of your attention in this session on the betrayed spouse who has just been hit with a bombshell. The straying partner usually understands and appreciates your doing so.

After making the disclosure, the straying partner usually feels help-less and has little to say other than apologizing or voicing guilt and pain. Whatever amount of guilt and pain is expressed by the straying partner, it will not be enough to satisfy the spouse. The spouse's demands for a greater expression of guilt are largely in hopes of avoiding the pain by closing the issue. Encourage the straying partner to listen without trying to fix the situation. Keep the pacing slow to ensure that both spouses take in the enormity of their situation. Couples are usually very glad to have the security and structure provided by the therapist in this session.

The Rest of the Session

Give the spouse space to react, to respond, to catch his or her breath. Slow the couple down so both spouses have space to pay attention to their pain. Many betrayed spouses are tempted to jump to a decision to end the marriage. After all, the myth is that an affair equals divorce. And the fantasy is that divorce means they won't have to deal with the reality of the affair. Highlight the fact that they are in crisis—not a good time to make any major decisions. Help them see that a decision to separate is premature. However, several short-term decisions need to be made before the session is over.

Help the couple talk about what they will do for the next few days. Start with their anxiety about the ride home together. They may want to talk, or they may want some separate space. It is important that both spouses are available to each other, even if the betrayed spouse doesn't want to talk.

Once the shock wears off, the spouse will want to know every detail of the affair. You will need to offer guidance about revealing details. The spouse *needs* to know who the third party is, how long the affair lasted, whether it is continuing, who else knows about it, whether it occurred in the couple's home or other "marital turf," and whether sexual protection was used. Often, most of these questions will be asked at the time of disclosure. When the straying partner resists providing this information, it may mean the affair is continuing. More detailed discussions about sexual positions and the like are not help-ful. With time and hard work, the spouse will become more selective about what details are needed. Until then it is the therapist's task to redirect the spouse who is pressing for details (see Chapter 5 about how to reduce the spouse's obsession).

Status of the Affair

You can usually rely on the spouse to address the question of whether the affair is continuing. The straying partner may have ended the affair or decided to end it. If the latter, help the couple discuss how and when this will occur. If the affair has not ended, a full discussion of this issue will need to wait for subsequent sessions. It may mean that the affair is a Split Self or an Exit Affair. Don't fall into the trap of insisting the affair end. Leave that to the spouse who has much greater power in this area than does the therapist. If we insist it end, it may just go underground. When an affair has not ended, couples can benefit from therapy for a period of time to sort out the direction in which they are going. They may need the help of the therapist even more than the couple who knows that they want the marriage and are going to work on it. Insisting that the affair end before you help the couple sort out their situation is counterproductive.

Avoidance Versus Space

Frame any proposal from the betrayed spouse to visit mother for the next few weeks as one more strategy to avoid the pain, conflict, and reality of the situation. However the spouse's demand that they sleep in separate bedrooms can provide some appropriate and symbolic space. If there is any talk of separating, you need to counter it with the suggestion that they take some time to find out how their relationship got to this point before they make any major decisions. Ask them not to make any decisions prior to the next session, or without talking about it in a session. Ask them also to delay saying anything to their children, family, and friends until they have a chance to talk it through in the next session. It is helpful—often essential—to schedule an extra session a few days later.

Offering Hope

For the spouse who learns of the partner's affair, it feels like the end of the world: "We can never get back from here." Offer a sense of the possible, giving hope where otherwise there may be only despair. Provide reassurance that they can come to understand what has happened, and that major decisions can be deferred until then. Stay balanced and supportive of both partners, reframing their definition of the situation to something more positive. The affair, for example, can be interpreted as breaking them loose from marital gridlock.

You might also suggest that the revelation of the affair is the beginning of healing. End the session on a hopeful note such as, "Let's talk next time about what this means for the two of you." Just the idea of being able to talk about this traumatic situation is hopeful. It also may be helpful to give them permission to not talk about the affair between now and the next session, although you can be sure they will.

Throughout this session be aware of laying the groundwork for developing a shared definition of the marital problem (see Chapter 5). The shared definition incorporates how they each contributed to making enough room in their marriage for a third party. The information they provide in this session about their behavior and communication patterns will be useful in future sessions in developing the shared definition. Once developed it provides hope and a framework for their efforts in therapy.

☐ Summary

Those who face disclosing an affair have varying histories, experiences, skills, and status. This is true even within a single type of affair. Whatever the type, factors that make a positive difference in telling about an affair include:

- Preparing carefully,
- Getting the whole picture out in the open, so that there are no more bombs in the wings waiting to be dropped,
- Being clear but gentle in disclosing the affair,
- Taking responsibility for the decision to have an affair,
- Ending the affair or committing to do so,
- Omitting anything designed to escape the betrayed spouse's pain or anger,
- Listening to what the spouse says,
- Wanting to rebuild the marriage,
- Love for the spouse.

Disclosing an affair is a critical turning point in a couple's history. Although they cannot possibly imagine it at the time, it may be the best thing that could happen to them, provided they accept it for what it is: a code red warning that says they are in serious trouble and need to take positive action.

CHAPTER

Managing the Crisis:
Cutting Through Obsession

The revelation of an affair precipitates a crisis for most couples. The crisis is an opportunity not to be wasted, but most couples have no idea how to use the crisis productively. They are caught up in the pain, anger, and guilt of the affair, and are unable to see beyond it. Many believe that there is nowhere to go but divorce. They desperately want something better for themselves, but seldom know what. This is the point at which many couples seek help from a therapist. Couples in therapy prior to disclosure of the affair enter this phase once the affair is out in the open.

Whether we see the couple a few days, weeks, or months after the affair has surfaced, the betrayed spouse's obsession about the affair is usually in full gear. Obsession can be the biggest obstacle to moving beyond the crisis. If not replaced with a more constructive process, it can slowly poison the couple's relationship. To be effective, the therapist has to quickly cut through the obsession with the affair and get to the underlying issues. This is the principal task of the crisis phase. It is a difficult task requiring persistence and a certain amount of single-mindedness.

Controversy among couples therapists about how to deal with the betrayed spouse's obsession is second only to disagreement among therapists about whether the secret affair needs to be disclosed. Some believe that the spouse's focus on the affair is appropriate and should be encouraged. Others believe that given enough opportunity to talk about the affair, the spouse will eventually get beyond obsession. Many think that empathy with the spouse's anger is what is needed. Still others, myself included, see continuing obsessive discussion of the affair as dysfunctional and destructive. That does not mean the affair doesn't need to be talked about.

This controversy stems in part from the fact that the nature and functions of obsession are not well understood. For example, some therapists regard obsession as the expression of emotion and thus regard it as desirable. Timing is also a factor—obsession that might be legitimate shortly after discovery of an affair is destructive as time goes on.

Values also come into play, evidenced by confusion about blame, fault, responsibility, and accountability. Some therapists view the betrayed spouse as an innocent victim, having no responsibility of any sort for the affair. After all, isn't the partner who chose to have an affair the one at fault? Therapists who view the betrayed spouse as an innocent victim believe it is cruel to put any responsibility on the spouse at a time when that person is in great pain. It seems to them like a second betrayal. Other therapists who think more systemically realize that affairs happen for reasons—reasons that have to do with underlying issues in the couple's relationship. The danger is that the affair doesn't get addressed at all.

Therapist bias and counter-transference are another part of the picture. As human beings, we too have our own experiences and emotional reactions to betrayal. Those having unfinished business with their own, their partner's, a parent's, or a friend's affair (or other betrayal) may find themselves aligning with one of the spouses. Those having no close-up experience with an affair may find themselves making internal judgments such as "I wouldn't put up with my spouse having an affair," or "You have to be pretty messed up to have an affair. That's something I could never do." We can end up taking sides or making judgments that interfere with our ability to deal with obsession.

Finally, it is just plain difficult to deal with obsession. The tenacity of the betrayed spouse, and the veiled nastiness and the repetitiveness of obsession are bad enough. It is easy to get annoyed, lose control of the session, or feel sick and tired of listening. For some therapists this may be preferable to getting into the deeper, more painful emotions underneath the obsession. Or it may simply be the result of not knowing how to effectively address obsession.

☐ The Nature and Function of Obsession

It is normal for someone who has just experienced a traumatic event (a spouse's affair certainly qualifies) to react first with shock. Shock may include disbelief, numbness, distancing, and dissociation. After the shock wears off, the next stage is obsession. Obsession has a useful function initially: it buffers the betrayed spouse from the pain and fear that come with disclosure of the partner's affair. The obsession is also a way of saying, "I'm an innocent victim." Anger, the one emotion expressed as part of obsession is a secondary emotion, designed to defend against a deeper and more difficult primary emotion. That is what obsession is all about—avoiding the deep pain and fear that are aroused by the partner's affair.

Obsession takes the form of endless ruminating (a thinking process and not an emotional one) about the affair, asking the spouse thousands of questions, looking for answers, trying to "understand." It includes questioning, blaming, and attacking the straying partner. It usually means picturing the straying partner engaged in sexual and romantic activities with the third party. Threats of divorce are thrown in. Obsession may be loud and noisy, but it is a search for rational answers in hopes of avoiding the pain, fear, and powerlessness that come with betrayal. Nothing the straying partner does or says is enough to satisfy the obsession. Incidentally, this is not a gender issue—men obsess every bit as well as women.

According to Lewis, Amini, and Lannon (2000), "Therapy's transmutation consists not in elevating proper Reason over purblind Passion, but in replacing silent, unworkable intuitions with functional ones. Patients are often hungry for *explanations* because they are used to thinking that neocortical contraptions like explication will help them. But insight is the popcorn of therapy. Where patient and therapist *go* together, the irreducible totality of their mutual journey, is the movie" (p. 179).

What fuels the spouse's intense rage and obsession after an affair is discovered? In addition to avoiding the deep pain stemming from the affair, obsession functions as a way of avoiding issues and emotions that the couple hasn't been willing to face earlier in the marriage, and that the spouse still doesn't want to address. The spouse takes the lead in this part of the drama, while the straying partner attempts to appease and apologize. No matter how much appeasing and apologizing, it is never enough.

Personal History and Obsession

Obsession occurs with all types of affairs. How extreme it is depends on the nature of the spouse's unresolved personal issues and how the obsession is addressed. Common themes sounded by betrayed spouses include rage that someone else is reaping the rewards of their efforts, a sense of being violated, victimized, or punished, pain at being rejected or abandoned, primitive feelings of jealousy, fear for the marriage, and overwhelming powerlessness.

The average level of obsession is difficult enough to deal with. In some cases the obsession seems out of control and unstoppable. When it continues at the same level for months, a history of unresolved emotional wounds and losses is usually part of the picture and individual therapy will be needed to get to it. If the marriage has been the primary defense against old wounds, an affair threatens the spouse's sense of self, and the fear of abandonment is defended against with even greater obsession.

Acceptance of traditional sex roles also has an impact on the emotions fueling obsession. With a man's affair, the woman's obsession may be a defense against her fear that she has been found wanting as a wife. A woman's affair is more likely to elicit in her husband a defense against the feeling his manhood is at stake, as opposed to fears about his performance as a husband.

Power dynamics between the spouses are important to keep in mind here. Prior to the affair, the straying partner was the more dissatisfied partner, and often the one with less power. The affair changes the power balance, and the straying partner shifts into the more powerful position. The spouse, upset by the shift in power as well as by the affair, attempts to regain the more powerful role by obsessing about the betrayal.

Obsession and Avoidance

The spouse's obsession with the affair provides another place for the couple to hide. It is much easier for the spouse to focus on the drama of the affair than to face all the issues and underlying emotions that have been avoided so far. The straying partner also is tempted to avoid the hard work ahead and in the beginning, appeasing the spouse can seem easier. This is an attempt to return to "the way it used to be," without facing the issues, let alone resolving them.

The implicit bargain is, "Okay, I'll obsess, you apologize, then I'll forgive you, and then we can move on and not really have to handle this mess." However, what follows is, "But you haven't apologized enough yet." The power switches back and forth as they try to strike a deal, with whoever is one-down making a move to regain the one-up position. Thus the system stays balanced and no change is possible. If this scenario is played out long enough, it may take another affair to upset the system sufficiently to surface the underlying issues. Real forgiveness can only come with emotional understanding, and this takes time, energy, and courage.

In some situations the straying partner comes alone to therapy, sent by the spouse to get fixed. If you suggest inviting the spouse to come, a common response is that the spouse won't come.

> I asked Tim who had come by himself, how he had asked his wife. He had said to Valerie, "I know I've really screwed up. You know, we talked a while back about going for couples counseling, but I don't suppose you want to go now." Valerie retorted, "I don't see why I should—you're the one with the problem." I talked with Tim about giving Valerie an invitation that was inviting. He decided to say, "Valerie, I know I've really screwed up, but I want this marriage and I think we have a better chance if we go to counseling together. I really want you to go with me. Please think about it overnight and let me know tomorrow."

Most spouses respond positively to such an invitation. If not, the spouse may decide to come several sessions later, after feeling left out or deciding that it is time to tell you how awful the straying partner has been. Once they both come in together, chances are good that they will continue couples therapy.

☐ Interventions to Reduce Obsession

Shock, followed in short order by obsession, is to be expected after the revelation of an affair. When the revelation occurs in the course of therapy, the betrayed spouse will probably need some time and space (one or two sessions) to take in the enormity of the situation and get beyond the initial shock before it is appropriate to work on reducing obsession. When the affair is the presenting problem, you can be sure that sufficient time and energy has already been devoted to obsessing about the affair. The spouse has repeatedly asked the straying partner the same questions, and found the straying partner's answers unsatisfactory.

The cycle goes like this: "How could you do such a thing to me? And then you lied about it. You don't know how much this hurts me. How could you? I just don't understand. What is there about her that's so much better than me? I can't deal with this." The spouse has probably repeated this a thousand times. She needs to repeat it once more, so she knows that you know, but subsequent repetitions are not going to change anything. It is helpful for everybody, ourselves included, to limit discussion of the affair during this early phase of treatment.

Some therapists suggest that the betraying partner share all the details of the affair with the spouse. This focus on the affair feeds the obsession, providing more grist for rumination. It also encourages the spouse in thinking that the affair is *the* problem. The affair is *a* problem, but more importantly, it is a symptom of the underlying issues that led to the affair. The focus belongs on the underlying issues.

Many of us have been taught that it is important for our clients to "vent," and to express their anger, or in other words, obsess. The rationale is that the spouse will get relief and the venting will end after it has run its course. Letting clients "vent," or encouraging them to do so, also feeds the obsession. Several problems occur as a result. Obsession is not an expression of emotions other than anger, and the anger is usually unleashed as an attack, not as an "I message." Since you get more of what you reinforce, this approach means more obsession for a longer period of time. Couples are not able to enter the rebuilding phase until the obsession has receded to a manageable level. When the obsession persists, it is extremely destructive to the person and to the marriage. The longer it continues, the more eroded the marriage becomes.

As therapists, we need to curb our temptation to protect the betrayed spouse who is obviously in great pain. We can be supportive, redirecting the obsession while acknowledging the anger, but we must keep the spouse moving toward recognition of the underlying issues and the underlying pain. If we are overly sympathetic or outraged, we are buying in to the idea that the problem resides with the straying partner. The corollary of this idea is that the spouse is the victim. Victims, of course, have little power. Adopting this framework makes effective couples treatment impossible.

Obsession with the affair is the betrayed spouse's biggest enemy— spouses who stay stuck in the obsession end up bitter and often alone. Spouses who get stuck usually get stuck here. Some become lifelong victims, focusing their life on the fact their partner had an affair. The spouse is usually less aware than is the straying partner that he or she has issues to face. The therapist's persistence in cutting through the obsession is crucial to getting to the spouse's issues.

Immediate Hazards

Obsession and premature apology can be considered opposite ends on a continuum, both promising safety. In reality, both are places to hide— neither is safe. Until the spouse moves beyond obsessing about the affair, and begins work on his or her own issues, neither the affair nor the underlying issues can be resolved. The only route towards a positive outcome is the hard one. Obsessing about the affair (or denying the problem) needs to be replaced with discussion of the real issues. Often neither spouse is consciously aware of the real issues at this point.

If the obsession is not quickly brought under control, the threat exists that the Conflict and Intimacy Avoiders will separate prematurely and get involved in litigation. A lot of people on the sidelines are urging them to get a detective, hire a "bomber" (piranha type divorce attorney), and "kick the cheater out." It may seem like evening the score for the spouse to get an attorney to counterbalance the alliance between the straying partner and the third party. However this is a strategy which can easily escalate and get out of hand.

Friends insist, "I'd never put up with someone who cheated on me." (Ironically, some of these friends discover later that they have been putting up with just that.) Female straying partners are even quicker to separate than are male straying partners. Slowing them down so that they have a chance to sort out their issues is important.

The "geographic cure" (moving to another community) is another route that tempts many couples, as does moving to a new home, or taking an expensive vacation. Help these couples realize that bribery only delays the day of reckoning, while interest charges accrue.

Alternatively, the spouses may continue the marriage despite the obsession. In these situations the marriage becomes further eroded, both spouses grow increasingly bitter, and the affair becomes the reason for everything that goes wrong. A man whose wife had an affair declared, "I feel angry with everybody, with life, with people, even with the system. I put most of the blame on women, because men are weak and stupid by nature, but women have more control. I do not think I will believe in people again." He clearly needs help in getting to the feelings underneath his obsession and he needs the therapist to hear him and be with him emotionally when he gets there.

With the Exiters, the immediate threat is a crazy legal fight. The straying partner is serious about separating, and is using the affair to justify leaving. The spouse knows an affair makes good ammunition in a legal battle. The spouse can disclaim any responsibility for the breakup of the marriage by focusing on the affair, especially by getting the court to validate adultery charges. Used this way the affair is another way to avoid dealing with the marital issues. A new issue is added at this point, because the focus on the affair precludes grieving for the end of the marriage.

The spouses of Split Selves and Sexual Addicts will probably obsess as much as anyone else when they first learn of their partner's behavior, and the same strategies can be used to cut through the obsession. These couples, however, are much less likely to abruptly separate.

Techniques for Reducing Obsession

In the initial period following disclosure, our hands are full. We are dealing with rage, guilt, betrayal, and humiliation, while trying to identify the type of affair, calm the situation, forestall impulsive behavior, reduce the obsession, and reframe the affair as a joint problem. We have no time to lose in cutting through the obsession. When an affair is the presenting problem start cutting through the obsession at the first session.

This is where managing the therapeutic process is crucial. It is well known that the person who holds the power in a situation is the one who defines the problem and gets those involved to agree to that definition. When dealing with obsession it is critical that the therapist be the one with the power. If either spouse takes the lead role in defining the problem, the other will not agree, thus precluding a shared definition of the problem. Without a shared definition, they will be unable to work on their mutual problems.

Connecting emotionally with the spouse's pain and fear lets the spouse know that you understand the depth of the wound created by the affair. This enables the spouse to trust you enough to begin working with you. Don't let yourself get trapped into discussing right and wrong or simple solutions, although there will be repeated attempts to pull you in. For example, when asked by the spouse, "Don't you believe it is wrong to have an affair?" ask "What are you feeling right now?" This sounds like a simple question, but the spouse who is in touch with inner emotions doesn't need anyone else to judge the affair. The straying partner needs to know that you understand his or her feelings as well.

Initially both spouses have their own definitions of the problem which tend to be mutually exclusive, framed as they are around innocence and guilt. The therapist needs to help the spouses shift from their no-win position to one that treats the affair as the symptom of a mutual problem. This is done by developing a shared definition of the marital problem, which then becomes the basis for therapy. The thinking here is systemic: Although one spouse is responsible for choosing to have the affair, both share responsibility for making enough room in the marriage for an affair. The shared definition must incorporate those reciprocal contributions of each partner which set the stage for the affair.

The strategy I have developed works well but it is not an easy one. It is a two-track process of reaching for the betrayed spouse's deeper emotions every time the obsession starts, and in between, getting an abbreviated history of their relationship. The marital history will enable you to formulate a tentative shared definition about how the two of them made enough room in the middle of their marriage for a third party. You will go back and forth between the two tasks: focusing on the spouse's emotions, and getting history with which to build the shared definition. The straying partner can tolerate and often welcomes being on the sidelines while you deal with the obsessing spouse. The betrayed spouse who is in such pain, whether in touch with it or not, cannot tolerate the reverse.

The moment the obsession starts ask the obsessor, "What are you feeling right now?" Note that this question is not, "What are you feeling about . . .?" which invites a rational response rather than an emotional one. The dialogue goes like this with Joe:

Joe: *Angry!*

Therapist: *Under the anger, what are you feeling?*

Joe: *What do you mean? I'm angry. Don't I have a right to be angry?*

Therapist: *Yes, I know you're very angry. I'd be worried about you if you weren't. But you also have some deeper feelings and I want to know what deeper feelings you're experiencing right now.*

Joe: *I can't get beyond the anger.*

Therapist: *What is your body feeling right now? Do you feel tension anywhere?*

Joe: *Well my stomach's upset and I've got a headache.*

Therapist: *So you're feeling upset and in pain. Your pain probably goes deeper than the headache.*

Joe: *I just don't understand. I trusted Jenny 100% . . .*

Therapist: [The therapist's interruption here is intentional—Joe is sliding back into obsession.] *I want to hear about your pain. Can you let yourself just feel your pain for a moment?*

Joe: *I just feel so hurt. I never thought Jenny would do anything like this.*

Therapist: *Just stay with your hurt for a few moments—let yourself feel it.*

Just like Joe, many clients will respond to the question, "What are you feeling right now?" by expressing how angry they are. Remember that anger is a secondary feeling, designed to defend against a primary emotion. With an affair, the primary emotion is usually pain or fear, sometimes both. Acknowledge your client's anger with a statement such as, "I know you are angry and I can understand your being angry, but I want to help you get to what you are feeling underneath the anger." It is essential that your client gets beneath the anger to the underlying emotion. When they do, be there with them.

Often a longer exchange of this sort is needed to cut through to the betrayed spouse's deeper feelings. Stay with the process until you get there. When your client is in touch with these deeper feelings, he or she becomes more grounded and the obsession gives way for the moment.

Developing a Shared Definition of The Marital Problem

When the obsession gives way, use these moments to get a quick and dirty marital history by asking the following questions:

1. How did you meet?
2. What attracted you to each other? (You want to anchor them in the long ago past, presumably when the attraction to each other was strong. Also, the primary source of attraction usually cuts both ways, and may be a major part of the problem. For example, a woman who is attracted by a man's strength, may grow to dislike his domination. Her husband, attracted by her accommodating nature, may get fed up with her inability to express her own opinions.)
3. Were those good things present throughout your courtship?
4. Were those good things there when you got engaged?
5. Were those good things still there when you got married?
6. For how long after you got married did things continue to go well? (Asking these questions reminds them that there are good aspects of their relationship, and provides a momentary buffer against their pain.)
7. When did things start getting off track for the two of you?
8. What else was going on around the time things started to change? (What were the stressors? Is there a new baby, a death, or other significant change? What outside factors contributed?)
9. How did you talk to each other about the changes and the stresses?
10. What did you say? This is the all-important question. Usually they haven't talked or haven't talked clearly about the changes. Instead, they may have criticized, complained, or withdrawn. Find out what was actually said—the message sent may be quite different than what they think they sent.

Assume there's a message in the affair, such as "I'll make you pay attention to me," or "You're getting too close, and I can't handle it," and probe for the message. As you begin to hear the message underneath the affair, tease it out, and highlight it. Interpret the message out loud as you're hearing it, or interpret the bits and fragments you're hearing. Assume interlocking behavior patterns between the two spouses. As you listen you can begin to identify the type of affair. Check out your hypothesis with additional questions based on the major issues for that type of affair. For example, if you think Joe and Jenny might be Conflict Avoiders you could ask, "How do you handle situations where you disagree?" If they sound like Intimacy Avoiders you might ask, "What happens when you both start feeling close to each other?" or "When you're feeling close, how long does it last? What happens to end the closeness?"

The obsession will crop up throughout this line of questioning. When it does, immediately go back to asking, "What are you feeling right now?" until the obsessor gets in touch with his or her emotions and becomes grounded again. Then back to this line of questioning, until you are able to formulate a statement about how they both set the stage for the affair. Normalize and support both spouses emotionally.

As you begin to define the problem, make it a definition that involves both of them. For example, you might say to Intimacy Avoiders, "It sounds like things went so well at first that you both got scared. You could be in real trouble if the two of you let yourself care too much." With Conflict Avoiders such a statement might be, "So both of you felt stressed after the baby came, and you both tried to protect the other from hearing about your stress, so you didn't tell each other how you felt and gradually you stopped saying much of anything important to each other." Or your definition might incorporate the reciprocal behaviors of the spouses, such as: "So you (to the spouse) had an affair with the baby, and you (to the straying partner) had an affair with Joanne." If they both agree that your statement is accurate, you have a working definition of the marital problem. If they don't agree with your statement, ask them to help you rephrase it until it fits.

Once the shared definition of the marital problem is established, you have a contract for therapy. Until you reach this point you can't really do couples work because you have one innocent victim and one bad guy, rather than two people who accept responsibility for their part of the problem and thus have an investment in making changes. Getting to this point won't end the obsession, so be prepared to jump on it immediately every time it comes up with, "What are you feeling right now?" Gradually the obsession will decrease.

Therapists can get into trouble by mistaking obsession for emotion. It is also easy to get side-tracked by the various things the spouse brings up in order to avoid the underlying emotions. These issues may be relevant at some point, but not now. The uncomfortable straying partner may attempt to rescue the spouse or distract you. In dealing with obsession it is critical for you to stay on course, focusing only on the spouse's underlying emotions and the history that set the stage for the affair. Effectively addressing obsession is the gateway to rebuilding.

A Typical Case

Let us look at a particular case to see how this actually works. Bob and Sue are both 32, and they have an eight month old son, Josh. They have been married for seven years. The presenting problem is Bob's affair with a woman he met at work. This is their first therapy session. My goals for this session are to identify the type of affair, calm the situation, forestall impulsive behavior, start reducing the obsession with the affair, and most importantly, to frame the problem as a mutual one, requiring work by both of them. After getting acquainted we begin to get to the heart of the matter. I have already asked them about their early history and their attraction to each other.

Bob: *Well, I'm glad we're coming in. I think it's a lot better to come in and get something done about this, because we don't deal with it very well at home.*

Sue: *We don't, I don't deal at all. I'm so angry! You know how home is, filled with taking care of the baby, working, getting through dinner, so we're not talking at all at home.*

(They admit to little communication. That suggests they are Conflict Avoiders. I decide to highlight this issue.)

Therapist: *I have this picture of you as living two separate lives in the same household. And that's the picture I have of how your marriage was before the affair. Is that accurate?*

Bob: *Noooooo, well—*

Sue: *I wouldn't say that. We had a full life and we had all of our activities. And now he's gone and ruined it!* (She gets teary.)

Bob: *Well, I think, probably it's the baby. Not so much since the affair, I think that's really changed—but the baby's where I think things began to get separate.*

Therapist: *How did you see that happening?*

Sue: *It's not the baby! How can you blame it on the baby? It's you! How* *could you do a thing like this? How could you have sex with some cheap tramp? And right after Josh was born?*

Therapist: *Sue, I know you're furious at Bob, and that you're really hurting. Tell me about your hurt.*

Sue: *Well he's blaming it all on the baby.*

Therapist: *I want to hear about* your *pain.*

Sue: *He's really hurt me. I don't see how he thinks I can trust him.*

Therapist: *You can't right now. The two of you have a lot of work to do before you'll be able to trust each other. Right now you're hurting, and I want you to tell me about your pain.* (By referring to "The two of you" I'm starting to frame their situation as a couples problem.)

Sue: (Crying) *It hurts so much.* (Sobs)

Therapist: *Yes, you are hurting a lot.* (Sue continues to share her pain as I listen and acknowledge her feelings. I also block her lessening attempts to blame Bob. Bob is fully involved but silent. When Sue's pain has run its course [for the moment], I remark that this is the time to begin working toward understanding what happened so that they do not have to go through this painful experience again. We go back to looking at the precipitants of the affair.)

Bob: *Well, there's this baby that came along, that's how it happened, and it just changed everything.*

Therapist: *What changed for you?*

Bob: *She's not fun anymore! I mean, we don't do anything together. There's no more romance. It's just like this, with her worrying about things. I mean, it's just—you know, the baby's a lot of work. We just don't do anything together anymore. It used to be different—the two of us together.*

Therapist: *When it started changing, how did you feel?*

Bob: *Well, scared, I guess.*

Therapist: *And then what? After scared?*

Bob: (Long pause) *Well, a little bit like there wasn't a lot of room there for me any more.*

Therapist: *Sort of left out?*

Bob: *Yeah, I guess so.*

Therapist: *Did you say anything to Sue about that?*

Bob: *Well, she's usually pretty good at sort of picking up things without me having to say it, so—*

Therapist: *So you were assuming she was picking that up.*

Bob: *Yeah, I mean she—Yeah, I thought she was picking it up, so—I guess not.*

Therapist: *Let's find out.*

Sue: *I—No! I thought you wanted to have the baby, too. No, how could I pick this up? We've been so busy! And the baby, and day care, dinner, and—*

Bob: *I know—*

Sue: *And working, and—*

Therapist: *So you agree that things have changed with the baby? I hear that implied in what you're saying.*

Sue: *Well, sure, how could it not change once there's a child in the house, and—but this is something we both wanted; something we talked about. He was excited when we got pregnant, and I—of course it's changed! How could it not change?*

Therapist: (They are beginning to admit the baby's arrival has changed their relationship, but I am sure there is more to the story.) *Have you done much talking between the two of you about the changes?*

Sue: *No, what was there to talk about? There are things to be done and we were just both busy—*

Therapist: *You're saying there wasn't time to talk?* (Conflict Avoidance for sure.)

Sue: *Well, I didn't think that there was a need to talk. What was there to talk about?! It was just a child was in our life, and we had—*

Therapist: *Did you miss some of the things that you used to do before?*

Sue: *Yeah, sure, I miss having more free time, and being more relaxed in my day, but I knew that was going to happen.*

Therapist: *Did you miss doing things with Bob?*

Sue: *Well I thought we were still doing things, we do things with the baby! It was just an addition that we had, someone else to be with.*

Therapist: *Okay, so you went from focusing on each other to focusing on the baby. I gather the baby's a larger focus for you Sue, than for you, Bob.*

Bob: *She spends more time. Yes.*

Sue: *We take care of Josh. We spend a lot of time with him.*

Bob: *Yeah. No, I know, but it's not the same.*

Therapist: (I decide it's time to switch the focus from the baby to the marriage.) *It sounds like you're both so busy being parents you've forgotten about being husband and wife.*

Sue: *I don't think that's any reason to have an affair!* (Sue still wants to avoid looking at the marital relationship.)

Bob: *Well, I mean, it's not like I planned on it.*

Sue: *Well, what—did it just happen?*

Bob: *Yeah, it just happened!*

Sue: *Oh, wonderful! That's wonderful!*

Bob: *Well, it just happened!*

Sue: *It just happened. Like magic!*

Bob: *Like spontaneity! Remember spontaneity?*

Sue: *You should have thought about that before you decided to have a child. I just can't believe you did that!*

Therapist: (I decide to begin sharing with them my formulation of the problem.) *It seems to me that the seeds for the affair were probably there from way back. I hear Bob, that you assume Sue is going to pick up on what you're feeling. And I hear Sue, that you operate in a similar way, sort of expecting that he will know that you're busy, or tired. I would imagine that goes back to early in your relationship. How did you deal with your different needs then?*

Bob: *No, we never really talked about problems, you know.* (Bob hears "different needs" as problems.)

Sue: *We didn't have any!*

Bob: *Yeah.*

Sue: *There was nothing to talk about.*

Therapist: (I decide it's time to push through the denial.) *You never felt angry?*

Sue: *Well, small annoyances, but nothing, nothing major.*

Therapist: *What did you do with the annoyances?*

Sue: *They'd pass. I don't like to dwell on things.*

Therapist: *So nothing that felt negative got dealt with.*

Bob: *Well, it didn't seem like there was a lot negative to deal with.*

Therapist: *You never got mad either?*

Bob: *Well, sometimes I'd get irritated at some little thing, but you try to accept that somebody's not the same as you are and there might be little things that you just have to accept about them. You know.*

Therapist: *Okay, so Bob, you tried to accept the differences, and Sue, you thought the annoyances weren't that important.*

Sue: *Well, they never really were.*

Therapist: *That's a sure way to lead to more important problems. It's like the underbrush and the weeds keep growing. It sounds like they blossomed into an affair!*

Sue: (Pause) *That's a lot of weeds! I sure didn't have weeds like that!* (She looks at Bob.)

Therapist: *Or you didn't know you did.* (Pause) *You were looking at Bob— put it in words, to Bob.*

Sue: *There just must be all kinds of things I don't know. I feel like I don't know you at all.*

Bob: *Yeah. Well, sometimes I feel like I don't know myself at all either. I mean, it's not like I feel good about what happened, you know. If somebody at work told me of some guy who had an affair when his wife was home with his baby, I would think the guy was a creep! But, you know, it's already done! I mean, we can't—*(voice breaks)

Therapist: *Bob, you were feeling a lot of pain there; can you share that with Sue?*

Bob: (Pause) *I can't take back how much I've hurt you by doing this. It's too late. And, I don't know what to do about it. And I don't feel good about myself—so I, I just don't know.* (Bob expresses some of the guilt that is characteristic of the Conflict Avoidant straying partner.)

Therapist: (Long pause) *Sue, can you respond?*

Sue: *Well part of me feels so badly that you are in such pain. I just hate seeing that.* (Now both have affirmed that they still care about each other.) *I thought about reaching out to you a minute ago, and trying to comfort you, and then I come back to why try to comfort you? And then I feel like I can't. How can I trust you?*

Bob: *Yeah, I don't blame you.*

Therapist: *So you wanted to comfort him and couldn't quite.*

Sue: *No, I came real close, but then I thought, What am I doing comforting you?! Who's comforting me? But I—I don't like to see you so unhappy.*

Therapist: (I want to reinforce Sue for disclosing some of her real feelings.) *It seems to me that it's a good sign for both of you that finally some of your real unhappiness is being expressed.*

Bob: *I just can't take it back. I'm sorry it happened. I don't know what to do. I don't know what the solution is.*

Therapist: (With their defenses coming down, it's time to restate the shared definition of the problem, and give them hope that they can resolve it.) *Well, I don't think there is a quick solution. It's going to take some time, and you're right, you can't take it back, but I think the two of you can work it through. It seems to me that the problem belongs to both of you. Both of you have been holding back from each other, and letting all the weeds grow. You each need to work toward understanding why you made room for the weeds, and on finding ways to get the weeds out of your marriage.*

Sue: *I just don't feel like that's me. I don't! I mean I have petty annoyances, but I don't feel as though anything's brewing in me that's led me to this point. I just don't.* (Sue is especially afraid of change, and would like to retreat to denying the existence of problems.)

Therapist: *I believe you. I think you're so in the habit of not letting petty annoyances get in your way that you sort of brush them aside and don't notice them to any extent. But then they don't get dealt with.*

Sue: *Well, I don't know. We don't want to argue about little things. I don't want to have to start arguing about little things—because I don't see that that's going to make things better.*

Therapist: (They're avoiding again—I'll remind them of their choices.) *You could have an affair.*

Bob: *That's a low blow!* (laughing)

Sue: *Yeah, but that way didn't work.* (Most of the energy seems to have gone out of Sue's obsession with the affair—for the moment.)

Bob: *Well, I feel the same way. But I don't think I had a whole lot of weeds there either. It's not like I was angry at her about things. I think I was just angry that life wasn't like that, that I couldn't have everything I wanted. You know?*

Therapist: *It's important to talk about that.*

Bob: *But, it's not like I blamed her for that. You know? I mean, that's why I'm not angry. If I feel angry with her about it, I know that it's not really her fault. So I don't want to be angry at her because I feel like it's not her fault, and that's not fair.* (Bob indicated later that when Sue understood how badly he felt about the whole thing, he felt worse: I don't feel worthy of her feeling bad for me!)

Therapist: *But if you're angry, you're angry, and you can tell her about it. You can tell her that you're dissatisfied, without blaming her for it. That's probably a very new idea to you. I think both of you have a lot to learn about how to talk about differences. I hear the notion that if you talk about differences with each other, it's a matter of blaming the other one. It doesn't have to be.*

Sue: *Well, why would you tell somebody you're upset unless you wanted them to be different? Why even bring it up?*

Therapist: *Sometimes you just want somebody to hear you.*

Bob: *Well, what do you think about people who are getting angry with each other in front of a little kid? I mean, it doesn't seem to me like kids should—*

Therapist: *Who says you have to bring the child in on it? He's only eight months old right now anyway, isn't he?*

Bob: *Yeah.*

Therapist: *Let's not get ahead of ourselves.*

Bob: *But I wouldn't want Sue to think it's because I don't want the baby. You know what I mean? But a lot of it is just because we can't do things like we used to do. I mean, you always have to have a baby sitter. She's more tired when I get—*

Therapist: (It's time to shift the focus from talking about feelings to sharing feelings. I prepare to coach them step by step, in this unfamiliar adventure. Bob is closer to his feelings, so I start with him, gently insisting that he share what he is feeling with Sue.) *Why don't you tell Sue now what some of those feelings are.*

Bob: *About the baby?*

Therapist: *About the changes.*

Bob: *I feel like we don't have as much time together. I mean fun time.*

Therapist: *Well, that's a fact. Can you talk about some of your* feelings? *Consider this an experiment to see if you can talk to each other a little bit differently.*

Bob: *Can you give me a hint?*

Therapist: *Do you miss her?*

Bob: *I miss you, and I feel real frustrated that we don't have time to be together, without it having to be doing chores and stuff. I enjoy being with the baby and you, but I need time with you without the baby* (tears in his eyes).

Sue: *You have that.* (Sue is still fighting her feelings.)

Therapist: *Can you, Sue, get in touch with what you're feeling right now?*

Sue: *I'm just angry! I'm just angry at him for—*

Therapist: (Good! Although Sue is still defensive, she is beginning to let herself feel. I want to encourage that, but without forcing her to respond to Bob immediately. She needs more support than Bob at this point.) *He told you he missed you. Are you afraid to hear that? Or are you not ready to hear it?*

Sue: *I'm afraid, because we have a child. Josh is a fact of life. He's in our lives. If he misses me, there is just nothing we can do about that. I'm scared that he feels this way at this point!*

Therapist: *What are you thinking he's asking you for?*

Sue: *My gosh, I guess the way things used to be! Like, like Josh is going to disappear!*

Therapist: *Check that out. See if that is what he's asking for.*

Sue: *Do you want Josh to disappear?*

Bob: *No!*

Sue: *Well, what do you want?*

Bob: (Long pause) *I want some of the time to be just you and me. I want some time with you. I want romance, you know? I want to go out to dinner with you, I want to leave all the routine work, I want to have some unproblematic time.*

Sue: *I'd like that too. I just—I'm too tired—* (Sue is backing off emotionally again.)

Therapist: *Finish that sentence: I just—*

Sue: *Just been like a whirlwind. I don't see how it can be done.*

Bob: *So is this it? I mean, is this what it's going to be like for 18 years, until he goes to college or something?*

Sue: *I don't think so!*

Bob: *That's really scary!*

Therapist: *Do you want what he's saying he wants?*

Sue: *Yes! I do. I just don't see how we're going to accomplish it.*

Therapist: *Okay, separate those two out.*

Sue: *I'd like it. I miss easy times too. I'm exhausted. I miss just being laid back and reading the Sunday paper, and going out to breakfast, and all of that* (tears in her eyes).

Bob: *Well, why can't we have some of that? I mean, why—*

Sue: *Do you know why?*

Bob: *No, I don't! And I don't understand—*

Therapist: *It sounds like the two of you are getting caught up on some logistics. Maybe we need to give some thought here to how you can get help so that you do have some free time. There's a practical problem, as well as the emotional problem. It sounds like you both want to spend some time with each other, although Sue, you have some reservations about it, not knowing how it can happen.*

Sue: *Well, and also if I want it. That's part of it, because when I look at you, I feel—*

Therapist: *So the baby's a good way to hide right now.*

Sue: *Yeah. It's—*

Bob: *Do you feel that way because of the affair?*

Sue: *Yes!*

Bob: *Did you feel that way before?*

Sue: *No. I didn't. I feel that way because of the affair. I feel like—I'm blown away.*

Therapist: (It's time for another restatement of their shared problem, and how they avoid it.) *It seems to me that to resolve this, both of you are going to have to take the risk of spending some time with each other and really talking to each other—including talking about your differences. Or you can hide behind the baby—he'll certainly give you plenty of ways to hide—or behind the affair, but the issue that the two of you need to address is how you can really share yourselves with each other. And until you're each clearer about how that will work, and until it's actually working, you won't be able to totally put the affair behind you. You certainly aren't going to put it behind you today.*

Sue: *No, I'm not ready to.*

Bob: *Well, maybe it's better if I—I mean, because she's so angry, right now, maybe it's better if I just stayed at my brother's for awhile. You know, until this kind of blows over.* (Bob is getting scared now, and he backs off further than Sue.)

Therapist: *This one isn't going to blow over.*

Bob: *How do we go about every day?*

Therapist: *How are you going to communicate in a different way unless you're there to communicate? You don't have much time together now.*

Bob: *It's just I think that now, because she's angry—I mean, I understand why she's angry, but I feel like that'll get me angry and then we'll just be angry at each other, and that's not going to make things any better.*

Therapist: *It might. Not being angry hasn't helped.*

Bob: *Well, that's true.*

Sue: (Sue is looking shocked. Her attempts to regain the upper hand are backfiring.) *You can't just leave me with all the responsibility for Josh— it's too much! I'm exhausted. What do you want from me?*

Bob: *I mean, you're so angry. I don't know what to do.*

Therapist: (Neither of them knows what to do at this point. They alternate between attempts at business as usual and grasping for a new way to approach their situation. It's time for me to provide some direction.) *You've got an opportunity to try things a different way. You've got a lot invested. It's obvious you both care about each other. It's also obvious that you both care about your son. You were able to share your real feelings with each other a few minutes ago, and you both lived through it. It seems to me that you've got what it takes to learn to deal with the hard stuff: your annoyances, and your irritations, and your anger, and your pain. At the very least, you owe it to yourselves to understand how you got to this point, before you make any major decisions. If you don't address this problem now, you're probably doomed to repeat it. Or the affair could be a real breakthrough for the two of you. Now what would you like to do?*

Bob: *I want to find a way out of this mess. I'm willing to do whatever it takes.*

Sue: *So am I. I don't ever want to go through this again.*

Discussion

My role here is an active one, pushing away the denial, supporting each of them, reframing the problem and playing it back to them.

Persistence is essential in cutting through the denial and getting the message across that this problem is serious and won't go away on its own. I try not to let anything slide because if I do, it reinforces their strong pattern of avoidance.

Throughout most of this session I used vertical communication (flowing between the client and the therapist), in order to gain information, to cut off unproductive communication between Bob and Sue, or to pursue an individual issue. As long as I stay connected with both, and give each an opportunity to be heard, "vertical communication" is productive. Horizontal communication (flowing between the spouses) is desirable when the spouses are expressing feelings, sharing information with each other, or problem solving. If the spouses feel they are being heard, their motivation to use the structure of the session and to stay connected with the therapist is high. After all, their marriage is at stake.

Additional Techniques

When a spouse's obsession is stronger, my role is similar, but requires even more persistence to get underneath the obsession to the real issues. At the same time, it has to be a gentle persistence that offers support, or I will lose the obsessive spouse. I want to elicit feelings from each spouse, not reactions. My role is active and directive. My interventions are directed toward identifying the underlying issues and offering emotional support, while restricting verbal attacks, obsessive questioning, and other destructive behavior.

Occasionally I need to focus on one or the other partner for a short period, to cut through the denial. When I am concentrating on the spouse, the straying partner usually understands what I am up to, but in the reverse situation, the spouse does not understand, and needs some extra support from me. A few words acknowledging how hard it is just to listen and assuring equal time, frequent eye contact, or the use of touch are all helpful ways of supporting and staying emotionally connected with one partner while focusing on the other.

Touch can also be an effective means of control, as when the hand on the knee conveys "be quiet." Touching must be used very carefully, for specific therapeutic purposes, and then only when the client is receptive to touch. If your client is of the opposite sex, additional caution is in order. If you have any doubts, refrain from touching.

Interventions that reframe the affair itself are sometimes useful. You can disqualify the affair by saying " that's not the issue," and return to the task at hand. If that does not work, turn it around and praise the affair: "That must have been a wonderful relationship for you to give it so much attention." With an hysterical spouse, usually a woman, suggest to her "You're having an affair with his affair. Is that what you want to do?" If there is anything she does not want to do, it is to validate his affair.

Glass and Wright (1989) suggest that the obsessive spouse make a written list of all the unanswered questions about the affair. Make it clear that the questions will not be dealt with immediately, but prior to the end of therapy the spouse will have the opportunity to ask and have answered any questions which remain. By the time the questions are allowed, the spouse is beyond the obsession, and the only unanswered questions are important in tying up loose ends of the affair.

Keep both spouses focused on their individual feelings and their individual needs. They know a lot about what they don't want, but what they do want is a lot less clear. Or they may just want the other one to make all the changes. If one spouse insists on blaming the other, a comment such as, "If things are that bad I wonder why you've stayed in the marriage for so long" reframes the situation. If the reframe doesn't take, and the response is "I should have left years ago," stay with it. You might say, "Well, maybe you should have, but you didn't. You're a smart person, so you must have had good reasons to stay." Then redirect them back to their shared issues and their individual feelings and needs. Throughout, you need to stay balanced between the two of them.

Other Tasks for the Early Sessions

In addition to cutting through the obsession and developing a shared definition of the marital problem, other tasks that need to be completed in the first few sessions include establishing whether the affair has ended and whether there are other secrets. The spouse can generally be counted on to ask whether the affair has ended, but may or may not feel ready to give the straying partner an ultimatum that it has to end. If the affair is continuing, couples sessions are often useful for continuing a dialogue with each other. You might consider this an interim phase for sorting things out and deciding on direction, rather than either marital or divorce therapy. If after substantial consideration, the straying partner is unable to end the affair, individual rather than couples therapy is indicated.

Additional secrets, such as other affairs, arrests, or the like, must be revealed during the crisis phase. It seems like a lot to handle, but think of it as emptying the bombs out of the wings. Bombs that are dropped after the couple begin to rebuild their relationship call into question the work done so far, making it much more difficult to rebuild a viable relationship. Westfall (1989) notes that the spouse reacts to secrets revealed late in therapy by reinterpreting the meaning of the therapy and disavowing responsibility for most of the marital difficulties.

Couples don't know during the crisis phase whether they will be able to resolve their issues. Fortunately they can begin resolving their issues before they decide whether they are going to continue their marriage. The work can be framed as understanding and changing the behavior that each contributed to the marital problems, with the knowledge that this will eventually lead to a decision about whether to continue the marriage.

The obsession is not over at the end of the initial sessions. It recurs frequently, though with lessening intensity, over the first several months of treatment and recurs periodically for some time after that. Continue to delve behind it in this manner to see what emotions are being hidden beneath the obsession.

Managing Persistent Obsession

An occasional spouse will have a harder time than others getting beyond the obsession. Persistent obsession may be active or passive; extreme nonresponsiveness is also obsessive. Obsession is more difficult to manage when the spouse lacks self-esteem, if the spouse's sole identity is tied to the straying partner, or the affair replicates in some manner unfinished business from the past. With these spouses, explore the underlying issues that make it so difficult to accept any responsibility for the marital problems.

Case Study of Unfinished Business

In the following case, unresolved losses and abandonments were surfaced by the revelation of the affair. The obsession persisted through much of the rebuilding phase and had to be continually addressed. The key to managing the obsession was identifying and addressing the feelings of abandonment that dated back to childhood.

Jerry and Carole came to see me a year and a half after her brief affair with a man she met at a conference. Carole was an extremely attractive, in-charge woman of 38, and Jerry was a quietly confident executive of 40. Jerry had been threatening to leave Carole ever since he found out about her affair, but hadn't taken any steps to leave. Carole was at her wits end, having apologized prolifically, answered hundreds of questions about the affair, and tried numerous other strategies to gain Jerry's forgiveness. Both of them were at the end of their respective ropes. Although they cared a great deal for each other and regarded themselves as "best friends," both despaired of getting the marriage back on track.

After a year of listening to Jerry obsess about her affair, Carole told him that she really did not like being the target for his anger. For Carole, saying this was a major accomplishment. Later, she told him she was fed up with his constant references to her affair. It was when Carole took a stand that Jerry began to worry that she might leave him, and this was what propelled them to seek therapy.

Jerry didn't want to take any responsibility for the marital situation. For a year and a half he had been reinforced by Carole for obsessing and playing the innocent victim. However, as long as he stayed the victim, he couldn't move and they couldn't move. He frequently tried to manipulate me into colluding with him with by demanding, "Don't you agree that what she did was wrong?" I repeatedly cut off talk of the affair, and shifted to Jerry's relationship with his parents.

I began to get a picture of Jerry as the only "adult" in his family of origin. His mother was affectionate at times, but drank too much and ignored any problems in the family. She seemed oblivious to Jerry's feelings and needs. Jerry's father was irresponsible and contentious when he did not get his way. At other times he flirted inappropriately with Jerry's girlfriends, which Jerry hated. Jerry coped with his parents' abdication by taking control of situations and creating success for himself where that was possible, as in school.

Jerry had picked Carole because she was responsible. He wanted somebody who was not like his father, somebody who had ideals, and Carole was bright, lovely, and very straightforward—until she had this affair. Her affair not only rocked their marriage, but it rocked the foundations of Jerry's approach to life.

Gradually Jerry's anger at his father's inappropriate behavior was surfaced as well as his rage at the abandonment he had experienced. Despite, or because of, the control he exercised, Jerry also had a number of issues with Carole that he had never mentioned. He didn't like it that she didn't talk more, and that she seldom voiced her own preferences, instead deferring to him. Parallels in the way Jerry had excluded Carole from his decisions and had kept his father at bay became apparent.

Carole had disliked Jerry's controlling behavior but she had never said so. She didn't share many of her feelings, having been taught that the proper role for a woman is to accommodate her husband. Thus she followed Jerry's lead. Carole was shocked that she had allowed herself to become involved in an affair, although with hindsight she realized that her unexpressed feelings about Jerry's control had been a contributing factor. She began paying attention to her own feelings. When she began to express her dissatisfaction, Jerry felt reassured. Although he found it hard to give up control, he preferred sharing the "bad guy" role rather than having it all to himself. As Carole began carrying her own responsibility for speaking up, Jerry's obsession began to subside.

Jerry didn't give up his obsession easily. Every week his obsession had to be moved out of the way by pushing through to his emotions, after which there was time for a little work. After a number of months, he could maintain the focus on his own issues between sessions and obsessing was at a minimum. If they missed a week, we were back to the obsession again! Couples therapy provided a relatively safe setting in which Jerry could begin disclosing feelings and sharing decisions with Carole, gradually learning to give up control.

After Jerry gave up most of his obsessing, occasional references to the affair were used to redirect his focus, "What is it you want to know from Carole, not about the affair, but about why she got into the affair." This strategy used the remnants of the obsession as a springboard to find out more about Carole, her childhood, and her feelings now, and worked fairly well as an interim step. Carole also was learning more about herself as a result of some of the questions Jerry raised. Gradually Jerry was able to talk directly to Carole without using the affair.

Next Steps

During the early phase when the obsession is greatest, stress taking enough time and examining all the options. Obsession contributes to a limited view of options: Couples tend to think they either must put up with the situation or end the relationship. Help them identify other options, such as delaying any decision for a month (better yet, several months), or exploring their ability to change those things they do not like. Challenge them by asking whether they are willing to confront this difficult problem. Convey a sense of hope that although they are at a bad place they can face and resolve their issues. Resist the many attempts to get you to take sides. To some extent you will need to be a communication traffic cop, insisting that each partner speak only for him or herself, ensuring that each listens to the other, and blocking interruptions. Redirect them, rather than allow them to continue unproductive or damaging skirmishes. Instead of asking "Why do you feel . . ., " pursue the feeling itself by asking "What are you feeling this moment?" When they are open for new input, you can suggest next steps.

Forestall premature decisions. You can suggest that there be no decisions about the marriage until they figure out how they arrived at the current situation. There is a real place for couples therapy that is neither marital or divorce therapy, but provides an open environment in which to identify and explore the underlying issues before making any decision about the viability of the marriage. This is a "containing" strategy and is good for this reason alone.

The crisis of discovery that brings many couples to therapy will limit opportunities for systematic history-taking initially, although history begins to emerge in exploring the meaning of the affair. As soon as possible, get a good family history including information about emotional, communication, and sexual patterns, and about other affairs in the family. Help the couple see the connections between family patterns and current issues. Genograms are a useful tool for highlighting patterns within the family (McGoldrick, Gerson, & Shellenberger, 1999). Not only does history provide insight into the situation, but more importantly, it helps the couple connect with the emotional experiences that have been important in shaping who they are.

Therapists can learn a great deal about the emotional mind, and how emotional change occurs in *A General Theory of Love* (Lewis, Amini, & Lannon, 2000). "All of us, when we engage in relatedness fall under the influence of another's emotional world, at the same time that we are bending his emotional mind with ours" (p. 142). "The first part of emotional healing is being limbically [emotionally] known—having someone with a keen ear catch your melodic essence" (p. 170). "When a limbic connection has established a neural pattern, it takes a limbic connection to revise it" (p. 177).

☐ Obsession and the Type of Affair

Initially the Intimacy Avoiders are often more persistent in their obsession about the affair than are Conflict Avoiders. The techniques for dealing with obsession are the same, though they require more energy from the therapist. Sometimes obsession about the affair is less, but the obsession is transferred to another issue. Intimacy Avoiders go down many paths in their efforts to avoid.

Some spouses of Sexual Addicts tend more toward denial of reality than toward obsession; others are just as obsessive as in any other type of affair. Split Self spouses, especially those with a long-standing investment in the marriage, also obsess as much as anyone else. In both these types of affairs, where much of the therapeutic work is individual, the obsession needs to be addressed in these sessions by cutting through to the underlying emotions. Developing a shared definition of the marital problem is done more effectively in a couples session with input from both spouses. When that is not possible, adapt the questions about the initial attraction and how things changed over time by asking about their own experience and their perception of their partner's experience.

The Exiters have a slightly different pattern when it comes to obsession. They usually come for help just prior to separating. The straying partner who is leaving the marriage is reluctant to engage in any real discussion of the situation. The spouse is obsessed not only with the affair but with being dumped. These are people who have difficulty with endings, and the obsession with the affair serves to obscure the ending of the marriage. The techniques for dealing with the obsession are similar, but the immediate focus for Exiters needs to be on confronting and discussing the ending of the marriage, rather than on where the marriage got off track (for a further discussion of this point see Chapter 9). The spouses need to learn how to channel their anger productively in the process of separation. They may not be able to address the underlying issues until the stress of separation lessens, but you can flag issues needing work in the future.

☐ Our Reactions to the Crisis

As therapists, in order to deal with obsession, we need to be both gentle and tough, persistent but sensitive, and empathic with the spouse's pain and the straying partner's guilt. At times we will feel helpless, bullied, annoyed, and exhausted. Our client's obsession can seem so overwhelming that we want to step back from it. If our own parents were often out of control, or if they were *always* in control, we will have a harder time stepping up to the obsession and confronting it. But confront it we must. It may help to keep in mind that we are confronting a behavior that keeps the spouse stuck, confused, and in pain. The spouse needs to apply the energy now spent in obsessing to facing and resolving the underlying emotions and issues.

Some therapists worry about putting too much pressure on an obsessive spouse. As long as the confrontation is done caringly, with respect for the spouse's pain, this is almost impossible. The spouse is not being asked to give up feelings of pain and fear, only the obsessive behavior. It is often difficult for us to keep the focus on painful issues when the spouse has been struggling with pain for some time. Certainly we need to provide time out for a brief and occasional breather, but then we need to refocus on the task at hand.

Every adult is sure to have experienced betrayal of some sort. Our success in dealing with that betrayal will influence our ability to confront obsession as well as other issues related to affairs. A desire to offer sympathy or to be protective of only one spouse warns that we are in danger of taking sides. When these and other red flags are in view, we need to explore our own issues and separate them from the couple's issues. Therapists who themselves are involved in an affair or its aftermath, are probably not able to deal effectively with obsession, and should refer the couple elsewhere.

Cutting through the obsession is exhausting work for us as well as for the couples with whom we work. Yet it is one of the most significant steps in the entire treatment process, because it opens up the possibility of working on those difficult emotional issues that the couple has not wanted to face, but because of which they have come to us.

The goal of handling the obsession is to get both spouses working on the issues they have been avoiding. Once the obsession is reduced, and a shared definition of the marital problems has been developed, couples are ready to work on resolving the underlying issues. During the rebuilding process there will be time to discuss important aspects of the affair in a different manner than obsessing.

The most difficult aspects of obsession for the therapist are being present with the pain and fear that lie underneath the obsession, and the tremendous energy needed to maintain control of the process, rather than letting the obsession continue. Although a great deal of work lies ahead for the spouses in rebuilding their marriage (or in ending it) half the battle is won when you begin to get the obsession under control. By pushing the obsession off center stage the real issues that led to the affair can now begin to surface. The real therapeutic efforts can now begin!

6

Rebuilding for Conflict and Intimacy Avoiders

As the obsession lessens, more energy is available for rebuilding trust. Now comes the hard work for Conflict and Intimacy Avoiders. It means getting into the issues that the couple has been avoiding over the years. Several factors threaten this important work. Some couples choose to sweep the issues back under the rug and pretend that all is well. Premature apologies serve as the broom. Sweeping the issues out of sight also can be accomplished by denying the existence of marital problems, viewing the affair as a one-time aberration, engaging in distractions, or buying off the spouse. Some people, believing that an affair means the marriage is doomed, start talking about divorce and need help in seeing that other options exist. A mild degree of narcissism often interferes with the spouses' ability to accurately perceive the situation, as when feelings of worthlessness, or defenses against such feelings, block out other truths.

Treatment of couples who fear conflict or intimacy centers on helping each partner identify his or her own inner language of feelings and on learning effective ways to express these feelings. Applying these new skills to old issues tests the couple's ability to rebuild a workable marriage. The family of origin provides the backdrop for this work, as current issues tend to replicate those of the past.

In the rebuilding phase, the pace slows down. Couples are beyond the worst of the crisis. After a brief moment to catch their breath, it is time to delve into working on themselves and their relationship.

☐ Therapists' Perspectives and Differences

Controversies among therapists regarding the process of rebuilding trust are much less intense than those about how to address hidden affairs and obsession. Differences among therapists at this stage have to do with the sequencing of issues, what to do if the affair continues, facilitating discussions about whether the marriage continues or ends, and dealing with the health care system's intrusions.

Couples can confuse their therapists about the direction in which the therapy is headed. When there has been an affair, "divorce talk" is common, even during the rebuilding process. In the early part of the rebuilding phase, the betrayed spouse is not yet fully committed to the marriage, even when that is the desired goal. "Divorce talk" is one way of saying "I don't want to be vulnerable right now," both to the straying partner and to one's self. Since trust has not yet been rebuilt, this stance is understandable. The extent to which the therapist engages with the couple in discussing divorce will depend on whether the therapist views the divorce talk as real or as a way of preventing emotional vulnerability. It also may depend on the therapist's own views about marriage and divorce, and the therapist's level of experience in deciphering divorce talk. Taking divorce talk literally early in therapy may reinforce the idea that divorce is the likely outcome. It is more helpful with Conflict and Intimacy Avoiders to suggest that they will be able to make a better decision a bit later and shift to the tasks of rebuilding.

Some therapists insist that apologies and forgiveness come before rebuilding in order to facilitate the rebuilding process. Others believe that real apologies and forgiveness can only come much later, after trust has been rebuilt. My view is that expressions of true remorse facilitate rebuilding but real apologies and forgiveness can only come after the straying partner fully appreciates the betrayed spouse's pain. Until some degree of trust is present it is not safe for the betrayed spouse to fully share this pain. Thus real forgiveness isn't possible at the early stages of rebuilding and is best left to the end of the rebuilding period.

Another difference has to do with whether the therapist insists that the couple commit to continuing the marriage at the beginning of the rebuilding phase or whether the commitment to the marriage is viewed as a product of the work done in this phase. I prefer to consider the earliest phase of rebuilding as an interim phase, neither marital nor divorce therapy, but a period to sort out in which direction to go. This phase can result in a commitment by both spouses to work on the marriage, or a decision by one or both spouses to end the marriage.

Even couples who want to continue their marriage and who choose to work on it can't fully commit until they see that they are able to resolve their issues. A commitment to the marriage that comes toward the end of the rebuilding phase is an informed one, based on reality and promising greater durability.

Couples therapists hold different perspectives on what to do when the affair has not ended. Many therapists refuse to see the couple if an affair is continuing. Some therapists insist the affair end. Other therapists may choose to continue seeing the couple, at least in some circumstances. An all or nothing stance may not be the best. My perspective is that there are times when it is important to see the couple even though the affair is continuing. For example, the couple may need help in talking about the situation and deciding how they will proceed. This is particularly true with Split Self couples. Couples sessions may also be useful with Exit Affairs, when the spouses need to talk with each other about the reality that their marriage is ending. With Conflict and Intimacy Avoiders who are undecided about whether to work on their marriage, it may be appropriate to use a couples format to discuss an affair that has not yet ended. As for the therapist insisting the affair stop, that is better left to the betrayed spouse who has much more leverage on this issue than we do. If we insist it stop, it may just go underground. I prefer to have affairs out in the open. These couples need a forum in which to talk about where they are as a couple and where they are going. If it becomes clear they are not ready to commit to serious work on the marriage, couples work can always be ended.

The health care system's intrusions into the therapy process are another problem for therapists. With many health care plans there is no coverage for marital work. If coverage does exist, it is likely to be extremely limited. However, brief therapy just doesn't work with affairs! Thus financial issues may affect the couple's ability to continue therapy. Compounding the problem is managed care's insistence on knowing all the details and on making therapeutic decisions despite never having seen the clients. In addition, in these days when medical records are computerized and privacy compromised, any information communicated about an affair can be damaging. Since employers provide most health insurance coverage, and the boundaries on information are so porous, employers may learn of an affair. The Uniform Code of Military Justice (1998) and its Manual for Courts-Martial, plus policies established at lower levels, make it clear that adultery is considered misconduct in the military, and that possible punishments include demotion or separation from the military. In the civilian sector, employers are beginning to notice that affairs, particularly those that have ended badly, can be costly for the company. Affairs at work lead to jealousy, charges of favoritism, and diminished work performance. Affairs that end badly leave the company open to charges of sexual harrassment. Better endings still leave a residue of tension and awkwardness between the affair partners that spills over onto co-workers and affects work performance. If one of the affair partners is reassigned, additional disruption occurs in the workplace. Some companies are taking steps to protect themselves, such as establishing relevant policies for the workplace and taking action when those policies are disregarded.

Therapists need to discuss with clients the pros and cons of using their insurance coverage. When clients want to use what coverage they have, the therapist needs to decide how to maintain privacy while giving managed care just enough information to gain approval. Even then, managed care's pattern of dribbling out approval for a few sessions at a time interferes with the therapeutic process.

On the positive side, a wide variety of treatment approaches can be used with success to help couples rebuild trust in their relationship. My sense is that whatever approach is used, the most important elements are the therapist's ability to connect with each spouse's emotions, to stay balanced between the spouses, and to provide a structure that keeps them exploring their difficult issues.

☐ The Process of Rebuilding for Conflict Avoiders

Conflict Avoidance Affairs occur when extra stress has been placed on the marital relationship. Often the precipitant is a new baby. Couples who function fairly well as a duo, may have difficulty incorporating the needs of a third person, especially a helpless baby, into their relationship. Other common precipitants include work pressures that compete with the marriage, the demands of an elderly parent, or a sense of inadequacy in gaining the spouse's approval. The conflict being avoided stems from dissatisfaction that a spouse is not sufficiently available, attentive, or approving. Many of these couples are struggling with the normal disappointment that comes early in marriage, when the honeymoon phase is over. Some expected that marriage would make them feel whole, and it hasn't done that. Others fear that voicing their discomfort could end the marriage. Rather than learning to interact with each other at a deeper level, these couples deny and avoid their uncomfortable feelings.

The partners have constructed their marriage to avoid conflict in the hope of gaining emotional security. As long as problems and conflicts are not verbalized, it is possible to believe they do not exist. It is this denial that forms the shaky basis for security. The affair is a clear message that the foundations of the marriage are not what they seemed.

As the obsession with the affair dies down, and the nature of the couple's issues becomes known, rebuilding can begin. Now there is room to explore the real issues and in the process to determine whether it is possible to rebuild the marriage. Guerin, Fay, Burden, and Kautto (1987) suggests that the most difficult phase of treatment is after the crisis, when both spouses understand the function of the affair, and they begin the difficult task of reestablishing trust.

The spouses are frightened about exploring previously taboo areas, frightened that they will find the marriage won't work, and frightened that it will. The panicked spouse declares "I can't forgive." As the therapist, you can reframe this comment while offering reassurance: "Of course you can't! It's too soon! You haven't done the work you need to do. The last thing you're going to do now is forgive." You can offer similar reassurance to the straying partner who declares "I don't know whether it will work." At this point the couple's commitment can only be to a process of exploration, not to continuing the marriage. They will determine as they work together whether they can build a solid foundation for their marriage.

Ending the Affair

A commitment to work on the marriage (as opposed to sorting out whether to work on it) comes after the affair ends or a decision is made to end it. If the affair was more than a one night stand, and there has been no real closure, this needs to be dealt with early in the rebuilding phase. The straying partner needs to close directly and openly with the third party. Help the spouse understand that without closure, the affair is still open. The spouse needs to know ahead of time when and how the contact will occur, and what the partner intends to say. Afterwards the spouse needs to hear what actually happened. Sometimes couples decide that the affair will be ended by phone. The spouse may or may not be in the background listening, but it is the straying partner's job to end the affair, not the spouse's. An affair ended by the spouse has not really ended. In other cases a note, an e-mail message, or a brief face-to-face contact is used to end the affair. Whatever the method, the message needs to be short and direct. For example, the straying partner might say, "I have decided to work on my marriage, so I am ending this affair. I do not want to have any future contact with you of any sort. Best wishes."

Optional contact with the third party needs to stop, so that the couple is not distracted from the work of rebuilding trust. When the third party continues to call or send notes, the straying partner needs to make it clear that the affair is over and he or she does not want any more contact. Subsequent behavior needs to match the words. Sometimes the clearest message that the affair is over is no response.

With these affairs, the emotional ties between the straying partner and the third party are usually quite slim. The loss is less the person than the fantasy. However if the affair was with a friend or if there are emotional ties of any significance the straying partner will need to grieve the loss. This is not easy for the betrayed spouse to understand. You can help by framing the grief as an important part of letting go, whether it is letting go of the third party or the fantasy.

If continuing contact between the straying partner and the third party is necessary, as sometimes occurs when they work together, the nature and the limits of this contact need to be understood by the spouse. Demands that the straying partner change employment to diminish the threat presented by the third party's presence can be viewed as obsessive behavior and treated as such. Changing jobs may not be possible or financially practical. The third party is not the threat; the shaky marriage is the problem.

In rare situations, it can be therapeutic when the affair continues for a while during the rebuilding phase.

Jane and Chris had been the ultimate Conflict Avoiders, but Jane was tired of it. She wanted change, but Chris was unresponsive. Jane then had an affair with a man living halfway across the country and told Chris about it. Chris was hurt, but also resigned himself to Jane's affair. They began marital therapy shortly thereafter, at Jane's insistence.

A few months later, Jane told Chris she was going to visit the man again. Chris again passively accepted Jane's plan. However, in Jane's absence, he began to get in touch with how hurt he was, and he experienced a glimmer of anger. As Chris made progress in paying attention to his feelings, he began to speak up more to Jane. Jane, too, was learning to assert herself in more appropriate ways. When Chris backslid for several weeks into his old passive behavior, Jane indicated she was again going to visit her lover. This time Chris got really angry, and for the first time they began to talk about Jane's affair, and what it meant in their relationship.

When Chris learned to assert his feelings and needs, Jane no longer needed to use the affair as a prod, and she ended it. If Jane had not found and used a prod that got Chris moving, he would have continued in his passivity. Marital therapy could not have been continued, however, if Jane's affair had been a secret one.

Goals and Treatment Formats for
Conflict Avoiders in the Rebuilding Phase

The shared definition of the marital problem, developed in the process of addressing obsession, provides an understanding of the specific ways in which the couple got off track, and thus sets a direction for therapy. The goals of the rebuilding phase of treatment are:

- Helping the spouses learn to talk about the uncomfortable issues they've been unable to discuss, with an eye to developing open, honest, and complete communication;
- Building trust, which means learning to share one's self emotionally and accepting the emotional experience of the other; and
- Making a well-considered decision about the viability of the marriage.

To reach these goals, the spouses must face together their problems with conflict. They must share feelings, positive as well as negative, that they have never confided in anyone before, and they must hear each other's real story. Tom, for example, admitted that he kept a part of himself distant from Marilyn—the part of himself that he thought would be a disappointment to her. Instead he kept returning to his obsession with her affair.

Couples therapy is the treatment of choice, with individual therapy as an adjunct, if and when needed. Individual treatment might be used to help a passive spouse learn how to stand up for him or herself, to provide temporary emotional support to an overstressed spouse, or to otherwise confront or encourage. It is essential that any individual therapy feed back into the couples therapy, an easier task when the same person provides both the marital and individual therapy.

Confidentiality between one spouse and the therapist runs counter to the goal of treatment and will sabotage the couples work. Consequently, the therapist must ensure, short of doing the work for the client, that the individual brings material from any individual sessions into the joint sessions. Clarifying this with couples before seeing them individually is important. Couples group is an option after they are clear about their real issues, and each owns their part of the problem (see Chapter 11 on The Use of Group Treatment).

As with all clients, clarify the goals of treatment with the couple. Outline what they need to learn, change, or address in order to resolve the problem identified in the shared definition of the marital problem and in subsequent sessions. The specific details will vary with the couple. Find out whether this is work that they want and are willing to do. Obtain their commitment to the goals and the process.

The Tasks of Rebuilding
for Conflict Avoiders

The tasks of rebuilding are directed toward differentiation of self and sharing one's self with one's partner. This entails working at two levels: the internal and the interpersonal. The internal level focuses on experiencing emotions, including those related to childhood wounds. The interpersonal level is concerned with using the here and now as a laboratory for changing the couple's interaction patterns. The tasks themselves are as follows:

- Paying attention to one's own emotions (differentiating between feelings, thoughts, and behavior)
- Being honest (giving up excuses, justifications)
- Giving one's self a voice (learning to express feelings and resolve differences)
- Owning responsibility (learning to set boundaries and take responsibility for one's own choices and behavior)
- Becoming emotionally vulnerable (asking for what is wanted, and accepting it when offered; sharing the real self)
- Developing reasonable expectations for the marriage (developing informed trust and accepting the inability to have it all)

Ambivalence about Exploring
the Marital Issues

Ambivalence expressed by the betrayed spouse about committing to the work usually has to do with resistance to owning a share of the problem, anxiety about being emotionally vulnerable, fear that the partner will leave if the spouse expresses dissatisfaction, or disliking change. If the straying partner is ambivalent, it may stem from confusing a commitment to work on the marriage with a commitment to continue the marriage, as well as anxiety or fear similar to that experienced by the betrayed spouse. For those who are reluctant to examine their situation, you might share with them a prediction that if they don't understand their own role in what has happened they are at risk of experiencing another affair.

A sense of hopelessness about the outcome, or a reduced reservoir of good feelings toward each other may also diminish the couple's willingness to explore the issues. A number of studies indicate that the loss of earlier levels of intimacy between the spouses is a key predictor of disaffection or divorce (Gottman, 1994a; Huston, 2001; Kayser, 1993). Peck (1975) writes that the early stage of game playing and raw manipulation, "collapses leaving the couple facing one another in a frightened, paranoid, vulnerable state. Once they become more personal with one another, the three of us can get down to the business of dealing with the ghosts" (p. 56).

Family History

If you have not already done so, get a complete family history of each spouse and a detailed history of the marriage. Chances are you were so busy cutting through the obsession that you learned only those details that were necessary to develop a shared definition of the marital problem. Be sure to get the family history in a couple's session. Each spouse will learn a great deal about the other, and each also may have something important to add about the other's family. As you learn about their families of origin, be sure to inquire about other affairs. Be on the alert for messages about sexuality, alliances, addictions, and family secrets, as well as themes of avoidance. Invariably, the current struggle replicates family of origin issues.

Ask for details about roles and relationships within the family. Was your client the "good kid," or the "outsider?" What was the relationship between the parents, and between each of the parents and your client? Look for ways in which their backgrounds have led them to the current situation, and highlight the interlocking nature of their issues. As you hear information that relates to the couple's underlying issues, share with them the connections you are making.

> With Chris I noted the similarity between his behavior and his father's passivity, and wondered aloud whether Chris had been instructed not to outshine his father or told to defer to his mother's wishes. Jane described a split in her family between the males and the females resulting from her father's affair. She had coped with the split by trying to prop up mother, who had deteriorated into seeming helplessness. When I asked how Jane was presently using this coping skill, she responded, "Oh, I know, I prop him up all the time." We went on to discuss how important it was for her to have control. I pointed out how each saved the other from having to feel uncomfortable: When Jane took control, Chris did not have to feel inadequate as he did when he was expected to act decisively. When Chris was passive, Jane had control and could avoid feeling helpless. Except that, as I observed, Jane felt helpless at being unable to change Chris's behavior, and Chris felt even more inadequate when tolerating Jane's affair.

If the relationship between one spouse and a child is presently overshadowing the husband-wife relationship, it is likely that this has been the case in previous generations. If the spouses have adopted reciprocal roles with each other, such as controlling parent/compliant child, this dynamic is also likely to show up in the family histories, as it did with Jane and Chris. Understanding how they learned dysfunctional behaviors reduces the self-blaming behavior that obstructs change. Also consider structural interventions that remove a child from the middle of the marital relationship and leave the spouses face to face to begin resolving their issues. For example, parents who communicate through a child can be directed to communicate directly with each other. Or parents can be instructed to make a particular decision between themselves, rather than asking the children what they prefer.

Reading is a useful adjunct for some couples; *The Dance of Intimacy* (Lerner, 1989), *Why Marriages Succeed or Fail* (Gottman, 1994b), *Affairs* (Brown, 1999), and *Are You the One for Me?* (DeAngelis, 1992) are particularly helpful for Conflict and Intimacy Avoiders.

Paying Attention to Emotions

Many clients who experience an affair do not know the difference between thoughts and feelings. Others learned early in life to tune out their emotions and need to learn how to recognize what they are feeling. With those who find this particularly difficult, ask them what their physical self is experiencing. Insist that they be very specific. For example, when Chris said he felt okay, I asked him to notice what was going on in his arms and legs, his stomach, his neck and shoulders. We hit pay dirt with his stomach—it was tied up in knots. Then I worked with him until he could make the connection between the knots in his stomach and feeling anxious. Sometimes clients' body language makes clear where the physical manifestation of emotions is located, as when someone's foot keeps moving.

Another common situation occurs when I ask, "What are you feeling?' and the response is, "Angry! I'm so disgusted. . . ." I interrupt to acknowledge the anger and to ask what the feeling under the anger is. The anger may or may not be part of the spouse's obsession. Many clients are unaware that anger is a secondary feeling that provides a defense against a deeper feeling, such as pain, fear, or helplessness. Help your client feel what's under the anger, in much the same way you would deal with obsession (see Chapter 5). Our clients also may use words such as "confused," or "frustrated," which are so broad that the feeling is not clear even to them, or words such as "betrayed," "deceived," or "ignored," which label what someone else has done but don't indicate how they feel when someone has betrayed, deceived, or ignored them. Insist that your client get down to the basic emotion.

Some Conflict Avoiders are afraid of feeling angry because they think it means having to attack one another. They fear "going out of control" because they fear the consequences of their own anger if it really comes out. These couples have an abundance of control, and exploding is not usually an issue. Help them find the location of their anger in their physical self, and then coach them in how to put their anger into words. Identifying the history of their fears, and noting that as adults they now have more choice over their lives also is helpful.

Being Honest

Conflict Avoiders are not used to being honest. Instead they are nice; they refer to small untruths as white lies. They openly declare that it is not nice to tell a person something that is going to be hurtful. They minimize the cost to themselves of withholding so much discomfort, insisting that those things don't really matter. Often they are unaware of how much they withhold. They also may tune out much of what they feel, so that they are not even aware of their dishonesty.

A discussion of what it means to be honest can be helpful. Some people believe that honesty means telling everybody every detail about everything. Others believe it means telling the other person what is wrong with them. Honesty really has to do with sharing one's own thoughts, feelings, and behavior that hold relevance for the other person. It is probably not relevant to Sheila for Adam to describe his musings about an office situation, unless he wants Sheila's help or needs her to listen. However if the office situation involves Adam's attraction to a colleague, that has a great deal of relevance for Sheila.

Learning to be completely honest means changing a habit—one that was learned as a child for good reasons, and has probably earned praise. Changing habits requires a series of steps:

* Monitoring one's thoughts, feelings, choices, and behavior constantly to get a clear picture of the dishonest behavior and to identify the cues and catalysts that put dishonesty on the front burner.
* Being aware in the moment of one's intent to lie, dissemble, or avoid the truth.
* Consciously choosing to be honest.

Owning Responsibility

Owning responsibility for one's own choices and behaviors means giving up blaming others, justifying bad choices, or avoiding issues. Difficulties in owning responsibility often stem from fears of abandonment, helplessness, or criticism. Sharing these fears and the history that engendered them is helpful as is looking at present day options for dealing more effectively with criticism, helplessness, or abandonment.

Sometimes resistance to owning one's responsibility comes from accepting responsibilities that are more appropriately left to others—in other words, not saying "no." Helping clients set better boundaries can facilitate their ability to take responsibility for what is theirs.

Giving One's Self a Voice

Giving one's self a voice means learning how to talk effectively about what one is thinking and feeling. Rebuilding also means listening to one's partner, and engaging in a full discussion of issues, even when painful. It also means calling one's partner on behavior that is hurtful.

Couples need a lot of help in breaking old communication patterns and replacing them with clear nonjudgmental messages. Help them recognize their interlocking patterns of avoiding conflict (they began this task when they contributed the data that you used to develop the shared definition of their marital problem) and teach them how to have a constructive fight with each other. They will learn that niceness is not as powerful as speaking up. In the process of learning, they can address old issues and begin to clear the air. You can help by not taking responsibility for setting the agenda—let them struggle with it. You may need however, to encourage them to keep digging until they get below the surface.

Becoming Emotionally Vulnerable

Increasing positive interactions between the spouses is essential. However the positive interactions often feel more risky than the negative. Positive interactions beget vulnerability which increases the fear of a negative response. Especially destructive negative interactions are contempt, defensiveness, and withdrawal (Gottman, 1994a). Gottman (1994b) instructs couples to "Accentuate the postive; don't eliminate the negative. . . . That magic ratio is 5 to 1. In other words, as long as there is five times as much positive feeling and interaction between husband and wife as there is negative, the marriage was likely to be stable" (pp. 56–57).

Doing this work in the context of changing learned behavior helps lessen self-defeating tendencies to blame one's self for whatever is wrong. Tying the present to what was learned in childhood also sets the stage for changing selected aspects of each spouse's relationships with parents. Selected reading is a useful adjunct for many clients.

As intimacy becomes more of a possibility the spouses have to struggle with boundaries. How close does either one want to be at a particular moment? How can they move closer and further apart in acceptable ways? What does each say to the other? The idea of voluntarily moving closer and further apart is a new concept for many couples. Akin to this is learning to ask for what one wants and accepting it when it is given. Learning to accept is often harder, because this tends to be associated with giving up control. However, reinforcement is built into the acceptance. For example, learning to tolerate her anxiety when she did not have control was necessary before Jane could accept Chris's offer to do the taxes, but she was delighted to be free of that responsibility.

Take it slow and easy when you ask the couple to expose their vulnerabilities. Use a gentle pressure so they don't avoid the task, but divide the task into small manageable bites. Humor is a great leveler, especially with Conflict Avoiders who tend to take everything seriously. Use humor to nudge a resistant spouse, or to redirect an unproductive dialogue. Tying humor to treatment metaphors can be especially productive. By the end of therapy, humor should be a daily habit.

> With a couple in their mid-thirties I used the metaphor of a brick wall between them (the division between them felt like a brick wall to me). They decided that each brick in the wall represented a problem they had not resolved. Rebuilding trust meant jointly removing each brick from the wall, examining it together, and deciding on a suitable resting place for it. The humor came from references to their peeking over the wall, or crouching behind it. At one point they decided the bricks were made of rubber, and they figuratively threw the bricks at each other. Progress was measured by their estimate of how high the wall was, and toward the end, by how many bricks were left.

Developing Reasonable Expectations for the Marriage

Even when the obsession dies down and the issue has been reframed as a joint problem, the spouse has a tendency to view her problems as less serious than those of the straying partner, and thus has a false sense of security. This spouse often assumes she has less work to do, when in fact she is a step behind the straying partner, who at least had the courage to make it clear that a problem existed. When the spouse doesn't do her work, the prognosis for the marriage is poor. Pressure needs to be kept on the spouse to address her own part of the problem.

Some therapists advise the straying partner to frequently reassure the spouse that there has been no contact with the third party. This approach is counterproductive because it keeps the affair in the center of the marriage as the significant reference point. Reassurance is better addressed by indicating where one is than where one isn't. The best form of reassurance for couples comes from sharing their thoughts and feelings with each other so that each has a sense of what is going on with the other.

Neither the marriage nor the partner can make either spouse feel whole. That is a do-it-yourself project. However the project is accomplished much more easily in the context of an open loving relationship with one's partner.

The dreams of "having it all" that couples so often carry into marriage, and the disappointment they experience when this doesn't occur, need to be replaced with acceptance that choices are necessary, that some choices are limited, and that choices have consequences. Dealing with an affair is difficult but can be an effective way to learn this.

Moving from Blind Trust to Informed Trust

Change for Conflict Avoiders means giving up fantasies and illusions about love and marriage—and themselves. These couples have confused trust with love. They believed that because they loved their partner they could automatically trust that person. The underlying assumptions are, "I love you, therefore I am one with you, therefore you would never hurt me." Lerner (1993) describes it thusly: "Denying that one's partner, or oneself, is vulnerable to powerful outside attractions is a form of sleepwalking" (p. 164). I call this blind trust. After the affair, the lack of trust in the partner is misinterpreted to mean that love no longer exists between the spouses. Low self-esteem may also be a factor in this interpretation. Nevertheless, grieving for the loss of this old belief system that promised so much is part of the work that the couple must do.

For those who trusted automatically, the idea of *building* trust is foreign. Trust is built by sharing one's emotional self, by accepting the reality of who the other person is, by making and following through on commitments, by positive interactions, by working together to resolve differences, and by having fun together. When these issues have been addressed, not only is trust rebuilt, but a stronger sense of self develops, one that is independent of the spouse. This self is able to face reality, to problem-solve, and to act responsibly, and knows it.

Rebuilt trust is of a different nature—it is "informed trust"—and is based on the realities in the relationship. Informed trust doesn't require the magical thinking or the denial of one's own observations that blind trust requires. With informed trust, problems are noted early and discussed so that they don't become secretly harbored resentments with the power to burst onto the scene and create havoc. Vaughan (1998) urges couples to regularly discuss their commitment to each other since, "The issue of monogamy is never settled once and for all" (p. 203).

Intimacy Issues

Conflict Avoidant couples hit plateaus where they are tempted to revert to old patterns, or at least not venture any further. When the once smooth surface of the marriage is disrupted, and the spouses begin to discuss and resolve conflicts, the underlying fear of intimacy begins to surface. Resistance increases again, and needs to be addressed.

Early in therapy, couples sometimes view an increase in emotional intensity or in lovemaking as a sign that their issues are resolved and decide that they no longer need therapy. They really are at the beginning of being more aware of their emotions. This is not evidence of having rebuilt trust. The opposite approach to rebuilding is taken by those who make threats and promises. Lerner (1993) states that "Threats and promises do nothing to guarantee fidelity or bolster trust. . . . What we can do, though, is work toward establishing increasingly greater levels of honesty and open communication . . . which is the only foundation on which trust can be built (p. 169).

Issues that come up at this time go to the heart of the matter. Each spouse is beginning to get in touch with their own issues and their contradictory fears about resolving the issues. Facing problems means they will have to take risks they've been afraid to take. Not facing the issues, means staying mired in the pain or reverting to the carefully balanced but emotionally numbing impasse. Help the spouses surface and discuss their ambivalence so that they can move past their resistance.

Glass and Wright (1988) note that, "It has been our experience that the less committed partners who are not sure of their love will be moved as much or more through their own caring behaviors as by those of their spouses" (p. 313). Lawson (1988) suggests that, "The 'feminine' qualities of nurturance, caring, and kindness are the qualities of *both* wife and husband most likely to make for the happiest marriages" (p. 311). She notes that gender scripts constrain both men and women in marriage.

Positive effects also can be generated by the affair itself. The affair may call on a part of one's self that is not being used in the marriage. Jim, whose sexual relationship with his wife had never been satisfactory, realized that sex could be different with a loving and responsive partner. Revamping the marriage meant repairing the sexual relationship.

When the rebuilding phase is going well, and each spouse is working on his or her own issues, it is time for a new courtship. Since Conflict Avoidant couples are serious, productive, and perfectionistic, they need to learn to play. Intimacy Avoiders have less difficulty playing. Couples like the idea of a new courtship; it sounds like fun and it sounds romantic. If they have a feel for what courtship means, you can send them off to explore on their own. Some couples, however, need guidance on how to court. Help them come up with ideas for small chunks of time that have the potential for fun and for learning something new about each other. Courtship is an essential bridge between therapy and the couple's everyday life. Some elements of courtship can and should continue after therapy ends.

Our Issues

With Conflict Avoidant couples, we can easily get caught up in their resistance and avoidance. It is sometimes difficult for us to keep the focus on painful issues when couples are courageously struggling with their pain. It is better that we help them face the full extent of their situation than that we protect them from pain. We need to be aware of our own difficulties with pain, our tendencies to want to protect, our own aversion to conflict, and our own issues around sex and betrayal. It is important that we process our own issues as we respond to our clients resistance, so that the decisions we make are therapeutically sound and not based on our own issues.

☐ Intimacy Avoidant Couples

Couples who avoid intimacy carry scars from childhood that make them wary of getting too close. The underlying issues tend to be more difficult ones than those faced by the Conflict Avoiders. There is a higher incidence of family histories that include abuse, neglect, alcohol, and other addictions. On the plus side, the Intimacy Avoiders are not afraid of conflict, and so they find it easier to discuss difficult issues. Once the conflict is reduced to a manageable level, these couples are easier to work with than the Conflict Avoiders because they are able to put the issues out on the table.

The presentation of the affair is sometimes low-key, such as "We've both had affairs." In other cases the affair(s) are a major focus of conflict and attention. In each case however, conflict is used to obscure emotional issues and to distance oneself from intimacy. The affair is not the major issue; the avoidance of intimacy is.

Techniques for Intervening
with Intimacy Avoiders

Much of the work for Intimacy Avoiders is the same as that for the Conflict Avoiders. However the continual battling of the Intimacy Avoiders interferes with getting to work. The therapist must cut through the conflict and push it aside to get to the real issues. Once these couples get to work, the good feelings that are generated toward the other spouse are experienced as threatening. A new round of conflict serves to forestall the risk of intimacy and must again be pushed aside for the work to proceed. Thus the process of working with Intimacy Avoiders is different than with Conflict Avoiders although the tasks are the same.

While these couples are not afraid of expressing anger, they need help in learning how to resolve differences. Control battles are common. These struggles need to be reframed to identify the real issues, especially the fear of losing themselves. Both spouses need help in identifying and safeguarding their individual feelings and needs. Their family histories will indicate why intimacy is so threatening.

Early in therapy, these couples will control the therapy session, given the opportunity. It is essential for the therapist to maintain control and act as a gatekeeper for communication, while providing emotional support designed to help the spouses become less apprehensive. Finding out where each one hurts provides a good beginning. Even here, it is important not to move too fast, so as to keep the vulnerability at a manageable level. Individual sessions as an adjunct to couple's work are often necessary with more combative couples who need greater support. Work on expressing intimacy needs to go very slowly. The sequence in working with Intimacy Avoiders is reflected in the following case.

Suzanne and Lowell, both 30 years old, came for therapy because of their continuing conflict over the six years of their marriage. They regarded themselves as friends, but both said that they each could be real SOBs. Lowell told me they both had recently gotten involved with other people and were getting from them what they were not getting at home. Their goal was to determine whether they could resolve their issues so that the marriage could work.

Getting a family history early in treatment helped me identify the nature and origin of their current issues and helped them better understand their difficulties. The fear of intimacy that each developed in childhood in response to family dysfunction was being played out in their marriage.

Suzanne's father was an alcoholic and her mother was unhappy and self-sacrificing. Lowell's father was demeaning and domineering and his mother was manipulatively dependent. Suzanne tries to prove she is good enough to be liked. At the same time she is tremendously afraid of caring, for fear of being trapped like her mother was, so she alternates between being provocative and charming. She can allow herself to be close to Lowell if he is angry. Lowell attempts to control so he won't be ridiculed for being wrong. He was angry at me because I wouldn't let him control the therapy session.

The shared definition of their problem was built around a metaphor: the gingerbread man. Suzanne's message was "Catch me if you can," and Lowell's was "I'll run as fast as I can." As they began to work on their issues, Lowell took the initiative in getting issues out in the open, while Suzanne was more expressive of her own feelings. Problematic behavior patterns were examined in the context of what that behavior meant in their families of origin, as well as what it meant now. As they separated their real feelings from their desire for approval, they began to spend some leisure time together again.

During the early months of therapy, they began each session with criticism of the other in an attempt to provoke an argument. I continually reframed this as a reflection of Suzanne's fear of being trapped and Lowell's fear of being abandoned. They were "dirty fighters" and we discussed in detail how that worked. Lowell was the first to be able to admit that he wanted his "new self," which he defined as loving, to win in the battle with his old combative self.

The issues around intimacy began to open up. Old behaviors, such as their little girl/big daddy routine became more pronounced. Suzanne's defenses against feeling trapped started to fall, when after a period of resistance, she began to realize that she hadn't given much attention to the hurt child inside herself. As she began to nurture her hurt child, she became able to enjoy sex as an adult for the first time. Lowell meanwhile located and talked with his sister (the family scapegoat) about the abandonment and isolation that each had experienced growing up.

Things were going so well between Suzanne and Lowell that they got scared. Each took a turn at sabotaging the intimacy that was developing. Lowell lapsed into his old domineering ways, criticizing Suzanne and telling her what to do. Suzanne stayed out with friends until 2 a.m. one night without calling Lowell to tell him she would be late. By this time, however, they couldn't kid themselves that this wasn't sabotage, and they shared with each other the feelings that had led to the sabotage. Concerns about intimacy became refocused on how to move closer and how to back away from each other.

Several months later Suzanne shared with Lowell the fact she was attracted to a man at work. She assured Lowell that she was not going to have an affair, but she felt there was something she needed to learn, and she needed to talk to Lowell about it. Lowell was scared, but was able to tolerate the situation. Suzanne began to realize that she wanted Lowell to be as seductive with her as was the man at work. Both became clearer about the difference between feelings and behavior, and Lowell began to be more playful and sexually creative.

Because of their strong motivation for change, the fact that they were friends, and their youth, they finished therapy in a year and a half. By then, Suzanne and Lowell could talk to each other about everything, and were doing so. Each was able to share their feelings, good and bad, with the other. Suzanne could tolerate feeling help-less and could lean on Lowell, without doing a little girl routine or fearing being trapped. Lowell was able to be loving and vulnerable without fearing that he would be abandoned. Affairs were not an issue because Suzanne and Lowell no longer needed to protect against intimacy.

Extreme Situations

If you think of Intimacy Avoiders as falling along a continuum of functioning, at the extremely dysfunctional end are a few couples where one of the spouses, usually the betrayed spouse, has a border-line personality disorder. In this situation, individual therapy is the treatment of choice for both spouses, supplemented with some couples work.

Our Issues

For the therapist working with Intimacy Avoiders, issues of control and timing are especially important. Taking a confrontive stance is not effective. The couple's inclination toward drama and impulsive be-havior is pronounced, and impulsive separations are common. It can be tempting for us to follow their lead and throw in the towel early in treatment when the control struggles are greatest. The most useful techniques are reframing the struggle to reflect the underlying prob-lems and helping them talk about their pain. When things are going well, we can be tempted to encourage too much intimacy too fast. For Intimacy Avoiders, this is terrifying. Small steps toward intimacy work better, especially when there is an opportunity to talk about each step before moving to the next one.

☐ Planned Separations as a Treatment Strategy

Some spouses need separate space to be able to do the work on themselves that is needed. These tend to be individuals who are not in touch with their emotions and who are extremely hesitant to speak up about anything, or couples who are so caught up in their cycle of conflict that they need some separate space in order to see and disentangle from their role in the conflict. In a planned separation, contact with each other continues although it is greatly decreased.

Trial separations are sometimes decided upon by a straying partner who doesn't want to give up the affair, but isn't ready to make a decision about the marriage either. Trial separations can be useful to provide a breather, or to play out fantasies about the affair, but they increase the risk of divorce. They are not useful when their primary function is to cut off the other person so as not to have to deal with conflict, or when they allow one or both spouses to run away from difficult emotions. The trial separation of the Conflict and Intimacy Avoiders can really be a trial, as opposed to the trial separation proposed by the straying partner in the Exit Affair who does not intend to reconcile.

Trial separations are planned, rather than impulsive. The terms need to be carefully laid out between the spouses, especially as to relationships with the opposite sex. The intended length of separation is usually several months and discussion of reconciliation comes toward the end of that period. During a trial separation a mix of individual and couples therapy facilitates individual growth while keeping the spouses working on their joint issues.

Some separations are not planned but in various cases they are productive anyway.

> With Nancy and Kevin, the separation was not planned. When one more secret dribbled out, Nancy had had enough and told Kevin to move out. He put his tail between his legs and did so. They continued to see each other and do some talking but the issue of honesty was a major problem. Then Kevin discovered in his individual therapy that he had dissociated since childhood. Dissociation was how he coped with the pain and pressure of a needy mother, an alcoholic father, and being the parent to his siblings. Kevin's lies were not really lies—he truly didn't remember. He would respond to many of Nancy's questions with, "I don't know," but under her continued questioning he occasionally remembered something about the affair and shared it with her. She perceived this pattern as intentional dishonesty.
>
> When Kevin's dissociation was identified, couples sessions were instrumental in helping Nancy understand what dissociation is, why Kevin

had learned to dissociate, and how he was working on it. With that information, Nancy was able to reach out emotionally to Kevin again, and after a few weeks they decided that it was time for Kevin to move back in. The separation was useful for Nancy because it gave her the sense that she didn't have to accept Kevin's lies, and it gave them both some space while Kevin was getting closer to the roots of his issues.

☐ Making Decisions about the Marriage

When the spouses understand their issues and have worked to rebuild trust, the time comes for them to consider whether to continue their marriage. Open discussions are needed, in which the spouses can explore how the relationship fits or does not fit them. Some couples easily decide that the benefits far outweigh the deficiencies. Others, for whom the benefits and disadvantages are more evenly balanced, need to weigh their decision carefully. Ask them to predict the course of the marriage if it continues, and to assess the gains and losses if it ends. At this point, unless both of them readily agree to continue the marriage, one of the spouses usually moves toward a decision to separate.

Talk about divorce toward the end of the rebuilding phase is quite different than earlier. Such talk at this time is usually quieter and accompanied by sadness. It reflects a realization by one or both spouses that they are unable to resolve their issues, or that they don't have enough emotional glue to stay together. Sometimes therapists are reluctant to accept a decision to divorce, but we need to remember that while we are responsible for the therapeutic process, our clients get to make the decisions about their lives.

Duration of Couple's Therapy

Treatment of Conflict Avoiders and Intimacy Avoiders usually takes from one to two years following the discovery of the affair, or sometimes longer. They are ready to terminate treatment when they have resolved their old issues and are addressing new issues as they arise. Suzanne and Lowell remarked that they were communicating so well that they were able to share everything, even Suzanne's crush on the man at work. Lowell wasn't totally comfortable, but because of their communication he knew that there was no danger to the marriage.

After successfully resolving the marital issues, one straying partner remarked, "I have come to realize that the trouble between myself and this woman—the fact I had affairs at all—has been because of the bad things left over, left unsaid" (Lake, 1979, p. 49). With couples who resolve their issues and stay together, forgiveness is usually the last big issue in therapy (see Chapter 12).

When Conflict Avoiders don't address their real issues, the following scenarios are likely. They will repeat the same experience (and hopefully resolve the issues this time); they will stay together despite obsession and unhappiness; the marriage will end with an Exit Affair; or the spouses will stay together and the situation will evolve into an Split Self Affair.

Intimacy Avoiders who don't address their real issues also are likely to end up repeating the experience, possibly using an Exit Affair to leave the marriage.

When the Marriage Ends

A decision to end the marriage may come at any point. Such a decision is usually made by the straying partner when he or she decides that the desired responsiveness is not forthcoming and will not be. This decision may be well considered or impulsive, depending on the degree to which the straying partner has dealt with his or her own issues. Sometimes the betrayed spouse is the one who decides to end the marriage, for similar reasons or to continue avoiding the issues. In some cases the spouses simply recognize that they have grown very far apart.

Impulsive decisions to separate are made by those who find that facing the issues is harder work than they bargained for. Signs that this is the case show up early: frequent canceling of appointments, dropping in and out of treatment, and not following through on commitments made in the therapy sessions. In these instances, the affair may resume, or another affair may begin. The prognosis for the marriage is poor, and therapy is usually short-lived. At this point the affair should be viewed as an Exit Affair.

When the decision to end the marriage is solidly based, the course of therapy changes to issues of ending. It feels especially sad when both spouses have worked on rebuilding their relationship and are unable to reach a resolution that will allow them to stay together. Hopefully as therapists, we are not so invested in their marriage that we can't accept their decision.

The process of discussing divorce is quite different with Conflict and Intimacy Avoiders than with the Exiters where the affair is used to shroud the fact that a decision to divorce had already been made. By the time a considered decision about ending the marriage has been made, each partner is able to own their own part of what has gone wrong in the marriage. They are in touch with their feelings, and able to talk to some extent about being disappointed that their hopes for the marriage have not transpired. Both spouses are deeply sad but their grief does not have the hysterical quality that is present in the Exit Affair. The spouses need to share their pain and their sadness with each other, as well as their disappointment and anger, and it is important that we facilitate this discussion. We, too, may want to share our sadness with them.

Separation Issues

With this kind of decision, and the absence of a rush to separate, practical matters of separating can be addressed carefully. The spouses will welcome your help in planning for the separation. Issues they need to discuss include telling the children of their decision, identifying the tasks that need to be completed before separation, and deciding when to separate. Since some practical decisions can have unintended legal consequences, couples should consult with mediators, financial planners, and attorneys prior to separating or taking other practical actions. To avoid negative legal and economic consequences, most couples work out the details of their separation agreement before separating. (See Chapter 9 for further information on preparing for separation.)

Before ending the marital therapy, review with the couple the many gains they have made. Discuss with them the issues, old and new, that each will need to continue to address and their various options for doing so. Help them anticipate and understand the emotional process of divorce. Take time to call attention to the feelings they are having now, as they are in the process of ending their marriage.

Therapy After Separation

Individual therapy can provide needed emotional support during the crisis of separation and throughout the grieving period. After the crisis, group therapy should be considered as soon as the person can tolerate a group setting. A divorce support group is another option for separated individuals.

An issue for therapists is whether to see both spouses individually or to refer them to other therapists. If the spouses have been seeing individual therapists, they will no doubt continue with them. If not, decisions need to be made as to whether they will continue with you or whether they need to start fresh with someone new.

At a time when they are losing each other, when their dreams for the marriage are ending, and when some of their friends are backing off, it may be too devastating to also lose a trusted therapist. Yet they may perceive a conflict of interest if you continue with both of them. For example, issues around dating, sexuality, or children may arise, and even if you are totally unbiased, your knowledge of one spouse's situation may be an impediment to your effectiveness with the other. Your understanding of them can also work in the opposite direction, with the result that both want to continue with you. Depending on the couple, this may be a viable option. Or is their desire to continue with you really a reluctance to let go of each other? If so, is this constructive (as in maintaining a friendship) or is it time for them to take another step alone? Sometimes it makes sense that one continues with you and the other does not, but if so, this needs to be agreed upon by all. They need to think this issue through with your help.

☐ The Therapist's Role in the Rebuilding Phase

The therapist's role is a complex one in working with Conflict Avoiders and Intimacy Avoiders. The major tasks are to help the spouses talk with each other about their feelings—their fears, anger, pain, and joy—and to help them learn new ways of communicating. Insist they share their feelings with each other in the therapy sessions. Surface all the underlying issues, rather than protecting them or letting anything slide. Continue to limit discussion of the affair, and keep enough pressure on so that the betrayed spouse isn't left behind. Offer emotional support to both spouses, and hold each of them accountable for themselves. Encourage small steps toward intimacy when both spouses are ready to explore their relationship. Use the energy created by the affair, the energy of the out-of-balance system, for rebuilding. This is an opportunity not to be wasted.

CHAPTER

Rebuilding for the Addictive Family

The stereotypical image of an affair tends to be that of the Sexual Addict. In reality, sexual addiction is not the typical type of affair. The image presented of the Sexual Addict is not accurate either. The image tends to be one of an outgoing man who loves sex, and enjoys pursuing women. Sexual addiction is much more complicated than that and has little to do with enjoying sex or women. This chapter focuses on the married Sexual Addict, who is most often male.

The married Sexual Addict who engages in affairs comes to the attention of therapists less often than do straying partners in other types of affairs. Some studies suggest that the number of Sexual Addicts is less than the number of straying partners in the other types of affairs (Hunt 1969; Kinsey, Pomeroy, & Martin, 1948). Schneider (1988) estimates that 10% of the married men who have affairs are sexually addicted. The figure for married women is not available but is probably much lower due to the different socialization and expectations for women. It is likely too, that men are less willing than women to put up with a sexually addicted spouse.

Some people deny that there is such a thing as sexual addiction, believing that a pattern of multiple affairs is a matter of morality or of men's nature. Others find sexually addictive behavior permissible or even expected for males, but encourage men not to put up with affairs on the part of their wives. Reinforcement of the addiction is provided when acquaintances envy the male Addict's "way with women," or chalk up his affairs to "Men are made that way." Our society colludes with the male Sexual Addict in denying the addiction. The cultural attitude toward female Addicts is quite different. At best they are viewed as playthings, but more often they are the target of harsh moral judgments. Women who are Sexual Addicts more often are unmarried third parties (see Chapter 10). They too, have great difficulty admitting their addiction and seeking treatment. Whether the changes presently occurring in women's sexual behavior in our society will be reflected by an increase in sexual addiction among married females remains to be seen.

The high of sexual addiction is in the conquest and the sexual fix. The excitement quickly gives way to guilt and shame. The roots of sexual addiction extend back to childhood, to experiences of abuse or extreme neglect that have never been reconciled. Dysfunctional sexual and relationship patterns were pervasive in the family of origin, and the Addict learned to substitute brief sexual highs for feelings of emptiness, isolation, shame, and low self-esteem. Addiction and codependency are issues for each family member. Acknowledgment of the addiction is a major step, and needs to be followed by intensive therapy, using several modalities, with the entire family.

Those who are addicted to affairs seek therapy for their addiction less often than do those in other types of affairs (Orford, 1985). In part this is because the concept of sexual addiction is still not widely understood. More significant however, is the Sexual Addict's immense denial, which resembles that of the alcoholic. While the alcoholic denies the extent of his drinking, many Sexual Addicts acknowledge their behavior but deny that the behavior is problematic. Some Sexual Addicts brag about their conquests (although not to their spouses)— that too is designed to fill up the inner emptiness.

When the Addict does come for help, therapists often overlook clues or do not see a need to treat culturally condoned behavior such as affairs. Bert, a 35-year-old computer whiz, told his therapist about his many affairs and wondered aloud whether he should tell his wife. The therapist, who was treating him for depression, said, "That's not necessary, they're not serious." When Bert's wife discovered the truth, the situation exploded. Bert's earlier query should have been an indicator to the therapist that Bert needed to explore this issue. Instead the therapist responded with the common male belief that a fling is not significant, missing the deeper issue.

The therapist's own background regarding sexuality has a significant impact on whether the sexual addiction will be addressed (Carnes, 1988). Not surfacing sexual addiction is in some cases simply a matter of inexperience or naivete. Training, or more accurately a lack of training, also is a factor. Few therapists have any training in the treatment of sexual issues, and even fewer have had the opportunity to learn about affairs, except from clients and friends, and through personal experience. Therapists trained in the traditional mental health disciplines often miss addictions, while those whose expertise is in addictions may not be familiar with the meaning of other types of affairs. The therapist's own denial stemming from unresolved or unacknowledged issues regarding sex or addictions will also interfere with recognizing sexual addiction.

☐ What Is Sexual Addiction?

Currently it is popular to ascribe sexual addiction to anyone who has an affair. This is a misuse of the term. Sexual addiction is a specific syndrome of behavior and underlying emotional issues. With addiction, the individual is preoccupied with one or more sexual behaviors to the exclusion of other areas of his life. Habits are not addictions. Just the opposite: habits allow some behavior to be put on "automatic" so that the mind can be used for other things.

Bradshaw (1988) defines addiction as "a pathological relationship to any mood-altering experience that has life-damaging consequences" (p. 15). Hunter (1989) says "Sexual addiction refers to the thinking and behavior patterns of a person who uses sex to cope with life and to defend against low self-worth and a shameful identity. . . . Sex is . . . a compulsive, often highly ritualized activity that ultimately adds to the pain and loneliness the Addict is already battling" (p. 1).

Some therapists use the term sexual addiction to refer to long term serious affairs (Split Self Affairs), with the inference that the straying partner is addicted to the third party. This is also a misuse of the concept of sexual addiction. A real relationship exists between the straying partner and the third party in a Split Self Affair. This is not true with sexual addiction, where the third party is regarded as an object to be used. The degrading sexual acts that are often part of sexual addiction are not present in Split Self Affairs. Sexual addiction does not refer to a frequent desire for sex per se, but to the compulsive pursuit of sex to assuage inner pain and emptiness.

Sexual addiction takes many forms. In addition to affairs it includes behaviors such as exhibitionism, pornography, cybersex, indecent phone calls, child molestation, incest, and rape. Affairs are regarded as among the least serious addictions in that they are victimless. Rape, incest, and child molestation are at the far end of the continuum of compulsive sexual behavior.

Elements of sexual addiction to affairs include the following:

- The behavior is compulsive.
- The Addict is increasingly preoccupied with the addictive behavior.
- The addictive behavior continues despite the cost to one's personal, family, and work lives.
- Risk and excitement are important parts of the preoccupation as well as the behavior.
- These feelings are a temporary replacement, a "fix," for the painful feelings being avoided.
- Usually, although not always, there are numerous affairs (another one every week or every business trip; fifty, a hundred or so, and counting).
- There is no emotional attachment to the sexual partner.
- The addictive behavior is hidden, which leads to greater isolation from the family.
- The behavior pattern is cyclical, with preoccupation and rationalization leading to efforts to engage in the behavior, followed by the behavior itself, followed by fear and shame and attempts to stop the behavior, followed by preoccupation and rationalization.
- Other addictive behaviors are likely, and each addiction reinforces the others.

Schneider (1988) distinguishes between affairs stemming from sexual addiction and those with other roots on the basis of whether the straying partner has the ability to act on his promises and control his behavior.

Although the focus of this book is on affairs, it needs to be kept in mind that those who are addicted to affairs are quite likely to have other addictions, possibly sexual in nature, which also serve the function of avoiding pain and gaining attention. Eighty-three percent of the Sexual Addicts treated by Carnes (1988) also had at least one other addiction. Forty-two percent of the Sexual Addicts in Carnes sample are alcoholics (Carnes, 1989b). The interlocking nature of addictions comes through in the case of Bill W., the founder of Alcoholics Anonymous, who gave up alcohol, but remained sexually addicted. At that time, sexual addiction was not understood, and help was not available (Carnes, 1989b). It should be noted that not all the Sexual Addicts in Carnes' studies engage in affairs. This chapter focuses only on those who are addicted to affairs, except where specified otherwise.

Underneath addictive behavior is shame, "toxic shame" as John Bradshaw (1988, p. vii) calls it. Children whose emotional needs are ignored in favor of the parents' needs learn to abandon their own feelings and display behavior designed to prevent abandonment. "Toxic shame is unbearable and always necessitates a cover-up, a false self. Since one feels his true self is defective and flawed, one needs a false self which is not defective and flawed. Once one becomes a false self, one ceases to exist psychologically" (1988, p. vii–viii). "The drivenness in any addiction is about the ruptured self, the belief that one is flawed as a person" (1988, p. 15).

Origins of Sexual Addiction

The making of a Sexual Addict begins early in life. A frequent theme in therapy is the emphasis the Sexual Addict's family placed on sexuality, either directly or by rigid avoidance of anything sexual. Addicts report growing up in families where no one is allowed to talk about sex or in which a family member is dedicated to controlling all expression of sexuality, or in families where sexuality runs rampant as when a father of adolescent girls walks around the house nude, or a mother keeps her son in her bed until he is 10 years old.

Sexualized attention is a common childhood experience for those addicted to affairs.

> From the time he was eight until he left home, Walt stepped into his absent father's role and assisted Mom by zipping her up, checking her appearance, and being her confidante after her dates. Such attention made him feel special, although it also felt a bit uncomfortable. Walt's mother justified her behavior, trying to make it appear normal to herself as well as to Walt. The result for Walt, however, was feeling stimulated much of the time, with an overlay of discomfort. His mother's use of him also deprived him of the freedom to attend to his own feelings and needs.

Abuse is a major factor in the development of sexual addiction. According to Carnes (1989b) 81% of Sexual Addicts have been sexually abused, 72% have been physically abused, and 97% have been emotionally abused. The latter category includes extreme neglect. Carnes (1988) theorizes that the more abuse as a child, the more addictions as an adult.

Rejection of the child's feelings is another factor contributing to addiction. Such rejection takes many forms, ranging from abandonment to engulfment. Engulfment by a parent is a subtle form of rejection which operates much like an addiction: The parent's needs take precedence, and there is no room for the child's feelings or needs. The child feels abandoned, and as children do, decides it must be because he is bad. He learns not to pay attention to his real feelings because they are so painful and instead devotes himself to behavior designed to elicit attention or to gain comfort.

> Frank's background is typical. He does not remember ever being hugged or touched by his mother. She was critical and withholding, and Frank's efforts to gain her approval failed. Frank reports a distant relationship with his father who was an alcoholic and womanizer. It is not surprising that once Frank discovered masturbation at the age of six he used it to relieve his loneliness and pain. Every night he rocked himself to sleep with his blanket and his penis. As he got older, he shifted to intercourse with women as a way to relieve his pain.

Based on clinical observation, families of origin provide some level of emotional attachment, however tenuous, for those addicted to affairs. This contrasts with the background of the child molester or rapist who has not bonded with anyone. The commonality is that the Addict has learned that people can be used for his own purposes. The cognitive component is, "My feelings are more important than your feelings, and if I don't take care of my feelings, nobody will. I have to satisfy my feelings" (T. Hodges, personal communication, November 25, 1989).

Family Background of a Sexual Addict

The typical Sexual Addict grew up in a family that is dysfunctional, secretive, and addictive. Boundaries pertaining to sexual behavior in the family are extreme: either rigid or flimsy. Another family member is probably addicted as well, whether to sex or another substance (Carnes, 1989b). The male Addict's mother is likely to be overprotective and controlling. His father is not available to him emotionally. Never having been allowed his feelings as a child, he is emotionally needy. It is this neediness that he attempts to fill with affairs.

Since addiction is a family disease, a family history of alcohol, drug, and sexual addiction is common. Carnes (1989b) found that 18% of the mothers of Sexual Addicts, 40% of their fathers, and 50% of their siblings have difficulty with sex. Because denial and secrecy are typical of sexually addicted families, the sexual problems and addictive patterns in the family are not discussed.

> John's childhood set the stage for his addiction. John, 34 years old and a manager on his way up in a large electronic security firm, is the oldest child and his mother's favorite. John's mother wanted him to be the man his father wasn't. Throughout childhood John performed well in

an attempt to live out the dreams his mother had projected on him (she had given up her own dreams when she became a mother). John describes his mother as intense, seductive, and the most important influence in his life. She was so powerful that at times he feared being gobbled up by her. As a young adult he found the relationship rather intrusive and uncomfortable, but tolerated it.

John's father was an alcoholic who eventually drank himself to death. When he was home, he was emotionally distant except about football. He expected big gains and daring touchdowns from John during high school and college games and was angry when John was benched. The home turf was arranged so that Mother was in control of the household and child rearing, father stayed away, and John stood in for father.

John's parents marriage was distant, stormy, and sexless. John's father coped by chasing women until he died. John remembers both parents questioning him about the other's activities. John's mother constantly disparaged his father: "You men can't be trusted, you never pay any attention to what's important," with an aside to John, "But you're not like that."

John reacted to his mother's sexual attention by building a secret life of fantasies, pornography, and masturbation. This also insulated him from his pain at being used by his mother and ignored by his father. As he got older he progressed from fantasies to one night stands and brief affairs as a means of escaping his pain. These became more frequent right after college, when John began living on his own.

In John's affairs he submerged himself in others. His fantasy was of being one with them, being loved by them. Then he wouldn't have to feel his pain or his rage at his parents' abandonment. If he was not merged with another, it was almost as if he was annihilated. Similarly, he feared that if he didn't perform well professionally he would disappear and be forgotten. John's struggle to be himself by losing himself had life and death implications.

He met Brenda through friends, and was intrigued by her old-fashioned virtues. He decided it would be a good time for him to settle down, and Brenda was devoted to him without being demanding. True she was not a real sex pot but marriage would change that. After ten years of marriage, their relationship, sexual and otherwise, has changed—for the worse.

The Pursuit of Sex, Love, and Power

The compulsive pursuit of sexual encounters is an attempt to avoid the pain of the Addict's inner emptiness. The Addict rationalizes his behavior, just as the alcoholic or drug addict does, and blinds himself to the risks he is taking and to the effects of his behavior on others. For the Addict, an internal process of bargaining goes on: "I need it, just this once, and then I'll stop. It won't hurt anybody, just this once." Prior promises, or concerns about the needs of others, are of little matter to the addict, compared to his "need." Yet the very nature of the pursuit, combined with his difficulty in experiencing his own feelings, prevents him from ever feeling satisfied as the result of a sexual encounter.

Cybersex is the newest "meet/meat market" for Sexual Addicts. The Internet does not create sexual addicts but its chat rooms and sexual sites cater to anonymity and to fantasy. Many Internet contacts result in face-to-face meetings, some of which are based on the pursuit of sex.

A search for power often coincides with the search for sex. Both have an element of excitement and both are designed to fill up the inner emptiness. Common arenas for seeking power are politics, law, entertainment, and religion (maybe power straight from God is best). The sexual activities of televangelists Jim Bakker and Jimmy Swaggart are instances in which the pursuit of power and money through religion became entangled with the compulsive pursuit of sex. These days it's the politicians who are making news with their sexual exploits. Their behavior, where the risk is immense, makes sense only when seen as sexual addiction.

The Addict is not all bad nor is all his behavior bad. Rather, much of his good behavior is serving the addiction. The Addict feels good about doing good deeds. These can be used to hide the affairs. They also help others overlook such behavior in light of all the good he does. The power inherent in the good deeds provides an emotional high.

The Kennedys

Nowhere is the relationship between power and sexual addiction illustrated more clearly than in the Kennedy family. The Kennedys were patriarchal with a tradition of men ruling the women, both financially and emotionally. It was part of the male rite of passage to seduce and have as many women as possible, and that pattern continued into marriage. The women who married into the family were basically outsiders with little power to influence the mores, norms, and traditions of the family. The men have affairs and do whatever they want, while the women stay home and raise the children.

Rose Kennedy's father, the mayor of Boston, was evidently disappointed with his wife's reserve. With Rose's birth, "He had the chance to love again, and into her he poured all the magnificent hopes and enthusiasms and all his remarkable vitality" (Goodwin, 1987, p. 106). Rose's husband, Joseph Patrick Kennedy, Sr., appears to have had many affairs, one of them being a serious emotional involvement with

Gloria Swanson. Rose's mother is reported to have told Rose about the affair, possibly as retaliation for Rose's closeness to her father. Goodwin (1987) paraphrases the message: "You see, you fool, your beloved husband is no different from your beloved father. Now you finally know what men are really like!" (p. 460). A friend of the family speculated that, "When Joe realized how close he had come to destroying his family, he determined that from there on in, he would keep his encounters with women at a more casual level. I think he simply decided that he would never again get so deeply involved with anyone, and as far as I know he never did" (p. 493).

Goodwin (1987) observes, "Jack seemed to be imitating the pattern his father had estblished . . . a pattern of keeping his relationships with women both superficial and numerous. It appears that the Kennedy children not only knew about their father's womanizing but fully accepted it, so long as their mother was protected from public embarrassment" (p. 837). With Jack, "So driven was the pace of his sex life, and so discardable his conquests, that they suggest a deep difficulty with intimacy. 'The whole thing with him was pursuit,' said one of the women Jack courted. 'I think he was secretly disappointed when a woman gave in. It meant that the low esteem in which he held women was once again validated. It meant also that he'd have to start chasing someone else'" (Goodwin, 1987, p. 838).

Jackie apparently accommodated Jack's womanizing. Botwin (1988) points out that Jackie Kennedy's father was "one of the most notorious womanizers of his day" (p. 39). Ted, Jack's younger brother, also had numerous affairs that Joan, Ted's wife, seemingly tolerated, though she developed an alcohol problem. Kathleen, Jack's sister, widowed during The War, later fell in love with a married man who is described as, "Like Joe Kennedy himself—older, sophisticated, quite the rogue male" (Goodwin, 1987, p. 848).

"History would later record a connecting link between the risks Joseph Kennedy took with Gloria Swanson and the sexual daring that would be observed again and again in his sons. It would seem almost as if, in repeating their father's behavior, they were unconsciously trying to gain some sort of mastery over this early trauma that had nearly destroyed everything they had" (Goodwin, 1987, p. 494). Many in the generation of Kennedy's coming into power now have continued the family legacy.

The Clintons and Harts

Politicians are not getting the free ride that used to be theirs. Recently the indiscretions of politicians are seized upon by those in the opposite party and news of the latest scandal is broadly disseminated by the media.

Gary Hart threw away his opportunity to run for president in 1988 for some "Monkey Business," when his political aspirations became intimately entwined with his sexual addiction. Gail Sheehy's (1987) account describes many elements that are typical of the Sexual Addict: Hart grew up in a strict Fundamentalist family with a demanding mother and a father who continually took care of her. With "a mother as continuously demanding as she was undemonstrative, Hart could not be expected to have any notion of a warm, close, friendly relationship with a woman. Sex and power could be sought only outside such a relationship. . . . It was buried in his earliest consciousness that one was either worthy or sinful. . . . One side of Hart, the rigid and controlling spirit of his Fundamentalist past, seeks perfection and inflicts harsh self-punishment for any natural pleasure. . . . The other side of him, the passionate and profane side, never saw the light of day as an adolescent boy—indeed, was imprisoned for his first twenty-five years. That delinquent side began beating on the cell floor and going over the wall as far back as 1972. . . . Finally it went haywire" (pp. 192–193).

Bill Clinton was already President when his addiction became blatantly obvious. Previously it had leaked out here and there but the "rumors" were managed. Most affairs spill over well beyond the members of the affair triangle, creating disillusionment, disappointment, distrust, anxiety, and fear. Efforts to help, fix, punish, and blame abound. The spillover of Clinton's dalliance with Monica Lewinsky is probably the greatest known to man. It cost the United States time, energy, money, respect, and lost opportunities. It has diminished Clinton's ability to be taken seriously. He too, came from a troubled family. His father was killed in a car accident before he was born. When he was two, his mother left him with her parents so she could return to school and become self-supporting, returning when he was four. She remarried at about that time to a man who was alcoholic and abusive. Bill Clinton then took on the responsibility of being his mother's protector.

Interestingly, Newt Gingrich, Speaker of the House of Representatives was having his own affair while leading the charge against Clinton. He did not receive the same level of public attention when his affair came to light. The difference may be that Gingrich did not make a public denial as Clinton did ("I did not have sex with that woman"), and his affair appeared to be an Exit Affair rather than one based on sexual addiction. He also resigned from office, thus removing himself from a leadership role where he would be under heavy attack.

Clinton's reckless behavior is typical of Sex Addicts, characterized by the narcissism that drives the sexual behavior and the grandiosity to believe it can be hidden.

☐ The Sexual Addict's Spouse—Codependency

The married Addict's spouse acts as if she does not know about his affairs. She is just as glad he is gone so much because she likes having total control over their household. He has tried to suppress his addictive behavior but has been unable to do so. He is deeply ashamed, yet preoccupied with his addiction. She ignores it, concentrating instead on maintaining control. Together they do a dance of codependency.

Carnes (1989a) contends that the spouses of Sexual Addicts (coaddicts) make three mistakes: 1) "They mistake intensity for intimacy . . . but there is no closeness. And it fills up one's life but leaves needs unmet" (pp. 131–132); 2) "Coaddicts mistake obsession for care. Like care, obsession focuses on the other, but makes the other into an object" (p. 132); and 3) "Coaddicts mistake control for security" (p. 133). With control, they believe they can make the Addict change, and thus prevent being abandoned.

The spouse and others who care about the Sexual Addict are faced with the Addict's dishonesty. The Addict will go to great lengths to protect the addiction, and in doing so lies about many matters, some important and some less so. The Sexual Addict's spouse knows something is wrong, but her needs and patterns of denial lead her to overlook the true nature of the situation. As the coaddict, she colludes with the dishonesty in order to present a picture that will gain the Addict's and the outside world's approval. Her "belief" in the Addict can be dangerous to her emotions and her health.

Coaddicts typically pick up the pieces for the Addict. Sally Quinn (1987) describes the enabling behavior of Lee Hart: "Of course she knew, they say. She had to know. You always know. By allowing him to get away with what he did, she only encouraged him to keep on doing it. By sticking by him once his indiscretions were revealed publicly, she only condoned his behavior. . . . We wanted her to scream! To stand up and say, 'That's it. I've had enough. He's betrayed me and the country, humiliated me for the last time. I won't be a part of this any more'" (p. B4).

Much of the public admired Hillary Clinton for her silence about Bill's sexual exploits. Others wondered why a bright and assertive woman like Hillary stayed with Bill. Some speculate that they had an arrangement; others say that she's power-hungry. It is clear that the marriage provided Hillary with access to pursue her interests that she would not have had otherwise (a route that woman have taken for centuries).

> Brenda, John's wife, is a typical codependent. She too learned early that her feelings were not to be trusted, so she turned her attention to meeting the expectations of her parents, her social group, and John. She was not particularly interested in sex, and not orgasmic, but she accommodated John sexually. She gloried in the traditional roles of wife and mother, taking good care of the house and their two children. When upset or feeling pressured she withdrew sexually and emotionally, devoting more attention to the house and the children. When disappointed, she blamed John for not caring about her, but collided with him to present a good picture to others.
>
> Their pattern is one in which John pressured Brenda to attend to his sexual needs, and Brenda reacted to the pressure by withdrawing emotionally and devoting herself to housework and child care. John's inner emptiness increased and, as he had always done in the past, he looked for some easy sex. This vicious cycle kept them both emotionally isolated, empty, and ashamed. For each it was a repetition of the emptiness and pain experienced in their family of origin.

The spouse who faces the partner's sexual addiction and her own enabling behavior may threaten to leave the marriage if the addictive behavior continues. This puts pressure on the Addict to admit the addiction and to get help. Sometimes separation is necessary before the Addict admits there is a problem. Many spouses are not ready to face their own issues and so are unwilling to take such a stand. Even when they do, it is not enough to get the attention of some Addicts.

When the spouse is truly unwilling to accept the addictive behavior any longer, matters come to a head. Even then the Addict often wants to see the problem as external, for example, rooted in the spouse's lack of interest in sex. If she stands her ground and insists on therapy for the Addict as well, there is a good possibility he will at least get to a therapist. Treatment for the spouse is just as necessary, a fact that she is often slow to recognize.

☐ The Treatment Process

Addiction does not mean that the problem can not be resolved or that it is biologically based, nor does it mean that the Addict is not responsible for his behavior. Just as with alcohol, facing the fact that one's behavior is out of control is the first step. The most useful approach is a systemic one that incorporates the principles of addictions treatment.

Sexual addiction is one of the most difficult addictions to treat. It embodies all three types of addictions: those based on fantasy, arousal, and satiation (Carnes, 1989b). It is most like the eating addictions in that abstinence is not a viable solution as it is with alcohol or drugs. The important elements of treatment include:

- breaking through the denial,
- reframing the behavior in the context of family of origin and the current family,
- identifying the addictive cycle and learning how to interrupt it,
- feeling and expressing pain, fear, helplessness, and rage,
- recognizing needs and learning how to get needs met, and
- involving family members in treatment.

What Brings Sexual Addicts to Treatment

Without negative consequences for the addictive behavior, the Addict has no reason to consider changing his behavior. Something of value to the Addict has to be at risk. Sometimes the Addict realizes the addiction may cost him his marriage, his family, his career, or his reputation. Too often however, the Addict rationalizes away the risks, and is joined in doing so by those around him. Breaking through the denial is difficult.

Because sexual addiction is more easily hidden than addictions such as alcohol or drugs it can be denied for longer. For example, the Sexual Addict's functioning at work may not be impaired in any obvious way. The spouse is likely to rationalize: "All men do that, but he comes home to me." Or the spouse may deny her knowledge in order to avoid feeling pain or shame; she too had a toxic childhood. Like the codependents they are, many Spouses defend themselves against seeing the addiction. Those who allow themselves to recognize the addiction sometimes dismiss it as inconsequential: "What's important is he works hard to make a good living for us, and he brings his money home." Some spouses are glad to be rid of the burden of sex. Others choose to put up with the situation because they are emotionally needy or economically insecure.

Because of the rationalization and denial that are part of the addictive cycle, the Addict seldom initiates treatment solely because he is concerned about his sexual behavior. He may however initiate treatment if he fears the consequences of his behavior. Crisis resulting from the addictive behavior, such as sexual harrassment charges, marital separation, or public exposure, are most likely to bring the Addict to treatment.

Occasionally other major crises, such as a heart attack or an accident, serve as a catalyst for entering therapy. In a few cases, persons addicted to affairs are ordered to therapy by the court for treatment of other addictive behaviors such as exhibitionism. Even then, the Addict usually believes that he can ameliorate some of the consequences while holding onto the sexual behavior. A typical comment is "I haven't done it for six months, since she caught me," implying his lack of understanding of his addictive patterns.

> John initially gave his reason for seeking individual therapy as his unhappiness with his wife's growing emotional and sexual distance. He soon let me know that he had engaged in hundreds of affairs with women over the years. What bothered him was his recent pickup of men at a gay bar. He realized that his compulsive need to pursue affairs was tied to his fear of being alone. The concept of sexual addiction was new to John, but one that he agreed fit.
>
> The affairs with women began when they pursued him. He found the seduction exciting at first, but soon it became uncomfortably heavy, much like his relationship with his mother. Sex with men also had the component of engulfment but with no lingering responsibility. He regarded these experiences as sordid and degrading, but was not sure he could stop. They also posed a huge risk to John's career if discovered. It was this risk that had brought John to therapy, a promising indicator for treatment.
>
> John experienced relief when Brenda refused to come with him to therapy. Without her he could keep his behavior a secret from her while more easily exposing his concerns to the therapist. For Brenda, not joining John in therapy meant she could continue denying John's addictive behavior and her coaddiction.

When the addiction is revealed in an individual session, insist that the Addict share this information with his spouse. With sexual addiction there is no question about whether affairs need to be disclosed. The risks to the spouse are immense. For the therapist, ethical concerns are also a factor as is the duty to warn (see Chapter 14 for a discussion of duty to warn and AIDS). As with other straying partners, the Addict needs to prepare himself to reveal his secret. Sometimes the spouse already knows about the Addict's affairs. In other cases the spouse "knows," but hasn't wanted to know.

The revelation is best done in a therapy session. Otherwise the therapist never knows if or how the Addict reveals, or how much. You can depend on the Addict to greatly minimize and justify the initial revelations to the spouse and family.

> John's secret began to be uncovered when a friend of Brenda's said she had seen John sharing drinks and intimate conversation with an

attractive woman a few nights earlier at a cozy restaurant. Brenda was disbelieving, and rationalized that it could not possibly have been John because he was working. John meanwhile was grappling in therapy with my statement that if there was any hope for his marriage it was in being honest with Brenda.

Paying bills a few weeks later, Brenda stumbled on four hotel receipts among John's papers. She confronted John, who then admitted to an affair. Under Brenda's questioning he allowed that he had been involved in six affairs. Brenda was devastated. John apologized, and promised he would never do it again. During therapy a few days later, I helped John explore the risks of further delays in telling Brenda the whole truth. Gradually, he decided to tell her the full scope of his sexual addiction: hundreds of affairs beginning before their marriage and escalating during Brenda's first pregnancy. Once he decided to make a full disclosure, I offered the possibility of using the next therapy session for that purpose and to help them begin dealing with the aftermath.

Goals and Treatment Planning

An essential component of treatment for Sexual Addicts is facing their addiction. Thus the choice of a therapist who is experienced in working with sexual addiction is critical. Sometimes an Addict chooses treatment that is not really treatment—it may consist of talking to a minister or rabbi, going to confession, or selecting a therapist who is not familiar with sexual addiction and unable to address it effectively. Addicts are often seductive with the therapist, attempting to win the therapist's approval or gain special favors. If you're not familiar with sexual addiction or don't like working with Sexual Addicts, make it a point to know who is skilled in this area so you can make good referrals.

Treatment of the Sexual Addict is directed to helping the Addict reclaim the real self that was buried in childhood. For the Addict, the goals of treatment are to stop the addictive sexual behavior, to reclaim his real feelings, to establish healthy relationships with others, and to make amends to the people he has hurt. The Addict's spouse also needs treatment for her codependency. Goals for her are reclaiming her real feelings and taking responsibility only for herself.

During the early phase of treatment, each partner needs individual therapy focusing on the self. When you are working individually with an Addict, suggest within a few weeks that he invite his wife to come to a session with him. Although she is not your client, she can be an ally in the treatment process, especially when she can confront the Addict's dishonesty and distortions. Occasional sessions in which she participates can be productive during the early phase of treatment.

"Old patterns between married co-addicts don't just fall away" (T. Hodges, personal communication, January 16, 1990). Even when the individual work is going well for each spouse, it is hard to sort out and heal the marital issues. These couples need to be seen together to work on untangling their codependency and to learn about respect, responsibility, boundaries, self care, and intimate communication. Couples therapy can be used parallel to the individual work.

When the Sexual Addict and the spouse present as a couple, codependent behavior is more obvious, and can be explored in depth, both with the couple together and in individual sessions. Since the Sexual Addict talks much more freely about his behavior when his spouse is not present, use individual sessions to assess sexual addiction. Use couple's sessions to identify reciprocal individual issues related to inner emptiness, pain, guilt, dependence, and responsibility.

Sexual addiction is a family problem so the treatment plan needs to address treatment for all family members. A typical treatment plan for a Sexual Addict includes individual therapy for both spouses, marital therapy every two weeks (or more often as the spouses are able to make use of it), and family therapy at selected times. Treatment of the Addict alone is likely to be ineffective, as the dysfunctional family patterns exert tremendous pull. Carnes (1989a) has found that relapse is usually tied to failure of the family to come for treatment. A twelve-step group offers added support.

Family therapy is fruitful at several points during treatment. During the crisis following disclosure of the addiction, family sessions provide a place for everyone to talk about the addiction and their shock, pain, sense of betrayal, and fears. An understanding of addiction can be gained by family members. Laying out a plan of action for treatment and encouraging everyone to talk about what they are feeling helps alleviate some of the worst fears. Later, family sessions can be used to troubleshoot issues and to help the individuals continue learning how to express and respond to feelings within the family in appropriate ways. When the Addict is ready to make amends to family members, family sessions for that purpose are a good option.

Effective treatment often involves several professionals: individual therapists, the couples and family therapist, and group therapists, plus twelve-step program leaders and sponsors. Some professionals will have more than one role, as for example working with each spouse individually and with the couple. When more than one professional is involved, it is important to share information so that the structure of treatment is solid and accountability is sustained.

Assessment

The Addict who is beginning treatment is out of control in regard to his sexual behavior and out of touch with his feelings. The therapist's initial emphasis with the Sexual Addict needs to be on cutting through the denial and justifications in order to reach the Addict's feelings. A good place to begin is by getting a detailed sexual history from the Addict. This can be done verbally, by using an assessment tool such as the Sexual Addiction Inventory developed by Carnes (1988a), or by having the Addict write his autobiography. The history should include an examination of relationship patterns in the family of origin and an inventory of other addictive behaviors.

The data is used initially to establish the fact that a problem exists. It also is used as an outline of issues for detailed discussion. Take enough time to focus on the Addict's feelings about each behavior or event. This process, which takes weeks or even months, begins to open internal doors that allow the Addict to bring new ideas and questions to therapy.

As part of his sexual history, the Addict needs to make a list of all his encounters: who the encounter was with, how he chose the person, and how he justified the encounter to others and to himself. The pattern of his encounters need to be examined in extreme slow motion so as to identify each element. Hodges (personal communication, November 25, 1989) suggests asking the following questions about a specific encounter:

> What were you feeling?
> What were you thinking?
> What were your physical reactions, down to details of your perspiration and heart rate?
> What were your fantasies?
> How did you get the other person to respond to you?
> How did you respond to the other person?
> How did you choose what you said?
> How did you choose what you *did not* say?
> How did you justify it?
> When you looked in the mirror at yourself, what were you trying not to see?
> What would your Mom have said?
> And your Dad?
> What would your closest friend say?
> Have you talked about it with any of them?
> Why was that?

In those instances when the Addict did not move ahead with the affair the following questions need to be addressed as well: Was it your choice or the third party's not to move ahead? What is your understanding of how that choice was made?

This level of detail personalizes the encounters, making justification less possible. It also illustrates to the Addict his distorted sense of reality. Examining numerous encounters in this manner gives a picture of the Addict's process as he moves toward another affair. It also provides ideas about how he stops himself. Help the Addict develop a specific plan for breaking his addictive cycle. Have him identify the tough periods and his sources of support. Guide him in learning how to use those factors that allow him to stop. By monitoring himself he becomes aware when he has started down the path to an affair, and he can choose to use one of his "stoppers" instead.

> For example, John's cycle began with feeling lonely or abandoned. Rather than pay attention to his loneliness, John sought to escape his feelings by turning to his porno collection. This was not sufficiently satisfying so he masturbated while fantasizing about his next sexual encounter. This fired him up for the active pursuit of sex, which he rationalized by telling himself it was okay this time because he was just going to help out a woman who would not otherwise have sex.

Intervening with the Sexual Addict

The feelings and issues that are uncovered in the process of examining the Addict's sexual history are generally those which the Addict has been avoiding through his addictive behavior. They have to do with basic self-esteem, pain, abandonment, and something as simple as allowing himself to care. Reframe the problem—it is not that he is a bad person. Rather, in reaction to feelings left over from emotional injuries in childhood, he has learned to soothe himself with sex. Separate the person from the behavior.

> As John struggled with his pain it became clear that his recent sexual encounters with men were not because of homosexual interests but a means of self-punishment in the context of addiction. Therapy with John proceeded on two levels: experiencing the pain and loneliness in his life, and interrupting his addictive cycle.

The therapist must not take away the negative consequences for the Addict. His motivation is derived from them. Negative consequences represent his first real boundaries, and are life saving. Instead the therapist needs to help the Addict realize that his justifications are inaccurate and that they keep him from feeling for others or for himself. With shame, the therapist needs to be careful. Tap into the Addict's own sense of shame, but without censuring or adding your judgment to his own. Instead help him use his shame as a motivation for change.

Paying Attention to Pain

Tracking the Addict's pain is one of the major tasks of therapy. What early experiences were so painful? What happened? Who was involved? How did the Addict experience these events? What did the experience mean to the addict? What does it mean now? What is the Addict doing now to continue the pain? What needs to be done now to resolve this painful experience? At first the Addict is likely to deny the importance of some of these early events, in an attempt to avoid his pain. Next he will become angry and resentful. Gently and firmly, the therapist needs to help the Addict find and stay with his pain. He needs to learn that his pain is important, that pain warns of danger, and that he can survive, even grow, from his pain. Help him identify constructive alternatives to the addictive behavior that he can use when the pain is too much. Tie the pain into its roots in the family of origin or in childhood. Help him see how he is still holding onto those roots, making the pain repeat.

Addicts (as well as other clients) are often tempted to sabotage themselves by making major decisions or changes which distract them from the most difficult part of treatment.

> John wanted to make a decision in the first few months of separation about whether to divorce Brenda. We discussed the negative impact this would have on the work of managing his behavior, and the probability that divorce would not change his feelings. John contracted not to make any optional major decisions or changes for the first year of treatment.

Residential Treatment

An innovative residential program for the treatment of Sexual Addicts has been developed by Pat Carnes, a pioneer in this field. The program incorporates assessment, information, and intense daily treatment using individual, group, and family therapy, combined with psycho-educational and twelve-step programs over a five-week period, which provides a jump-start on recovery. Family week, in which family members participate, opens up needed dialogue. Before leaving the residential program, an aftercare plan is developed for the Addict and the family, again utilizing individual and group therapy and a twelve-step group immediately upon discharge. "We emphasize the restructuring of the relationship with self as the essence of recovery," states Carnes (2000).

Few communities offer inpatient programs of this sort, and financial and time constraints limit those who can take advantage of such a program. Many people, however, are able to change their behavior with good outpatient treatment.

Relationship Issues

The Addict does not know what normal and legitimate dependency needs are or how to get these needs met. During the middle phase of treatment the focus on relationships grows, and the work on feelings which was started earlier continues. The Addict needs now to talk to people, both those he knows and new acquaintances, about his addiction and his pain. This is also a time for expanding the Addict's ability to form healthy relationships. Opportunities to do so are provided in group therapy, twelve-step groups, and marital therapy.

He needs to continue monitoring his behavior and be constantly aware of whether his thinking is clear or distorted. Keeping a daily log of his acting out cycle is useful. The question to be answered is, "How close did I come today to having an affair or otherwise engaging in the old addictive pattern?"

Group Therapy

Group therapy is a powerful and essential treatment modality for sexual addiction. The group needs to be designed specifically for sexual addicts. A group is often the first opportunity for the Addict to talk openly with his peers about his sexual secrets and his addictive process, and hear others do the same. In group he will meet others who are ahead of him and realize that it is possible for him to make similar changes. The older members in turn see how far they have come by talking with him. The focus of the group is on honesty, building healthy relationships, sharing pain, learning how to get needs met in healthy ways, and holding each other accountable.

Twelve-step groups play an important role in the Addict's recovery. A few therapists believe that twelve-step groups constitute the primary treatment for a sexual addict. Most see twelve-step groups as an adjunct to therapy (Carnes, 2000; Hodges, personal communication, November 25, 1989; Schneider, 1988). Twelve-step groups allow the Addict to talk with peers about the addiction, check reality, be confronted when in danger of relapsing, learn how to build relationships, and gain emotional support. Other group members are always available for assistance and support when the Addict is struggling to break out of his addictive cycle. Twelve-step groups are intended to offer a community of support in contrast to therapy groups that work on older and deeper aspects of feelings. Many Sexual Addicts have found Adult Children of Alcoholics (ACoA) groups to be a sound alternative when twelve-step groups focused on sexual addiction are not available.

> Without Brenda, John was particularly vulnerable to yielding to his old patterns. He began monitoring himself in order to recognize his loneliness in time to make different choices. We identified a number of alternative behaviors which John could turn his energy to when feeling tempted to soothe himself with sex. He had a few slips, but learned about his vulnerabilities from them. He went to meetings of Sex Addicts Anonymous regularly, and being able to call group members at any time helped bridge the gap created by his separation from Brenda. The group's support and its emphasis on understanding and taking responsibility for one's self felt accepting, not shaming. Any treatment model that increased John's shame would have reinforced his desire to again find a hidden refuge.

Marital Therapy

During the middle and later phases of treatment, when the individuals have a greater understanding of and are addressing their own issues, regular couples therapy can be quite productive. The spouses need to become acquainted with each other in a way they never have before. Concerns and feelings that are being surfaced in the individual work, which continues, can be explored in terms of their ramifications for the couple. Dysfunctional dependency patterns between the partners, including flip-flops between addiction and dependent behavior on the part of each, are evident in the session and can be addressed on the spot. Couples work at this point also provides a forum for discussing information and feelings about the affairs that have not yet been addressed.

Couples who have separated may begin to explore reconciliation if both have been in therapy. When only one has been in treatment, reconciliation can be a step toward relapse.

> After a year's separation John began talking with Brenda about reconciliation. He told Brenda that he had been able to stop having affairs. Brenda had recognized her codependent behavior and was making efforts to change. They negotiated terms for reconciliation which included a commitment to sexual fidelity and to honesty, and an agreement that both would continue their therapy.

Couples group also is an option once these couples have begun to make good use of couples work. Criteria for participation in the group should be a history of sexual addiction, or at least of addictive behavior. (See Chapter 11 for a discussion of group therapy.)

Celibacy Contracts

Some therapists believe that a celibacy contract is essential in treating a Sexual Addict (Schneider, 1988) while others use it in selected cases. (Hodges, personal communication, November 25, 1989). A celibacy contract is an agreement to engage in *no* sexual behaviors for a specific period of time. This includes masturbation and intercourse with the spouse. The intent is to allow the Addict to decompress from the pursuit of sex so that he can experience other feelings, and so that he can begin to learn about his sexuality anew. Celibacy also tells the Addict that he can control his sexual behavior. Selective use of a celibacy contract might be made with an Addict who is still using sex as a fix after the initial period of treatment.

> When John and Brenda reconciled, John wanted to have sex several times a day. Since this sexual preoccupation was another manifestation of John's addiction, a celibacy contract was established between the two of them for ten weeks. During this period, John and Brenda were obliged to find nonsexual ways of meeting their emotional needs. Though difficult at first, celibacy provided an exciting challenge which helped them discover such pleasures as quiet conversation, or sharing an evening of music. When the celibacy contract expired, they decided to resume their sexual relationship gradually, making sure that they continued to enjoy the new forms of intimacy they had developed. They know that in the future, any big increase in the desire for sex is likely to be masking other emotional needs.

Later Phase of Treatment

The Addict needs to make amends to those he has hurt with his addictive behavior. Making amends means going to his wife and his children, acknowledging his behavior, answering questions openly and completely, and apologizing for the pain he has caused. He needs to make himself available to listen and to talk about whatever the other person needs to discuss. His wife may still have questions about his affairs or need information about his internal process (at this point questions should be constructive, not obsessive). His children may express pain and embarrassment. When he knows he has control of his addictive behavior he can reassure them that this will never happen again because of the work he has done, while acknowledging his past behavior.

Amends also need to be made to others he has injured in his pursuit of sex (for example the woman who filed sexual harassment charges against him, and those friends and colleagues who have covered for him). He is not ready to make amends until he is in touch with his feelings, understands the pain he has caused, and truly regrets his behavior.

The danger point for the Sexual Addict comes when his desire for an affair decreases, usually because he is meeting his emotional needs in other ways. It is when the conscious desire for an affair decreases that the risk of relapse increases.

> For John this occurred nine months after he and Brenda reconciled. His relationship with her was better than ever, and he was not even feeling like cruising for women. John decided he was cured and stopped monitoring himself. "All of a sudden" he found himself having a drink with a woman he met at a management seminar and fantasizing about getting her in bed. The sudden recognition that he was back in his old cycle was a shock. With mixed feelings he told his companion that it was time for him to go home, and proceeded to do so. When he got home he told Brenda what he had done. Although upset by his close call and the evidence that he was not "cured," John felt a sense of pride that he had chosen to handle the situation responsibly.

The Addict is ready to end therapy when he is meeting his emotional and dependency needs in healthy ways on a regular basis. He will need to continue monitoring his behavior for the rest of his life. Twelve-step groups are useful for this purpose, especially after therapy ends.

☐ Factors in Effective Work with Sexual Addicts

The therapist who works with the Sexual Addict needs to be tough, yet compassionate—tough enough to confront denial and seduction whenever it occurs, and compassionate enough to feel the Addict's pain and care about his person. Patience is necessary, as is the willingness to examine details under a microscope. A systems approach coupled with knowledge of addictions provides a solid background for understanding and working with the dynamics of addiction.

Working with Addicts is fascinating, but we need to be sure we are there as a therapist to help in healing, and not as voyeur or judge.

Honesty in working with the Addict is essential. Without it, we can not confront the Addict's dishonesty. We must examine our own affairs, our fantasies, and our close calls. We especially need to be clear about how we honor our own commitments so as to prevent becoming involved in affairs or other addictive behaviors.

As therapists, we need to take an active role in addressing sexual addiction. This means recognizing sexual addiction as such, confronting the addiction, and offering, in conjunction with other professionals, the network of services that are needed by the Addict and the Addict's family.

8
CHAPTER

Rebuilding and the Split Self Affair

Split Self Affairs signal a marriage held together by belief in Family and in doing things right, rather than by strong emotional bonds between the partners. Family refers to a constellation of feelings and beliefs: at its heart lie feelings of abandonment related to the family of origin, and the determination to create a "real family." Problems that occur in the marriage are perceived as something to be fixed in order to achieve the desired family structure. It is as if by constructing the ideal family that the marital partners believe they will become whole.

But Split Selves are not whole. As young children they had to sacrifice their own needs and feelings, and that pattern has become a way of life. Life is about performing well and doing things right in the hope of gaining love—but approval will do for now. Typically, both spouses grew up in families in which their emotional needs were not met. Their families of origin may have been chaotic, out of which arose the urge to build a perfect family. Alternatively, their families of origin may have been organized around the pursuit of perfection, with constant demands for performance and extremely high expectations for the children's success. In neither case did the parents take responsibility for their own emotional lives, and their offspring learned to hide their real feelings and behave in ways to avoid pain and gain approval. It was a lonely way to grow up.

Split Selves are survivors in the best sense, having coped successfully with parents who didn't parent. Quite often the Split Self became the

161

parent in the family at a young age, raising self and siblings, and parenting a parent as well. Since Split Selves learned not to attend to their own emotional needs, they are underdeveloped emotionally and overdeveloped rationally. In the workforce their willingness to assume responsibility combined with rationally-based coping skills is highly valued and the Split Selves tend to be successful professionally. They don't understand why these skills don't pay off in their personal lives—and many therapists wonder why as well.

Of the different types of affairs, this is the most complex and one of the most challenging for therapists. In the past this has been primarily a man's affair, but that is beginning to change. The male straying partner usually picks a younger woman as an affair partner; the female straying partner is more likely to choose someone around her own age. A strong emotional bond flourishes between the affair partners. These are the affairs that often continue for years, sometimes until death, despite efforts to end it. The 29 year affair of Charles Kuralt of On the Road fame is a classic Split Self Affair (Williams, 1998).

☐ Origins of the Split Self Family

In the Split Self family, issues are dealt with by attempting to make the marriage, the partner, and the self fit the desired image of Family. Anger at childhood experiences is buried deep beneath the surface, and the emphasis on family is used to keep it there. Each family member is invested in the myth that this is a perfect family. Perfection means performing well. The spouses are able to put aside their anxieties by devoting themselves to the well being of their children. The children are called upon to validate the family myth, and mostly they perform their assignment well. A great deal of caretaking behavior occurs—but the particular type of care may not fit the recipient since it is based on the Split Self's idea of what should be done and not on what the other person wants or needs.

Building the Perfect Family

The Split Self family is similar to the "perfect family" of the bulimic as described by Carter (1988). Both families attempt to suppress the past and force the present into a narrow mold. Achievement is emphasized, but it must fit within the rules of the family. The ghosts of family secrets and prior unresolved losses float in the background, unwelcome and unaddressed. These families differ in terms of where the greatest performance pressures are placed. In the bulimic family, they are placed on the children. In the Split Self family, the greater pressure is on the husband and wife. Thus the symptomatic family member in the bulimic family is a child, while in the Split Self family one of the spouses carries the symptom, in this case an affair.

It is more important that the marriage be perfect than that the children be. Neither spouse however, has any idea of how to build an intimate relationship or even what one is like. The spouses push and pull at each other, much as parents often do with children, to perform the reciprocal role in the perfect family script. Feelings are put aside, as secondary to doing what should be done. The children attempt to fill the gaps and alleviate pressures in their parents' marriage by acting as the middlemen, carrying the depression, or smoothing over any upset. Everyone focuses on the positive, and anxieties are not discussed. The facade of the perfect family remains intact.

The quest to develop the perfect family allows the spouses to cover up their sense of themselves as insufficient, incomplete, or lacking. The expression of pain or disappointment is disallowed because it feels like an admission of failure. The spouses are often high achievers in other aspects of their lives, no doubt because of the energy they pour into "doing the right thing." The male straying partner is usually successful in his occupation, which is one that is valued by the family. The female spouse, believing that her success depends on her performance at home, devotes herself to the roles of wife and mother. These days she may have a career as well. She takes pride in doing it all herself, keeping those who try to help at arm's length. These successes reinforce each spouse's belief that they can construct their family to fit their ideal. They pat themselves on the back for their hard work and for each tangible success, and paste a smile over their depression.

Denial of Hurt and Disappointment

When despite their extensive efforts, the approval each had expected from their marital partner is not forthcoming, the spouses have great difficulty handling their hurt and disappointment. The typical Split Self spouse has been brought up to believe that any marital problems are her fault. Rather than talk about her disappointment, she works harder at the marriage, prodding and prompting her husband as she attempts to move him toward her ideal. Her husband doesn't talk about his hurt or disappointment either, instead deciding that since he "can't ever please her," he will protect himself by limiting opportunities for further disappointment. He withdraws, staying longer at work or busying himself with the yard, church, boat, or other matters. When attempts to force the other spouse to play the role of ideal partner are met with failure, the tendency is to deny the pain and turn to the children or to work. The devotion to children and work is cited as further evidence of the essential goodness of this family. The truth is that neither knows how to pay attention to their emotions or how to talk about what they are feeling.

Underneath the myth, the experience begins to feel like that in the family of origin. In time, the partner begins to be viewed as similar to the withholding, demanding, or uncaring parent of childhood. Each spouse becomes more depressed, but projects it onto the other, using the other as the excuse for why it is not possible to act in one's own interests. Thus each becomes a further source of disappointment to the other. The children become the primary link between the spouses. Any success the children achieve is used to validate the myth of the perfect family.

When the children leave home, the in-house escape from anxiety and depression is gone. Even though the myth has been crumbling internally for some time, it is a shock for these spouses to be left alone, disappointed and disillusioned, with each other. Occasionally the myth cracks at an earlier point in the marriage when an event occurs that rips loose the cloak of perfection. In either case, a substitute is sought to prevent against anxiety and depression.

☐ The Split Self Affair

The Split Self Affair develops when one spouse, most often the husband, develops a strong friendship with someone else, often with a work associate. In many cases the third party is a generation younger. She awakens his dormant emotional self and stirs his passion. His emotional self has been so neglected that it is impossible for him to resist. Gradually, the friendship evolves into a serious long-term affair.

The third party, who is usually single, offers affection and understanding. The straying partner, now emotionally awakened, assigns his lover the role of ideal partner, the role originally assigned to the spouse. He leaves his anxiety and depression at home and makes excuses for his frequent absences to see his lover. Any negative feelings are directed toward his spouse.

The promise of the affair isn't dulled by the demands and disappointments of daily life, so the straying partner can continue to view his lover as ideal. As long as she seems totally loving, thus implying he is loveable, she protects him from his depression, just as his spouse probably did in earlier days. In many cases, even the affair is structured as family—the Split Self straying partner is protective of his young lover, much the way a father looks after a daughter.

The Straying Partner's Dual Emotional Ties

The inner split between the rational and the emotional selves is projected onto the two women. The spouse represents family and doing things right, the third party represents the emotional self. The straying partner doesn't understand that his split is an inner split, and not a matter of choosing the right woman. The straying partner externalizes his internal conflict, seeing the issue as choosing between his wife and his lover. His struggle is actually between his real feelings (anger, disappointment, anxiety, and the like which have been pushed into the background for a lifetime) and his approval seeking self (who is heavily invested in the myth of the perfect family). The emotional self wants to be loved, the rational self wants approval. He cannot choose one woman because he has deposited only a part of himself with each. He can not do without either woman until he incorporates the divided parts of himself into a whole.

The affair is a serious one. It has the power to disrupt the marriage, although if the affair successfully relieves the tension between the spouses, the marriage may go on as usual, parallel to the affair. The affair may even keep the marriage together. The affair between Ayn Rand and Nathaniel Branden was a particularly dramatic version of the Split Self affair which lasted for years (Branden, 1989). Alternatively, the straying partner may leave the marriage to pursue the relationship with the third party. Or this affair may impel the straying partner to seek therapy.

Why not simply leave the unsatisfactory marriage and then look for a more satisfying relationship? That would be too dangerous emotionally. The straying partner would be left on his own with the feelings he has been avoiding. Why then is it so hard to leave the spouse when the third party is providing validation? Giving up on the myth of the perfect family feels like giving up on life. Hanging on to the spouse keeps alive the opportunity to prove one's worth and lovability in the face of adversity, which holds the promise of ending the internal pain forever.

Sometimes the Split Self Affair continues until one of the trio dies, as was true for Franklin Delano Roosevelt (Ross, 1988). Franklin and Eleanor were a typical Split Self couple. The increasing tension in their relationship was eased somewhat by Franklin's affair with Lucy

Mercer. While Eleanor was preoccupied with raising the children, Franklin had someone else to meet his companionship needs. When Eleanor found out about the affair, a battle ensued over whether Franklin would give up Lucy Mercer. Franklin's mother settled the issue, by threatening to disinherit Franklin unless he got rid of Lucy. Franklin and Eleanor never dealt with what the affair meant to their relationship, and although they decided to stay together, they subsequently led separate lives, not sleeping in the same bed, or even spending much time in the same house. They were political partners but were no longer really marital intimates. Incidentally, Franklin and Lucy got back together a few years before he died, reconnecting with the help of their daughter Anna (Gerson, 1989).

Timing of the Split Self Affair

Many Split Self Affairs occur in the middle or later years of the marriage as the children are leaving home. For many couples this constitutes a major crisis because little is left of their relationship. It also is a time when awareness of one's mortality grows, as parents become ill or die. It is a time for reflection and for decisions about how to spend the rest of one's life. It may be the last opportunity to make midcourse corrections. If intimacy and affection are lacking, now is the time to change things. Other crises, such as a serious health problem, or loss of one's work identity may also crystalize dissatisfaction with the marriage. The crisis may generate enough energy to rebuild the marriage or to end it, or it may be the catalyst for a Split Self Affair that provides the missing emotional connection. The long serious affair is about exploring one's emotional self and developing a relationship based on passion rather than on doing things right.

Some Split Self affairs occur earlier in marriage. If the wife is the straying partner, the affair is likely to occur earlier in the marriage, before the nest empties. Women tend to pay greater attention to their emotional life than do men, and are often aware of their dissatisfaction at an earlier point in marriage. Because of children or financial issues, they frequently find it more difficult than do men to leave the marriage. The basis of the affair, the desire to maintain the myth of the perfect family while relieving anxiety and tensions, is the same. My observations and those of other therapists suggest that more men are becoming involved in Split Self Affairs before reaching middle age than in the past, but this is still a small group.

Although the attachment to the spouse continues through the shared devotion to the concept of family, emotional satisfaction is lacking.

When the energy towards change is little, or when the ambivalence between the shoulds and the wants is evenly balanced, the affair may continue for years. Sometimes the straying partner engages in a series of Split Self Affairs, each one lasting a number of years. When this is the case, the straying partner is still pursuing the dream of the perfect partner and avoiding his own uncomfortable feelings.

What Brings Split Selves to Treatment

Split Self individuals and couples come to therapy when their anxiety can no longer be contained by focusing on a third party, whether it be the children, the lover, or another person or object. The crisis that ensues results in real change when one or both spouses are forced to try something new.

With a Split Self Affair the prognosis for the marriage is poor, especially if the marriage has been a long one. The partners know only the other's public self. The original positive feelings toward the partner (which were directed primarily to the public self) have eroded, and years of disappointment have piled up. In a great many cases the spouse sees no need for any sort of therapy, believing as she does that if something is wrong it is her fault, and so denying the existence of any problems. The outlook for the individuals is better, but only if they address the issues underneath the affair. Since Split Selves are usually in their late forties, fifties, and sixties, this is often their last opportunity for resolving personal and relationship issues successfully.

Because of the long history of trying to make the marriage what it "should" be, and the years of overriding feelings, these people do not have the capacity to be emotionally honest, even with themselves. The focus of therapy needs to be on reclaiming their feelings and their emotional integrity, or in other words, helping the underdeveloped emotional self (the five year old) to develop. When the emotional self of both husband and wife gets into the teens you can begin to tackle the marital issues.

Treatment is focused on understanding and resolving family of origin issues (understanding, disentangling, and eventually forgiving) and reclaiming one's own feelings and using them to live one's own life. The rules and scripts of the perfect family, which were a way of living life for someone else, are replaced by making one's own choices. Issues that need to be addressed include dependency, buried rage, dysfunctional family patterns, the divided self, and patterns of avoidance. Rebuilding centers on the individual in the early stages, while marital therapy is appropriate later on for couples who decide to work on their relationship.

Split Selves may present as a couple or as individuals. Those who present as a couple usually seek help because the straying partner has decided to leave the marriage but has difficulty operationalizing that decision. The straying partner's request to the therapist, which is not clearly verbalized, is, "Please take care of her so that I can leave." The spouse wants the therapist's help in preventing him from leaving. These couples look similar at first to the Exiters. However the Split Self straying partner is attached to the spouse and this attachment persists, sometimes preventing separation and in other cases leading to reconciliation. The straying partner is just as attached and just as divided with the third party. Some straying partners end up leaving, some never leave. Most flip-flop a number of times in their decision about whether to stay in the marriage and many of these move out only to move back in at least once.

Straying partners who are most troubled by their double attachment usually come in alone to sort themselves out. Betrayed spouses who have been dumped also may seek individual help to recover from their emotional devastation once they realize the separation is real.

☐ Treatment of Split Self Couples

Some Split Self couples arrive under the guise of wanting marriage counseling. The spouse wants marriage counseling, but the straying partner has another agenda. He is looking for someone who will take care of his wife for him so he can leave. He seldom wants to explore his own issues at this point. However he is conflicted about what he *should* do versus what he wants to do for himself. His identity is tied up with doing the right thing. He is concerned with leaving in the right way, the nice way, and tries to convince his wife that it is the "right" thing to do for both of them. Approaching separation in such a way is in accordance with the myth of the perfect family. His wife however, who feels she has little left to lose, is not as willing to "make nice."

The spouse feels cheated and panicked. As you clarify the situation, it becomes apparent to her that the straying partner is planning to leave her. She may become somewhat hysterical, or icy angry. When she realizes that her hsuband is intent on leaving and that you are not stopping him, she may become angry at you. This is true even when she is quite depressed or agitated. She may drop out of therapy at this point. When she realizes he is really gone, she may find another therapist who she perceives as supportive of her, or she may tough it out alone.

Roger brought Estelle, his wife of 27 years, in for marital counseling a few weeks before he left her. They came from different cultural backgrounds, but held many similar values about the importance of family. They had married when Estelle discovered that she was pregnant.

Roger's father had been extremely angry and critical throughout Roger's childhood. Roger coped by going his own way and keeping his turf separate, which was what he did in the marriage. Estelle was the oldest of six children, and like many oldests, was a substitute parent during frequent family crises. Her style of relating was accommodation, though she deeply resented how little it got her with Roger (or with her mother).

Estelle had discovered Roger's affair three years earlier, and had gone into a rage. With marital counseling, Roger had agreed to end his affair and the tensions in the marriage had eased a bit. Three months ago things had come to a head with Estelle's discovery that Roger was again seeing the same woman.

In the initial session, Roger led off. He complained that Estelle was living in another world and that he was tired of listening to her berate herself and him. He was not going to put up with it anymore. He had wanted her to change, but now it did not matter anymore. Estelle tried desperately to come up with something positive and hopeful that would satisfy Roger. Roger felt scared by any hopeful remarks or suggestions for change and shot them down. Estelle then became angry and told Roger to choose between her and the other woman (her intent was to force Roger to end the affair). Roger expanded on his complaints and mentioned feeling trapped. When I asked about his goals for therapy, he was again vague.

As I pursued what they wanted from therapy, it became evident that Roger was reluctant to work on the marriage, but that he was concerned about Estelle. He had decided to leave, but he couldn't bring himself to be fully honest with Estelle, so he was hoping that I would somehow make his leaving possible. Estelle, knowing that Roger was thinking about leaving her, wanted my help in hanging on to Roger. I focused on getting Roger to talk to Estelle about his plan to leave. When Estelle realized Roger was serious, she increased her pleas to me: Why wasn't I trying to talk Roger out of this crazy idea? After all, she was the one who had made the home for him, who took care of him, who had worked like a dog to raise their children.

Staying or Leaving: Considering Separation

The most useful role for you initially, as the therapist with this couple, is to help the husband state his real agenda clearly. He needs to own his decision to leave, and his wife needs to face the reality of it. Provide space for his wife to respond, and help her express what she is feeling.

Once the straying partner is clear about his intentions to leave, ask him to share, step by step, his expectations of how things will go following the separation. Raise questions about those elements that seem unrealistic. Help his wife ask questions if she is ready to do so. Point out behavior that is repetitive in some way of the couple's pattern or of experiences in the family of origin, and inquire how these behaviors will change.

Whether the decision appears to be imprudent or well considered, separation will destabilize the system, and the resulting crisis may induce self-examination by each spouse. The crisis will occur only if the spouses really separate, not if the only change is that the straying partner puts a different address on his driver's license, but continues to drop by when he chooses (as he has been doing before he moved out). One therapist suggests to Split Selves that they take turns moving out for two weeks at a time, so that each knows what it is like to be alone. Lee Raffel (1999) advocates controlled separation as a tool for couples in crisis that allows them to slow down sufficiently to examine and resolve the marital stalemate. Marriage counseling (counseling that assumes they are working on rebuilding their marital relationship) is not appropriate at this point, but working with the couple on their separation for a few sessions helps them clarify the situation and sort out their next steps.

> Roger later commented to Estelle, "I guess that's an explanation of why I need to move out. It's a way of truly expressing my independence, and getting out of this reactive mode. When you express affection to me, I know that you're taking a risk, but I just feel boxed in, like I'm expected to do something. Does it make sense to you that I would feel under your thumb—sort of, you know, like you've been my mother in some ways?"
>
> Roger, like so many other Split Selves, learned early that when someone expresses anxiety, he is supposed to fix it.

Legal Aspects of Separating

Too often lawyers and others trying to be helpful suggest that the betrayed spouse use detectives or pursue litigation. The obsessive Split Self spouse is especially vulnerable to acting on such advice when given by authorities. The legal contest is the ultimate triangle: all one's own anxiety gets put aside in order to pursue litigation. This backfires when the contest is finally over and each spouse is still stuck with their anxiety and the lawyers have their money. Generally however, Split Self couples decline a full fledged contest; it does not fit their image of the perfect family.

If they intend to separate, refer the couple to mediation to work out the terms of their separation agreement. Mediation is a more supportive process than is litigation. It is a process that helps both partners identify and examine their financial needs and resources. Mediation encourages wives (and husbands as well) to negotiate as full partners with each other in settling the practical matters between them. The spouses do not have to be amicable to use mediation. In fact, mediation can make the greatest difference for couples who are conflicted.

Help them separate safely so that they don't burn bridges. If they heal their internal split, they may want to take another look at the marriage. Whatever you do, don't refer the wife to an attorney who is a gladiator or a "bomber." This type of attorney treats the woman as a helpless victim at a time when she needs to be learning how to actively promote her own interests.

Preparing for Separation

Identify issues that each spouse needs to address, but be aware that neither is likely to explore the underlying issues right away. The straying partner is hopeful that by ending the marriage and moving into the new relationship he will have resolved his issues. His wife still holds hope that, "He'll come to his senses, and be back. He's always done that before." In addition the stress of separating is so great that neither spouse will have energy for much else at first. Flag issues for the purpose of planting seeds that can lie dormant until the individual is beyond the immediate crisis.

It is likely to take much longer to cut through this wife's obsession than that of any other spouse. She has 20 or more years invested in the family, and she is hanging on for dear life. She is so overwhelmed by the fear of losing her husband and family that she is unable to process anything that doesn't fit her conceptual framework. Help her understand how her reactions to this crisis are similar to patterns in her family of origin, and suggest that she can use this crisis to learn some ways to cope that feel better than what she has known in the past.

Parallel to the couples work, each spouse needs to begin working on him or herself in individual therapy, addressing the underlying pain and anxiety, tracking the patterns of coping with tension (including avoidance) in the family of origin, and learning new ways to share one's real feelings with another person. The individual work needs to be the primary treatment format for Split Selves.

Post-separation Ambivalence

With some straying partners, ambivalence about ending the marriage is likely to surface not long after separation. Just about the time his wife accepts the fact he is gone, he begins to feel an emotional tug toward her. He goes over to her house on the pretext of fixing something. Before long they drift into bed, and now he is cheating on his woman friend. Concerns about his relationship with his lover are beginning to surface, as is his realization that the issue goes deeper than being married to the wrong person. He consults a therapist about his mixed feelings, and his "need to make a decision."

What goes on here? He was afraid of displeasing his wife and creating more tension (stated as "I don't want to hurt her") so he avoided conflict during the marriage. Now he is doing the same thing with his woman friend. He is puzzled. Previously he saw his wife as "bad" and his woman friend as "good." Now he's beginning to see his lover as "bad" and his wife as "good." He is confused that his lover has become the "mother," and his wife is now the girlfriend. He is afraid to tell either his wife or his woman friend what he wants or doesn't want, and he is not at all sure himself about what he wants or how he feels. He does know that he does not want to be alone.

The self he presents is designed to please without becoming too intimate in areas where he fears being vulnerable—or too separate in areas where he fears being rejected or abandoned. He walks the balance beam. If both women are willing to continue a relationship with him, he has the perfect system. He can play out each side of himself, and each woman serves as a distance regulator for the other relationship. If he feels overwhelmed by his lover, he can use responsibility for his wife as a reason to distance. If his wife is critical or makes too many demands, he can raise the specter of the lover.

Individual therapy that focuses on untangling family of origin issues and reclaiming one's own real feelings is indicated for each spouse. If both spouses are interested in exploring the marriage, a combination of individual and couples therapy is possible. Sometimes only one partner, usually the straying partner, makes use of individual therapy. This has a mixed impact, on the one hand destabilizing the old marital system and thus facilitating change, but at the same time lessening the possibility that the couple will resolve their shared issues successfully and increasing the chances of divorce.

Exploring Whether to Work on the Marriage

Couples work (not marital therapy) can supplement individual therapy. Even though the affair is a continuing shadow in the background, an assessment of whether they want to salvage the marriage can be initiated. Even though the affair is continuing, taking a look at the marriage together can be extremely useful.

Help the couple explore what has gone wrong, and encourage them to share the pain of their past experience. In this process the wife may talk of ending the marriage, but much of her behavior is likely to be directed to pleasing her husband (her issues are similar to his). Help her express her pain, her dissatisfactions, and her desires for herself in relationship to her husband and her marriage. Help him express his pain and his ambivalence and difficulty in being too close to either woman. Address the underlying issues such as fear of dependency, buried rage, and his struggle between what he should do and how he feels. Highlight ways in which the present replicates the past.

Help the spouses comprehend the intricately balanced system they have developed, and the factors that contributed to the current crisis. Let them help you identify the underlying dynamics that keep each in the system. What is the symbolic meaning of the triangle? The functional role? What similar triangles have they used in the past? What triangles of a different sort have they used? Who was the triangle with before the affair? How did prior generations use triangles?

This exploration of triangles focuses the work on the self and the self in relation to others. It also breaks down some of the illusions about the affair. Provide support to each spouse as they expose real feelings. This work will take a number of sessions and will result in a decision about whether to work on the marriage. Individual therapy must parallel the couples work during this period, so that the underlying issues are addressed, and the system does not restabilize prematurely around the old patterns. If they decide to work on the marriage the affair will need to end, precipitating a grieving process for the straying partner. If they decide not to work on the marriage, help them focus on the emotional and practical aspects of ending it.

Reconciliation

If the couple has separated, thoughts of reconciliation early in treatment are usually a response to anxiety generated by the separation itself and by the issues surfaced in therapy. The key question in assessing the motivation for reconciliation is whether it is an attempt to avoid change (to recover the security of the old system) or whether it is based on successful mastery of change. A premature reconciliation is bound to fail, because it is another attempt to resolve anxiety by choosing the "right" partner. The emphasis in the early phase of treatment needs to be on each spouse's individual work on developing the emotional self, as described later in this chapter.

☐ Working Individually with the Straying Partner

Those straying partners who are most troubled by their inability to end the marriage or the affair tend to come in individually, rather than with their spouse. The affair has continued for years. Promises to the lover to leave the marriage have come and gone. The spouses barely tolerate each other, but the straying partner is stuck. He is unable to leave. He views the problem as not being able to decide which is the right woman for him.

The straying partner knows he is stuck. He comes to treatment for help in deciding which relationship to pursue and developing the ability to act on his decision. He has probably not told his wife that he's seeing a therapist, and he is clear that he doesn't want marital therapy—he wants to work on himself. Later in therapy he is more likely to want to bring in his woman friend than his spouse.

He needs to own his feelings before he can address his relationship issues. Thus the client is the individual and not the couple, although the spouse and the family of origin provide an important context for the work of therapy.

Typical treatment issues are illustrated in the following case:

George Reynolds came for individual therapy at the age of 58. He is physically imposing, but gentle in demeanor. He is a successful corporate executive, but has a long history of marital problems. He requested help in understanding why he has stayed in the marriage, and help in leaving.

George's parents split when he was three years old. After that he lived with his mother and a succession of stepfathers and live-ins. He never saw his father again. His mother was critical, unpredictable, and unavailable. "She was so God damned involved in how she looked and whether she was attractive!" She was also a heavy drinker and probably a sexual addict. George learned not to make any demands of her, in an attempt to avoid punishment and humiliation.

George liked his first stepfather, but lost him at the age of seven when his mother became involved with another man and the marriage ended. He knew that the marriage was ending before his stepfather did because he had met mother's boyfriend and realized what was about to happen.

George reports many embarrassing scenes during his childhood involving his mother, her current man, and too often, the police. Mother subsequently married several more times, had numerous affairs, and generally deteriorated. Throughout his childhood, George tried to save his mother, by doing what he thought would please her. The underlying fantasy was that if he could save her, he would prove to her he was worthy and then he would get the mothering he so desperately wanted.

It was this pattern that George later used with his wife, who responded to him much as his mother had.

At 17, George left home permanently, entered the Army, and later went to college. He says he wrote off his mother when he left home, returning at the age of 21 when she was dying. He didn't stay for her funeral—rescue and redemption were no longer possible.

Relationship Between Marital and Family of Origin Issues

George's concern about belonging was a major factor in choosing Vivian for his wife. Vivian was the indulged daughter of a privileged family. When he was 25, he married her in hopes of belonging—to a good family. They have two daughters and a son, all grown.

George has had a number of affairs during his marriage, but became seriously involved with Paulette eight years ago. Paulette is 36, and has never been married. She is her father's favorite.

George prides himself on giving people what they want or need, "making it right for them," as he tried and failed to do with his mother. His self-esteem is tied up with being a "different kind of man than those who used and abused mother. Real men protect women, no matter what the women do." He believes that if he is not taking care of mother/wife/women, he is like the uncaring men with whom his mother had affairs. He believes that if he is loving enough, that will prove he is loveable. His savior fantasy comes through in his attempts to control, fix, make things better. The control serves to keep him from feeling vulnerable, and prevents his repressed rage from surfacing. If he exposes his feelings, he fears Vivian will ridicule or denigrate him, just as his mother did, and he avoids risking that. Better to stay in control than allow Vivian to spoil things.

At the same time he is afraid that if he attends to his own feelings he will be selfish—like his mother and his wife. He cannot help his wife live up to her potential, and he could not save his mother. He can not get angry about his powerlessness, because that would prove he is like his mother. The guilt instilled by his mother can only be dealt with by being a success, and success is defined by others.

George's struggle is apparent in his demeanor with Vivian. He desperately wants her to acknowledge that he is her equal, that he is different from the men who treated his mother badly, that he is loveable. He is furious that she will not do this, but immobile. He rationalizes his anger by finding fault with Vivian, and his anger turns to depression. He tries to prevent what he regards as his weaker self from being touched, and in the process he disowns his scared and helpless feelings. His dislike of Vivian provides a channel to release fragments of his anger, usually in the form of carefully justified complaints to others about her behavior.

Treatment Goals and Formats
for the Split Self Straying Partner

With Straying Partners like George, the work initially is with his emotions and with the original family of origin issues—no one has touched these for generations. It requires giving up the fantasy of building the perfect family, and replacing the myth with reality and with behaviors that build intimacy. The goals are honesty and ownership of himself, a reclaiming of his ability to feel and to validate his own feelings, including the pain of the past. As he gets in touch with his feelings the issues related to the chronic depression surface, and can be treated. This is slow, slow work—an inch at a time, and it is long term work.

Initially individual therapy is the treatment of choice. Once he is moving, group therapy as an adjunct to individual treatment is extremely beneficial. Eventually group therapy can become the primary form of treatment. In a few cases, couples work is viable in the middle and later stages of therapy if both spouses want to explore facets of the marital relationship, discuss whether or not to separate, or move toward rebuilding or toward separation.

Many Split Selves do not know what they are feeling, or even what a feeling is. When this is the case, it is essential to teach the person how to pay attention to their feelings before doing anything else. Most are able to identify physical sensations located somewhere in their body. Instead of asking, "What does your body feel?" which is too broad, review with the person what is going on physically in their neck and shoulders, their head, their legs, their stomach, their breathing, and so on. Once they identify a feeling, such as the stomach feeling tight, ask what color it is, and whether it is hot or cold. Help your client link the physical feelings to what is going on inside emotionally at that moment. Comment on changes you notice in facial expression or body posture, and ask about the emotions related to those changes. Don't accept comments that begin with, "I feel that," as feelings—you are about to hear a report or a thought. In the future, when they are able to respond with an emotion to, "What are you feeling?" make sure you don't change the question to, "What are you feeling about X?" That question invites a rational response. When you want a rational response, ask for it more directly, as in "What are your thoughts about X?

Early Phase of Treatment

Identifying issues in the family of origin and linking them to both the marital problems and the affair provides the straying partner with an understandable framework for therapy. This approach reduces the fear that he will be discovered to be defective, a common expectation of those beginning treatment, especially those who have been aiming for perfection.

The therapist must keep the straying partner attending to his own feelings and not allow him to focus on pleasing you. Because he is so attentive to indicators of what he "should" do, it is important to refrain from giving him advice or even strokes. Instead, be with him emotionally when he is attending to his feelings.

> George couldn't leave his wife until he could say goodbye to his mother, and saying goodbye to her meant first dealing with his pain and his anger at her. He couldn't do that until he was able to pay attention to his pain and his anger. Thus the first piece of work for George was to learn to pay attention to his feelings, not an easy task with a man whose professional life was built upon successful wheeling and dealing.
>
> George wanted to use therapy to *analyze* his situation. He needed to use therapy to learn about his feelings. We struggled many times as I insisted that he pay attention to his feelings. Gradually the nature of his comments about Vivian began to change from criticism to a description of his reactions. He described a tremendous fear of arguing with his wife:

George: *I'm just terrorized. It's like I'm a bad boy. I avoid arguing with her so I don't feel this way. I just can't tell you what she does. I guess I don't care too much what she does. I just couldn't tell her how I felt.*

Therapist: *Your fear of disappointing her, or of being a disappointment may get in the way.*

George: *There is that element of it.*

Therapist: *Let's focus on that.*

George: *Or a fear of being inadequate, or losing her, or something bad she will do or react.*

Therapist: *Does that go back to Mother?*

George: *It certainly does. Certainly those are the kinds of things that go on. Well, I mean, isn't that the "saving Mother" part really?*

Therapist: *Spell that out.*

George: *If you make mother see how wonderful it is out here, rather than where she is, then you can save Mother. You gotta show Mother that you can produce happiness for her, you know, produce good stuff, so that she wants to be with you and be aligned with you. I mean all of that goes into that lump.*

Therapist: *That you're worth being with?*

George: *Yeaaah, something like that.*

Therapist: *Desirable to be with?*

George: *Yeah, you've got to demonstrate it is what I'm saying, and then bring her with you and then that saves Mother. It takes her away from wherever she is, and then* . . . (voice trails off)

Therapist: *When you can't do that, how do you feel?*

George: *I don't know, it's sort of—it's inadequate is what you're really saying. Failed again.* (This is said with great sadness.) (George is starting to understand and to feel his pain. He is just beginning to explore whether he can give up fixing things. The pain of feeling unloved hovers over him. He is still afraid to trust.)

It is hard for him to relinquish his belief in family, and especially his belief that he has the power to make his family fit his image of family. This is true even though his family is primarily structure, with little substance. Giving up his belief means giving up his image of himself as savior, and facing the reality that he can't save his wife, any more than he could save his mother. He needs to grieve this loss. The bonus is that by giving up the savior fantasy he also gives up the role of the ineffectual savior, the failure. The rage he has buried since childhood begins to surface, and can finally be addressed.

As George began to experience his real feelings, group therapy was added to individual treatment. The group provided a safe place for him to voice feelings of pain, powerlessness, and rage, to struggle with control issues, to examine his attempts to prove his worth, and to explore his idealized view of others. In a sense, it was the family he didn't have, with acceptance, with limits, and with interaction that helped him know himself. (For more on George's group therapy, see Chapter 11.)

Middle Phase of Treatment

The marital relationship is impacted when the straying partner begins to take responsibility for voicing his feelings to his spouse, as for example in responding "No, I don't want to go to the theater," instead of "Yes, dear." He dares to explore how he wants to interact with his spouse instead of pushing her to take care of him, or expecting her to accommodate to his desires. His anxiety increases as he tells his wife how he feels.

George was delighted when he discovered he could talk about his feelings without having to take responsibility for fixing the situation, although he did not easily give up fixing. He began to tell Vivian how he felt by saying, "Vivian, I just don't care what you feel about that. I'm just telling you that I'm tired of being screamed at and I'm tired of living this way. You aren't listening to me, but I'm telling you that, and you'd better hear it." By choice, he spent less time with Paulette and more at home so that he could experience his reactions to Vivian. Gradually he shared a wider range of feelings, including his helplessness. Progress was mixed, with backtracking when the pain of vulnerability seemed too great.

Following a period of exploring family patterns George remarked, "I look back and I could say two things: I could come up with times my mother belittled me. I also say to you something I've come to realize that she must have done a lot of it because somehow I found a woman to marry who I either trained to do the same thing, or who brought the tools to the job." A few weeks later he acknowledged, "I don't love my mother. I really can get very angry at my mother, I don't love her, and yet I lived my whole life thinking that I should and wanting to—or wanting to care like that for someone."

He was stunned to realize he had been treating Vivian much like he treated his mother, coming and going as he pleased, and cutting conversations dead. He realized that he had wanted both his mother and Vivian to notice his absence and reform. George decided to work on honoring what was due to others from him. He decided, for example, that it was appropriate that he escort Vivian to an important community function, rather than hiding behind work. This led to the realization that he too, was due certain things, and he began work on taking what was due him. This was more difficult because it meant feeling entitled. As he learned to acknowledge and trust his own feelings he gave up looking to Vivian for validation. During this period he initiated more frequent contact with his children and began to build adult relationships with them.

George is a man who likes words, who feels them, and experiences the nuances of meaning in a word. Earlier in therapy, dissertations on the nuances of words were disallowed as another way of avoiding feelings. However it was important that the words I used fit George's feelings. Later, when George consistently paid attention to his feelings, word play, and in particular, reframing, became useful. An early verbal self-portrait that George shared was being "immobile" and "terrorized," with Vivian. As he began to speak to Vivian about his reactions "immobilized was reframed as "rock-like," connoting George's solidity rather than paralysis. A later reframe moved to "grounded."

Last Phase of Treatment

The final phase of therapy is a time for resolving old issues and for integrating and applying the gains that have been made. The straying partner needs to talk very directly to his spouse about himself, his anger, his pain, and his concerns about the marriage. Acknowledging what was good is as important as pinpointing what is not working. It is out of such discussions that decisions are made, usually by the straying partner, about the future of the marriage. If parents are still alive, issues with them need to be resolved to the extent possible, and peace made.

> Before George voiced his anger to Vivian, he began telling group members when he was annoyed with them, carefully at first, and then more directly. He then moved to tell his children when he was irritated, being careful to own his irritation, and fighting his temptation to give advice instead. He also set clear limits with Paulette, letting her know what she could and could not expect from him and why.
>
> Gradually he brought up the idea of separation to Vivian, at first to let her know what he was thinking, and later to tell her he was moving in that direction. At first, Vivian did not take him seriously. When she realized that George was sincere she panicked, and made threats designed to scare him into staying. George stuck by his decision to leave, but went about planning for separation in a very deliberate manner, inviting Vivian to participate with him in the planning.
>
> George was quite clear that he was not leaving for Paulette, and that he was going to live on his own for a period. He was aware that Paulette had her own work to do, and that it was possible that he might choose in the future not to continue with her either.
>
> In the last phase of treatment George integrated the many changes he had made into a coherent and positive self-image. When men like George are able to validate their own feelings, they are free to decide whether to continue the marriage, and are able to carry out their decision.
>
> George was ready to end therapy some time after he separated, when he was consistently and appropriately expressing his feelings to those he cared about and setting appropriate boundaries with them.

☐ Working with the Triangle

With straying partners who have some sense of self but are unable to end an affair, another type of intervention can be useful. This strategy, which is designed to unbalance the system, can be used in the context of either individual or couples therapy. Thinking systemically, the situation calls for a meeting with all three corners of the triangle. The goals for such a session are to identify the dynamic that keeps the straying partner stuck, to replace fantasy with reality, and to unbalance the stuck system.

The normal pattern of interaction in this triangle is between the straying partner and one of the women, leaving out the other. By bringing the trio together the interaction pattern changes, and the unbalancing begins. This meeting is a reality test for the straying partner. The lover becomes a real person to the spouse, rather than a larger than life fantasy. Often she turns out to be similar to the spouse in appearance or personality.

Frame the situation as one that the three are in together, and which they will have to resolve together. The straying partner, hoping to get unstuck, will usually agree to this plan. His wife may protest the idea of ever sitting in the same room with the other woman, but she is likely to become intrigued by the idea. She must have moved beyond obsession, and be in the process of reclaiming her own identity, to be able to risk this kind of meeting. The woman friend, generally, is amenable to the idea of meeting together, sometimes believing this to be an opportunity for him to see she is a much better woman than is his wife. Both women believe he is weak, and want to save him. At the heart of the matter though, is the fact that they are entangled with each other and will continue to be until one of the three risks changing the pattern. Think of the session as a mini-group, but instead of stand-ins for the important roles, they are filled by the real people.

To prepare for this session, the man needs to ask both women to meet together with him and his therapist. The request is framed around helping him, not therapy for them. You, the therapist, will need to meet with each woman, possibly more than once, to prepare for the session. You will need to decide whether you want to meet with each woman individually or with each of them, in turn, with the straying partner. You will want to learn something about the meaning of the affair to each woman, their fears and their desires, and what they hope to gain from the meeting of the triangle. You can help each to clarify their own agenda and identify those approaches that are most likely to be productive.

This is a powerful strategy and should be used carefully. It is not to be used early in treatment—only when your individual client continues to be stuck over a considerable period of time. Its success depends on each person having sufficient support, both within and outside the session, to be able to explore the meaning of the triangle and to tolerate the attendant pain. You need to provide a structure that feels safe for all three people. The principle components are your understanding and concern for each person, and your control of the session. Your role is to manage the process which allows them to explore and understand their situation in new ways.

Alan's therapist used this technique about a year into therapy, to help Alan separate his work from his father's unfinished work.

Alan, age 56, grappled with his love for two women: "Nancy was that part of me that I sent to the grave when my father died when I was 19

. . . I can walk into Nancy's home and her children are there and we all feel that this is a family. It was just one of these powerful attachments. I never wanted to leave my wife. I went to therapy to sort out which of these women I wanted to be with."

The therapist wondered whether a connection existed between Alan's current struggle and his father's life. "Was there anything that your father wanted to do that he hadn't done?" Alan talked with family members to find out more about his father's life and what had been left unfinished when his father died. An uncle revealed that Alan's father was in love with two women before he went off to the war. One of those woman was Alan's mother, Dorothy, who married Alan's father after he returned from the war. Alan described to his uncle what the other woman must have been like—smart, energetic, and pretty—"Like the women I always get attached to."

Another relative spilled the secret of the mystery woman: "Everyone knew your father was going to marry Catherine McCormick." Alan realized that his father believed he had married the wrong woman! He also recognized that he was acting out his father's unfinished business in his affair with Nancy. In fact, Catherine McCormick was like Nancy and the women before her that Alan had been attracted to.

So that Alan could sort out his relationships, the therapist saw him with his wife and then with Nancy in alternating weeks, culminating in one session with all three. At this point, Alan had to weigh his alternatives. "To leave my wife was to leave too much of my life. To leave Nancy was to leave the old fables, the romance of Tristan and Isolde, the pursuit of the myth, of passion. I weighed the fun, the relaxation, the whole encounter of my life with my wife and children. I chose to stay with my wife. I like her. And I'm going to have to process the same stuff with anyone. Why not stay with the one you've got a lot of it clear with?"

This technique is usually not needed when the straying partner is female. Once the affair is known, the male spouse is less likely to tolerate a triangle that continues over time. The biggest issue for the female straying partner is revealing the affair to her spouse.

☐ **Working Individually with the Abandoned Spouse**

The issues of the abandoned spouse are similar to those of the Split Self straying partner. Until her partner left, her pursuit of the perfect family helped her avoid the painful feelings from her past. Now she has the pain of being rejected, plus the pain of losing her major role in life—the wife and mother who created the perfect family. In many marriages she has been mother to her husband as well as to the children. It is part of what is expected of mothers in perfect families. Her struggle to hold on to her husband is in large part an attempt to stave off the loss of her dream of the perfect family and her role in that dream.

Treatment Goals and Formats

The treatment goals and formats for the abandoned spouse are similar to those for the straying partner: reclaiming the ability to feel, addressing unresolved family of origin issues, and learning how to connect at an emotional level. In addition she will embark on the grieving process, which her obsession has, to some extent, held at bay. Her grief is not just for her marriage but also for her dreams of the perfect family. (Her husband also grieved, but in ending the marriage he had the advantage of grieving before he was faced with separation; and he wanted the breakup whereas she did not.)

Individual therapy is the treatment of choice initially. In many instances she also can benefit from medication for her depression, which is likely to have deepened with the separation. As she gets in touch with her emotions the issues related to the chronic depression surface and can be treated. When the obsession subsides it is time to consider group therapy as an adjunct to individual treatment. By the middle phase of therapy, group can become the primary form of treatment. Sometimes couples work (not marital therapy) is useful at a later stage if both spouses want to explore facets of the marital relationship, discuss reconciliation, or reach closure with each other.

Early Phase of Therapy with the Abandoned Spouse

The Split Self wife who has been abandoned comes to therapy when she realizes her husband is not coming back. She is "bloody," seriously depressed and obsessed with the other woman. Her obsession is especially poignant, focused as it is around what she believes is lacking in herself. The early work with the abandoned spouse addresses the grief and the family of origin issues.

The first task for the therapist is to cut through the obsession, which is not an easy job. Acknowledge her anger but pursue the emotions underneath the anger: pain, fear, and helplessness. Disallow or insist that she reframe victim statements into "I" messages about her feelings. Use the same techniques described in Chapter 5 and Chapter 9 to help her get in touch with her dissatisfactions and disappointments in the marriage. Explore with her how the marital patterns are similar to patterns in her family of origin.

One of the primary goals of the early phase of treatment is to help the spouse reclaim her real feelings so that she can develop an internal sense of self. Support her in her pain, but keep her working on her own issues. She has no time to spare.

> Betty's husband left her just after her 55th birthday for another woman. She and Jim had been married for 32 years, and their two children were grown. Five months later she made an appointment for therapy at her boss's suggestion. She was severely depressed and obsessed with thoughts of her husband and his rejection of her. This was the second time he had left her. He had left eight years earlier, also for another woman, but returned after two months. This time he did not return.
>
> To the outside world, Betty and Jim presented a picture of a very close family. The truth, however, was that Jim had withdrawn from Betty early in the marriage. Betty kept trying to give Jim what he needed, trying to make the marriage work as she believed it should. When the kids came along, she became very involved with them and tried to do for them what she wished her mother had done for her. Each protected the other from angry or upsetting feelings within the family, and as the children grew, they joined in the protective patterns.
>
> Jim's leaving had raised questions for Betty about whether her mother was right after all: "My mother said I wasn't attractive to men—Jim was proof that Mother was wrong." The separation was devastating to Betty, for it exposed to the whole world that hers was not a perfect family, thus threatening her fragile sense of self.

The therapy goes back and forth, untangling the present from the past, as in this conversation with Betty:

Betty: *You know the thing I think of immediately is that I wasn't female. You know, I see that. That's interesting because she* [Mother] *thought of herself* (long pause) *well, I thought of her, as the ultimate female. That's absolutely right.*

Therapist: *So you're not feminine. Is there part of you that believes that?*

Betty: *That's right! Yeah, sure!*

Therapist: *How did that effect what you did with Jim?*

Betty: *Well I defined what I thought was feminine, which was sort of help-less, flirtatious, the housewife, putting whatever he wanted first,* doing what he *wanted to do, trying to figure out what he wanted* (pause).

Therapist: *So you tried to be feminine with Jim, as you understood it.*

Betty: *As I understood it. Not as I felt. (pause) Some of it I felt, some of it I didn't. And I guess—what I hear my mother saying is that it really is a woman's fault when a man leaves. You have not been what he wanted.*

Therapist: *So Jim left because you weren't feminine. Is that how it feels?*

Betty: *Yeah.* (tears)

Therapist: *No wonder you're hurting. Did you ever feel like this when you were a little girl?*

Betty: (tears) *Oh, I did. My mother never had anything good to say. When I was upset I would go and hide in the corner of the basement. I remember going down there and just hiding for hours.*

Therapist: *You were really alone.*

Middle Phase

When the abandoned spouse has some understanding of how she has arrived at her current situation, group therapy can be added. Here she can learn to share her feelings with others, and experience what it is like to be a member of a group, rather than assume responsibility for the others.

> Betty continued to explore her femininity, her fears related to men, and her pain. Group therapy was added and was helpful in surfacing Betty's reluctance to share the hurt part of herself and her difficulties with intimacy (for more information on Betty's group therapy, see Chapter 11). The group helped her separate her mother's negative judgments from her inner knowledge of herself. Group therapy also was a "lab" in which she could explore her fears about men and about her femininity, and test out new behaviors.

Last Phase of Treatment

During the final phase of treatment, different threads of inquiry are woven together. Letting go of fantasies—about the former spouse, one's parents, the perfect family, and even oneself—is painful, but is freeing.

> Betty's father came off his pedestal during the final phase of treatment. Where previously Betty had idealized her father as the "good parent," she became aware that he had kept his distance from her so as not to displease her mother. She grieved for the father of her fantasies, and began to let go of him. In the process she was able, for the first time, to put herself in her mother's shoes, and understand how angry her mother must have been at being stuck with the "bad guy" role. Seeing her

mother as human allowed Betty to be easier on herself and more comfortable in her femininity.

Betty began to understand that she had picked Jim because he was similar to her father in his remoteness. This spurred her to work on being less remote herself with those she cared about. Several years after separating Betty was ready to meet with Jim to talk about their unfinished business (see Chapter 12), and to gain closure with him. Then she was able to shift her focus to the present and the future. She was ready to terminate treatment when she was able to share herself without becoming entangled in what the other person wanted or expected, when her sense of femininity had been repaired, and when she had rebuilt her life to fit her own preferences.

☐ Outcomes

It takes longer for Split Selves than for many others to work through the issues surfaced by the affair. Split Selves are older, with habits reinforced over a lifetime, but motivation and maturity are in their favor. When they decide to do some serious work, they work hard. It is slow work, but it is exciting. The fact that time is running out provides strong motivation. For those who are able to replace the myth of the perfect family with their own sense of self, and who develop the ability to enjoy and to be intimate with others, their final years can be very satisfying.

CHAPTER

When the Marriage Ends with an Affair

An affair at the end of a marriage inflames the spouse, and provides an instrument for continuing destruction. For those whose marriage ends, important though painful lessons can be learned from the experience, whether or not the affair continues. The therapist's role is preventive as well as therapeutic. Helping the couple discuss the real issues behind their separation so they can say goodbye reduces their need to seek emotional closure in the courts.

☐ The Function of the Exit Affair

Exit Affairs are viewed as the cause of divorce by friends and relatives, by the public at large, and by the spouses themselves. However, a review of research on extramarital sex indicates that "the suspected powerful influence of extramarital sexual relationships in the termination and aftermath of marriages has probably been exaggerated" (Thompson, 1983, p. 47). Gottman (1994a) suggests a cascade model of marital dissolution: "decline in marital satisfaction, which leads to consideration of separation or divorce, which leads to separation, which leads to divorce" (p. 88). It is likely that a decline in marital satisfaction is also a precursor of Exit Affairs. A slight restatement adds affairs into the model: decline in marital satisfaction, which leads to consideration of separation or divorce, which leads to an affair or other behaviors that distance one from the marriage, which leads to separation, which leads to divorce.

The reality is that Exit Affairs are used by the couple to rationalize or implement a decision that has already been made by the straying partner. Putting the blame for the marital breakup on the affair and on the third party is a defensive maneuver. For observers it feels safer to blame the split on immoral behavior or unethical people rather than realize that people who once loved each other can drift to a point of no return.

For the couple the emphasis on the affair obscures their responsibility for the marital situation. Prior to disclosure of the affair, both spouses probably engaged in an intricate dance to avoid facing their deteriorating situation. The dance is described in the following group therapy conversation.

> Joel remarked, "I knew things were bad in my marriage, although I didn't ever admit it to my wife until she found out about my affair." Christine admitted knowing but not wanting to know that her marriage was bad. "I didn't have the skills to talk about it back then. If I had admitted there were problems I would of had to do something and I didn't know what to do." Mary said, "When I found out he was having an affair, I could blame everything on him." Christine added, "I did too! I didn't want to be the one left holding the bag. The fact he had an affair made it okay to end the marriage. It wasn't like I just said 'I want out" for no good reason. Now there was a good reason."

Clinical experience suggests that when the straying partner is female, she makes more attempts to persuade her husband that the marriage is bad, and cues about the affair are fewer. The male straying partner drops numerous cues about the affair, hoping his wife will discover the affair and end the marriage. The spouse looks the other way when cues are dropped so as to avoid knowing that the marriage is ending. Following disclosure, neither spouse takes responsibility for the marital problems or for the individual issues that contributed to the crumbling of the marriage. Denial is tremendous as each tries to pretend that the breakup of the marriage is not their fault.

The Exit Affair as a Defense against Loss and Guilt

Both spouses are invested in the fiction that the third party caused the split. It is a way of saying, "I didn't do anything wrong, I'm not a bad person. I'm not rejecting you or being rejected because I'm bad." Both spouses know at some level that they share responsibility for the demise of their marriage but they are a long way from admitting it. The straying partner usually feels some guilt, but justifies and ministers to it with the affair.

These couples have difficulty with endings generally, and great difficulty in facing the issues of separation. It is not just that endings are painful; prior unresolved losses are usually a factor. Experiencing the current loss (the marriage and one's hopes and dreams for it) would surface lingering emotions from prior unresolved losses. Instead, the affair obscures feelings, both present and past, of pain, loss, and abandonment. Unfortunately these efforts to avoid pain usually increase and extend the pain, rather than alleviate it.

For the straying partner the desire to avoid feeling guilty about ending the marriage often leads to excessive blaming.

> Jack alleges, "Mary is so totally hostile; she hasn't cared about me in years—she's a mess; she's revolting." Thus he establishes that Mary is without merit and that leaving for a loving partner is both desirable and justified. Mary counters by verbally eviscerating Jack and his "friend," Kathleen, to everyone who will listen. She's harder on Kathleen than on Jack—if it's Kathleen's fault then Mary has less responsibility for the demise of her marriage. She hires a gladiator (a litigious lawyer) to fight Jack for her. For Mary, blaming is a defensive reaction that protects her from the pain of rejection and prevents her from having to face the knowledge that she too contributed to the demise of the marriage.

Issues for the Therapist

Some therapists are very uncomfortable with the intense hostility that is so often a part of Exit Affairs. Such discomfort may stem from inadequate training or experience in dealing with such intensely negative emotions, misperceptions about the meaning of the affair, biases about affairs or divorce, or the therapist's own issues. In therapy, this may play out as the desire to ally with one or the other spouse, impatience with the obsessive spouse who isn't ready to move on, doomed efforts at marriage counseling, an inclination to make judgments, or just plain exasperation. If your discomfort level is high, supervision with someone who is comfortable and experienced in working with such cases can be very helpful. Or, it may be better to refer these cases to someone else.

☐ Intervening Before the Separation

Several issues bring the Exiters, either individually or together, to a therapist around the time of separation: the straying partner's desire to leave, the spouse's desperate attempt to hang on to the marriage, the need for guidance with practical aspects of separating, and the hope for emotional support. Sometimes it is only to be able to say, "We went to marriage counseling, and it didn't work," much like getting a doctor's excuse for missing a day of school. Any couples work is short term, and is directed to surfacing the decision to separate and addressing the specifics of separating.

The marital partner making the decision to end the marriage, most often the straying partner, generally wants short term help with the crisis. The spouse wants help with the crisis too, but may be open to examining the underlying issues as well. It's important to flag the real issues as you hear them, even if neither spouse wants to tackle them at this time. You're laying the groundwork for future development of a shared definition of the marital problems (which each will develop individually at a considerably later date).

Determining Whether a Decision to End the Marriage Has Been Made

A decision to separate may have been made by the straying partner, but has not yet been shared with the spouse when the couple arrives for their first appointment. When this is the case, the therapist needs to help surface this decision. The major indicator that a decision has been made is the straying partner's lack of personal involvement in the "marital" therapy. Although expressing concern for the spouse, it becomes clear that the straying partner is not interested in exposing his or her own concerns or feelings. Although the physical self is present in the session, the emotional self is not present in the session nor in the marriage. In addition to diminished involvement in the marriage, the straying partner is afraid that any show or feelings will be misunderstood, making it even harder to leave. Some straying partners do not trust themselves, fearing that any positive feelings for the spouse mean that they should stay in the marriage.

As you get clues that a decision to separate has been made, feed back your observations to the couple. You can for example, state to the straying partner, "Anne, you don't seem to be here in the room right now," or "Your heart doesn't seem to be involved in talking about your marriage." Escalating this tack with an uninvolved spouse, you might say, "I wonder if your lack of involvement is a comment about where you are in the marriage?" You also can inquire of the spouse, "Is Anne usually this uninvolved? What do you make of her lack of involvement?" You may even need to inquire whether the emotional absence reflects a decision that has been made about the marriage.

Readiness to Face the Decision

If your client is the straying partner or the spouse, and not the couple, you can adapt this strategy accordingly. The spouse who is ready for an honest answer, even if it is not the desired one, is able to inquire at length about the meaning of the straying partner's lack of involvement. Alternatively, the straying partner can begin to volunteer thoughts about separating, whether or not the spouse is receptive.

Another opportunity to get at the hidden decision arises when the straying partner makes a veiled statement about the intent to leave, and the spouse doesn't seem to hear it. Ask the spouse what he or she heard, and suggest asking the straying partner what it means. If the spouse is reluctant to do so, ask what he or she is afraid of hearing. Keep both spouses on task until whatever is going on is clearly stated and understood.

Many therapists find it painful to surface a decision to divorce, and wonder if it would be kinder to let the decision emerge gradually. Other therapists find it hard to accept a decision to separate, without at least attempting marriage counseling. The danger in either of these approaches is that everyone continues the pretense that nothing serious is going on, while the situation deteriorates. The therapist who buys into this is not addressing reality, which is that one partner has made a decision to leave the marriage. If a decision to separate (or divorce) has been made both spouses need to face it, and turn their efforts toward coping with this painful reality. A decision made for all the wrong reasons is still a decision, and the spouse deserves to know when a decision of this nature is in the works.

The Ambivalent Straying Partner

So far we have focused on the straying partner who has decided to leave, not on the straying partner who is still ambivalent about separating. The same approach is useful in both instances, as it will surface ambivalence of one or both spouses about staying in the marriage. If the thought of separating is uncovered at the stage of ambivalence, the couple has an opportunity to thoroughly discuss the pros and cons of separating and plan accordingly. A decision to separate, however, is still likely. When it occurs it will be the choice of one spouse, rarely of both.

Some affairs might be considered Almost Out the Door Affairs. Instead of resolving the ambivalence, the straying partner defers to an external situation. Jean for example, became pregnant by her husband shortly after talking individually to a therapist about her extramarital involvement and her desire to leave her husband. The pregnancy reflected Jean's ambivalence, and allowed her to postpone decisions about the marriage. Jean then changed therapists (to one who did not know about her affair) and began marital therapy with her husband. Sometimes the external situation that settles the matter for the moment is beyond the couple's control, as when the straying partner loses a job in a company cutback and can not afford to leave. These marriages often break up later, after continuing to deteriorate.

The Decision to Separate

When the straying partner acknowledges having no interest in working on the marriage and has made a decision to leave, the spouse feels devastated. The decision to end the marriage is more traumatic than the affair—the affair was a place to hide from the decision. In some cases the spouse wants the therapist to make the straying partner stay. It is as if the spouse is saying, "Do something—anything—to keep her from leaving." When it becomes clear that the marriage is ending, the really desperate spouse will run from therapist to therapist, trying to find someone who will prevent the straying partner from leaving.

When a decision to end the marriage has been made and clarified, the therapist's role is to help the couple address practical aspects of separation, forestall impulsive or destructive behavior, reduce the spouse's obsession, be empathic, and keep them talking about the pain of separating. Flag issues for future work, as you go, such as the need for control, a poor self image, fears and inhibitions, or other unresolved losses.

The straying partner may want to act on the decision impulsively, walking out on a moment's notice or simply leaving, or dropping out of couples therapy. In the latter instance, the motivation for therapy may have been to justify leaving or to get help for the spouse who is about to be dumped. It is easier for all concerned, however, when the couple takes enough time to make basic plans about living arrangements, parenting, and finances. Many couples prefer to separate after they have signed a separation agreement (also known as a property settlement agreement) so that the details of their arrangements are clear and binding.

Clinical experience suggests that female straying partners in the Exit Affair are more apt to separate quickly than are males. They often try to separate before their spouse discovers the affair in hopes that decisions about property or children will not be effected by the affair. Women also seem more apprehensive about their spouse's anger. Love, or the lack of it, is frequently the stated reason when a woman leaves, as in "I don't love you anymore." At the same time, she may be telling friends about her "love" for the man with whom she is involved.

Lawson (1988) found that married women who have affairs separate more often than do women who remain faithful. "Only the 'serious affair' led to a man's divorce, but if women had more than three 'extramarital relationships,' her chances of separating were very high indeed" (p. 288). Women who divorced and married their lover, as opposed to women who had strayed and stayed in their marriages, had a much greater belief that sexual fidelity is important in marriage, supporting the idea that female straying partners who leave the marriage may be those who are most likely to connect sex with love.

Practical Aspects of Separating

Initially, when the couple is in the process of splitting up, see them together so they can talk to each other about the process and the emotions of separating. Walk them through the process of separation so that they can anticipate what the experience of separation will be like, both practically and emotionally. Start them thinking about living arrangements and other practical matters. Flag issues that have legal implications so they can get expert advice in these areas. Coach the couple in how to tell their children about the pending separation, and suggest books such as *Mom's House, Dad's House* (2nd edition; Ricci, 1997), and *Children of Divorce: A Developmental Approach to Residence and Visitation* (Baris & Garrity, 1988). Guidance regarding the children is useful especially when the relationship with the third party is continuing (see Chapter 13).

You will probably want to refer the couple to mediation, a much more appropriate way to make decisions about practical issues than fighting it out in court. Couples do not have to be in agreement to use divorce mediation. Although used by couples who are amicable, mediation is of most benefit to those who need help in resolving their conflicts. Many courts provide mediation services, usually limited to parenting issues. Mediation offered in the private sector generally addresses support and property issues as well as parenting arrangements.

You are in a key role to educate your couples about mediation and help them prepare for it. Make it your business to know who the good mediators are in your community, as well as who the responsible low-key attorneys are, so that you can make competent referrals. Make sure that the mediators you refer to are good *mediators*—mediation is a very different process than the practice of law. (Present day turf battles by the legal profession to exclude all but attorneys from practicing mediation sometimes obscures the nature of mediation and the qualifications of those equipped to practice mediation. For more information on choosing a good mediator see www.affairs-help.com or www.mediate.com)

Reducing the Spouse's Obsession

The spouse's obsession is greater in the Exit Affair than in any other type of affair. With Conflict Avoiders and Intimacy Avoiders, the obsession is held down somewhat by the fear that the straying partner will leave. In the Exit Affair, this fear is a reality. Since there is little left to risk, obsession flows more freely, and is compounded by the issues of separation and divorce. Obsessing about the affair is a way of denying any responsibility for the marital breakup. For some spouses, it is impossible in the midst of the crisis to admit that they had a hand in their own rejection. The obsession functions to cushion the emotional shock of separation, by keeping the pain one step away. Obsessing, however, prevents the acceptance of any comfort which is offered.

Use the same techniques described in Chapter 5 to deal with the spouse's obsession, but with some modifications. Most likely, you will see the couple together for a very short period. Rather than attempting to develop a shared definition of the marital problems, focus on the fact that the marriage is ending. That is the shared reality at this moment, and the one that must be dealt with by both spouses. Help them pay attention to the pain and sadness that both feel in ending a relationship that has been so important. Facilitate talking about how it feels to lose their dreams as well as their partner. Acknowledge the obsessive spouse's anger but insist that the spouse owns it as in saying, "I am so angry at you," rather than, "You are a no-good cheat." Persist in cutting through the spouse's obsession and the straying partner's reluctance to express feelings. These sessions are highly charged and exhausting for all. The therapist walks a fine line, on one hand furthering a very difficult and painful discussion, and on the other hand exercising control so as to limit destructive interaction, while providing emotional support throughout.

The Secret Affair

Issues for the therapist are compounded when the Exit Affair is hidden from the spouse. Although the affair is not the real reason the marriage is ending, if it is revealed it will draw energy that is needed to address the issues of ending. If not revealed, it is a land mine that can explode at any minute. Affairs are often used in our legal system as the basis for making decisions about parenting and family finances, an approach that does not consider anyone's needs or take into account the fact that both spouses cooperated in making enough room in their marriage for the affair. When the spouses seem litigious, it is probably best that the therapist not initiate revelation of the affair. Questions raised by the spouse about an affair, however, need honest answers. When an affair is revealed in the midst of discussions about separation, the spouse's response will be obsessive. The net effect may be to push the straying partner out the door more quickly.

When the secret affair is discovered after separation the spouse feels humiliated: "How could I have been such a fool not to figure it out? I should have known! He's wandered in late for the past year, but I always thought it was his work. I feel so stupid!" Offsetting these feelings is the recognition that earlier intuitions were correct, even if they were ignored at the time.

☐ Intervening After Separation

Pain is a major catalyst for initiating therapy. Being dumped by one's partner and replaced by a third party is one of life's more painful experiences. Those not in therapy or who have never seen a therapist often seek help at this time. Those already in therapy can continue their work, although in a different format if the prior modality was couples therapy.

Treatment Goals and Formats

To continue couple's therapy after separation would keep fantasies of reconciliation alive, and delay the work of grieving and letting go. Therefore once the couple separates, use individual or group therapy as the primary treatment modality. Couples sessions can be used on occasion to address practical issues such as parenting problems, or to explore reconciliation, should that possibility arise. Much later, when both spouses are emotionally ready for closure, couples sessions can be arranged for this purpose. (Chapter 12 describes interventions with divorced couples for gaining forgiveness and closure.)

Each spouse needs to manage the transition to single status. How well each moves ahead depends on the degree to which old issues of loss and abandonment are understood and resolved. The goals of treatment after separation include grieving, understanding one's own contribution to the end of the marriage, resolving old issues of loss and abandonment, and developing the ability to be intimate and independent. Steps in the emotional process of divorce are shown in Figure 9.1 (Brown, 1976). As shown in the diagram, the spouses are out of synch with each other as they go through the emotional process of separation and divorce, accounting for much of the tension and conflict.

☐ Steps in the Emotional Process of Divorce with an Exit Affair

For the straying partner, understanding why an affair seemed necessary is essential. The spouse needs to examine the tendency to avoid facing painful issues. The spouse, pushed by the pain of separation, usually moves faster than the straying partner in the period immediately after separation. Straying partners may not realize for some time that they also have work to do. Some spouses get stuck along the way and don't rebuild their lives. Betrayed spouses are most likely to get stuck in the obsessive phase (incomplete grief work). Straying partners who become stuck are likely to focus on the new partner and stop short of examining themselves and their contribution to the demise of the marriage. Along with moving through the emotional process when a marriage ends, both spouses also need to accomplish the tasks of rebuilding outlined in Chapter 6.

Working with the Betrayed Spouse

Individual therapy for the abandoned spouse after separation may be a continuation of work begun prior to separation. For many however, this is their first experience with therapy, or the first after an abortive attempt at couples therapy. These spouses tend to be seriously depressed

Initiator	Phase	Non-Initiator
• Deny problems/possibility of split	Decision-making	• Deny problems/possibility of split
• Consider possibility of separation		
• Grief: Loss, helplessness, guilt, failure, anger, and blame	• 1–2 years or more preseparation	
• Detachment—Affair		• Learn of affair
• Decision to end marriage		• Obsession
• Separation	End of marriage	• Separation
• Cope with massive change in living patterns	Crisis phase	• Double whammy: grief and change Anger, blame, rage, obsession, helplessness, guilt, and failure
• Enjoy affair	• Marriage still primary reference point	
• Affair ends or remarriage to 3rd party		• Acknowledge reality of separation
		• Manage day-to-day activities
If affair ends:	• 1 year postseparation or more	• Sadness
• Develop new social relationships		

Figure 9.1. Steps in the emotional process of divorce with an Exit Affair.

(*continues*)

Initiator	Phase	Non-Initiator
• Explore new opportunities and changes	Rebuilding	• Reassess values and needs
• Accept responsibility for own actions	• Marriage not primary reference point	• Explore new opportunities and challenges
• Understand marital breakdown, including own contribution		• Develop new social relationships
• Reassess values and needs		• Accept separation/divorce
		• Accept responsibility for own actions
• Set long-term goals	• 2–4 years post-separation	• Understand marital breakdown, including own contribution
• Develop capacity for independence and intimacy		• Set long-term goals
		• Develop capacity for independence and intimacy

Movement can be in either direction as the individual struggles with each step, and it is possible to get stuck at any point in the process. The most common places to get stuck are in the anger and obsessive part of the grief process for the noninitiator, or in "new social relationships" for either.

Figure 9.1. (*Continued*) Steps in the emotional process of divorce with an Exit Affair.

and stuck in the most painful part of the grief process. Their "moral superiority" is getting them nothing. Be firm, but gentle, and facilitate the grieving process. The initial emphasis needs to be on the spouse's real feelings—the full range of them—and not on the obsessive ideation. You can validate the spouse's pain and rage at being dumped in this manner, but also help the person explore ways in which the marriage was not meeting his or her needs. Tread lightly here, because the spouse will protect the unfaithful partner from perceived attack by others, including you, for as long as there is any shred of hope for reconciliation. Arriving at a definition of the marital problems will have to wait until the worst of the grief process is over.

Grief and Obsession

Self-esteem and saving face are of greater concern for the betrayed spouse in the Exit Affair than for those in other types of affairs. Expect the obsession to be more intense, and to continue for longer than in other types of affairs. Obsessing, particularly righteous obsessing, is a way of trying to raise one's self-esteem and save face with others, as well as to avoid pain. Like many defensive behaviors, prolonged obsessing is self-destructive. Obsessing also delays moving into the grief process. Spouses who obsess heavily need help in order to shift to more productive methods of coping. Keep working toward redirecting the energy spent on obsessing to better purposes, such as attending to one's own pain. Keep in mind that the amount of anger is directly related to the degree of pain. Use the anger as a bridge between the obsession and the pain.

> Joan, in the early stage of therapy, raged about how awful her former husband was: "He's low life, he doesn't care who he hurts, he's robbed me of everything that matters, even his mother agrees with me, and the kids. . . ." Just below the surface was great hurt. I reached over to Joan, grabbing the hand that was thrashing about, and commented, "I know you're really furious at Sid. I'm glad you're letting yourself feel just how angry you are." I held her hand in a firm but comforting way. "Tell me about your anger." She again started attacking Sid. I asked, "What else are you feeling along with your anger?" As she started in on Sid again, pointing with her free hand, I grabbed that hand too, and held each of her hands firmly in mine. We continued:

Therapist: *I want to hear about* your *anger, not about Sid.*

Joan: *I am furious! I am so angry I could just scream!*

Therapist: *Go ahead if you want.*

Joan: (Muffled scream).

Therapist: *Sounds like there's something else there too.*

Joan: (Begins to get teary).

Therapist: *Tell me what you're feeling right now.*

Joan: *It hurts so much* (cries).

Therapist: (I continue to hold her hands). *Tell me about your hurt.*

> Joan proceeds to share her pain, shifting occasionally back to obsessing, but I continue to hold her hands and pull her back to her pain. When she protests that it is too painful, that Sid is the one who should be in therapy, I gently talk about how important it is for her to understand what has happened so that she never has to go through this again. She cries as we talk, and begins to relax. I let go of her hands when we finish, for today, focusing on her pain.

Touch can be comforting, even grounding, with clients who feel out of control, as does the abandoned spouse. Touch can also lend control. It needs to be used carefully however. If I sense that a client is not open to being touched, I respect that message and do not touch the person. Asking permission to touch her when she is obsessing is not useful because she cannot admit her need for comfort at that moment. Be especially careful about touching anyone who has been sexually abused. Most of all, trust the non-verbal messages you are getting from your client about receptivity to touch.

Women who are dumped adopt the role of victim more frequently than do men, no doubt because of cultural conditioning that encourages women to accept the role of victim. Provide extensive emotional support to the spouse *except* when she plays victim. When she is obsessing or is in passive victim mode, help her shift gears before you offer emotional support. She needs to let herself feel her anger, which can then lead to her pain. If you support her in her victim stance you will reinforce her obsession, thus encouraging more of the behavior that makes it hard for her to cope.

Men, as a rule, are more demanding in their obsession, which is easier to redirect because it has to do with active, rather than passive behavior. Some men, however, are stoic in the face of pain. With them, the therapist needs to be gently persistent to reach the pain, teaching them how to get in touch with their feelings when that is needed.

Making Changes

Bowlby's (1979) ideas about effective treatment of the bereaved can be applied equally to couples whose marriage ends with an affair.

They need to "review everything surrounding the loss but to review also the whole history of the relationship, with all its satisfactions and deficiencies, the things that were done and those that were left undone" (Bowlby, 1979, p. 151). Only by reviewing and reorganizing past experience is it possible to accept one's new status and consider future possibilities and make the best of them without subsequent strain or breakdown.

When grieving is coming to an end, it is time for the client to begin serious work on the underlying issues that were flagged earlier. The goals of this phase are to understand one's own contribution to the deterioration of the marriage, to resolve old issues, and to learn more productive ways of relating to others.

Margie, a 31-year-old with a three-year-old daughter, first came for help three weeks after her divorce was final because she was depressed and couldn't seem to get herself going again. Eighteen months earlier, her husband had announced on the way home from the grocery store that he was leaving, and an hour later he left to move in with his lover. Margie became a recluse for six months after Herb left, hoping he would come back and no one would be wiser. At the time of our initial session, Margie's parents had still not told any of their friends about her separation.

Margie had always tried to meet her parents exacting expectations, and had done quite well although her parents didn't acknowledge that. Her parents talked about the sacrifices they made for their children, and expected Margie and her brother not to reflect negatively on them. Margie was not sure what the sacrifices were, remembering instead that they never had family meals, and that her parents did a lot of drinking after her father got home from work.

Margie feared doing the wrong thing, and believed she was not entitled to feel angry toward others. She coped by trying to stay in control, and by not sharing how she really felt. In fact, she was very angry, but directed most of it against herself. The act of seeking help was a major step in itself.

Initially the focus of therapy was on surfacing and validating Margie's pain and anger and on helping her find safe and acceptable ways in which she could express her anger. We determined that if unbridled, her natural physical style of expressing anger would be to throw things. We set up an exercise where she would throw ice cubes at the cement block wall in her basement, during which she could yell and scream. She was given permission to visualize Herb's face on the wall, and instructed to limit the exercise to one minute, and to feel rather than think. She could repeat it as often as she liked within those limits, and could expect it to provide her with some temporary relief. She reported at the next session her relish at physically expressing her anger. During this early phase of therapy she could tolerate feeling and expressing her anger at Herb because it was "justified," but she could not yet get to her deeper emotions.

As she began to explore at a deeper level Margie struggled with the issue of control and her need for safety. Rather than directly confronting her resistance, questions were posed such as, "If you felt angry toward your mother when she belittled you, what would that mean?" and "If your mother really didn't pay attention when you were hurt, what would that mean?" This technique of trying on the question allowed her to try on the answer. Recognizing that the answer fit allowed her to acknowledge its truth.

At this point Margie began to realize that she defended against feelings of helplessness and abandonment by becoming more controlling and passing judgment on the issue at hand. She defended this behavior as necessary and right, and only gradually became willing to explore her feelings of helplessness. Brief time limits on feeling helpless allowed her to experience the feeling in bite size doses, and reassured her that she would not lose total control as she feared.

Margie described her father as meticulous, always in control, and wanting to keep everyone happy. A few months later she confided that he was not trustable, as he had an affair for four years and had lied about it. Her mother had done nothing about it, preferring instead to maintain her social status. Margie was furious at both of them. She used this betrayal to justify her distrust of men and her desire to stay in control. It also opened the door to work directly on Margie's sense of abandonment and helplessness.

As Margie began to sort out her contribution to the end of the marriage, it became clear she had replicated her mother's pattern of self-sacrifice, even to the point of ignoring signs of an affair. She had decided when she became pregnant, that it was time to give up single pleasures and she expected Herb to see it the same way. Herb, however, had expected his freedom to continue. It was fine with him for Margie to handle the household, making few demands on him, but a totally different matter to be expected to give up his freedom. When Margie changed and expected more from Herb, he found someone else to take care of him. They never talked about the changes that were occurring.

By learning to understand and use her feelings, Margie took less responsibility for pleasing others. She started holding the line with Herb, putting an end to his "dropping by" to see their daughter, and very gradually began to set limits on her parents' intrusions into her household. Without the old charge of anger and distrust, and with less fear of sharing her feelings, Margie found new satisfactions in her friendships and dating relationships.

The affair, as well as the separation, looked very different to Margie after getting her own life in order. She declared, "Herb did me a favor. I could never have made the decision to leave but we were in trouble from the day we got married. I just couldn't admit it back then."

Working with the Straying Partner

Although the betrayed spouse often has a more difficult time immediately after separation, some straying partners find themselves in trouble as well. Most experienced some grief before separating, but believed their anguish would be over once they separated. Instead of relief, they are shocked by another wave of grief. Learning that their grief is normal, that positive memories do not necessarily indicate a poor decision, and that guilt is not useful to anyone helps in finishing the grief work.

Others experience much less grief, but are alarmed when the same patterns begin to occur with the third party. They seek help to keep the new relationship together or to explore the problems that are surfacing. If the relationship with the third party ends, and a great many of them do, the ensuing discomfort may also be the catalyst for seeking therapy.

This is the time to explore and resolve the issues that contributed to the deterioration of the marriage. What or who did the betrayed spouse symbolize? Why was an affair used to force an end to the marriage? Why are endings so difficult? Such issues usually stem from prior losses and abandonments, and a sense of being unlovable. For some straying partners, this work is a continuation of work begun in couples sessions. For many others, the first experience with therapy comes when they find that separation does not lead to what they had hoped. Vic, for example, thought his life would be better when he got out from under his wife's demands and criticism.

Vic's affair with Nancy was his way of saying he was leaving Bernadette. Although he had tremendous guilt about leaving his son, age five, and his daughter, age eight, he moved in with Nancy. In an attempt to assuage his guilt, he volunteered to pay two-thirds of his net income in alimony and child support. More than half his free time was spent with his kids, although Bernadette had custody of them. Nancy pressured Vic to spend more time with her and less with his children, but Vic maintained his schedule with them.

Although Vic was able to separate physically from Bernadette, he did not want to lose his children. His own father had been gone a lot and when he was home, he drank until he fell asleep. Vic was ashamed of him, and their relationship was minimal. Vic tried to fill his father's shoes, attempting to please his mother, and helping raise his younger sisters. His mother was demanding, critical, and down on men. Vic took on the responsibility to prove to his mother that not all men were bad. He wanted his children to have a different experience than he had.

Vic had picked a wife who was similar to his mother in her demanding and critical behavior. She needed someone to take care of her and Vic needed someone to care for, since he had learned early to sacrifice his own needs in order to be the caretaker for the rest of his family. Now he was trying to take care of everybody: his children, Bernadette and Nancy, and it was tearing him apart physically and emotionally. By the time he sought treatment he was quite depressed.

When Vic first came to see me, he denied feeling any anger, but his internal tensions were reflected in his thin tense body, and his great hesitancy in speaking. He apologized for everything, and stated that the divorce was all his fault. About his feelings he could say only that he was miserable.

Early in therapy, the focus was on providing Vic with emotional support while helping him find and experience his pain and his anger. These he could tolerate only in small bites. As his tendency to sabotage his own interests became apparent, Vic was asked to examine the meaning of this behavior. He began to talk about his resentment at being loved only for his performance, not for himself, and to understand the sabotage as his way of refusing to perform. He decided to cut off conversations with Bernadette when she was critical of him, rather than appeasing her and becoming more depressed.

The next area of exploration was how Vic was using his close relationship with his children to keep Nancy at arms' length. His fears about intimacy were now being played out in the new triangle with Nancy, the children, and himself. This issue provided fertile ground for learning to pay attention to how he felt and what he wanted.

Speaking up about what he wanted was harder, especially when he wanted time alone. Guilt at not wanting to do what Nancy or his kids wanted him to do often resulted in "changes of mind." He was more aware, however, of his resentment at giving in, which created a shift in his previous equilibrium. Further exploration ensued about painful events in his childhood and how he was replicating many of the situations he found most painful, unconsciously hoping to change the end of the story.

After six months, group therapy was initiated as the primary treatment, with individual sessions on an as needed basis. Group was selected because it could offer Vic considerable emotional support, honest feedback from peers, a safe place to try out new behaviors, and an opportunity to be one of the kids in the "family," rather than the substitute parent.

In group Vic began to explore his confusion about love and betrayal.

He was able for the first time to talk about his self-doubts, his feelings of abandonment, and his struggle to find his own path. Gradually he learned to pay attention to his feelings, a luxury he had never known before.

☐ Resolution of the Affair

The affair is over when each spouse understands the meaning of the marriage and the affair, the issues of loss have been addressed, and the former spouses are able to talk to each other respectfully if not affectionately. Guilt about the affair, or obsessive anger, are far in the past.

> Understanding the affair meant Vic could own responsibility for the pain it caused, that he understood the mixture of reasons that led him into the affair, and that he had the ability to resolve problems in a different manner. Because he was paying attention to his feelings, he could share them with his new partner. He was able to say the hard things that needed saying as well as the easy ones. As he learned about himself, his guilt about the affair lessened. Internal changes for Vic had to do with a greater sense of freedom and increased self-esteem. No longer was he his mother's partner.

When the former spouses are both ready, however long that takes, meeting together is important in order to talk about any unfinished business and to discuss what was good about the marriage as well as where they got off track with each other. In this way, they can gain a more complete perspective on the marriage as well as reach closure with each other (see Chapter 12). If the marital problems and the issues of loss are not addressed, the risk is great that they will recur, either in one's own life or in the next generation.

Sometimes only one spouse makes significant changes and the other continues along a path of bitterness or avoidance. In such situations, meeting together may be relatively unproductive or impossible. However, even an unproductive meeting may give added perspective and validation to the prior decision to end the marriage.

Treatment that addresses more than the crisis aspects of the affair and the separation generally takes from two to four years, or occasionally longer, depending on the severity of the underlying issues. Those who have greater self-esteem, fewer losses, and who are younger find it easier to change, but those who grew up in dysfunctional families are often more motivated to change.

An Exit Affair doesn't have to mean the marriage was a failure. If it begins a period of reworking one's life in a better manner, and if the children's needs are adequately addressed, the affair can serve as a difficult but positive turning point.

The Unmarried Third Party

Treatment of the unmarried third party centers on dependency issues, boundary confusion, and oedipal conflicts. The struggle between the desire for intimacy and the fear of what it will cost is a difficult one. Sexual addiction may be an issue as well. Many unmarried third parties prefer a married lover because that fits their damaged sense of self. The affair provides an arena where unresolved issues from the past can be played out once again. These include dependency, denial of self, abandonment, and abuse. Reclaiming one's own feelings and the right to act in one's own behalf helps in letting go of relationship patterns that hurt.

The general public often views the unmarried third party as a home-wrecker, someone who is 100% responsible for the affair, as if the married affair partner had no choice but to be seduced. Some therapists get caught up in this type of thinking too, viewing it as a morality issue for the third party rather than as stemming from childhood wounds. Females who are unmarried third parties experience more shame than do males, probably as a result of different societal expectations. To oversimplify a bit, women are supposed to be pure while men are supposed to be virile. Some female therapists have a hard time refraining from judging female unmarried third parties, especially those who are sexually addicted, because of gender beliefs and expectations.

☐ Patterns of Unmarried Third Parties

In Chapter 2 we looked at the different types of affairs in the context of the couple relationship. Here we are looking at the different patterns that are typical of unmarried third parties. These patterns range from involvement in a series of brief affairs or one night stands, to transitional affairs, to long term serious affairs. The pattern chosen has to do with the depth of the pain being avoided. Is closeness more of a problem, or is distance more difficult? Those who choose long term affairs are less damaged by their difficult childhood experiences and less likely to have been sexually abused. Those whose sexual pattern is brief affairs and one night stands have experienced such pain as children that they are unable to risk emotional attachment. They are quite likely to have been sexually abused as children. In between are those involved in situational affairs.

Serious Long Term Affairs

It appears, based on clinical experience, that the role of unmarried third party in a long term affair is taken much more often by females than by males. Unmarried men generally see themselves as having many options in the choice of a partner plus the prerogative of taking the initiative, and for an ongoing relationship they tend to prefer someone available. In contrast, a particular group of unmarried women with Oedipal issues finds the married man most attractive. The Oedipal conflicts that men have may be played out more often in marriage, where the traditional gender roles can enable a mother–son relationship. Pittman (1989) suggests that female philanderers, "In their determination to avoid coming under male control . . . will make themselves as independent of marriage as possible. In this way, they differ from male philanderers, who seem best able to protect themselves from female control by staying married, at least in name" (p. 175).

Other reasons ascribed for being the other woman in a long term affair include the reality that after the age of 45, single women greatly outnumber single men (U.S. Bureau of the Census, 1998). Women who might prefer to marry may settle for a relationship with a married man. Richardson (1986) points out that many single women today want the freedom to pursue personal goals as well as an intimate relationship, and believe that, as the other woman, they can have both. "But what mostly happens to these 'new' Other Women is what happened to previous generations of Other Women. They lose control and their relationship ends up benefitting the man more than the woman: Being a new Other Woman has the same old consequences" (Richardson, 1985, p. 145). Richardson is talking here about the Split Self Affair.

Unmarried third parties also become seriously involved in Exit Affairs. These affairs however have a much quicker and clearer resolution than do Split Self Affairs. Exit affairs provide a quick escape route for the married person. Once the divorce is final the affair couple may head toward marriage or, in most cases, the formerly married person ends the relationship some months after the affair has served its purpose. The unmarried third party in an Exit Affair won't be spending years and years as the third party.

Situational Affairs

Situational affairs, used most often as a bridge between being married and being single, are also more common for women than for men. An example is the recently separated woman who deliberately chooses to become involved with a married man because "It's safe. He can't make any demands on me." She implies that she is not yet able to assert her own feelings and needs. Sometimes this is a comfortable choice, but often what was comfortable at first becomes painful later. If she is moving through the divorce process in a normal manner, she will soon move beyond the need to protect herself in this way and will choose a partner who is available. Separated and divorced men generally have less fear about whether they will be able to assert themselves so once they are ready to become involved with a new partner they pick someone who is available.

Brief Affairs and One Night Stands

Unmarried men and women seem equally likely to engage in brief affairs and one night stands with a married person. This may be a one-time experience, an occasional activity, or a way of life. When the pattern of affairs is compulsive, the problem needs to be viewed as sexual addiction. Engaging in a series of brief affairs and thus escaping the risks of intimacy is linked to childhood wounds.

Unmarried males with a pattern of brief affairs with married women seldom seek therapy for this issue. If in therapy, they usually come for other reasons. The behavior pattern has a macho edge to it, and in many quarters is viewed as normal. The underlying issues for those who engage in brief affairs and one-night stands are similar for men and women. With men, however, the dislike or distrust of the opposite sex is more prominent. With women neediness and distrust are usually present.

Variations on the Theme

Many women profess to be happy in their role as unmarried third party. A writer to Ann Landers (1989a), an unmarried third party, described her lover: "'Faithful' is a word that is not in 'Lover's' vocabulary. It didn't apply to his first marriage or his second one, either. I believe, however, that he is confining his amorous activities to his present wife and me because Father Time is catching up with him. . . . I'm sure he was attracted to me because I have a good reputation, am much better educated than he is, am well-dressed, have money and don't mind spending it. I'm also a good listener" (1989a, p. D9). Clearly, she is devoted to filling "Lover's" emptiness on many levels, and sees herself the winner, at least for now.

Our concern as therapists is not with those who are satisfied, but rather with those unmarried third parties who are becoming increasingly uncomfortable or who are hurting. They tend to be women whose fling turned into an attachment or who adopted the role of unmarried third party to ward off the pain of unresolved issues stemming from childhood experiences.

Family History

Women in our society are given strong and repeated messages encouraging them to please men, to appear sexually attractive, to sublimate their own interests to those of the family, and to disregard their own feelings and needs. These messages encourage women to be dependent. Some families counter these messages with consistent nurturing and respect for their daughters. In other families, neglect and abuse reinforce the cultural message. Those women who become unmarried third parties are at the dependent end of the continuum although they commonly describe themselves as independent.

Patterns in the family of origin are similar for those in brief, situational, and long-term affairs: The child's emotional needs were pushed aside in favor of the parents' needs and desires. The families of origin diverge however in *how* the child's needs were dismissed. With brief affairs, the child's pursuit of nurturing was often crushed by abuse, whether sexual, physical, or emotional. With long term affairs, an inappropriately close attachment to the opposite sex parent is more common, such as when a daughter becomes her father's primary companion and confidante.

Typical childhood experiences of the unmarried third party are as follows:

Received too much inappropriate attention from opposite sex parent
- Closer to opposite sex parent than was the same sex parent
- Overwhelmed or abused by a parent
- Role confusion and/or reversal was expected and valued

Not supported or protected by same sex parent
- Same sex parent was absent due to death, divorce, or other reasons
- Same sex parent dependent or afraid of opposite sex parent
- Same sex parent does not like self or those of same gender

Boundaries diffuse
- Emotional needs were ignored, neglected, or ridiculed
- Family was overtly or covertly incestuous

As a result the unmarried third party is emotionally needy but afraid of being dependent, seeks approval from others, ignores, denies, or dismisses her own feelings, and has difficulty trusting.

In contrast to many female straying partners, the female unmarried third party often takes an active role in pursuing an affair. It may be an active pursuit or a passive strategy arranged to get an invitation, but it is clear that it is a campaign to win a particular man. For example, Rose decided she wanted to get involved with Dave, a work colleague. Rose deliberately made sure she dropped by David's office just before lunch, or after he had a tough meeting. She arranged to be on a committee with him, and she showed him the nudes she painted in art class. She did not initiate the affair itself, but "waited until he got the idea." Monica Lewinsky adopted a similar strategy with Bill Clinton.

☐ Unmarried Third Parties and Long Term Affairs

The unmarried third party who is in a serious long term relationship with a married man—most likely a Split Self—is more likely to seek therapy than those who engage in brief affairs. Often her primary agenda is finding a way to free her lover from his marriage. In many cases she has picked a replica of her father, to whom she was attached or from whom she still wants approval. She expects to beat out her lover's wife, just as she beat out mother. She pays more attention to her lover's feelings than to her own. She and her lover reinforce each other's avoidance of emotional issues, sometimes even to the extent of becoming alcoholics together. She denies her pain and loneliness as long as she can.

Choosing a Married Lover

In the background are issues dating to childhood that contributed to her choice of a married lover. She pursues, as do those in the Split Self affairs, an idealized mate who she believes will give her the attention and approval she seeks. Richardson (1988) notes that "Secret relationships provide a harbor from the normative world where an apparently ideal relationship can be constructed and individuation and trust created" (p. 218).

> Connie, a 35-year-old accountant, initially came in to talk about her married lover's impending separation and the repercussions she anticipated with her family and with his grown children. In part this was wishful thinking in that Ross, 56 years old, was not at all ready to leave his wife, although he had been making promises to do so throughout the four years of his and Connie's affair. However, this provided an entree to therapy for Connie, allowing her to explore similarities in how she related to Ross and to her father, and eventually to make better choices for herself.
>
> Both Connie's father and Ross are forceful, opinionated, and used to doing what they want. When Connie doesn't agree with her father's "proposals," he refuses to talk to her, sometimes for days. Ross's reaction is similar: He pouts and withdraws. Connie feels extremely agitated when this occurs and explains, "I avoid creating that reaction."
>
> Connie was attracted to Ross by his strength—he is strong enough to take care of her—or so she believes. She talks about "waiting for him to come home" but the flavor is of playing house. In her family, the women run the household but the men are permitted to venture forth into the larger world. The marital relationships are marked by distance, in contrast to the overinvolvement of the parents with their children. Connie's father, uncle, and two brothers have each had an affair at some point.
>
> Connie's father long ago gave up on getting attention from his wife, and turned instead to Connie. She was the child who took care of father, who gave him the attention he wanted, but never quite got his approval. She also was responsible for preventing her father from going off on angry tirades. She proudly claimed "I'm quite good at preventing him from going out of control."
>
> Connie's choice of Ross as her partner embodies several functions: Ross provides another opportunity for Connie to play out her unfinished

business with her father. (Maybe this time she can win full approval.) Ross also is a symbol of rebellion against her father. (Her father pretends that Ross does not exist.) If she wins Ross, it will prove she is better than her mother (thus no need to feel guilty about taking over her mother's role). Winning Ross also will prove she is in control (she does not like dependent women and denies her own dependency needs).

The splits in Connie's life are many: She is divided between being in control and getting her dependency needs met, between Ross and her father, between her mother and herself, and between her real self and the false self she presents.

Serious Affairs and the Loss of Power

Richardson (1988) notes that in these affairs, which are constructed to protect the straying partner's marital status, "the unmarried third party deepens her sense of intimacy and commitment because she decreases the opportunities for publicly testing the relationship and/or increases her dependence on it. . . . The more dedicated she is, the more disempowered she becomes. . . . Because the relationship is forbidden, it is not socially tested, thereby contributing to its longevity" (pp. 216–217). Richardson also notes, "because his free time away from family obligations largely determines their time together, the Other Woman gradually loses control of how her time is spent. . . . Some of these women lose dreams as well as time. When they find that they cannot manage these secret affairs as well as they thought, when the relationships begin to damage other areas of their lives, the women suffer a loss of self-esteem; they are unable to hold onto the ideal image of themselves as women with mastery and control" (Richardson, 1986, p. 27). This is often when they come to a therapist for help.

Long, Serious Affairs and Treatment

By the time the unmarried third party comes to a therapist she has doubts about whether her lover will ever leave his wife and her sense of personal power is eroding. Only the tip of the iceberg shows when the presenting problem of the female unmarried third party is how to get him to leave his wife. Initially she rationalizes or denies the pain she is experiencing in this relationship: "We don't have any issues between us, it's just that his wife won't let him go, and I want to see what I can do to help him." She may try to regain control by calling his wife, attempting to shake her lover loose. She will ask your guidance in how to advise her lover's wife to let go of him. Full exploration of this issue gradually leads to her recognition that she cannot make him leave his wife.

Sometimes she comes for help because the pain is so great that she is ready to leave, but needs help to do so. Theoretically she has a choice between staying in the relationship or ending it. Realistically, she probably will not be able to end the affair until she has some understanding of her own issues.

She also may seek therapy if he ends the affair, for example, to work on his marriage. She is likely to struggle against this loss, trying to prevent herself from the feelings of abandonment that linger from childhood.

Treatment Goals and Formats with the Serious Affair

An early and continuing goal of treatment for the unmarried third party is reclaiming her real feelings. Thus the thrust of therapy is on helping her learn to pay attention to what she is feeling. Pain is often the feeling that is most accessible, and although she avoids it, her pain can be tapped with simple inquiries. As she admits her distress she becomes more willing to explore her needs, her fears, and the factors that keep her in the affair.

Initially individual therapy is best so that she can begin to learn about her issues and can gain support from the therapeutic relationship. Group therapy can be added when she is ready to tackle issues of dependency, intimacy, and competition.

Exploring the Family of Origin Issues

Getting a detailed family history early in therapy helps in understanding the specific meanings the affair holds for her. How did family members relate to each other? What were the alliances? Who colluded with whom about what? How were sexual matters dealt with? What needs and feelings were ignored or dismissed, and how? How did she cope when this happened? What episodes stand out? As painful experiences emerge, help her take plenty of time to attend to these long neglected feelings. Explore connections between the past and the present, particularly in regard to the affair.

Sooner or later the fantasy of winning father's love and approval surfaces in such a way that she comprehends the parallel in the relationship with her lover. Moving ahead means exploring issues around dependency and intimacy, and eventually giving up her fantasies and grieving her losses. When her lover does not make significant changes himself, which is typically the case, she usually ends the affair and develops a more rewarding relationship with an available partner.

Connie began to explore her divided self and her struggle between pursuing her own interests versus remaining "on hold." As the patterns of control and avoidance in her family of origin became clear, Connie began to feel her anger at her parents. This was tempered by the realization that she feared her parents' disapproval and had coped by avoiding her parents and withholding information about herself. She was tempted to confront her parents for the purpose of forcing them to acknowledge her relationship with Ross. I wondered aloud whether this might not be using Ross to do a "hit and run" and then to hide behind. She decided not to confront her parents, and began to discuss taking her life with Ross off hold.

A few weeks later she talked of feeling like an undeserving little kid, but quickly moved away from this. Gradually she began to examine her feelings of powerlessness and the ways she accommodated, yet rebelled against authorities. With her father, and with men in positions of authority, Connie focused on preventing criticism, not on getting what she wanted. Nonetheless, when she did not get what she wanted she plotted subtle ways of sabotaging the other person.

When Ross had been particularly attentive for several weeks, Connie confided that she did not know how to react to being wanted rather than needed: "I feel out of control. I should be doing something." This led to a deeper exploration of her fear that not being in control meant jeopardizing the relationship. Certainly with her parents, being needy meant being abandoned or ridiculed. As we explored the flip side, being in control, Connie began to see that her control did not get her what she wanted; it only helped her avoid pain. Even then the costs were high: She still had the pain of not getting what she wanted, and the isolation that was a by-product of her control.

Connie embarked on a deeper level of work. She mentioned a closet that she kept locked, so that she didn't have to see "all the losses." Inside the closet were the lost years in which she had not had her emotional needs met. The closet became the working metaphor in therapy. Was she going to open the closet door? How far? What was she going to take out of the closet today? Or put into the closet? How full was the closet? Who else knew about the closet?

When she realized that she had been raised to remain single, so that she could continue to be available to take care of her father, Connie became incensed. After considerable discussion, she decided to confront her father, telling him that she was no longer going to be available on demand.

As Connie learned to pay attention to her feelings, she struggled with letting go of control. She wanted to be accepted on her own terms, yet she withdrew and kept her terms hidden. She surprised herself one night when Ross "was acting weird, and I didn't like it, and I told him to go home." For Connie this was momentous: She paid attention to her feelings of dislike, she voiced them, and stated what she wanted, without regard for whether Ross would withdraw from her. She continued to see Ross, but with growing awareness of her own emotional responses to him. A few weeks later, Connie confronted Ross as to whether he had come to see her only to avoid being with his wife.

Her anger and pain were now out of the box and open to full view. I remarked that her feelings about Ross were much like her feelings toward her father. Connie sadly agreed: "My childhood went to my father and now my adult life is spent waiting for Ross." This painful recognition became the catalyst for gradually developing a social life of her own. She told Ross that he needed to do so as well so that she did not have to carry the whole weight of his social needs. Group therapy was added at this point to provide emotional support and feedback, and as a catalyst for exploring Connie's competitive and approval seeking behaviors.

Ending the Affair

Unmarried third parties need a safety net of support before they can end a serious affair. Their own feelings provide a significant source of support once they learn to pay attention to them. It is important that the pain from childhood has been sufficiently dealt with so that unmarried third parties are free to face and grieve the loss of their lover. Friends with whom they share their selves and their struggle are vital in providing comfort and emotional support when they are lonely.

Around the time Connie was tired of hurting, her sister confronted her, "with a family voice," about the affair. This time Connie felt supported by her family's concern for her. A few months later, with other options in place, Connie ended her affair with Ross. She missed him greatly and grieved for him, but she also was relieved at putting down the burden and excited by the opportunities opening up in her life. She continued in therapy for some time longer, working on what it means to be a woman, examining her competitive behavior, learning to relate to men as equals, and enlarging her ability to share and trust.

Connie's last task in therapy was forgiving her parents for the pain she had experienced as a child. "I understand why they couldn't be there for me. Yes, it hurt, but I know now they were only trying to protect themselves from feeling their pain just like I was doing. It's sad, I feel sad for them—it's such a waste. But I don't need to hold them accountable any more. When my mother gets on one of her kicks, I know it's her and not me. And I don't need my father to say 'You're wonderful.' I can say it to myself now."

Richardson (1985) found that many single women felt that "The painful feelings associated with their relationship have so changed them that being an Other Woman has no future place in their lives" (p. 148).

Other Outcomes

The affair with a Split Self may play out in other ways. In some cases the Split Self partner ends the affair, having decided to stay in the marriage. Sometimes one member of the affair triangle dies. In a very few cases the Split Self partner leaves the marriage to pursue the relationship with the third party. When this happens some third parties get scared and end the relationship. In other cases the affair partners may move toward marriage.

When He Ends the Affair

Some Split Selves, particularly those who have been working on their own issues in therapy, decide that they really want to make a go of their marriage. For the third party this is very painful. Those who are in touch with their emotional selves will go through a grieving process. Those who are not will probably cope by replacing the affair partner with another unavailable person. In either case the unmarried third party may seek therapy to help her through her loss. It will be important to help her look at the parallels between the affair and her relationship with her father: being special, competing with her mother and her lover's wife, and being abandoned. The abandonment, painful as it is, provides her with an opportunity to resolve her issues with her father.

When a Member of the Triangle Dies

Because these affairs are largely hidden, the death of one of the affair partners makes grieving difficult. The secrecy means an absence of people with whom to grieve. No one brings food, or calls to offer condolences. No one is there to listen to the pain. If it is the Split Self partner who has died, going to the viewing or to the funeral is usually out of the question. That is the prerogative of the spouse and the family. If the unmarried third party dies, the married affair partner is unlikely to have people with whom to grieve, although he may be able to participate in the funeral.

The 29-year affair of Charles Kuralt, the TV journalist of "On The

Road," and Pat Shannon came to light after his death (Williams, 1998). She was able to attend his funeral as one of the 1,600 people to do so. The difficulty started later when it was discovered that he had left her the land in Montana that they had shared together. This was how Kuralt's widow learned of the affair. Pat Shannon was taken to court when Kuralt's widow contested the bequest. This ending was messier than most since it was played out in public, and the rituals provided by courts are not ones that facilitate mourning a loss.

In working with bereaved partners, the therapist can encourage them to design a goodbye that has personal meaning for them, in addition to facilitating the grieving in other ways. One woman actively sought out others who were in the same situation so that they could share their grief. Another, who had kept her network of friends and shared them with her affair partner, decided to have a memorial service for him at her house and invited all their friends.

When He Leaves the Marriage for the Third Party

This is the ending that most unmarried third parties dream of. The affair partners have talked about it from early in their relationship. It doesn't happen very often, but it does happen.

The third party needs to be sure that this is not just another flip-flop out of and back into the marriage by the straying partner, and this requires time. The couple also will need to address the extra problems created by starting their relationship with an affair: shame, family disapproval, moving from a relationship that was sheltered to one that will encompass all the stresses and dailiness of everyday life, and questions about trust (see Chapter 15).

☐ Unmarried Third Parties and Situational Affairs

A number of newly single women become involved in situational affairs with married men. These affairs are of relatively short duration, usually four to six months or so. They begin some months after separation, when the woman is getting lonely but is not ready for and does not want a serious relationship.

These women have left or been left by a dominating spouse to whom they acquiesced. They are not sure of their capacity to set boundaries in a relationship and so choose a partner who has built-in limits. If he has a wife, he will have to go home sooner or later, and she won't have to push him out. Recently separated men are much less likely to begin a relationship with a married woman, probably because they are less concerned about setting boundaries.

As these women move through the steps in the emotional process of divorce (see diagram in Chapter 9) and enter the singles' world, they no longer need someone else to set limits for them and become impatient with the constraints of the situation. This usually occurs before the end of the first year following separation.

Situational Affairs and Treatment

These women are anxious and not sure they are strong enough to take care of themselves in the world. Thus, the primary focus of treatment is on learning to set boundaries and to take care of themselves. This means learning to pay attention to what she is feeling, giving herself a voice, and setting limits with others. A psycho-educational divorce counseling group can provide an understanding of the process she is in and offers emotional support. Individual therapy is useful in resolving family-of-origin issues that have made setting boundaries so difficult. Group therapy also may be be important.

> Christine began attending a short-term divorce counseling group three months after she separated. After the fifth session, she confided that she was seeing a married man. She was not comfortable that he was married, but at the same time it made her feel safe—nothing could get out of hand because he would have to go home. She wanted to talk about her discomfort, so we added individual therapy.
>
> We traced the roots of Christine's willingness to accommodate others back to her childhood. Her mother, a relatively passive woman, had done much the same thing, especially when Christine's father was drinking. Her father hadn't really gotten out of control, but Christine's mother had feared he would and urged everyone in the family to walk on eggshells so he wouldn't drink.
>
> Christine didn't want to be like her mother but hadn't learned the skills to be different. Much of our work together was focused on how (giving herself a voice) and when (paying attention to what her feelings told her) to set boundaries. After several months, she decided that she no longer needed the safety of the married man and ended that relationship. By now she had a support system comprised of several other singles so she felt she could truly be on her own, and take her time before getting into another relationship.

These women are relatively easy to work with. The danger is that they will drop out of treatment before fully addressing their issues, for fear of being too selfish or too demanding. The therapist who keeps the issues out in front, but with a light touch, can be very helpful in helping clients like Christine stick with the work they need to do.

☐ The Unmarried Third Party and Brief Affairs

Unmarried third parties who pursue many brief affairs are sexually addicted and are attempting to fill their inner emptiness while avoiding the risks of emotional attachment. Protection against the emotional abandonment they experienced as a child means suppressing their real feelings and substituting a false self which is designed to gain approval. The false self also protects against loss. After all, if the other person never knew your real self, it is not you who is being rejected. On the other hand, if the best you have to offer (your false self) is rejected, you are in real trouble.

All this leaves the unmarried third party feeling empty and isolated, and affairs are a way of numbing internal pain by settling for fragments of attention. Although sometimes enjoyable for the moment, brief affairs leave in their wake another abandonment.

Brief Affairs and Patterns of Behavior

The unmarried third party in brief affairs is more afraid of intimacy than the unmarried third party in the long serious affair. She may present a tough facade, but she is skittish, wanting attention and affection but backing away from it quickly. Intimacy has been too costly for her in the past. It is likely that her relationship with her father was more punishing than enticing, and she may have been sexually abused. She may be flirtatious or needy, volatile or quiet, but she is devoting her life to the quick fix of sex in the hope of gaining love.

Her affect swings abruptly between little girl and adult. The little girl presentation is often higher pitched, giggly, and says, "Come here— but I'll hit you if you get too close." The adult is serious, troubled, and bewildered by her ambivalence about intimacy. Her physical appearance may also be girlish, almost virginal in some cases, or it may be sexually suggestive. She craves nurturing but is terrified of it. She is unable to ask for what she wants, even when it is as basic as a condom or a cup of coffee.

Monica's experience is typical.

Monica, a 26-year-old computer analyst, was upset that another relationship was disintegrating and came to therapy at the suggestion of a friend. Monica had a history of short relationships with men, and in addition had been relatively promiscuous between relationships. She distinguished between men she likes, who are usually single, and those she has sex with, who are often married.

Monica attracts men with her sexuality, and gets hooked by their flattery. "The men I fall for are charming—although they usually drink too much—the others aren't exciting enough." The men she likes are usually in their late 30s or 40s. Initially they appear to be warm and generous, but soon turn out to be needy, allowing her to stay in control. She turns her attention to saving them, attempting to prove herself so that they will care for her, and in the process replicating her experience with her father. In most situations, Monica ends up drained and dumped. The few times when the man responds appreciatively, Monica panics and sabotages the relationship. After all, it is not permissible to win Father. What would you do with him then?

She felt lonely and empty after having sex with someone whom she did not want to sleep with. These sexual encounters and one night stands were usually with someone that she found unattractive, arrogant, or even threatening. Later she admitted "It's something that just happens when you're not in control, though you're doing it to get control."

The marital relationship between Monica's parents appears rather calm to the outsider, but inside the family it is another matter. Both parents are workaholics. Monica's mother assists her husband with his business, and tries to avoid his displeasure by anticipating and accommodating to his desires. With Monica she is intense and negative, severely criticizing Monica and her brother about minor details, lecturing them about the need for education, but ignoring their emotional needs. Monica's father alternates between being flirtatious and charming, and raging at minutiae. He is a dry alcoholic, and the son of an alcoholic mother. He is extremely needy and the attention he demands results in cutting Monica off from all her friends. The experience of spending her free time listening to her father is overwhelming. She can see why she wants some distance in relationships.

Monica's brother is the major target for both parents' underlying rage, which alternates with short periods of pseudo-solicitous behavior. Monica avoided much of her father's rage by sitting on her father's lap and hugging him, coaxing him to feel better. She was always concerned however, with whether her mother would get mad. Mother's nonverbal message was be sexually attractive to your father (so I don't have to) but do it in a girlish way, not too sexual. Monica confided that her mother gets angry when Monica wears slacks, claiming that it ruins her sex appeal to men and her attractiveness to her father. For Monica, physical affection is tied to rebellion—that is the only safe place for it.

Monica was sad and lonely, desperate for love but unable to trust. "I worry that I'm too much for one man to handle and that I'll never be able to be faithful to one man for the rest of my life." She was unaware of the many mechanisms she used to distance those to whom she was attracted. She covered her sense of emptiness with a facade of competency.

She was angry at her parents but feared acknowledging it. Her behavior with her parents is replicated in her relationships with men: She doesn't share her feelings with men because "that would be a demand, and it's not fair to demand." In reality, she was afraid she would be punished for making demands. She protects the man's need to see himself as nice, while her feelings of defiance alternate with anguish over not having done well enough. On the outside, she smiles and is solicitous.

Brief Affairs and Treatment

The unmarried third parties who engage in one night stands and brief affairs seem less likely to seek help, but when they do come to a therapist their own issues constitute the agenda. Some are disturbed about their own behavior and want help in changing their lives. Others are referred because of other addictions such as alcohol or shoplifting, or because of recurrent infections or venereal diseases, or depression. They may have seen a therapist in the past, but the sexual behavior was missed or misdiagnosed, as often happens with other compulsive behaviors as well.

Getting to the Issues

Unmarried third parties often have great difficulty telling the whole story, or even the real story, largely because they do not understand their own behavior or feelings. They have no awareness that the difficulties they are experiencing are related to their painful childhood experiences and tend to think of themselves as flawed. Thus the presenting problem may be expressed as distress over the fact that relationships keep ending, concern about a current relationship, or in other euphemistic ways. Occasionally the true situation is described in the initial interview, but most often the therapist has to pursue hints and hunches for a number of sessions before getting to the truth. Denial often further clouds the situation. Frequently the affect, or even the substance, of the person's history is dissociated.

Early in therapy, the unmarried third party often tries to stave off the depression that is becoming more pronounced. If her depression disappears instantaneously, it is usually because she has gotten involved with a new man, one with whom she hopes to have more than a one night stand. Kasl (1989) points out, "You can't get over depression that easily. On the positive side, being cared for and feeling the power of her sexuality [brings] energy back to a body that had felt lifeless" (p. 88). Her energy can be put to use in learning about her emotions and her behavior patterns. When this affair ends, as it is bound to, she will again be depressed, but will have a slightly better understanding of herself on which to draw.

With the unmarried third party who engages in many brief affairs, the issues of abandonment and seduction are foremost. Included here are themes of betrayal, rebelliousness, power, irresponsibility, neediness, dependency, and abuse. Sexual addiction is likely to be part of the picture. Those who have lost control of their choices and their life should be regarded as sexually addicted, defined as compulsive sexual behavior over which one has lost control. Compulsive sexual behavior is self-destructive, even suicidal. Many women however are not searching for sex, but for touch or affection to fill their emptiness. They may not even be orgasmic—being orgasmic means letting go of control. Sometimes she loses orgasm as a defense against the anxiety associated with intimacy or with her fear of merging with another and thus losing herself.

Treatment Goals and Formats with Brief Affairs

As the result of childhood experiences the need for physical affection may be paired with hostility or shame. Treatment needs to center on helping the unmarried third party reclaim the ability to feel. With that process underway, second stage goals include letting go of relationship patterns that hurt, and learning to build safe and caring friendships. A component of this is learning to ask for what she wants. Then comes the development of intimacy with a desirable, available partner. If her ability to enjoy a normal sexual relationship is impaired, as it often is, she also will need to learn about her sexuality.

The focus here is on the treatment of female unmarried third parties who are as likely to be searching for attention and affection as for sex. Treatment of sexual addiction, particularly in married men, is described in more detail in Chapter 7.

Intensive therapy is needed, but the therapist must proceed slowly and carefully. The absence of a marital relationship, even a shaky one, indicates that she is more vulnerable and more wary than the married sexual addict. She usually has few social supports. She does not trust anyone, and for good reason, and it will be difficult for her to develop a trusting relationship with the therapist. When she does feel close to the therapist, she may feel like fleeing therapy. To feel safe enough, especially at first, she may need to work with a female therapist.

Individual therapy is the basic modality in the first phase of treatment. Here the unmarried third party can begin to get in touch with her feelings, or when necessary, learn what a feeling is. She will be reluctant to experience her feelings in certain areas because of the pain in doing so and her fear about what will happen as a result. Giving voice to her feelings is even scarier, for it makes her vulnerable, and triggers all the old baggage that was denied or dissociated.

As soon as the unmarried third party is able to express some of what she is feeling, and can tolerate a group situation, group therapy should be considered as an adjunct to individual therapy. She needs to be in a group with both men and women, at least a few of whom also have issues regarding sexuality and addictions. Later on, when she has begun to heal, group therapy alone or with occasional individual sessions may be sufficient.

Sex Addicts Anonymous, Adult Children of Alcoholics, and similar groups can be used to supplement individual and group therapy. These groups, which are based on the twelve-step model, can be instrumental in helping the unmarried third party understand and interrupt her compulsive pattern, and they provide emotional support from others who share the same issues.

Brief Affairs and the Early Phase of Treatment

The development of a strong and caring therapeutic relationship is the first priority in treatment. Listening, accepting, understanding, and responding are the keystones in building trust and creating an environment in which it is safe enough to explore her frightening feelings. The therapist's responses which validate her feelings, help her know that she is moving in the right direction, and that she is not crazy. Eventually she will be able to validate her own feelings but for now she needs the nurturing and reinforcement of her fragile sense of self that the therapist can provide.

A detailed family history is essential, but at first the unmarried third party may be able to share only a part of her history. As she talks about her family of origin, encourage her to share any difficult feelings that arise, while being careful not to make comments that prompt her to put up a protective wall around her family. She will want to do so anyway, because the injunctions of an enmeshed family are: don't think, don't feel, and don't tell.

In her desire to be liked and her fear of rejection and shame, she has difficulty telling the whole story at times. When she resists discussing a particular issue, give her permission not to do so, but ask why it is important for her not to share. Many times, after describing why she cannot discuss the issue, she proceeds to discuss it after all. If not, ask if she has a time in mind when she will be ready to talk about it. She needs reassurance that her feelings provide her with important information but that they do not have to be acted upon literally. Taking enough time for this work is important; it can not be rushed.

Taking a Sexual History

Getting a good sexual history is equally important. Who was her first sexual experience with, and at what age? How did she feel about it? What experiences have followed, and with whom? What was her relationship with the person? What was she feeling that precipitated her sexual involvement? How did she feel during the experience? Afterward? Who did she talk to about it? Additional questions for sexual addicts are listed in Chapter 7. Normalize not remembering it all now— the memories will likely come later.

> Monica first sought help at the age of 16 after she had "gotten stuck" in several "awful and dangerous" sexual encounters. She learned from that counseling experience that she had the right to choose who she had sex with, but she did not deal with the roots of her sexual behavior. At 19, when the relationship with her first serious boyfriend ended, she went to Al-Anon and found it generally helpful in letting go. She has had a number of relationships since. Between relationships she has frequently turned to one night stands to avoid being alone and lonely.
>
> Now at 26 she is feeling hurt and abandoned by the most recent breakup, but trying to stay away from sleeping around. "When life gets rough I want to go back to my old ways. I've been craving something for the past month." We worked on learning to monitor her feelings and behavior so as to become aware of how and for what purposes she used her sexuality, and to gain insight about how to redirect herself. She decided to be celibate for the next month, taking it a day at a time.
>
> "I want to be with someone with whom I can be as comfortable as with my cat who sat on my chest and licked my tears away. I want to be able to cry with a man and have him comfort me." The goals that Monica established included replacing her old sexual patterns with healthy relationships, learning to pay attention to her feelings, becoming an adult

emotionally and sexually, and resolving the unfinished business of her painful childhood.

Like many clients, Monica was initially protective of her family: "My parents did the best they could." The close relationship she claimed with her father turned out on closer inspection to be Monica performing as her father's audience, listening to him talk at length about various issues. She liked the special attention but felt obligated and trapped.

With Monica, the words and the music were often at odds. She had herself tested for AIDS, then denied the possibility that AIDS was a real threat. When she did well, she panicked and handed over all power to another person. Then she panicked again because she was sure she could not please him or her. She described a humiliating experience with a boyfriend, punctuating the story with little girl laughter. She covered her pain with a blanket of denial. We focused on this experience and others, until she got in touch with her pain and began to cry. She stayed with her pain for several minutes, and I stayed there with her.

Addressing Issues of Seduction

Issues of seduction need to be addressed throughout therapy. Seduction is a pattern that is known and that has offered some protection from pain. Attempted seduction of the therapist may take such forms as attempting to shift the relationship to a personal basis, using her neediness to get the therapist to do her work, or trying to maneuver extra time or special privileges. With a therapist of the opposite sex, seduction is likely to include flirting, touching, or other behaviors with sexual overtones.

To ignore the seduction gives a message that you, the therapist, are not on to her tricks, and thus may not be able to help her. Going along with the seduction tells her you may be like all the others she has seduced. The therapist needs to identify the seduction and help the woman explore the meaning of the seductive behavior. The therapist also needs to set clear and firm limits with the client. The idea of closeness without sexuality will initially be viewed as foreign, or even viewed with suspicion and doubt.

It is not the therapist's responsibility if the unmarried third party acts out sexually. It is the therapist's responsibility to help the woman examine her feelings and motivations for her self-destructive behavior. Kasl (1989) relates her approach: "When it is clear to me that a client is definitely going to act out sexually, I do not use my energy trying to stop her. She needs to learn to stop herself. I do ask that she stay conscious while engaging in her addiction and come back and talk about it. I say to her, 'Be aware of what you were feeling or not feeling beforehand. . . . Be aware of your body and your connection to the other person when you are being sexual. . . . Check your feelings about yourself and your partner after being sexual.' Being conscious destroys the addictive high" (p. 302).

Let yourself care about your client. She does not need another uncaring experience. Be careful however, about the use of touch, especially with a client of the opposite sex. Unmarried third parties are people whose boundaries have been violated, often by sexual abuse, and touch can be misinterpreted as seduction or worse. Ask first, and respect her answer. Many therapists are used to comforting with a touch or a hug, and it can be difficult not to do so when our client is in pain. We need to make sure that touch is what she needs and wants, and not a way of avoiding our helpless feelings. This reinforces the message that she has the right to set the boundaries around her physical self.

Middle Phase of Therapy

When the unmarried third party has started paying attention to her feelings, the hard work of exploring her pain, both present and past, can move ahead. It is during this phase that she will re-experience the painful events and relationships in her family of origin. She will be anxious, apprehensive, and resistant. She will be tempted to flee toward any available, or unavailable, man. She will also be excited, motivated, and gratified by the opportunity to resolve her issues.

> When Monica was frightened I used the analogy of standing at the end of the high dive board, and standing . . . and standing . . . afraid to jump off. The longer she stands the longer she remains frightened. If she jumps, she will be in the water, but she knows how to swim. Monica made the jump by letting herself look at her parents collusive use of her. She was furious at all the confused messages, the betrayals, and the emotionally abusive behavior of her parents. A few weeks later she related dreams of killing her mother.
>
> Group therapy was added at this point so that Monica could begin to work directly on relationship issues. She began to understand that her ways of competing with women were designed to prove that she was better than her mother; thus she must be acceptable. She discovered that her self-sabotage was an outgrowth of her attempt to remain a little girl, to be sexy but not sexual with her father. She also said, "I slept with men because I didn't have self-respect or esteem. I didn't think there was anything I was good for—except flirting." She was learning that she had strong feelings and opinions, and that it was safe to talk about them.
>
> Throughout this period the focus was on identifying her feelings and using them to construct a more accurate picture of her childhood (she

had been hurt but she was not bad), and as a guide in relating to others and to herself. She became less anxious about being alone, even choosing at times to be alone with whatever feelings she was in the process of sorting out. She continued her earlier efforts to develop friendships with people she liked, and "practiced" new behaviors with them as well as in the group.

Concluding Phase of Treatment

During the final phase of therapy the unmarried third party separates herself from her parents, having confronted them, possibly several times, and finally accepting their limitations. By now she has her own feelings to trust, and most of the time she remembers to use them as her guide. She explores her sense of what it means to be a woman, bringing together her emotional, rational, and sexual selves. The enormity of being on her own, of being grown up, is exhilarating and frightening. She worries about how she will handle future crises, and is reassured by the fact that when crises occur, she is better at handling them than she ever was in the past.

> Monica was ready to end therapy when she understood and had made peace with her past, when her feelings, thoughts, and behavior were integrated, and when she had close friends with whom she was able to talk freely about what was on her mind and with whom she could play. She was not in a relationship with a man at the moment, but her most recent relationship had been significantly different than earlier ones, and she felt certain that she was not going to settle for an unsuitable partner, nor were her expectations unrealistic. She had also forgiven herself and no longer accepted being mistreated.

☐ The Aftermath

Unmarried third parties who decide to address the issues underlying their use of affairs, and who have the courage to address their pain, are usually successful in changing their lives. With commitment and persistence they gradually free themselves from the past, becoming women in the fullest sense. Those who never commit to change are likely to choose unavailable men or to pursue brief sexual encounters for the rest of their lives. They run a great risk of ending up alone.

The Use of Group Treatment

Groups are a powerful tool for treating the issues underneath the affair. Because of societal taboos and preconceptions about affairs, those involved in the affair triangle have few healthy outlets for discussing their situation. Thus groups can be particularly beneficial in working with affairs.

Therapists, however, seem less likely to offer group therapy these days. Short term special focus groups such as those for cancer or divorce are popular, but ongoing therapy groups that address the deeper emotional issues are hard to find, in large part a result of the current pressure on therapists to provide brief therapy. Nonetheless, if affairs are common among your client population, consider using group therapy as one of your approaches. Not only is it a powerful modality, but it is usually more affordable for clients.

Different group structures are appropriate for different types of affairs. Considerations for the therapist include composition of the group, and rules that provide sufficient safety for group members. To be effective, the therapist needs a keen awareness of seduction in all its forms, and the ability to be both tough and caring in confronting it.

A healthy therapy group acts much like a functional family, and thus offers the opportunity to learn relationship skills that were missed in the family of origin. It has clear rules about limits and expectations, and within those boundaries provides numerous opportunities to try out new behaviors, to get honest feedback, and to share feelings. Group therapy can supplement individual or couples work, or may be the primary intervention.

Therapy groups can be structured to focus on a single issue or on broader issues, with participants chosen accordingly. In considering whether to form a group around a single issue (such as sexual addiction) or broader issues (such as intimacy, dependency, and other relationship problems), explore how the criteria for selecting group members will effect the process of the group. What perspectives need to be represented in the group to reflect the underlying issues? Can this be achieved within a single focus group? If so, a single focus group may be preferable. If not, a group focusing on a wider group of issues is preferable.

A couples group, focusing on broader issues is the most appropriate group format for Conflict and Intimacy Avoidant couples. Retreats for couples who have moved beyond the obsessive phase in working on their marriage are another possibility. A broadly focused group comprised of individuals is generally best for members of the Split Self triangle, Exit Affairs, and unmarried third parties. Twelve-step groups having a single focus are particularly useful with addictions. Short-term special focus groups, focusing on only one type of affair or one aspect of it, also can be used in a variety of situations.

☐ Couples Groups for Conflict and Intimacy Avoiders

Couples group is an option after both spouses are clear about their real issues, and each owns their part of the marital problem. The classic couples group, with four couples, meeting for 90 minutes once a week, with a single therapist or with male and female cotherapists, works well for Conflict and Intimacy Avoiders. The goals of such a group are to explore the feelings and behaviors of each participant, to examine the dynamics of each couple's relationship including factors that contributed to the affair, and to learn satisfying and effective ways of interacting as a couple.

Couples groups do not need to be designated as affairs groups, and it is probably better if they are not. Billing it as an affairs group reinforces obsession and gives too much attention to the affair. It is not necessary that all the couples in the group have experienced an affair, but everyone should share the experience of betrayal (lies, disloyalty, or the like)—not a difficult criteria to meet.

Readiness for Group

All the couples need to be committed to working on the marriage, but they don't need to have decided that the marriage will work. Group is especially useful for those couples without a network of friends, those who were outsiders or were too close to their families of origin, and those who need to learn how a functioning family works.

Prior to beginning group therapy, couples are seen for varying periods of time in marital therapy. Several factors need to be considered when assessing whether a couple is ready to move into a couples group. Couples who are ready for group have some understanding of their issues, they are open to learning more about their interaction with others, they can tolerate group pressure, they are not in the throes of a crisis, and they have rapport with the therapist. Because each spouse has the other for support, couples are less fearful of group therapy than is the typical individual. They can often benefit from the group experience at an earlier stage in therapy than could an individual with similar issues. However the flip side is that couples sometimes collude to hide their dirty linen.

Once couples move beyond the get-acquainted stage, group therapy becomes the primary treatment modality. Group may be the only treatment modality used with a couple, or it may be augmented by individual therapy for one or both spouses, occasional couples sessions, or by groups such as Adult Children of Alcoholics (ACOA), as needed.

Group Selection

In selecting couples for the group, match for age group and general level of functioning but mix Intimacy Avoiders and Conflict Avoiders. Include at least two couples whose marriage is likely to continue (insofar as it is ever possible to predict), to provide an element of hope for the group. Include at least one and no more than two Intimacy Avoidant couples. A group comprised solely of Conflict Avoiders is deadly: when everyone colludes to avoid conflict the real issues are slow to surface. Similarly, a group comprised entirely of Intimacy Avoiders is so chaotic that getting to work is difficult. Selecting both Conflict and Intimacy Avoiders builds in a constructive tension between rationality and emotion which facilitates an effective group process.

Group Structure

Since these couples have walked to the edge of the precipice in their marriage before addressing their issues, they need more than brief therapy. An open ended group provides an intensive treatment experience and maximum flexibility. It allows couples to take the time they need to resolve their issues. As couples leave the group, members gain experience with handling endings in a positive manner. This contrasts with the denial or distancing typically used in the past to avoid the pain of endings. Fresh perspectives materialize as new members join the group. Trust has to be established anew with each couple that joins the group, and the loss of old members grieved. For couples where trust is an issue, recurring opportunities to build trust can be therapeutic.

The standard group rules that include confidentiality, speaking only for one's self, and no outside socializing with other group members, are appropriate. Because these couples have had difficulty with boundaries the latter rule needs to be carefully monitored. Newly formed couples groups can take longer to coalesce than a new group of individuals because the spouses collude to protect each other. Once the couple facade is cracked, group is supportive, normalizing, revealing, and healing. Groups always provide models for new behavior, and opportunities for reality testing.

Obsession is just as out of place in a couples group as it is in a couple's session. If it occurs, and it sometimes does, it can be addressed by asking the obsessor what he or she is feeling at the moment, in the same manner described in Chapter 5. An advantage of group therapy, however, is that group members as well as the therapist can be instrumental in disallowing obsession and refocusing the obsessor on the real issues.

The therapist's main task is to keep the couples addressing the issues that they used the affair to avoid. Self-disclosure, vulnerability, managing conflict, moving closer and backing off, and the desire to avoid responsibility for one's self are continual themes in the group process as well as within the marital relationships. Highlighting the parallel processes provides group members with a here-and-now opportunity to examine and change problematic behaviors. If a group member is also in individual therapy, the issues and feelings stirred up in individual sessions need to be flagged as issues to be brought to the group.

Couples Group Case Study

Occasionally an affair will be discovered during the life of the group. If the affair has ended and the spouses want to work on the marriage, the affair can be explored in group in much the same manner as in couples therapy, but with the additional input of the group. The couples in the following group were in their thirties and early forties, and had been married from eight to fifteen years.

Dave and Jessica were Conflict Avoiders. Jessica's affair had disrupted the old balance. In the past, Jessica took most of the responsibility for their life together. In exchange for having control, she did not hold Dave accountable for his behavior. In fact, she expected that Dave would procrastinate or "forget" those things he had promised to do. In those instances when Jessica was upset by Dave's behavior, Dave played to her expectation: "Who me? I didn't do anything wrong." Jessica's affair was symbolic of how tired she was of Dave's passive "Can't you see what a good boy I am?" routine.

This was the second marriage for both Annie and Bert and these Intimacy Avoiders were having a tough time of it. Both had grown up in dysfunctional families, and their efforts to solve problems frequently ended in long chaotic arguments. Each was quick to blame the other, and slow to explore his or her own feelings. Their fighting over Bert's recent affair, Annie's previous affairs, and a variety of other issues had brought them to therapy.

Doris and Sam found it very difficult to talk about themselves and about their feelings. Sam's father had exercised strict discipline over his family and Sam was following in his footsteps. Doris' family was a quiet one, with family members living separate lives within the same household. A vague but growing unease brought them to therapy. The therapist believed group therapy would provide them with needed stimulation and with new models for interacting, so they began group after five couple sessions.

About two months after joining the group, Doris and Sam seemed still to be stuck in their silence and passivity. During the last session Doris had pushed Sam to tell her what he wanted. Sam responded with requests that she keep the house cleaner and that she be more spontaneous. Doris agreed and the matter dropped. This was the third time that virtually the same scenario had been repeated. The therapist wondered aloud why the group avoided confronting them. Bert and Annie began fighting about whether Bert was going to work late the next night, and Jessica began to play therapist with them, while Dave silently withdrew. The therapist observed to the group that whatever was going on must be powerful and scary, because the group seemed to be protecting a secret, much like their families of origin did.

Because newcomers to a group are unlikely to risk revealing a major secret in the group, the therapist decided to meet individually with Sam and Doris during the week in an attempt to identify the secret. Sam revealed his secret early in the individual session: He was having an affair with a secretary who worked for one of his colleagues. He was ready to tell Doris, but was afraid of her reaction, so the therapist helped him prepare to reveal his secret. He told Doris in the beginning of the next group session about the affair, including the fact that he had ended it two days earlier and that he wanted to work on their marriage. The group gave Doris space to react, and supported her in her anger and pain. They also supported Sam for having the courage to reveal the truth and for deciding to work on the marriage. (If he had decided not to end the affair or not to work on the marriage, group members would have felt threatened and the therapist would have helped them attend to their fears of betrayal and abandonment.)

The group was instrumental in helping reduce Doris' obsession with Sam's affair. Because the other couples had been there themselves, they knew how necessary it is to get beyond the obsession in order to have any chance at rebuilding the marriage. The other couples shared their perceptions of what the affair in their relationship had meant, facilitating Doris and Sam's self-examination.

In reflecting on why they had been so slow to confront Doris and Sam, the group realized that one of the legacies of family secrets is paralysis. Dave asserted: "The next time any of us feel paralyzed, we've got to remember it means there's buried treasure here."

Progress in a couples group is up and down, just as in individual or marital therapy. Periods of fast movement alternate with periods of slow plodding work or regressed behavior, both within the group and within the marriage. Healing aspects of group include the bond of sharing similar problems, learning alternative ways of relating to others, and the validation that comes from exposing one's real self and finding acceptance.

Termination Issues

If the affair is continuing, decisions need to be made by the therapist in conjunction with the couple and the group about whether it is appropriate for the couple to continue in the group. Usually it is not appropriate because the straying partner is not sufficiently committed to working on the marriage. If the straying partner decides to continue the affair, leaving both the group and the marriage, allow the spouse to stay for a short period. Losing the group and the partner at the same time can be too great a loss. Some spouses leave in a few weeks; others are ready to leave after the worst of the grief process is over. A new couple entering the group will make the spouse very aware of being single and alone, and will surface the issue of whether it is time to move to a different treatment format, possibly a group for individuals. Ideally this issue is addressed before a new couple joins the group.

As a result of their work in group, some couples decides to separate. This arouses a mixture of feelings among group members, ranging from sadness and hurt to fear for their own marriage. These feelings need to be discussed with the separating couple before they leave, and with the remaining group members afterwards. Helping the separating couple identify their next steps provides a bridge for them and for the group's concerns about them.

Other couples leave group having resolved their major issues and having rebuilt trust. Couples generally give several weeks notice (as established in the group rules) to the group of their intent to leave. These weeks are used to review progress, pinpoint remaining issues, and prepare for leaving the group, or in some cases, to question the wisdom of the decision to leave group at this time.

During the couple's last session, group members acknowledge the significant events they have shared, their feelings about leaving, and hopes for the couple and for themselves. The group experiences sadness at losing the couple, but is delighted and encouraged by their success.

Benefits and Limitations of Couples Groups

Both Conflict Avoiders and Intimacy Avoiders can benefit from participation in a couples group. It is a more demanding format than regular couples therapy because group members as well as the therapist hold each other accountable. It is hard to dismiss issues when others who are in similar situations all convey the same message. The group's effectiveness comes in part from this dynamic. In addition, the varying perspectives of the group members provide rich feedback, opening up more avenues for exploration. The inclusion of both Conflict Avoiders and Intimacy Avoiders provides balance (neither too depressed nor too chaotic) and offers couples a first-hand look at other ways of relating. This type of group is not suitable for Split Self couples who need first to work on themselves individually, for Exit Affair couples about to separate, or for Sexual Addicts and their spouses who need a somewhat different group.

☐ Couples Groups for Sexual Addicts and Codependents

Groups available for Sexual Addicts and their spouses range from therapy groups for couples or individuals to groups that are part of a larger treatment program, to twelve-step groups. Whatever the group's stated purpose, the focus needs to be broad because addiction touches all aspects of life.

Most groups are based in the community and are offered by mental health professionals, addiction treatment programs, or twelve-step organizations. The Meadows in Wickenburg, AZ, headed by Patrick Carnes, a pioneer in developing treatment for sexual addiction, provides a comprehensive inpatient treatment program for Sexual Addicts, their spouses, and their families that uses several types of group treatment (Carnes, 2000).

Couples groups for Sexual Addicts and their spouses share some similarities with groups for Conflict and Intimacy Avoiders. They have many similar goals, and a similar structure. The groups are different however, in significant ways. The addiction group is comprised only of Sexual Addicts and their spouses. The roots of addiction tend to go deeper than those of Conflict and Intimacy Avoiders, so group is not the only or the major therapeutic modality. Generally group is combined with individual therapy, and with participation in a twelve-step group.

Because breaking the addictive cycle is a major goal, group discussions emphasize each person's responsibility for understanding and changing their own pattern, both within and outside the group. The focus is on feelings and issues that were previously avoided through the addiction. Particular attention is placed on experiencing one's own pain, which the addict has avoided by means of the affairs, and which the spouse has avoided through the codependent behavior.

It is essential that each spouse understands and is working on their own piece of the addictive pattern, before becoming involved in a couples group. Typically the group is led by male and female co-therapists who have extensive experience in working with addictions, as well as in working with groups. See Chapter 7 for a detailed discussion of treatment for Sexual Addicts and codependents.

☐ Groups for Individuals

Group therapy is an excellent tool for confronting issues related to affairs, particularly when the group is structured to address betrayal and its underlying issues. A group comprised of straying and betrayed Split Selves and Exiters along with unmarried third parties is such a group. All the players in the affair are present so multiple perspectives can be addressed. As with the couples groups described earlier, this group does not need to be described as an affairs group, but is simply a therapy group. However group members need to be clear that addressing the issues underlying the betrayal in their own lives is on the agenda.

Goals of such a group include helping group members gain insight, resolve internal conflicts, change dysfunctional behavior patterns, set boundaries, and resolve the issues underlying the affair. To reach these goals, participants need to learn a different process for approaching problems: one based on understanding one's own emotions and motivations and letting other people do the same, rather than assessing right and wrong.

Another group for individuals is one comprised only of Sexual Addicts. Commonality among group members is important here because the roots of sexual addiction go so deep and the shame is so great. For the Sexual Addict, participation in group therapy is one part of a multipart treatment program including individual therapy, family therapy, and a twelve-step group. Much of what follows about groups comprised of individual Split Selves, Exiters, and unmarried third parties also applies to groups for Sexual Addicts.

The Individual's Readiness for Group

To be ready for group, individuals need to have some understanding of their own issues, and the ability to tolerate a group situation with the attendant pressures for self-disclosure. Group is particularly useful for those who need to learn to stand their own ground, to learn how to share themselves, and to get honest feedback from others, and for those with a history of feeling like an outsider or of sabotaging relationships.

The time to begin group is not during the throes of a crisis, but on the downhill side of it. Individuals who are fearful of a group situation need a longer time to prepare than those who are comfortable in groups. Exploring the potential benefits, including the possibility of resolving the fear of groups, is useful. Group also can be presented as the "advanced course."

Group replaces individual therapy as the primary treatment format for many group members. Individual therapy can be used as an adjunct to group in times of crisis, when the individual is stuck, or when the individual is moving very rapidly. When important personal issues or issues pertaining to the group come up in individual sessions, they need to be fed back to the group. This is particularly true of attractions between group members. The therapist can flag these issues and assist the individual in bringing them to the group.

Group Selection

Including different personality types provides constructive tension in a group. It is widely agreed (Berne, 1966; Yalom, 1975) that heterogeneity is necessary in a group if change is to occur, but too much heterogeneity can impede the work of the group. Yalom recommends selecting group members based on their heterogeneity for conflict areas, and homogeneity for ego strength.

In selecting individual members for this type of group include straying partners, betrayed spouses, and unmarried third parties who have been involved in Split Self or Exit Affairs. Ideally, the straying partners will be both male and female, as will the spouses. Individuals who experienced an affair while unmarried but in a committed relationship also might be considered for the group. Participants should be within a similar age range, but the older the age of the members the broader the age span can be. For example, members of a group ranging in age from 38 to 62 years functioned as peers most of the time, but occasionally found the age differences within the group helpful in addressing generational issues.

Group Structure and Rules

These therapy groups are open groups, with new members joining as old members leave. The group is limited to a maximum of eight members. The average stay in the group is about three years, although the range for those who complete the work they came to do is from two to five years. Most groups follow the classic therapy design and meet weekly for an hour and a half. The group can be led by a single therapist, by male and female co-therapists, or by same-sex co-therapists.

Groups are a place for people to try out new behaviors, test boundaries, share themselves, and otherwise learn to take responsibility for themselves. When affairs have been part of the behavior pattern for individuals in the group, attention to boundary issues is especially important.

It is essential to monitor adherence to the group rules, particularly the prohibition on contact with each other outside the group sessions. Group members will test the rule, sometimes deliberately and other times not. When even a hint of outside contact between group members drifts by, such as a comment about a parking lot conversation, insist that the conversation be discussed in group. Facilitate a group discussion of the rule and the reasons for it. Generally group members want the protection offered by the prohibition on socializing and will strongly support it. If adherence to this rule is shaky, group members will increase their socializing in order to determine where the limits are, and will decrease their participation in group, eventually leaving group because it is not meeting their needs.

The ban on socializing is not just to protect against affairs, (a very real possibility in this type of group) but also to make the group as risk free for its members as possible and to protect against collusion, coalitions, and avoidance. Group members need to be able to talk openly about their attractions and frustrations with each other, which is facilitated by knowing that they will not have to act on these feelings. It is hard enough for members to risk expressing themselves honestly and fully; with real life consequences it would be impossible. Group is an opportunity for members to live out their issues in a controlled environment with opportunities for new responses. Out of group socializing draws on old behavior patterns.

Group Process

Group process is of prime importance. The group, serving as a surrogate family, can provide a nurturing and healing experience. Feedback, support, confrontation, and interpretation are among the techniques used to help participants explore the meanings and feelings attached to their behavior, while at the same time providing a corrective experience.

Exploring issues related to affairs is facilitated by the group members' understanding of the affairs in their lives. One of the difficult issues for clients relates to dishonesty within the marriage (including the affair), the subject of this group discussion:

Bernie: *I knew I was having an affair and that's not what you're supposed to do. I didn't want to be bad, so I lied about it.*

Margaret: (whose husband had an Exit Affair) *I knew the marriage was bad, but I didn't know what to do. I was scared to say anything—I didn't know what to say—I couldn't handle it.*

Eileen: *I didn't want to know—I was sure if I said the wrong thing he was going to leave—and he did.*

Jack: (recently separated) *I'm really pissed at you guys! My wife went out and screwed around on me, and then she lied, and I'm left holding the bag—and all you can say to Bernie is you didn't want to know! Well I did!* (Honesty with himself and with the group is an issue for Jack.)

Bernie: *I still feel guilty about lying.*

Therapist: (to the group) *It sounds like it was easer to lie than to talk about the problems in your marriage.*

Eileen: *If you don't talk about it maybe it'll go away. If you talk about it, it's real.*

Carrie: *If you talk about what's not right, you're complaining. Nobody likes you then. I felt like a nag. Yeah, for a long time I thought he had the affair because I was such a nag. It took me ages to realize that* he *wasn't straight with me.*

Jack: *Well my marriage was ok, until that deceiving bastard came along and sweet talked her into going off with him.*

Margaret: *Once I knew Al was having an affair, I was furious. I blamed him for everything, for ruining our marriage, for being a shit, for hurting me like this, for never paying attention to me. He didn't deserve to be alive after hurting me so much. . . . But looking back, honestly, the marriage was awful by then. And I didn't know what to do about it* (sadly)—*so I just pretended that everything was okay.*

Therapist: *So you're suggesting that Al actually did you a favor?*

Margaret: *I hate to admit it, but yeah.*

Carrie: *Jack, tell us the truth—were you happy? What was going on in your marriage?*

Jack: *Well . . . things weren't great.*

> Honesty with himself was necessary for Jack to be a functioning member of the group. The other group members understood that and worked with him to that end. By sharing their own experiences the group indicated to Jack that it was safe to own up to how his marriage really was. They pushed him, gently, to drop his angry defense and let them in on his pain. At this point Jack began to admit to problems in his marriage and to own some of the responsibility for what happened. The group supported him and encouraged him to stay with his pain, offering the hope that he too would be able to move beyond his pain in the not too distant future.

Group Themes

Usually one or two themes dominate each group therapy session. Themes are multi-layered, relating to the issues discussed (which are current but also have ties to patterns in the family of origin) and the process of the group. Examples are membership in the family, power and control, shame and vulnerability, betrayal, opportunities lost, and love and acceptance.

Themes normally recur periodically. A group that is working well will reach some level of closure on a theme and move on to the next theme, coming back in subsequent sessions to the same theme to do additional work. The group that is stuck does not reach any closure and goes round and round with the same issues in the same ways. Each group has its own ways of avoiding work, such as engaging in rescue behavior, or reciting the latest developments in boring detail. The therapist's recognition and confrontation of these dodges are important for an effective group process.

Good group notes (distinct from notes in individual case records) are helpful in understanding the development and flow of the group, and in diagnosing the problem when the group is stuck. Notes that include the themes for the session, the patterns of interaction, and a phrase or so about each participant are sufficient.

Group Case Study

The discussion that follows occurred in a group comprised of straying partners, spouses, and unmarried third parties, age 40 to 60. In this session they are struggling with an issue that lies at the heart of an affair: the desire for intimacy. As this discussion begins, Betty (Split Self spouse, see Chapter 8) is seated next to George (Split Self straying partner, see Chapter 8) and is turned toward him. Her body language suggests she is allying herself with him. Beth (unmarried third party) is sitting across from George. (Some group members' comments have been edited out in the interest of brevity and focus.)

Beth: *I am— I'm going to pieces! George is getting on my nerves tonight! And I have no idea why! I wish he'd shut up, and I don't know why. George is my favorite person and he's driving me crazy. He just goes on and on.*

Therapist: *Say more about how that feels.*

Beth: *It feels terrible! I'm ready to explode! I'm not kidding you! I mean—*

Therapist: *Go ahead and explode!*

Beth: *This is it, folks. I mean, I'm really, it's grating on me tonight and I don't know why.*

Alice: (Exit Affair spouse) *Have you talked to him about it?*

Beth: *Yes! It's just, I'm just churned up inside. Like you wouldn't believe! I want to get out of this room! And I have no idea why!* (giggle—looks at George) *Because if you say one more word . . .* (giggle) *He's just getting on my nerves!*

Group: *Nervous laughter.*

George: *You can count on that!*

Beth: (pause) *I don't know if it's because I don't want to hear what you have to say, I don't know what it is! I just don't even want to be close to you tonight. And I'm—and you're one of my favorite persons.*

George: *Well I could tell you why I have so much of it to say. If that would be of interest to you?*

Beth: *No.*

George: *Well, I'm going to tell you anyway.*

Group: *Laughter.*

Beth: *Don't do it; I don't want to hear it.*

(Great, she is serious about pursuing this!)

George: *But it scares me . . .*

Beth: *See, there you go.*

George: *No, it does, it scares me. I, I mean, I get really terrified.*

Eddie: *Of? Of?* (Eddie shifts his focus to George. I wonder if he is protecting George or is uncomfortable with the coming conflict. Other group members are silent but attentive, giving Beth the space to pursue her issue with George. Betty continues to be attentive to George.)

George: *Well, you know, I feel like you go down this road and you've got to go through these various things; you've got to get that business undone. You just can't live without doing it. I don't . . .* (George tends to be a talker. Will Beth stay with her issue or let George take over?)

Beth: *I tell you, when I was on the way over here from the Metro station, the one thing in my mind is "I wanted to get a hug from George." I really wanted to get close to George. And I don't know if that has anything to do with it, you know, because I'm not getting—I'm running. Just about as fast as I can. I can't breathe, even.* (This is a big risk for Beth—she has never talked before about feeling close to any of the men in the group. Her father, her previous husbands, and the men in her life demanded her attention but were not emotionally responsive to her. Beth needs a genuine response from George. I also want to make sure that this discussion is completed and not derailed.)

George: *I am so happy to hear you say that.*

Beth: *That I can't breathe?*

Group: *Laughter* (reduces tension)

George: *That just simply makes me feel so wonderful.*

Beth: *Well, I really missed you. And—and I don't know why I'm running from that, but I am. And I—I don't know.* (very quiet, serious)

Therapist: *Scared to realize you really care about him?*

Beth: *I don't know if that's involved in it or not. I'm not ready to admit it.*

Therapist: *You've been admitting it for the last few minutes.*

Beth: *Yeah. . . then why did you ask me?*

Therapist: *He's one of your favorite people . . .*

Beth: *Because you just wanted me to say it, that's all!* (laughing) *In a more direct manner!*

George: *Oh, I love it!*

Beth: *I hate this sometimes. No, I don't know. But why did I, why did I decide to run? That's what bothers me. I mean, I just—I couldn't ask George for that hug.*

Therapist: (I realize I am getting into a one-on-one with Beth. I believe that the nature of the issue combined with Beth's vulnerability mean that resolving this issue in this session is critical. I decide to stay with Beth for the moment rather than focus on getting more input from the group.) *Was there anything about where he is tonight that especially put you off, or was it where you were tonight?*

Beth: *I don't know. I think it had to do more with me; however, what he was saying was getting too close to me as well. That was really setting me off. Because I was getting closer to him, and I didn't want to. I mean, that scares me. All I wanted was a hug.* (nervous laugh)

Therapist: *That could be pretty scary.* (pause) *Did you feel like that sometimes with your father?*

Beth: (very low voice) *Yeah.*

Therapist: *Talk some more about that.*

Beth: *I hate to talk about that. It's always felt that any closeness I had with my father was going to cost me, more than I wanted to pay.*

(Betty abruptly switches her attention from George to Beth, turning her body toward Beth and listening to her attentively, nodding her head in agreement.)

Therapist: *Such as?*

Beth: *The isolation, that if I—if I was affectionate, then, I'd be cut off. I know I've told you about that. I felt very cut off from my own siblings, let alone my friends—that I'd have to be—it was a commitment of some sort. I'd have to spend the rest of my time with him.*

Therapist: *That he wanted more than you wanted to give.*

Beth: *Yeah, all I wanted was a hug.* (She is seeing the connection between her pattern with her father and with George.)

Therapist: *And no more.*

Beth: *Yeah. And I couldn't get just a hug.*

Therapist: (Now that she understands her reaction she can work out her issue directly with George and the group. I begin to shift the focus to the here and now.) *So one of the things then about George is you want a hug and no more. Maybe you need to tell him that.*

Beth: *But I have difficulty with this!* (nervous laugh)

Therapist: (She is still not ready to deal with George. Why is that? Is it because she wants more than a hug?) *Well are you sure that you're that clear?*

Beth: *I am that clear. That's all I wanted. In my mind that's all I wanted. I wanted a hug. And then I wanted to step back from that.*

Therapist: *Okay.* (pause)

Beth: *But, when I got here and he was here, I felt I would have to pay more in some emotional way than I really wanted. I thought he might—I don't know—I thought he might overreact to my reaction, thinking that I wanted more out of him than just a hug. Because that's the reaction I've had from him in the past.*

Therapist: *And if he thought you wanted more, and he tried to give you more, you couldn't say no. Without hurting his feelings.* (Now that Beth has exposed her dilemma, it is time for her to talk directly to George. I am going to pull back and see who initiates the exchange.)

Beth: *I didn't get beyond that.*

George: *Well you've done that in the past, though.*

Beth: *What?*

George: *That's interesting! You've become angry. I can think back on times when you would send me a "save me signal" and I would get busy and save you and everybody would get busy and jump all over me for doing it. I mean, I just said that, you know, in a generalized way, but you know what I mean, that, that business of—*

Beth: *I know, I know I've gotten on you for trying to save me, but I—I was not conscious of wanting you to save me.*

George: *Well, you know, it could be my misunderstanding and my misreading, you know.*

Beth: *No, maybe I did, I'm just saying—*

George: *I'm not trying to lay that on you. I'm just saying, I read that, and then having done what I thought you wanted, you got angry. You see, I think that's something I would have trouble with.*

Beth: *What?*

George: *I'm not sure. Well, you say something, and I'm okay with what you want. I think a part of me would get busy and say I really want to be right for Beth. I want to be right where she wants me to be. And I wouldn't know necessarily where that was. And I can easily stumble on that.*

Beth: *I know. But I don't need you to save me. All I wanted was a hug.*

Betty: *When you were talking about your father I wanted to jump in, but I didn't want to interrupt you.*

Beth: *Go ahead.*

Betty: *I could really identify with what you were saying. My father—he tried to make me—make with me something he didn't have with Mother.*

Therapist: *Gave you too much?* (pause)

Betty: *And I ate it up!*

Therapist: *No wonder Mother didn't want you to be feminine!*

Betty: *Shhheew! That's absolutely right!*

Beth: *My mother actually would—the way she controlled me: "Your father won't like it," and God help me, I wouldn't do anything that displeased my father, so I cut myself off from the things I wanted to do in order to please my father. I mean, it was a very conscious thing at that age.*

The emerging theme is "I want to feel close to you, without having to take responsibility for you." Closeness in the past has been entangled with rescuing: save Father (Beth and Betty), save Mother (George), save Wife (George), save Beth (George and Betty), save me (everyone). Affairs were an attempt to gain intimacy without paying too high a price, but they exacted a different price. Beth, George, Betty, and the other group members continued for the rest of the session to grapple with their feelings for each other, their fears of becoming too close, and the ways in which they tend to rescue others and sabotage themselves.

Beth's difficulty in asking for a hug illustrates how important it is to ensure that the group remains a safe place. A major component of safety is the prohibition on out of group contact. Group therapy is an excellent way of getting these dynamics into the open. It provides a safe setting to expose and work on uncomfortable feelings and issues.

Issues of Ending

Just as in the family, group members grow up and are ready to leave "home." Leaving group, or graduating, is an important experience. Most group members have little positive experience with endings. Affairs clouded the end of their marriages, resulting in sudden death or a lingering final illness. Prior experiences with endings tend to be similar: either no real ending or an abrupt cut-off.

Planned endings offer an opportunity to demonstrate and participate in a healthy ending and to learn how it feels. Planned endings are discussed ahead of time. Group rules commonly require a month's notice when someone plans to leave.

> When Beth announced she would be leaving group, she talked about the issues she had resolved. No longer having the urge to flee from intimacy, she had developed several close friendships. She was handling issues as they arose, and had come to terms with her parents' limitations. "This has been the best year I've ever had, and it's been the most painful one. Growing up is a bitch!" The other group members confirmed Beth's assessment of herself, and joined with her in reviewing the work she had done and the mountains she had climbed.

When the end is at hand, closing rituals can heighten feelings of closeness. Group members are often surprised to find that hope and encouragement outweigh sadness in healthy endings. In subsequent sessions, group members need to express their feelings about the person's absence and the continuing emotional connection with the person who has graduated.

Unplanned endings, or those that are premature, arouse the anxiety of others in the group. Common concerns that need to be surfaced and discussed are "If I leave, will anybody care?" "Will they even notice?" "I can't deal with this either." "Maybe nothing will help anyway." While a mature therapy group may be able to take responsibility for confronting and discussing the urge to flee, other groups need the therapist to help them address the feelings and the issues involved. Time and attention need to be devoted to each ending, and any group efforts to deny or avoid the feelings of loss need to be met with a quiet insistence on sharing the feelings of the experience.

☐ Special Focus Groups

Groups work best when the participants are functioning at similar levels. Diversity of perspectives enriches the process, but a commonality of interests and purpose also is necessary. When commonality is the prime consideration, a single focus group may be best. Split Selves and Sexual Addicts for example, may not have sufficient commonality to make good use of the same group.

Groups for Sexual Addicts

Many cities have twelve-step groups specifically tailored to the issues of sexual addiction such as Sexaholics Anonymous for the addict and

COSA (Co-Dependents of Sexual Addiction) for those involved with the addict. These are similar to therapy groups in the honesty that is expected and the emotional support that is offered. Feedback to the other participants may not be permitted however. These groups also differ from standard therapy groups in that twelve-step groups are self-help groups, members are encouraged to call each other at any time to get support, the focus of the group is on working each of the twelve-steps, and the persons attending may vary from session to session. Addicts are counseled to attend meetings and to go through each of the twelve-steps, which are adapted from the twelve steps of Alcoholics Anonymous. When a twelve-step group focusing on Sexual Addiction is not available, some addicts have found ACOA (Adult Children of Alcoholics) groups a useful substitute.

The first step in recovery for many Sexual Addicts and their spouses is attending a twelve-step group. Even when the group is focused on alcohol or on addictions other than sexual addiction, the similarity of the addictive process and the struggle to interrupt the cycle strikes a chord. The Addict begins to realize that he or she is not alone and that help is available. Typically, after the awakening provided by involvement in a twelve-step program, the Addict seeks individual therapy to address the underlying issues.

Other Special Focus Groups

Groups focusing on a particular population or issue also can be helpful. These are usually directed to individuals rather than couples, and may be brief therapy, psychoeducational, or self-help groups. Generally, affair-related special focus groups are time limited, meeting for a defined number of sessions.

Brief therapy groups are best used for a specific and limited purpose. For example, straying partners in Split Self Affairs often see their situation as unique, rarely knowing that others are in a similar situation. If you have several of them among your clients, consider bringing them together for three or four sessions for the purpose of sharing their experience and learning from each other. The ground rules need to include confidentiality and no contact with each other outside the group. Depending on your clients, this could be an all male group or a mixed gender group.

Groups also exist solely for the other woman who is involved in a long, serious affair with a Split Self. Although the brief therapy group can be very helpful as a strategic intervention, the primary treatment format for the Split Selves and the unmarried third parties needs to be ongoing individual or group therapy. Preferably the ongoing therapy group is for individuals, includes both genders, and reflects all three sides of the affair triangle.

I would suggest *not* putting together a group of betrayed spouses because they tend to elicit and reinforce each other's obsession. They too will do better in an ongoing therapy group for individuals that incorporates the other poles of the affair triangle, as described earlier in this chapter.

Psychoeducational groups offered by mental health professionals can be quite helpful in providing a framework for thinking about affairs, offering opportunities to talk about one's own experience, and hearing how others are coping with similar circumstances. However, our society's negative attitudes toward affairs make some people reluctant to show up in such a setting. Typically, little advance screening is done so there is the chance that an undisclosed affair could surface if both spouses show up. To prevent against this, consider offering separate groups for males and females. Typically such a group meets weekly from 3 to 6 times, for 1½ or 2 hours. Here too, an agreement to maintain confidentiality is important.

Self-help groups span a broad range of issues. Some are for couples who have survived an affair. Others are for individuals whose spouse "cheated" (the same caveat about reinforcing obsession applies here). At least one group has been developed for female third parties whose affair partner had died. Bulletin boards on some affair-related Internet sites serve as another type of self-help group. These boards offer opportunities to share one's own experience and to learn from others. Since face-to-face contact is not a factor, the vulnerability of exposing one's self is lessened. On the other hand, contacts made on these boards sometimes develop into affairs. Nonetheless, Internet bulletin boards have become an important part of self-help opportunities available to those who are part of an affair triangle. Good boards on affairs include www.affairs-help.com (my site) and www.dearpeggy.com the site of Peggy Vaughan, author of *The Monogamy Myth* (1998).

☐ Factors in Effective Group Therapy

Group therapy is exciting in its possibilities for change. To make the most of the group's potential, the therapist constantly needs to be aware of the group process and to surface issues that the group is reluctant to address. To be effective the therapist needs to:

- Facilitate the sharing of feelings between group members,
- Identify and help the group address attractions and betrayals within the group,
- Highlight key issues,
- Be tough enough—make sure no one slides without addressing it,
- Understand the meaning of different types of affairs, and
- Monitor and enforce group rules.

New members in a group provide old members with a measure of how far they have come. The latter remark "You are where I was a year ago," and offer encouragement. For the new members, seeing others who are resolving issues similar to their own, provides a sense of hope.

The universality of the issues in a group is so powerful that nothing else can compete. We all have to deal with the same issues: being accepted, going after what we want, coping when we do not get what we want, experiencing hurt, and trying to be understood. Group clarifies that these are universal issues, not one person's burden.

CHAPTER

Trust, Forgiveness, and Closure

Forgiveness is the last phase in dealing with an affair. Forgiving each other comes after confronting and resolving the painful issues that were avoided earlier. With forgiveness comes closure on the affair. True forgiveness opens the door to a new and more intimate partnership. Couples often devise a celebration or a very personal ritual to mark this transition.

Forgiveness is also possible for couples who decide to end their marriage, and it helps in finalizing the emotional divorce. Although forgiveness comes more easily to couples who have worked out the issues in their marriage, it is equally important for couples who divorce.

What is forgiveness anyway? It is not about undoing what happened. Reality is that what has happened, has happened—there has been an affair. It is not about forgetting what has happened. An affair will never be forgotten—and shouldn't be. It is not about going back to the way things were. Even if it could happen, most couples don't want that. Forgiveness is about taking the affair off center stage and putting it in its proper place when the time comes to do so. And the timing is different for each couple.

Smedes, in *The Art of Forgiving* (1996), identifies three stages of forgiving. First is rediscovering the humanity of the person who hurt us. This is an important aspect of the early rebuilding period after an affair. Next is surrendering our right to get even. This comes at the end of the rebuilding period. Last is revising our feelings toward the person we forgive. This too develops during the rebuilding period.

Therapists generally agree that genuine forgiveness is a good thing. Differences surface regarding what's the right time for forgiveness. Some therapists believe that an apology, no matter what its timing, is sufficiently humbling that it should be accepted or at least considered seriously by the spouse. The problem with early apologies is that most straying partners are too quick to apologize. They say they are sorry even before they tell their spouse what it is they are sorry about. They apologize while their spouse is still numb with disbelief or in the early stages of obsession and has not gotten to the underlying emotions. They apologize at every turn.

Some therapists regard an apology as necessary before the work of rebuilding can begin. Even when the straying partner is genuinely sorry, and many are, they do not yet understand how they helped set the stage for the affair and they have not yet fully listened to their spouse's pain. They are more concerned with avoiding the feared consequences of their behavior than with understanding what has happened and coming to terms with it. Hearing the spouse's pain is a necessary and major part of moving toward forgiveness.

My experience indicates that moving through the process of rebuilding is necessary before couples can truly understand the concept of forgiveness. Apologies and forgiveness on the heels of disclosure block the possibilities for growth, rebuilding, and meaningful forgiveness.

☐ Forgiveness for Couples Who Stay Together

Forgiveness is a two-way—or maybe four-way—street. It includes forgiving each other and one's self. Forgiveness is possible when the hidden issues have been resolved and the marriage rebuilt. When the time is right and the message is real, forgiving each other gives new life to the marriage.

Readiness for Forgiveness

Couples are ready to forgive when they complete the tasks of the rebuilding phase. This means that they have developed a new pattern of open, honest, and complete communication, and thereby regained each other's trust. In fact, trust between them is usually greater than before the affair. The obsession with the affair is long over, and neither one feels an urgent need to talk about the affair any more, although they may refer to it occasionally. Their expectations of each other and for their marriage are more realistic. Any other secrets have been shared and dealt with. Both spouses know how the affair related to their individual and relationship issues, and to patterns in their families of origin. They accept the fact that life holds losses and mistakes. And they know their danger points—those situations in which they are most likely to ignore reality, in hopes of avoiding pain or gaining comfort.

They have courted each other anew. The old marriage no longer exists (they wouldn't go back to it if it did exist). This is probably the first time in their lives they have allowed themselves to know and be known by another person. The intimacy is exciting and rewarding, and the scary aspects of it are tolerable, especially when the spouses share their fears. They are enjoying the fruits of the hard and painful work they have done since the affair was revealed. Occasional setbacks occur but are dealt with in more productive ways. Together they are able to get themselves back on track.

This is the time for the therapist to ask about the affair to determine whether there are any loose ends. After all the earlier work to eliminate the obsession, it may seem ironic that you are now encouraging them to talk about the affair. However it is an essential step in putting the affair in perspective. Occasionally you will find a piece of unfinished business. If so, help them finish it before moving to forgiveness.

> Val had made a list of questions about Peter's affair that I would not let her ask early in treatment. Most of these questions had been answered in the course of therapy, but one remained: Was the other woman also controlling? Peter responded, "Back then I would have said no. With what I know now, yeah—she was. She certainly had ideas about what she wanted with me, but I was so caught up in myself I couldn't see it. I was really upset with you, and feeling real guilty about being upset. She offered me an escape, and I took it. I know too much now—I couldn't ever kid myself like that again. (teasingly) But you'll never have such power over me again." Val countered with a laugh: "Power like that, I don't want!"

When they are ready to forgive, the typical response to an inquiry about the affair is, "We've dealt with that pretty well," or "I think that's finished." Sue (see Chapter 5) commented, "This has been tremendously painful, but we've really come through it together. If we'd stayed on the track we were on, we would have split up, or I'd be in the loony bin. Bob added, "My affair really made us look at things we hadn't wanted to face."

In preparation for forgiveness ask each of them to identify how they might sabotage the work they have done. Once identified, neither spouse can engage in sabotage without being aware of it.

> Val indicated that sabotage for her would be ignoring her own pain and instead criticizing Peter's behavior. For Peter, sabotage would mean not sharing his feelings and letting Val be the "bad guy."

When you believe the spouses are ready to ask for forgiveness, review their progress with them. Encourage each of them to talk about the changes they have made, the problems that they have resolved, and the work that they are continuing to do. If the couple runs into any snags in reviewing their issues and their progress, they are not quite ready for forgiveness. Shift then to the issues that have been surfaced. When these issues are resolved, again review with them their progress, preparatory to moving to forgiveness.

Sometimes couples decide they're ready before that is the case. Couples who are afraid of the work ahead often claim they're ready to forgive long before that is possible. With others, in the process of reviewing their progress, your gut may say they are not ready. Trust your gut. Help them understand why you believe they are not ready and what they need to work on to be ready. Forgiveness is too important to allow a cheap imitation.

Resolving Unfinished Business Before Forgiveness

Occasionally the idea of forgiving surfaces issues of power and control that haven't yet been fully explored.

> Sherry was ready to talk about forgiving Ian, but not ready to forgive him. With the affair, the balance of power in their relationship had shifted. Sherry had leverage for the first time and she knew forgiving Ian meant giving up the leverage that came from the affair. She was enjoying her new sense of power and wanted to keep it. She took a long time to decide she was ready to forgive Ian and during that time she introduced some additional changes in their relationship to make sure she never went back to her old pattern of just going along.

Forgiveness

When the couple has completed the tasks identified above, and no loose ends are identified in the review, the next step is forgiveness. Just as the events that led to the affair were framed as marital problems, the request for forgiveness goes in both directions. It involves each of them owning their own responsibility for having let their marriage deteriorate to the point of crisis.

When the couple is ready, a discussion of the meaning of forgiveness is useful as a transition into this final phase of work. The idea of forgiving one's self needs to be part of this discussion. Forgiving one's self is part of accepting forgiveness from the other. In order to ask for forgiveness, or to accept it, forgiveness of one's self usually needs to come first. For a few people however, forgiving themselves is the last step. In either case, forgiveness is not complete without forgiveness of self.

Structuring the situation can be done by suggesting that they seem ready to forgive each other. A positive response from each means you can move ahead. Invite each of them to formulate a request for forgiveness. They should be able to do this fairly easily. Usually the straying partner requests forgiveness for the affair, and the pain it has caused. The spouse's request has to do with that person's contributions to setting the stage for an affair (back to the shared definition of the problem once more).

Roger and Kathy began marital therapy eighteen months ago. The presenting problem was Roger's affair, which was the Conflict Avoidant type. We are reviewing their progress:

Kathy: *It's much nicer now with us.*

Roger: *It really is.*

Therapist: *You've done a lot of good work with each other.*

Roger: *If you hadn't asked those questions about where my head was—it certainly wasn't in the marriage!*

Kathy: *It really did help us to have someone else kind of showing us the way.*

Therapist: *Let's do some reviewing about where you are now and the kinds of things you've accomplished.*

Kathy: *I think the most exciting thing for me is that there's a warmth that's different. It feels good!*

Therapist: *I can feel the difference!*

Roger: *It feels as if there is a life beyond getting married and having kids.*

Therapist: *And you didn't used to believe that.*

Roger: *No. That's right.*

Kathy: *For me it's much more exciting because, I don't know, I really like to dance and I like music and, I'm finding out I like to make love. That's really been important for me because it was as if I was dead. Something was dead.*

Roger: *I know—for me too. I still don't like to dance, though. But, I manage.*

Kathy: *You'll suffer through it. (grins)*

Roger: *I want to do it for you; it's not suffering.*

Therapist: *One of the things that I've noticed recently is how much different your communication is.*

Kathy: *Well, I consciously try to do what we talked about, and that is to tell him what I want, or what I feel, or what I'm thinking. And I find that it makes a difference because he really does listen to me now. That really makes a difference.*

Therapist: *So Kathy, you say more, and Roger, you really listen to her. Is that also true when you fight? Let's look at how you're keeping your fights on track. First of all, how are you allowing yourself to get to the fights, because you never used to fight?*

Roger: *Well, I was afraid. I thought that if you fought, it meant that you weren't committed, that something was going wrong. I was really afraid of it. But now, it really clears the air. I still don't think we scream and yell; it's not my way of doing it, but we do have disagreements, and it's okay that we don't agree. It's really okay.*

Therapist: *That's something new too.*

Roger: *Well, for example, Kathy wanted to buy this awful, awful chair. And she went ahead and did it. And I have said I am not going to sit in it. But she did it. And we survived. And we argue about—*

Kathy: *And it looks wonderful! It looks just wonderful!*

Roger: *It looks awful! It looks awful!*

Kathy: *I love it!*

Roger: *But it's okay. I guess what concerns me is that it's a chair. What happens in a real serious fight? Maybe this is practice.*

Therapist: *This is practice for the big stuff—and the more you deal with the little stuff, the less big stuff there is.*

Roger: *I guess we were so organized before, we never argued about who paid the bills because Kathy always paid the bills. Now Kathy thinks that I should pay some of the bills, so we argue about the little things, too, but—*

Kathy: *And I think it's important because I used to feel that I had to worry about the money alone all the time. And then I would sort of nag you about the little things. This way, I think you're more aware of what things cost and where the money is going, so I don't even feel like nagging you anymore.*

Therapist: *It seems to me that as long as you're talking about what you're experiencing, and you're talking about your differences, that you're doing the work that's most important for the two of you.*

Kathy: *Well, we've been thinking a lot about differences. We never used to argue about where the kids would go to summer camp. Last week we had a pretty good heated argument about whether they would or whether they wouldn't,* *and if they did, where would they go. I don't think that would have happened before.*

Roger: *No. We just always sent them to the same place.*

Kathy: *And resented it, or—*

Roger: *Well, it's almost scary, because you can argue about anything.*

Therapist: *I get the idea that you are almost enjoying your new ability to argue.*

Roger: *I'm having fun. I hope Kathy is!*

Kathy: *Well, the whole thing I said, about dancing—it's as though the arguments are a new dance. I mean, there's the ability to argue as a new dance. Everything isn't so held down. We don't have to keep everything in, so there isn't that feeling of being so tight. I don't know what's going to happen. Sometimes I get a little nervous. Because it's scary. But it's much better. It's more open. And it flows better. I feel better. I can get excited when he's coming home. I don't just resent that he's expecting dinner, and he doesn't always expect dinner the same way any more. Now we talk about going out once in a while, and, you know, I don't feel like he's going to have a fit if he comes home and there's not dinner. I can go and buy chicken at the Deli and he's not going to get angry. I can just do whatever I want.*

Roger: *That's true. And it feels better to me too. I don't try to figure out ahead of time whether Kathy will disapprove, and she tells me a lot more so I don't have to guess. I can relax more. Sometimes I think it has to do with the children, too. As they're getting older they seem to require less, and it gives us more of a chance to make decisions that have to do with us. It feels something like what it was like that first week when we were married.*

Kathy: *It's a little nicer because I think I was kind of scared that first week.* (pause—they exchange loving glances)

Therapist: *I think you talk to each other about a lot more now than you ever could have then, partly because you're older and you have some life experience, but mostly because of the work you've done in these last months. You have learned how to be husband and wife with each other. I wonder if this isn't the time we need to finish talking about the affair, and see if there are any leftovers there.*

Roger: *You know, when you said that, my stomach just tightened up. I don't know what happened to you Kathy, but—*

Kathy: *Well I did give a big sigh, like "oh, here we go again."*

Therapist: *Well is there anything here to talk about at this point?*

Kathy: *I don't feel so hurt. I'm not sure I'll ever forget, you know, but the way I live now is a little different in the sense that I try and enjoy more of what I'm experiencing instead of remembering history and being angry about* *this, that, and the other thing. I really try to enjoy the moments and when I see myself start thinking about it or if something triggers it for me, I sort of say, "Well that was before," or "That's not part of us now." I don't want to be there anymore. I don't want to hurt. It just was too painful. I do believe Roger loves me, that he cares about me, and that's what I want to believe and that's what I want to enjoy. So it's very different for me now. And Roger, I hope you don't stop all the nice little things you're doing now. It feels very good.*

Roger: *It feels good to me too.* (pause) *I am still shocked that I could be so blind as to get involved in the affair. In some ways I may be avoiding thinking about it now.*

Therapist: *Or maybe it's over.*

Roger: *Well it is over. I just don't—I'm the sort of person, I don't rehash, intellectualize everything, think about it. It is over, and it was over when I told Kathy it was over. It's left a mark on me though. I've seen what happens when you don't work on your own life and you try to bring someone in to make things better. I think that's what I was doing.*

Therapist: *It was a red flag that said "We've got a big problem."*

Roger: *I thought it was the answer and I just sort of shut Kathy and the children out, and that bothers me. I still don't like to think that it is something I could do. But I did it. I've learned a lot, but I don't ever plan to learn this way again. And now I've got some better ways to work things out. That's where I am with it.*

Therapist: *Maybe it's time for the two of you to ask for forgiveness from each other.*

Roger: *Well, there's nothing that would make me happier, really.*

Therapist: *How do you want to ask her?*

Roger: *Will you forgive me Kathy?*

Kathy: *I . . . Yes, I will forgive you. I have forgiven you.*

Roger: *Thank you.*

Therapist: *And Kathy?*

Kathy: *I have to ask you to forgive me for keeping myself a secret for so long, for not letting you know who I was or what I want.*

Roger: *Well, I have the easier job. I do forgive you.*

Kathy: *I love you very much.*

Roger: *I love you too.*

By the time of this session Roger and Kathy knew what their issues were and understood their reciprocal roles in setting the stage for an affair. Kathy's request for forgiveness was specific to her contribution to the marital problems: keeping herself a secret and not sharing with

Roger who she was. Roger referred to his use of the affair to avoid working on the marriage. How hard they had worked to achieve this kind of mutuality was reflected in the ease with which their language flowed, as well as in the intensity of their feelings.

This session was emotionally powerful for the therapist as well as for Roger and Kathy. The tenderness, the love, and the honesty were intense, and each of us was moved to tears.

Rituals and Celebrations

Rituals can be important as part of forgiveness. Most couples spontaneously come up with the idea of a ritual or a celebration. Couples with little history of family celebrations, however, can benefit from your suggestion that they might want to celebrate their renewed relationship in some way. Talk with them about the kind of celebration they want, its symbolic meanings, and whether it will be private or shared with others.

Rituals and celebrations tend to symbolize either the ending of this painful period in the marriage, or a new beginning, or both. One type of ending ritual is burial of an item symbolizing the affair. Peter and Val (see Chapter 5) together wrapped up her notes describing her pain and anger over his affair, and buried them. They spent the rest of the day at home with each other (without the kids), and then went to their favorite restaurant for dinner. A month later they went away for a long weekend by themselves, which they referred to as their second honeymoon.

Rituals symbolizing a new beginning often take the form of a second wedding ceremony or a renewal of the marital vows. Sometimes the children are involved in the celebration, sometimes not. Often the couple chooses to renew their vows in private without any official ceremony. Any sort of ritual is fine as long as it holds meaning for both spouses.

Roger and Kathy shifted their focus from forgiveness to celebrating:

Kathy: *Let's talk about a celebration!*

Roger: *That's a neat idea! That really is!* (pause) *Maybe I should ask you to marry me.*

Kathy: (playfully) *Yeah, then I can think about it.*

Roger: *The only thing that I want to be different is—remember that jerk you were going out with when I asked you out for the first date?*

Kathy: *You mean Freddie?*

Roger: *Yes, I don't want there to be a Freddie this time.*

Kathy: *No there's no Freddie.* (playfully) *There's just this old husband of mine.*

Roger: *Well maybe we can ditch him.*

Kathy: *OK, sounds good to me.*

Roger: *So will you marry me?*

Kathy: *Yes, I'll marry you. Yeah, that would be fun. I love to have celebrations. Let's have a real ceremony.*

Roger: *Sure, why not? We'll get married all over again.*

Kathy: *You know the Audubon Society? I'd love to get married outside.*

Roger: *Why don't we do that, okay? What about June?*

Kathy: *OK, I'll be the June bride.*

Roger: *Is that corny?*

Kathy: *It sounds good to me.*

Roger: *And the kids will be in the wedding.*

Kathy: *That's right.*

Roger: *How about your family?*

Kathy: *You mean how they will react to it?*

Roger: *Are you going to invite all of them?*

Kathy: *What do you mean all of them? Yes! I love it when they all come.*

Roger: (teasing) *Remember what happened when we got married, how rowdy they were?* (teasing)

Kathy: *Yeah, well? That's part of my family.*

Roger: *I guess.*

Kathy: *If they can accept us getting married again we can accept them.*

Roger: *That may be a problem.* (giggles)

Kathy: *What?*

Roger: *Them accepting our getting married again.*

Kathy: *You think they're going to think it's funny?*

Roger: *Funny?* (with a grin) *They may not approve.*

Kathy: *They don't know what happened. I didn't tell anybody anything.*

Roger: (with tears in his eyes) *Okay, it's set.*

Kathy: (with tears in her eyes) *Great!*

Forgiveness gives some closure to an extremely difficult period and moves the affair from the couple's immediate agenda to their shared history. The affair becomes an event that, like other past events, can be talked about when it's relevant to do so. With forgiveness, one phase of the marriage ends and the door opens to another.

Termination

Termination of therapy is separate from the forgiveness which comes near the end of therapy. It marks a major triumph for the spouses. They are well aware, however, of the need to continue their work. As part of termination, a check-in session can be scheduled three to six months into the future. This provides an opportunity for trouble-shooting, helps allay anxiety about being totally on their own, and establishes a specific point at which they will again review their progress. Most couples are doing well at check-in, needing only minor tuning up, if that.

Some couples do not make it to closure. They decide along the way that it is time to leave therapy or to end the marriage. Many of them will again seek therapy, as individuals or as couples, to resolve their unfinished business. In assessing their issues, inquire about a lack of closure on past affairs or marriages that ended in divorce. Closure may be possible, although in a somewhat different manner.

☐ Closure for Couples Who Divorce

The need for emotional closure between former spouses is not well understood in our society today and is under-addressed. Institutionalized means for helping divorced couples reach closure are lacking. Couples whose relationship ends search desperately for closure, often without clearly understanding what they're searching for—after all, they are not supposed to need anything from the "ex" any more. With the Exit Affair in particular, couples are not ready for closure at the time of separation. They are preoccupied, and appropriately so, with separation issues, and they have little perspective on their own issues. Nor is closure provided by the legal divorce. For the most part, the final divorce hearing is a brief and empty ritual, with only one spouse present. When the final hearing is significant, it means the spouses are still at war, and the emotional work of letting go has yet to be done.

When couples marry, they bring together two separate stories and begin to develop a shared story. When the marriage begins to disintegrate, the stories start to diverge. Fleshing out the story of how they began to diverge, tying in threads from the two original stories, and accepting the divergence is the work of closure. Ex-spouses need to meet face to face when they're ready, for the purpose of reaching closure with each other in regard to their marriage. This is not a ritual, but a meaningful dialogue between the two of them that clarifies what happened—that brings the two separate accounts of the marriage together, validating the good parts and the painful ones, so that both share a common understanding of the marriage.

As every therapist knows, many divorcing spouses resist letting go of their "ex." They hassle each other, go out of their way to avoid each other, insist the other has victimized them, or if they are really stuck, they litigate. These are all forms of obsession and they all keep the "ex" in a special role, although the spouses passionately deny this. It is possible for any couple to gain closure, but only if they do the necessary work of resolving their own issues first.

Real closure comes much later, usually several years after separation. If closure has not been reached, it is never too late to explore whether the spouses are ready or can move to a state of readiness. Couples whose marriage ended with an Exit Affair are very likely to need help with closure, but many other couples whose marriage has ended also can benefit from help with closure.

Usually it is the need for acknowledgment and closure that underlies continuing harassment, or even litigation. More often the search for closure takes the form of a sense of something unfinished hanging in the background. Couples who look to the final divorce hearing for emotional closure are disappointed, especially when the hearing is five minutes long and the decree arrives in the mail a few weeks later. People are not necessarily ready for closure just because the divorce decree is granted.

Readiness for Closure

Forgiveness is best understood within the context of commitment and mutual betrayal. It is crucial that both spouses be emotionally ready to close with each other. This means that each understands and owns his or her contributions to the marriage, both positive and negative, and that each can openly acknowledge the other's positive contributions.

How do you know if your client is ready for closure, or if your client's ex is ready? Several signs indicate readiness to begin thinking about closure. Feelings toward the former spouse shift from anger to sadness. Rather than muttering about reparations, your client is sad about opportunities lost long ago. Hope grows of reaching some sort of peaceful accommodation with the ex, and consideration is given to talking with the ex. There is a sense of recognition that they were in it together.

Your client may have indications from the ex of a desire to move the relationship to a more comfortable place. Lacking that, your client can initiate a discussion with the ex about the client's need to resolve old issues. It is important that both have moved far enough in the emotional process of divorce to understand their own contribution to the deterioration of the marriage (Brown, 1976). Typically this takes two to four years or more after separation.

Closure comes through understanding and acknowledging how it really was and how it is now, with each owning and sharing their own piece of the story, good and bad. There is great sadness, almost bittersweet, that they are doing now what they wished they could do during the marriage. The sadness also reflects the letting go that comes with closure, a necessary part of the grief process.

Preparation for Closure

As one or the other gains an understanding of what the affair was about, and how it tied in to difficulties in the marriage and to the split, it is possible to arrange a joint session. To begin the process, talk with your client about the possibility of a session with the ex for the purpose of gaining closure. Typically your client will want to think about it, talk with you about it, and then begin to prepare for it. In preparing for closure, your client needs to identify the issues that are still hanging and any questions that remain.

An early step is inviting the ex. The invitation needs to be given by your client, and is framed around the client's need for closure. The ex is not being invited to engage in marital therapy, but to help your client gain closure. It is an opportunity for the ex to gain a sense of closure as well, and the session should be therapeutic for both of them, but the basis for the session is your client's need. Reasons why the ex may agree to participate include assuaging guilt, a bona fide desire to help the former spouse or the children, or to gain closure for one's self. Most former spouses are willing to come in for at least a single session. If the ex declines to participate it may be a matter of not being ready yet. Leave the door open for a closure session at some later date.

These sessions work best when both former spouses are ready for closure, so that together they can review and acknowledge their connected stories. Prior to this session, each needs to identify unfinished business with the other: What needs to be said, what questions need to be asked and answered, what needs discussing, and what is desired from the former partner now. Offer the ex a session or two prior to the joint meeting in which to identify concerns about the meeting, feelings now and in the past about the partner, unfinished issues, and if the ex is willing, his or her needs regarding closure. During this preparation the ex will be assessing whether you are sufficiently sensitive and skilled to make the joint session beneficial.

It is helpful if each spouse is able to acknowledge what was valued in the ex and what was good about the marriage, to admit to failures and transgressions and the reasons for them, and to share feelings as they occur during the session. Closure means making peace with what the marriage really meant and forgiving each other for past hurts and betrayals. It often means forgiving one's self as well. If the ex also has been in therapy, the prognosis for meaningful closure is excellent. Even without therapy, success is likely if both spouses are ready for closure.

Closure

Closure may be attained in a single session or may require several sessions. When the first session is on track but the discussion is unfinished, the ex who has agreed to only one session is usually willing to come back again. The ex-spouses will have a sense about the proper timing of any additional sessions.

The agenda can include one or more of the following:

- Reviewing the purpose and goals for the session.
- Asking and answering questions about feelings and events during the marriage.
- Discussing unresolved issues of ending.
- Identifying and discussing how the marriage got off track.
- Identifying and discussing marital problems that led to the affair.
- Assessing their current relationship with each other.
- Acknowledging the importance of each other and of the marriage.
- Sharing feelings about the demise of the marriage.

Part of the reluctance to close is the desire to cling to one's personal fantasies about life and marriage. This was certainly true for Betty and Jim (see Chapter 8) who had invested years in building the perfect family.

Betty and Jim were ready to talk to each other three years after separating. Jim had seen another therapist for two years, beginning six months before the separation, and Betty had been in therapy (a combination of individual and group) since a few months after the separation. By the time Betty was ready to meet with Jim around issues of closure, she had addressed most of her issues with her mother and had started to remove her father from his pedestal. She had learned to pay attention to her own feelings, rather than ignoring them and performing as she thought was expected of her.

As we moved toward this meeting, Betty identified issues she wanted to discuss with Jim: Had Jim really liked *her* or was it her stability he liked? Was he as turned off sexually to her as she thought, and as she was to him? Had he ever been attracted to her physically? What had enabled him to decide to leave her? She wanted information from him that would help her make sense of her experience in the marriage, that what she experienced had a basis in fact.

After Jim accepted Betty's invitation, I met with him individually to help him prepare for the joint session. Jim's reason for agreeing to meet with Betty was a combination of concern for her and a desire to settle things. He was pessimistic, however, about having a useful discussion with Betty. We discussed his perceptions of the marital problems, and identified unfinished business as he perceived it. At this point I realized that they had identified the same areas of unfinished business, even though their perceptions were different. I asked Jim what he needed from the session. He stated that he needed me to deal with Betty's tears, and that he wanted to know why Betty had been so obsessed with having a son. We scheduled the session when Betty was clear about her questions for Jim and was ready to listen to answers which might be painful.

At the beginning of the joint session, I encouraged Jim to be absolutely honest, telling him that the truth would be most beneficial for Betty and that she could handle it. Betty emphatically agreed. They began by discussing the type of relationship they would like with each other. Jim emphasized his desire for a cordial relationship with Betty. Betty expressed the hope that it be like a casual acquaintance. "After all, we've got two kids that we raised and we spent 32 years together. That's an important piece of my life—that's almost all of my adult life."

They moved next to what had originally drawn them together. Betty indicated that she had always thought he picked her for her stability. Jim agreed, adding that he was ready to get married, and that Betty had seemed to be the "right person." He observed that Betty had picked him because he was fun. Betty replied, "Yes, I hoped that you could pull that from me, but it didn't work. Probably to balance the stability."

Next they got into more difficult terrain, their sexual relationship. Each asked and answered questions carefully, being painfully honest without attacking. Their perceptions of the sexual relationship meshed, both agreeing that the physical attraction was present but not primary, early in their relationship, and that it had not endured for long. Jim described his affair as the turning point. "With Erika I found that sex really could be exciting. I hadn't known that before for sure. Erika was not around long, but that experience helped me make the decision to leave. I knew I had to leave no matter what the people around me felt." Betty admitted, "Only after you left did I realize what a box I'd created for myself. I was always trying to be what I thought you wanted me to be. I'm sick of living a lie." Both admitted their profound disappointment that the marriage had never provided the emotional connection they had wanted.

For Betty, this session underscored her growing recognition that she could not get from Jim what she had wanted from her father—a man who would make her feel feminine. By taking Jim off the hook, she accepted responsibility for working directly on her own femininity. Jim closed the session by saying that it had been much more productive than he expected, and he volunteered to come back again. His offer was accepted and the potential session was "put in the bank" to hold for a time in the future when it might be needed.

Closure was handled in a somewhat different way by Brad and Allison:

Allison had an Exit Affair after three years of marriage to Brad, when they were both 29. Brad was stunned—obsessed with righteous rage one moment and pleading a lack of understanding the next. He tripped over his strong religious beliefs, assessing Allison's morality rather than working on himself. Gradually he began to explore his own issues with trust, control, and intimacy. As his focus changed, he became interested in talking to Allison about why she had left him. When asked if he would like Allison to join him in a therapy session Brad snorted: "Oh she won't come in." I agreed she might not, but on the other hand, she might. Brad's invitation to Allison made clear that the purpose was to help him, not change her. She agreed to come in for one session. Brad discussed with me what he wanted to say to her, and I reminded him of the need to listen as well as talk. When Allison came in she was able to talk about some of the issues, but without much depth. Although Brad was disappointed that she could not share more, he was surprised to find that he was much more in touch with his feelings than she.

Over the course of the next year, Brad developed a serious relationship with Jenny. He still sought closure with Allison however, and six months later he arranged to bump into her. They had a casual conversation in which she indicated she would like to have a talk with him. He prepared for their meeting in therapy, anticipating and clarifying what he wanted to say to her. They arranged to meet over dinner. This time both were ready to talk about their marriage, its pluses and minuses, and how they had gotten off track with each other early in the marriage. Brad ended the evening feeling great. He had achieved what he wanted: a sense of closure. Along with closure, he felt he could be friendly to Allison again—he no longer felt angry or hurt, or held hostage.

No matter how long they have been separated, when there is unfinished business between former spouses, consider arranging a closure session. After reaching closure, former spouses are able to treat each other as well as they would treat any other acquaintance. The bitterness and resentment are gone. They may or may not be friends, but they are able to discuss and resolve parenting issues, share information about family members, and otherwise acknowledge each other as decent human beings. Closure brings a continuing sense of peace.

For some, closure with the former spouse is not possible—the ex is not emotionally available, is unwilling to meet, is physically unable to meet, or is deceased. In such cases, Gestalt or other techniques can be used to help your client gain closure.

☐ The Aftermath

The pain and the ghosts endure when there is no closure. A sense of that is conveyed by Jonathan Coleman, author of *Exit The Rainmaker*, in an interview (Trueheart, 1989). In describing the book's subject, who abruptly walked away from his wife and his life of success, Coleman says, "[Carsey] still gets agitated when [Nancy's] name is brought up. I don't think it ends until he can sit down and write her a note, or better yet speak to her on the phone, or better yet see her face to face. I think it would release both of them" (p. C2).

Forgiveness is not about forgetting. To forget the lessons learned because of the affair would be a great loss. Forgiving means moving the affair from the present to the past. The affair is part of the couple's shared history, but not a current focus.

Children and Affairs:
Issues and Interventions

Extramarital affairs always create waves in the family. Children, with their finely tuned antennae, know a lot more about a parent's affair than some parents suppose. In other families, parents tell the child more than they want to know. Issues for the therapist center on decisions about what the children need to know, their reactions to learning about a parent's affair, and intervening so as to lessen the fallout for them. A family systems perspective is used to examine children's reactions to their parents' extramarital affair, and to formulate appropriate ways of intervening.

Parents often err by choosing one extreme or the other: telling the children nothing about a parent's affair, or everything. Those who promote keeping the affair secret rationalize their own shame or embarrassment by arguing that children won't understand, that it is harmful for children to know, or that it is possible for the affair to remain hidden. Parents who tell in an attempt to form an alliance with the child against the other parent lack the ability to set appropriate boundaries, relating to the children as if they are peers or pawns, or parents themselves, able to confer forgiveness, understanding, and acceptance.

The impact of parental affairs on children varies with the type of affair, the child's age, prior family functioning, and the parents' handling of the affair. The impact of a parental affair may continue through childhood, and often does not end when children leave home. Many of our adult clients have unfinished business regarding a parent's affair. The legacy is reflected in comments of adults, such as, "You never know the real truth," and, "There was so much lying. I think that hurt me the most."

☐ What Should the Children Be Told?

Whether to tell the children about a parent's affair is almost as big an issue for therapists as whether the straying partner needs to tell the spouse. While most therapists would agree that the children need to be protected, they disagree on what that means. The major difference centers on what parents should tell their children when there is an affair in the family. Some therapists advocate saying nothing at all, based on the belief that an affair is private information between the parents. A number of therapists believe that knowledge of the parents' sexual life is inappropriate information for children. Some want to protect children from disillusionment and pain. Others believe that children are better protected by age appropriate information than by silence.

Marcia Lebowitz, Director of The Children's Divorce Center in Woodbridge, Connecticut (personal communication, September 6, 2000) thinks that children should generally be told. However, an exception can be made if the parents can absolutely guarantee that the children will never learn of the affair. An out-of-town Conflict Avoidant one-night-stand or very brief affair that is being handled with great discretion by the parents might meet this standard. With most affairs, an absolute guarantee is not possible.

Decisions about whether to tell the children are often more complicated than tell or don't tell. All things being equal, I think it is best for the children to be told in an age-appropriate way about a parent's affair. However "all things" are often not equal. Therapists wonder about whether children should know of a parent's affair when the community is a small one, when the third party is a close friend or relative, or when the children of both affair partners go to school together. On the other hand, what will the legacy be of keeping the affair a secret? And is it really a secret, or instead is it something that is taboo to talk about?

When divorce is in the offing, consideration needs to be given to what it would mean to tell the spouse and then the children of an affair. With our adversarial legal system it could mean that decisions about custody and parenting arrangements are made on the basis of adultery, which assumes a guilty party and an innocent victim, instead of basing such decisions on the children's needs.

In many cases, secrecy itself ensnares the children in the parent's unresolved issues. Children are much more attuned to emotions than are most adults. They absorb it all, from the smallest nuances of annoyance to the most profound emotional fallout of family secrets. They feel the tension, and experience the changes in their parents' relationship. "Without the truth, children suspect the worst. When they only know that by asking to pass the corn flakes at breakfast makes mommy and daddy grumpy, kids worry" (Stapen, 1989). In trying to defend against helplessness, children often conclude that they are the problem. They may take on the responsibility for resolving the parental problems, a hopeless task at best, but magnified when the true nature of the problem is unknown. Other common reactions of children include depression, failing grades, or acting out behavior.

What do the children need? Ideally, children need honest information from their parents that is age-appropriate and not overwhelming. They need an opportunity to share their feelings and their confusion, without reprisals. They need to know whether divorce is in the works, or whether their parents are attempting to stay together. They need space to grieve their losses, whether the loss is of innocence, of parents on a pedestal, or of their family as they have known it. They need the freedom to pursue their current developmental task. They need a relationship with each parent. And they need their parents to face the real issues rather than hold the children hostage in a war that cannot be won.

Thus the issue of telling the children needs to be dealt with in the context of the situation. Sometimes the decision to tell the children will not be a clear yes or no, but a question of when. For the therapist the issue around secrecy is not whether to tell the children but how the parents can provide the children with appropriate information that helps them deal with the situation in which they find themselves. The therapist who can help parents sort through all the considerations so that they can decide how best to help their children through the crisis is invaluable.

☐ Telling the Children

If the therapist is seeing one or both parents at the time the affair is disclosed, it is important to get the parents' agreement that they will refrain from talking about the affair with their children or in front of them until the parents and the therapist have discussed how to approach doing so. A full discussion of the children's needs and how best to talk with them about the situation should occur as soon as possible. It is often useful to schedule the next session in a few days so that this issue, plus others, can be discussed

If the child already knows about the parent's affair, having previously been told or having suspected or discovered it, it is still important that the therapist discuss the children's needs and reactions with the parents and guide them in developing a plan to help their children deal with the situation.

Parents need guidance about how to help their children talk about their feelings and how to meet the children's needs. They need to be aware of their children's needs and reactions related to their current developmental stage, issues about the affair, changes in the family, and in some cases, the emotional process of divorce.

Planning to Tell the Children

Karpel's (1980) argument that secrets are best dealt with from a stance of "accountability with discretion" is applied by Reibstein (1990) to adolescents and the secret parental affair. In making a plan to tell the adolescent, "the therapist needs to understand the function of the affair's secrecy: what other secrets are thereby being kept. That is, there are usually 'secrets' prior to the one of the affair which fuel the 'secret' as 'symptom'. Often the adolescent knows or suspects the obvious 'secret'—the secret of a sexual infidelity. However, what he or she most worries about is whether the parents' marriage is at stake. This fear and the unmanaged marital dysfunction may be the important underlayer, or the real undisclosed 'secret'. . . . It is easy for the therapist to be drawn into the drama and to collude with both levels of secrecy, with the result that the critical therapeutic question gets lost" (p. 14).

Obviously, telling the children in this manner can only be done if the spouse also knows about the affair, and has some understanding of its function in the marriage. When a shared definition of the marital problems has been developed (see Chapter 5) and both spouses are able to give priority to the child's needs, it is time for a family conversation about the affair and the marital problems. Parents may choose to talk to their children at home or they may prefer to do so in a family session. In either case, this conversation needs to take place as soon as possible. The therapist's assistance in helping the parents decide what to say and how to say it is crucial. Parents need to be ready to speak honestly about the overall marital issues including the affair, to share their pain, sadness, and guilt, and to demonstrate their commitment to working on solutions to their marital problems. Children need space to respond, both during the conversation and subsequently. This discussion can begin the process of freeing the children from the middle of the marriage.

Schneider (1988) reports that "couples who have talked openly with their teenage or older children have found it beneficial to their relationship with the children and often helpful to the children" (p. 197). Especially with teenagers, openness helps them recognize their own patterns more clearly, and validates the child's perceptions and experience. "Being open with our children is part of *our* recovery" (Schneider, 1988, p. 199).

Essentially the same approach is useful for latency age children. With younger children, who can not understand the meaning of an affair, it makes more sense for parents to tell the children in simple words that Mom and Dad are upset with each other, and that they are working together to help stop the hurt. Or an analogy can be used—even little kids know what it feels like to be left out. The parents might say that Mom and Dad have been having a hard time talking together and Mom has been spending a lot of time with a man she works with and Dad is feeling left out. They can follow this with a statement that Mom and Dad are getting help from the therapist so that they can feel good with each other again. The therapist can be very helpful in guiding the parents to choose language that meets the child's needs and in deciding when and where the children will be told.

As with other issues, parents should give information and watch the child's response to see if it is sufficient or whether they need to say more. There is a fine line between sharing enough with the children, and overburdening them. Parents need to let the children know that the door is open for further questions or future discussions. For real healing to occur, the parents need to reestablish themselves as the team in charge of managing the family, whether the marriage continues or not.

Damage Control with Children Who Have Already Heard Too Much

While secrets in the family are destructive (Bradshaw, 1988) so is making children part of the fight. Children who know about a parent's affair although they have not been told, worry about whether divorce is in the offing. Loyalty conflicts are common, especially when the straying partner confides the secret of the affair to the child and not to the other parent. Children caught in these ways react by attempting to protect one or both parents, by ignoring their own needs in order to please their parents, by withdrawing or becoming depressed, or by regressing or misbehaving. For example, Justin, age 16, had three fender-benders within two months before his parents were able to accept the fact that this was Justin's way of trying to get a response from his parents about what was going on in the family—what was going on was his father's affair. Children who continue to be burdened in this manner pay a high cost in terms of diminished self-esteem, delays in development, confused sexual identity, and difficulty with intimate relationships (Wallerstein & Kelly, 1980; Westfall, 1989).

The therapist in this situation needs to help the parents refocus their attention on the children and their needs, and put aside their own anger and desire to retaliate or self-validate. This can be a tough task for the therapist, as parents who have lost sight of their children's needs are usually the more dysfunctional ones.

☐ A Systemic Approach to Issues and Interventions with Children

Issues that are particularly difficult for children are various forms of secrecy about the affair, the seductive or the obsessive parent who allies with the child against the other parent, separation and divorce issues that are neglected because of the affair, and remarriage (or cohabitation) of the straying partner and the third party.

Adolescents are particularly upset by a parent's affair. Teens whose major developmental task is separation, are unable to proceed normally if they fear their family or one of their parents will fall apart without their presence. "Adolescents . . . felt betrayed by the parent's 'immoral' conduct. Needing the external presence of the parent . . . these youngsters sometimes became overwhelmed with anxiety in the face of their own heightened sexual and aggressive impulses, and in the absence of the familiar external limits. The response of these young people was sometimes dramatic, and the changed behavior included delinquent acting out, flight, and acute depression" (Wallerstein & Kelly, 1980, p. 93).

Loyalty, the need for approval, and the lack of power make it hard for children to tell parents about how upset or worried they are by the parent's affair. Instead, children become symptomatic. One child withdraws, the next becomes a super-child, while another becomes sullen or starts picking fights. A drop in school performance, delay in developmental tasks, or frequent illnesses are other common symptoms. In working with children, it is important to determine the family roots of the symptoms, rather than to assume the problem resides in the child.

Thinking systemically offers the therapist the best perspective from which to understand and intervene with children experiencing the distress of a parental affair. When the child's behavior is sufficiently problematic, therapy for the child or the family is indicated. A systemic base allows the therapist to assess the interlocking patterns among family members in regard to the affair and the issues underlying the affair. Treatment goals established from this base will be different than when the therapist examines and treats only the child's behavior. A systemic base gives the therapist more flexibility in considering who should be involved in the treatment process, a distinct advantage when a parental affair is creating problems for a child.

The therapist may work directly only with the child, with one or both parents, or with all family members. If more than one therapist is involved with the family, they need to consult closely with each other, whether they are working as a team, with different family members, or in different settings.

Intervening with Parents

Interventions that help are those that allow the child to express feelings of anger and disappointment in appropriate ways.

> Tom, angry and disappointed at learning from his rather hysterical mother of his father's affairs, took matters into his own hands. Physically strong for his eleven years, he began punching his father as hard as he could when they were "rough-housing." His father accepted Tom's hits, feeling they were his due, but commented to the therapist that it seemed as if Tom really wanted to hurt him. The therapist helped this father understand that Tom needed him to set limits and that Tom could not feel good about himself by hurting his father. Moreover, Tom's anxiety was increasing because it seemed that no one was in charge.
>
> The father was coached to respond to Tom's attacks with comments such as "You must be really angry at me," with the goal of providing Tom with opportunities to verbalize his feelings instead of acting them out. He was asked to imagine himself as Tom, feeling both anger and love toward his dad, and instructed to feel his way to what Tom needed from him at those times. Gradually, and with some help, this dad decided Tom needed a big immobilizing hug, followed by a verbal acknowledgment of Tom's anger.

When a parent cannot set limits, it may be because the parent wants to give the child what he wishes he had as a child. Parents who were brought up by harsh or unloving parents often go to the opposite extreme in an attempt to be different, setting no limits on the child's behavior. Therapy for the parent is needed to resolve this issue.

Parental Acting Out

Parental acting out around an affair can be viewed in terms of dysfunctional triangles within the family structure. Who is siding with whom for what purpose? Who is in charge? What is the family history regarding boundary issues? Parental acting out can be defined as behavior by a parent that is designed to secure the child as an ally, whether in support of that parent or in opposition to the other parent, or both. The child is treated more like a spouse than a child. Bradshaw (1988) regards this as emotional sexual abuse.

Abandonment, actual or anticipated, underlies most parental acting out. Most commonly the acting out parent is the spouse who feels abandoned and is obsessed with the affair. Some straying partners act out by using the child as a confidante or as an ally against the spouse. In the latter case the child may be a substitute for a spouse who has already emotionally abandoned the straying partner, or a defense against experiencing the abandonment.

Betrayed spouses who involve the children in their obsession about the affair don't trust that their children love them. They act as if they expect the child to abandon them as well. Sharing the obsession with the child, however, is one of the most damaging things a parent can do. Such a stance asks the child to betray the other parent. This in itself, is hostile and intrusive.

Probably more than any other behavior, the attempt to gain control of the child's affections exacerbates parental conflict. In reviewing research on the effects of parental discord on children, Emery (1982) found that "Inter parental conflict has been associated with behavior problems in children whether that conflict occurred in intact marriages, before a divorce, or after a divorce" (p. 313). The straying partner who attempts to draw the child into an alliance against the other parent has a significant problem with boundaries. When the straying partner is the opposite sex of the child, oedipal issues compound the situation. Teenagers, who are very conscious of sexuality, may experience this situation as seductive or repulsive, or both.

In summary, parental acting out means that the boundaries and hierarchical structure within the family are distorted and disrupted, leaving the children to push and pull at the structure as best they can in their attempts to cope.

To prevent parents from dismissing the effect of their behavior on the children, use your knowledge of their children, and the children's concerns and issues to personalize your remarks. With particularly resistant parents, spin out your fantasy of the future schism between the parent and the child, and ask if that is what they want as their legacy. You also can ask what kind of legacy they want to leave their children.

Intervening When Parents Are Dysfunctional

When parents are acting out, interventions need to be made with both the parents and the children. In working with the parents, developing a shared definition of the marital problems is essential. This provides the basis for the parents to take charge of their marriage and work toward solutions. The real issues are easier to tackle than the out of control feelings that accompany the spouse's belief that the affair and ensuing upset is all the straying partner's fault. When one or both parents are unable to participate productively in couples sessions, individual sessions are needed for a brief period of time until the underlying issues are addressed sufficiently to make active participation in couples sessions possible.

The therapist can help the child understand that the parents have turned to the child because they are so hurt. Explain that now the therapist is helping the parents, the child does not have to. The therapist also can help the child find a way to tell the parents that it is not fair to be saddled with such responsibility, while coaching the parents on how to let the child be a child. Individual therapy for the child can provide an outlet for anger, guilt, and fear. Until the parent's alliance with the child against the other parent is resolved, the therapist provides a reality base for the child, affirming the child's perceptions and supporting the child's feelings. When the child feels guilty about keeping the secret of the affair from a parent, the therapist can support the child's feelings, acknowledging that such secrets are too heavy for a child. It is essential that the therapist not contribute to the good parent/bad parent split that so often occurs. Later on the therapist can help the child make peace with the unknowing parent. The therapist also can give permission for the child be a child, and give up the responsibility for holding the marriage together. This of course assumes that the parents have taken charge of the marriage, or that the child is old enough to be able to begin separating from the parent.

> Marcy's was a particularly difficult situation. Her father didn't know about her mother's affair, but at 14, Marcy knew more than she wanted to know. Marcy's mother, Ann, had begun therapy to explore whether to separate from Marcy's father, Steve. Ann was not willing to invite Steve to join her in therapy. Ann's therapist was concerned with what

she was hearing about Marcy's depression, school problems, and social isolation, and referred Marcy to another therapist.

Marcy shared with her therapist her anger and disgust that her mother was having an affair, and didn't have time for her except when Ann wanted to confide the details of her affair. Ann meanwhile, was concealing the affair from her own therapist. Ann's therapist learned about the affair from Marcy's therapist in a discussion of the case. The information about the affair could not be used directly with Ann however, for fear it would incur Ann's wrath and jeopardize the therapeutic relationship between Marcy and her therapist. Yet it was essential to get this secret into the open in therapy and subsequently in the marriage in order for Marcy to move out of the middle.

The first step in flushing out the secret was to identify its function. Based on knowledge about Ann's history, the therapists theorized that the affair was Ann's most recent attempt at an oedipal triumph. During her parents' five year separation, Ann had lived with her father and attempted to gain his approval by her school achievement and her homemaking efforts. When her parents reconciled, Ann's hopes of gaining a special role with her father were dashed. Ann's secrecy about the affair was a way of hiding her oedipal fantasies and protecting the current "victory." It also was an "I'll show you," to her father as well as her husband.

Ann's therapist focused next on Ann's adolescent sexual acting out which followed her father's reconciliation with her mother. Ann had engaged in this behavior at some cost to her self-esteem, and although the "I'll show you" was directed to her parents, Ann also was ashamed and had successfully hidden her sexual behavior from them. After focusing on Ann's pain about that experience and others in which she had operated from the "I'll show you" standpoint, the therapist wondered with Ann how her hidden "I'll show you" was getting played out now, and what it was costing her. A few minutes later Ann slid in a comment about the man with whom she was having the affair. The therapist responded "So that's how it's getting played out now, with Brad." Ann agreed, but was still rather evasive. The therapist pressed Ann about why she had needed to hide the affair, and gradually the door opened on Ann's deep sense of shame. She retaliated for feeling bad about herself with nonverbal "I'll show yous," usually in a form that had self-destructive components. Ann indicated at the end of the session that she disclosed the affair because "I know how I played it out with my father, and I know what my agenda was with Steve, but I don't know what it is with Brad and that scares me."

The therapist attempted to achieve structural change by pursuing disclosure of Ann's affair. Once disclosed, Ann could explore it in therapy rather than with Marcy. The therapist used Ann's confusion about her role with her own parents to begin talking about the kind of parenting Marcy needed.

Family sessions were used to reinforce Ann's parental role, to provide

Marcy with an opportunity to share her anger and pain, to bring Steve into the parenting decisions, and to reduce opportunities for Ann to retreat to a hidden "I'll show you." By this time Ann had told Steve that she had decided to leave him, so an additional task for the family was to talk about the reality and the emotions of the impending separation. They were also referred to mediation to work out the details of their financial and parenting arrangements.

Ann's "I'll show you" was another dimension of the family's system of secrecy. By hiding, Ann felt she had power over others; they did not know what she knew.

Karpel (1980) warns that such secrets are "unused ammunition" because the secret must eventually be disclosed for the secret-holder to savor the full effect. Thus there is always pressure toward destructive disclosures (p. 297).

Interventions with Young Adults

Young adults who experience a parental affair find it almost as difficult as adolescents. Just as they are making the commitment to marry and are setting up their own households, they are given an unsettling reminder that impermanence and betrayal occur in families. The young adult who is pressed to be the emotional support for an obsessive parent finds it a heavy burden, and one that drains energy from his or her own relationship. The strategy described above, with the emphasis on the parents taking responsibility for their own issues, can be modified to use with young adults. In particular, young adults need to be encouraged to move away from taking undue responsibility for consoling or resolving their parents' problems.

Family sessions, with adolescents as well as with grown children, can be useful in replacing the image of the perfect family with reality and in letting the children off the hook. Invite each family member to contribute to the agenda. If the family is a large one, schedule a longer session. Often these young people want to know if their parents will survive (sometimes literally) if they don't take care of their parents. It can be useful for everyone to talk about how the affair has affected them, both emotionally and practically, and to share how each is working on their own situation.

Even if the parent's affair is in the long ago past, if the issues are unresolved for the young adults, a few family sessions can be extremely useful. Such sessions get the issues into the open, provide a forum for talking about the facts and the feelings, and set the stage for future discussion and support among the siblings.

☐ Issues Specific to the Type of Affair

The risks for the child are related to the type of affair, how it is handled within the family, and whether the parents resolve the underlying issues.

Conflict Avoiders

The children who are least effected by a parental affair are those whose parents are Conflict Avoiders and who use the affair as the catalyst to work on their own issues. When the issues are swept under the rug, as they often are, the children have a much more difficult time. In time, many of these unresolved situations evolve into Split Self Affairs.

Intimacy Avoiders

The conflict that is central to the Intimacy Avoidant Affair can be the most damaging factor for the child. Study after study reports that parental conflict, especially conflict that pertains to the children (and children are always triangled into the conflict in these families), has detrimental effects regardless of family structure (Depner, Leino, & Chun, 1992; Emery, 1982, 1988; Furstenberg & Cherlin, 1991; Wallerstein & Kelly, 1980). In addition, these families are likely to be more dysfunctional than are the Conflict Avoiders. Amato, Loomis, and Booth's (1995) study on parental divorce and marital conflict indicates that, "If conflict between parents is relatively high, offspring are better off in early adulthood if their parents divorced than if they remained married" (p. 911).

Interventions with these families should be directed toward moving the children out of the conflict. Thus as Margolin and Christensen (in Emery, 1982) suggest, marital therapy may be more appropriate than family therapy to help children in conflicted families.

Sexual Addiction

When sexual addiction is an issue for a parent, children in the family face all the issues previously identified plus the issues of addiction. Everyone in the family needs to be in treatment. Children, who are frequently in codependent roles already, need guidance and support in developing their individual selves. They also need opportunities to talk with their peers and with their families about feelings and behavior. This suggests a combination of individual, family, and group therapy for the older children. Some programs offer multi-family groups, with everyone meeting together for part of the session, and breaking into peer groups (teens, latency age children, straying partners, and spouses) for another portion of the session. Groups such as these provide children with a safe forum for expressing their sense of shame, betrayal, and fury, both to their peers and their parents. Groups also help in changing family patterns of secrecy to more open communication.

Even more important than therapy for the children of addictive parents is therapy for both parents, and participation in Sex and Love Addicts Anonymous, Sexaholics Anonymous, or another of the twelve-step groups. If the family patterns remain unchanged, children are at great risk for becoming addicts themselves. With comprehensive family treatment (see Chapter 7) the children have a chance to understand the legacy of addiction and to learn how to make healthy choices.

Split Selves

The children of Split Selves have, in many cases, left home and are embarking on their own lives. Having grown up with the formula for the perfect family, they are now attempting to apply it in their own lives. Revelation of a parent's affair, especially when the straying partner leaves the marriage, sends shock waves through the family. Grown children are appalled, horrified, and angry at the parent who has fallen off the pedestal. After all, this was supposed to be the perfect family. Not only are the children angry at the straying partner, but they are impatient with the spouse who can not quickly recover and return to her observance of the family rules. At the very time that these young adults have expected to rely on the family values they have carried with them into the outside world, these values are being called into question. Some of these young people hang onto the family values and attempt to live them out more successfully than have their parents. Others are shaken, with outcomes ranging from depression to rethinking family values.

> Betty's daughter (see Chapter 8) became angry at her mother's grief. Her message to her mother was, "You've always been the strong one. How come you're not being the woman I thought you were? You're letting us down."

Many of these young people are already heading in the same direction as their parents: building the perfect family and repeating the cycle of disappointment and loneliness in one more generation. Un-examined, the parental Split Self Affair can reinforce the tendency to build a more perfect family than did one's parents.

Exit Affairs

The Exit Affair is used by the straying partner as a way to leave the marriage, and by the abandoned spouse as the rationale for separation. Thus both spouses deny any responsibility for the disintegration of the marriage. People who don't own their problem are reluctant to participate appropriately in resolving the problem, though they often make attempts to resolve the problem as they have defined it. Parents often defend against their seeming powerlessness by attempting to control the children's affections and loyalties. The tentacles from these affairs create very difficult situations for many children.

Parents who use an affair to separate have a lot at stake in maintaining the camouflage. They feel protected by it, and don't realize the damage that occurs as a result. Children are particularly vulnerable in this situation. They are faced with all the normal pain and disruption that occurs when parents separate, and in addition may feel betrayed and ashamed of their parents' behavior. There is seldom adequate planning for separation, decisions are based on anger and guilt, and betrayal spreads as children are asked to take sides.

Intergenerational boundaries are skewed when a child is over-identified or over-attached to one parent and insecurely attached to the other. Long term risks for children include diminished self-esteem and problems with trust and intimacy, which can extend for generations. Wallerstein (Squires, 1985) commented that she had been startled to find "young adults who are intensely preoccupied with a parent's infidelity 10 years earlier" (p. 10). Of course the affair is not the sole issue, nor the underlying issue, but parents' dysfunctional reactions to the affair add a significant burden to the child's load.

In summarizing research on parental conflict and divorce, Emery (1982) advised, "Current evidence suggests that interparental conflict, not separation, may be the principal explanation for the association found between divorce and continuing childhood problems" (p. 313). Not surprisingly, open hostility was found to be associated with child behavior problems more than apathy, notable here because clinical observation suggests that marriages that end with an affair display more hostility than those that end for any other reason. Wallerstein and Kelly (1980) note that, "Guidance for parents is needed, welcomed, and well used if offered appropriately at the right time and within the right context. The timing of the help early in the divorcing process is crucial to its success" (p. 318).

Intervening with Divorcing Parents

Parents need a great deal of help in reaching beyond their own feelings to do what their children need. The first step for the professional working with the Exit Affair is to help the parents talk about the very thing they want to avoid discussing: the end of the marriage. The spouse who is being left needs to face the fact that the other parent has decided to leave, fair or not. It is essential to acknowledge how painful this is for all concerned. Parents who are unable to face their own pain are unable to recognize their children's pain. They cannot parent appropriately until they do.

Next, parents need to learn how the breakup of the marriage is affecting their children and what their children will need from them. *Mom's House, Dad's House* by Isolina Ricci (1997) is packed with sound and detailed information for parents on how to help children through the process of divorce.

When the marriage is ending with an affair, discussion of the affair as the reason for the breakup is not useful because it reinforces the bad guy/victim mythology. Instead, the therapist needs to help the parents define the situation as one in which both parents own a piece of the problem. Both contributed, though sometimes unwittingly, to the end of the marriage. Listen for ways each has neglected or wounded the other, such as being a workaholic, or spending all free time with the children. Acknowledge how sad and how painful it is to have arrived at this point, and then use this information for balance in defining the problem: "You (to the wife) had an affair with Kevin, and you (to the husband) had an affair with your work—it sounds to me like you were both feeling pretty dissatisfied with your relationship. Now let's talk about how the two of you will manage the ending of your marriage so that your children will come through this with as few scars as possible." (See Chapter 5 for a more detailed discussion of developing a shared definition of the marital issues.)

Most separating couples can benefit from meeting together with a therapist or mediator to plan parenting arrangements for their children. To make joint sessions such as these productive, the professional must demonstrate concern for each parent as well as for their children, all the time maintaining control of the session. A few parents cannot tolerate being in the same room with each other without resorting to abusive behavior. In these cases consider functioning as a go-between when working on parenting arrangements. The most contentious parents also need individual help to resolve old issues that are rekindled by the trauma of divorce. With contentious couples, it is easy for our own fears about intervening in family fights to surface. A steady diet of working with contentious couples is difficult and emotionally draining and we need to make sure that we have balance in our lives so that we are not overwhelmed by it.

The situation is more difficult when only one parent is available to discuss parenting, which is too often the case with the Exit Affair. Sometimes an invitation to the other parent by the therapist is effective. An "authoritative invitation" works with some parents; others need a gentle inviting approach. Being authoritative can be difficult because it raises issues for the therapist about boundaries, coercion, and the appropriate therapeutic role. If the other parent is not responsive or does not live in the area, work with the family members who are available, focusing on grief, communication patterns, and responsibility for one's own behavior.

Many parents who could benefit from therapy when their marriage is ending will not see a therapist, for a variety of reasons. Filling this gap to some extent are court counselors, divorce mediators, and school personnel. California courts have taken the lead in mandating mediation when parents are having difficulty deciding on or carrying out appropriate parenting arrangements. Many local courts also mandate or offer parent education on the impact of separation and divorce on children. One study found that with as little as four hours of parent education, a higher percentage of parents reach agreement on their parenting arrangements without going to court. Co-parenting classes and counseling, usually available in the private sector, may be recommended, or even ordered, by the court. More information is provided at www.courtinfo.judca.gov. Many other states are following in the path of California. Consider referring some of your therapy clients to similar services in your area for additional help.

Intervening with Children Whose Parents Are Divorcing

Children can benefit from individual therapy while their parents are preoccupied with the affair and with separating. Therapy provides a safe place for the child to share pain, anger, and disappointment and to learn coping skills. Adolescent concerns about parental sexual behavior and about one's own sexuality can be safely discussed in this protected setting. The emotional support offered by the therapist provides a bridge for the child across the period when parents are not available.

Group therapy is particularly helpful for adolescents. The group can be viewed as a substitute family in that it provides its members with emotional support, validation, and socialization experiences. It also can help teens learn how to confront their parents effectively about their own concerns.

Divorce groups for elementary age children can also be helpful. Neil Kalter reports that groups for elementary school children "can significantly reduce aggression and depression, enhance self-esteem, and increase understanding of what is normal and all right for children to experience after divorce" (Mann, 1986). The groups Kalter refers to were conducted in school. Such groups, however, must not be viewed as a substitute for effective parenting, but as a supplemental resource during a time of severe stress.

Children of divorce benefit from having dependable adults to lean on while parents are regrouping. Therapists may take this role as may a relative, teacher, or friend (Wallerstein & Kelly, 1980). Children can be encouraged to reach out to others, and coached in how to do so, with good results. Discuss with the child his or her desire to protect family secrets in order to relieve the child of that burden, and help the child think through who might be safe to talk to. Follow up on the outcome of these efforts.

While all of these interventions with children are helpful, they do not fully protect against the effects of parental conflict. Research indicates that parental conflict is the most significant factor in the impairment of children's functioning (Emery, 1982; Johnston & Campbell, 1988; Kalter, 1987; Wallerstein & Kelly, 1980). Thus, when parents are dysfunctional or conflicted, children may benefit most from successful interventions with the parents. This does not mean interventions with the children are not helpful, but with more conflicted parents, they are not enough. Only when parents assume their own burdens are children let off the hook.

The Overburdened Child

With divorce, sometimes a child is burdened by responsibility for the abandoned parent, usually the mother, and the siblings. This burden may include physical responsibility for running the household and caring for younger siblings, as well as emotional responsibility for the parent and the other family members. Vic said years later about his mother, "I had to be fine for her to be okay." Children so burdened have no time for friends, no time for fun, no time to be a child. If in so doing they gain the parent's approval, they learn that they are loved for their performance and not themselves. If despite their efforts, they fail to gain the parent's approval they are likely to decide that they are inadequate, or adopt a "what's the use" attitude. Alternatively, some children who hold things together especially well, ignore their own emotions, having learned that performance is what matters. They are on the road to becoming Split Selves, which may play out in adult life through an affair or in some other way.

With many affairs, and especially with an Exit Affair, oedipal issues add to the child's emotional burden. For the opposite sex child who is burdened with the emotional responsibility for a parent, the question arises as to whether the child is filling in for the same sex parent, thus becoming the companion and confidante of the opposite sex parent. Rob described such a relationship with his mother as "covertly incestuous." Confusing the matter still further may be the situation in which the opposite sex parent, for example the mother, hates all men, and advises her oldest son and confidante "Don't be like all those other men."

Again, interventions need to be made with both generations. The parent needs to grieve and resolve the other issues that are interfering with normal functioning and effective parenting. The child needs a place to share feelings and gain support in letting go of the emotional burden without experiencing undue guilt.

Custody Issues

Custody fights tied to an affair ("adultery" as it is called in the legal arena) are attempts to resolve the emotional pain by "winning" the children. Sometimes the battles are purely punitive; in other cases the battle is an attempt to prevent against abandonment. The spouse may even say, "He has a lover, he's not going to take the kids too." She protects herself by holding the children close, making them her fortress so that she is not totally deserted. Parents who take this stance are feeling desperate. Freeing the children from the battle will be a slow process, as it hinges on the parent's resolution of his or her own dependency issues.

When a parent is threatening to cut the children's relationship with the other parent, include the children in discussion of parenting arrangements. Help the children talk about their love and need for both parents, and their fears of being disloyal to either parent. Help the parents learn about their children's needs in your sessions and through reading and parent education groups.

It is important, if it is at all possible, to keep the Exiters from engaging in custody litigation. Whatever you do, do not refer these couples to attorneys known to be litigious. Refer these couples instead to divorce mediation. Divorce mediation provides a forum for the children's and each parent's needs to be considered in deciding upon parenting arrangements. Children are sometimes included in mediation sessions so that they can speak about their concerns and preferences. The mediator will not make decisions for the parents, but will help defuse the emotions and guide the parents in considering all relevant factors. Consultation between the therapist and mediator can be helpful in devising strategies and deciding on the timing of interventions in either area.

☐ When a Parent Is Living with the Third Party

An extremely difficult issue arises when the straying partner moves in with or marries the third party, especially if this occurs right after the separation. The therapist needs to take a strong role in helping both parents understand the children's needs and how to meet them. It is inadvisable for the straying partner to immediately introduce the children to the third party. The children need time to grieve the loss of the family they knew, and they need time to rebuild a new relationship with each parent, unencumbered by the presence of the third party (or new romantic interests for that matter). It is not that the third party is hidden from the children, but that the children are not ready to develop a relationship with the third party at this point.

Involving children prematurely may just set up a repetition of the old scenario. It is another relationship where the partners do not know each other well and do not have established patterns of handling problems. Thus the likelihood is high that it too will end.

Protected Space

You can suggest to parents that they consider setting up "protected space" for their children. This is a specified time period in which the children have no contact with the third party or any other romantic interests. It provides space for the children to grieve for their family as they knew it, and to develop new routines of daily life and new relationships with each parent. A six month period of protected space is usually sufficient. At the end of that period the parents meet to discuss whether the children are ready for contact with the third party. If so, a plan is developed for gradual contact. If not, a decision needs to be made by both parents about how long to extend the protected space before again seeing whether the child is ready.

If the child is to visit the straying partner's residence, "protected space" requires cooperation of the third party, who will need to leave the residence during the child's visits. It is up to the parent living with the third party to ask for that support. If the third party does not agree to leave, the parent will need to take the child to other venues for visits.

Decide when to involve the children in the relationship between the straying partner and the third party by considering whether:

- the new relationship has a solid emotional base,
- the new relationship has lasted for a significant period of time and is expected to continue,
- the children have grieved sufficiently (parents often underestimate the children's need to grieve),
- relationships between the children and each parent are being rebuilt,
- the motivation is not to hurt or replace the other parent,
- at least six months have passed since the separation, and
- both parents agree to the plan.

There are always exceptions. Bert's four-year-old daughter, Amy, had visited the apartment he was sharing with the third party a number of times in the two months since the separation. As agreed, the third party wasn't there. Amy began to ask, "Daddy, who is taking care of you?" She knew Dad was living with someone, but at her developmental stage she couldn't quite understand. In discussing her question, Amy's mom, dad, and I decided that Amy probably needed to meet the third party in order to understand. Dad arranged to take Amy to a park and meet the third party there. He introduced the third party to Amy as the person who is taking care of him. They spent less than an hour together and Amy's questions ended.

Sometimes the children already have a relationship with the third party. The straying partner can benefit from guidance about the children's need to grieve and their need to have time alone with that parent rather than only "family" time in which the third party is always present. The latter situation occurs when the new couple attempts to validate their relationship by being together constantly.

Structural interventions that have as their goal the restoration of a functioning parental team are important when the straying partner is living with the third party. To gain sufficient cooperation initially from the parents, it is usually necessary to provide opportunities for controlled and directed expressions of pain and anger about the marriage and the affair. Sometimes individual sessions with each spouse prior to a joint meeting are useful in preparing each to talk to the other.

Mitch and Bonnie had been separated for six months when they first met with the therapist. They had not yet worked out the terms of their separation agreement, and they were having numerous arguments about their children, Carol age 8 and Ted age 11. Mitch was living with Linda, with whom he began an affair nine months before the separation. Bonnie was furious at Mitch, not just because of the affair, but also because she had discovered during marriage counseling that he was seeing Linda again. That discovery precipitated the separation. Bonnie refused to let the children go to Mitch's house, because Linda was there. Mitch and Linda however, were taking the children on various Disneyland Daddy excursions. Transfer time was often fight time for Mitch and Bonnie.

Both parents had a long history of being abandoned, and both were afraid of intimacy. As a child, Bonnie had done pretty much what her mother wanted. If she didn't, her mother cried and went to bed. Her family was shielded by the armor of secrecy and emotional cut-offs. Mitch, the oldest of five children, was pretty much on his own growing up. His parents were too busy to notice his needs, and Mitch was shy and didn't ask for help. The strongest family pattern was reserve, both emotionally and verbally. Both Bonnie and Mitch had made changes in themselves that they liked, but they hadn't shared their feelings about these changes with each other, and each misinterpreted the meaning of the other's changes.

One of the first interventions was to structure a time for Bonnie and Mitch to talk when the children were not present. They agreed to consult with each other on simple issues, such as visitation schedules, and school activities. Large issues, such as the children's contact with Linda would be discussed only with the therapist. Separate sessions were scheduled with each parent to identify the underlying issues that made them so reactive to each other. These issues centered on their fears of abandonment, which for Bonnie had come true with Mitch's departure to live with Linda. Mitch's feelings of being abandoned in the marriage were not obvious to Bonnie. In subsequent joint sessions the therapist helped each verbalize these fears rather than defend against them through conflict. The therapist also made sure that the other was listening before either expressed vulnerability.

A reduction in the children's contact with Linda was negotiated in order to give the children time to grieve, to rebuild their relationship with Mitch, and to adapt to the many changes. Plans were made to examine this issue in six months, and decide then what modifications were in order. "Check-in sessions" were scheduled every two months with the proviso that if a problem arose that they could not resolve, either could ask for an extra session.

After five months, Mitch decided unilaterally to take Linda and the children to the mountains for the weekend. He was shocked when Bonnie was outraged upon hearing about the trip, and contended "It just felt right." Individual sessions were needed with Mitch to help him see why he had sabotaged his agreement with Bonnie. She meanwhile, was threatening never to meet with Mitch again. An individual session was scheduled with Bonnie to help her unload some of her pain and anger, and to appeal to her sense of competency as a parent, so that she could continue to work with Mitch for the children's well-being.

The next joint session was difficult. Mitch apologized for acting unilaterally, and committed himself to joint decisions in the future. Bonnie told him how hard it was for her to trust him. They worked out some small decisions, and the question about changing the amount of the children's contact with Linda was deferred for another month. The therapist pointed out that Mitch would need to keep his commitments over the next month if he expected Bonnie to negotiate with him again. Bonnie was reminded that it was in her interest and that of the children not to give Mitch any excuse to sabotage the situation.

The month between sessions was a quiet one, and at the next session Bonnie and Mitch agreed to specific changes regarding Linda and the children. An appointment was made for the following month to assess how the changes were working. Timing is important with this type of issue. By buying time, the heat around the issue of Linda was to some extent diffused. Waiting also made it easier for Bonnie. Once she was beyond the worst part of the grief process and had started dating she was not so directly consumed by feelings of abandonment. This improvement usually occurs by the end of the first year after separation, and for Bonnie it took just over a year.

Helping the Parents Move On

Often the spouse is angry because the straying partner has not yet owned responsibility for leaving the marriage in a destructive manner. When the parents have not dealt with the affair, it comes up everywhere: in therapy, mediation, the courts, the child's school, and of course, at home. It ends up being an issue for the children.

The abandoned spouse in these situations often finds it difficult to let the children visit the straying partner, because the third party is there. For example, when the straying partner is a man, the wife and mother feels that she is being replaced not only as the wife, but she fears that the woman who "took her husband away" is also going to take her place with her children. Because children cannot tolerate the loss of a parent without negative consequences, this mother needs help in facing the fact that it is detrimental for her children if she refuses to let the children see the straying partner. If she feels she is giving in or giving up to let the children see their father, she needs help in finding other sources of inner strength. You can reassure her that her children know she is their mother, and that they will not let anybody else take her place. If issues exist that are interfering with her relationship with the children, family sessions with the mother and children are in order.

These parents need help in learning to communicate with each other, in understanding their children's needs, and in developing workable arrangements. The father may need a reminder that he needs to consult with the children's mother regularly about parenting concerns, rather than with the third party. In this kind of situation it often helps to bring both parents together for the purpose of negotiating with each other about the children. When the parents are contentious, you will need to help them identify and resolve the underlying issues. You may want to refer each of them for individual therapy as well.

In some situations, issues around the third party continue long after divorce. This means that the former spouses have not reached closure with each other. They need to talk with each other about the marriage, and the issues that led to its demise. The therapist needs to help them acknowledge to each other the importance of the marriage, and the things they valued in each other and in the marriage. This can be done long after separation and divorce, and provides necessary closure. In fact real forgiveness only comes after time—and after talking with each other about what happened. (See Chapter 12 for a detailed discussion of forgiveness and closure.)

In summary, the therapist's role when the marriage ends with an affair is to take the affair off center stage, and help the family address the issues of ending so that they can move beyond the separation in ways that are beneficial to their children and themselves.

☐ Adult Children of Affairs

When a parent's affair is never addressed, the child's burden extends into adulthood. Marital problems and affairs are a common result. Many adult clients, whatever their agenda for therapy, have unresolved feelings about a parent's affair that occurred in childhood. In obtaining a family history, be sure to inquire about affairs in the family, determining if you can what type of affair it was. Particularly when your client's parents are divorced, ask whether the marriage ended with an affair. Find out what the parent's affair meant then, how it was (or was not) handled, and what it means now. When affairs are part of the picture, issues of secrecy and loss may still be unresolved. Facilitate grieving, and provide permission and assistance in removing emotional burdens that remain.

Issues stemming from a parent's affair and the way it was handled fall into several categories: the overburdened child who is now an overburdened adult, use of an affair to cope with a problem, loss of a parent, loss of one's own childhood, pretense and secrecy, difficulty with intimacy, and low self-esteem. The sense of loss among these adult children is great.

> Frank felt thrust into a parental role when, during his junior year in high school, his mother told him of his father's affair and asked what she should do. At first, Frank was able to step back, feeling that the issue was between his parents and would not bother him much. It was a different matter when his mother demanded they move to another community, and Frank had to change high schools for his senior year. As is common, Frank did not know about his mother's ultimatum or her threats to prevent Frank's father from ever seeing Frank again until many years later. Following the model provided by his father, Frank had three affairs during his first marriage before acknowledging that he could not live the life he had chosen and be happy. Subsequent therapy, including couples therapy with his third affair partner (to whom he has now been married for 15 years), helped him change the pathways of the past.

The children of parents who have an addiction are at risk for addictive behavior themselves.

> Al (see Charlotte and Al's story in Chapter 7) who struggled as an adult with sexual addiction and codependency, had a father who as he put it, "chased women," and a mother who didn't like men. Interventions with Al focused on finding his real self, and on parenting his two children.

Family secrets are often the legacy of those who experienced a parental affair, especially if the affair was never addressed, or quickly reburied.

> Rob knew something terrible was happening when he was in sixth grade. "Suddenly our life as a family changed, everything changed." He remembers a terrifying all night fight. A few months later his family moved to another state. Nobody was talking about anything. His parents continued to argue, but their cruelty and withdrawal from each other were even more scary. Rob and his younger brother feared that their parents would get a divorce any day. Indeed it seemed as if divorce was impending for 20 years. Rob's brother withdrew from the family and created a life for himself with friends and activities, leaving the door open for Rob to be the lightning rod for the family.
>
> Years later, just after Rob left his first wife because of her affairs, his mother confided that she had an affair. He felt profoundly disillusioned, and very uncomfortable with his mother's desire to share this type of secret with him, even though he was close to her and had been more of a companion to her than had his father. He began to set limits on his mother's confidences.
>
> His mother had seen therapists briefly over the years. Their primary recommendation was medication. Eventually Rob's mother became

severely depressed and was referred to a family therapist, and 20 years after the affair, things begin to change. After many months of marital work, Rob and his brother were invited to join their parents for a few sessions. Questions about the past were answered and intuitions validated.

Although Rob had been strongly opposed to affairs, he became involved in an affair himself during a period when his second wife was preoccupied. Rob ended the affair by moving to another community, but kept it a secret from his wife. After the positive results of his parents therapy emerged, he told his wife of his affair. Within a week Rob and his wife began therapy. Their relationship has become much more intimate as a result of examining the issues underneath the affair and the patterns inherited from their families of origin.

About his mother's affair Rob says, "It had a tremendous impact on our life, but it was a secret from us." He advises parents to get into therapy and deal with the underlying issues: "That would have made the biggest difference to us as a family." He also wishes he had someone to talk to. "It would have been very reassuring if they confirmed that my parents were having problems and that they were getting help."

Alexandra is a therapist who works with couples and families. Her experience is a little different.

For the first time since her parents separated 12 years ago, Alexandra spent a week with her father and the woman with whom he became involved ten years before separating. Although her father had never talked to Alexandra about the affair or the woman, "I was supposed to accept their relationship as legitimate, as no big deal." She spent the week coughing, and had trouble breathing. The experience reminded her of a period in late elementary school when she cleared her throat constantly. No physical cause was ever found.

The next piece of the puzzle fell into place when she was discussing a case involving an affair. She began to get stirred up, feeling helpless with the spouse, angry at the straying partner, and even more upset with the third party. The coughing began again. In a flash of insight, Alexandra realized the cough and the throat clearing were her way of expressing what could not be said in her family about her father's affair. As we talked, she said, "It's in my chest again. My heart, my love for him—It feels like I'm being crushed . . . . All the stuff I don't say collects in my chest."

She went on to talk about her father's pattern of fleeing, attributing the fact that he has never gotten a divorce from her mother to his fear of becoming close to anyone. "I don't trust him—he's good at deceiving—it's not conscious on his part . . . . I could never trust what I heard about his affairs. The seed of deception was there from the beginning." Actually, very little was said, but much was assumed.

Alexandra's mother is still very bitter at being "wronged." In recent years Alexandra and her siblings have developed a relationship with their father, which her mother interprets to mean that they do not support her. Of the four siblings, Alexandra has done the most to examine the family issues and get her life in order. "It took me years to grieve the loss of my family. I kept going to the door and knocking. It took awhile to realize it was the wrong door. My family never experienced any intimacy. That's what I had to learn to do on my own." She is currently talking with her siblings about the possibility of getting the family together to discuss what has happened since her father's affair began 25 years ago. "Now is a time that I think we can handle talking about it." If Alexandra's family is willing to talk, it will be a momentous event in the family's history.

Family sessions can be very powerful. If you think such a session would be useful, talk with your client, whether an older adolescent, a young adult, or one or both parents, about the possibility. Getting everyone together at the same time is often more of a problem than willingness to meet. If only part of the family can get together, meet with them and arrange to meet later with your client and the rest of the client's family. Ask everyone to contribute to the agenda. If the family members are willing, tape the session for anyone who can't be there. Family sessions can start a deeper dialogue among siblings or between parents and their grown children. Such sessions also can help siblings with the realization that one or both parents is stuck, and that they are not responsible for making either parent change. Sometimes it is not possible to open discussions with family members that get to the heart of the secret. Even so, these adult children of affairs can examine their own patterns of secrecy, changing those that are confining or destructive.

☐ Outcomes for Children

The best outcome for children following a parent's affair is when the parents perceive the affair as a warning and work seriously to resolve the underlying individual and marital problems. This is most easily done with a Conflict Avoidance Affair, but is not impossible with any type of affair. Intimacy Avoidance, Sexual Addiction, and Split Self Affairs, as a rule, have deeper roots in dysfunctional family patterns, requiring a greater degree of change. Exit Affairs are the most disruptive for children, requiring that they not only deal with the affair but also with the changes brought on by their parents' divorce.

Children sometimes fear that they are doomed to be just like the parent whose behavior they found shameful. Alternatively, they may put a disproportionate amount of energy into being different than that parent. If they see parents working to resolve their own issues, there is not such fear nor such a need to be different.

Additional factors that help children weather the storm of an affair include honesty, cooperation between parents in regard to the children, a support system for the family that encourages open communication, reassurance that parents are working on their problems, an opportunity to grieve, and the freedom to be a child. Peck (1975) writes, "It is particularly important that in the process of therapy the children regain some faith in the marital bond so that they too can get on with their own play. Their dilemma is that they cannot ignore their parents stress until they are sure that Mom and Dad are in good hands and will see the struggle through" (p. 58).

The most detrimental factors for children ensuing from a parent's affair include parental conflict, avoidance and secrecy, being overburdened, and not having an outlet for feelings of shame, anxiety, anger, or grief. When these factors persist, the child is at risk for problems with intimacy, affairs (a repetition of the parents' behavior), addictions, performance deficits, low self-esteem, and hostile behavior.

The best prognosis for the child, however, is when the parents tackle their individual and marital issues. This can mean that parents are working toward reestablishing trust or toward separating, but the parents are in charge as opposed to defaulting on their role as leaders of the family. Parents who struggle with their own issues provide their children with a positive model for problem solving that is an alternative to the previous model of using an affair to avoid facing problems.

CHAPTER

Affairs and Violence

Novels and newspapers constantly remind us that romantic triangles are volatile, and that violence is a real possibility. Some of these deadly triangles take on the attributes of a folk tale because of the prominence of the participants. One of the better-known deadly triangles was that of renowned architect Stanford White, who was murdered by Harry K. Thaw in 1906 over showgirl Evelyn Nesbit. Both White and Nesbit were married. The story made big news at the time, much like the Clinton story, and has never stopped. Stanford White's story was made into a movie, *The Girl in the Red Velvet Swing*, was the inspiration for *Ragtime*; and has been written about for the last century in papers, magazines, and on the web (www.crimelibrary.com/classics). Betty Broderick's murder of her former husband and the third party in 1989 continues to be written about (Meloy, 1992). This kind of violence tends to be viewed in our society as a crime of passion. It is not that at all. There is a personal history that has put the spouses on the path toward violence.

Rage at being betrayed is not lessened by money, education, or status. Any betrayed spouse can be expected to be angry upon learning of a partner's affair. The question is how the anger will be expressed. Will it come out as obsession about the affair, as some form of punishment, as physical violence, or as homicide or suicide? Cultural, situational, and personality factors influence how intense anger is expressed.

Violence may mean anything from a single shoving incident to homicide or suicide. As therapists, we need to assess the potential for violence with the individuals and couples that we see regarding an affair, and make appropriate interventions to prevent violence, whether or not the people involved have been violent in the past.

In this chapter we consider factors that contribute to the potential for violence following discovery of an affair and explore strategies for preventing such violence. The focus here is on couples with no prior history of violence.

☐ The Link Between Affairs and Violence

Although most betrayed spouses feel like wringing the partner's neck or torturing the third party, only a few actually do so. However, betrayal combined with an overwhelming sense of powerlessness can easily precipitate violent behavior. On occasion it isn't the betrayed spouse who becomes violent but the third party or the betraying partner.

Cultural Influences

Our society's attitudes about affairs can encourage violence. Talk of violence is rampant, not just in response to affairs, but generally. Violence is glorified and justified as a fitting response to acts of betrayal, especially sexual betrayal. Many states' divorce laws still incorporate extra punishment for adultery. Murder mysteries abound with affairs that result in homicide. At the personal level, whether it's an acquaintance's or a public figure's affair, there is much judging, jesting, and speculating about who is to blame for an affair and what the punishment should be.

The American melting pot brings in other cultural perspectives on punishment for an affair. For example, those with an Arabic heritage may accept, even expect, a man's affair but have an extremely negative reaction to a woman's affair. In some Muslin countries a woman's adulterous behavior, once proven, is punished by stoning her to death. Similar codes hold in some South American countries. In Asian countries a wife's affair is extremely shameful for the husband and for the larger family. When public accusations are made that an Asian man is having an affair, that too may evoke shame. Among the many responses to such shame, suicide is more likely than homicide. Members of ethnic communities in this country often hold to the values of their homeland and these values influence how affairs are experienced and addressed. We need to ask about the values and customs that our clients bring regarding affairs.

Incidence of Affair-Related Violence

Although we frequently read about affair-related violence in the news, only fragmented data exists on its incidence. We can assume that for every affair-related homicide, there are several incidents of serious violence, many episodes of lesser violence, and numerous other situations where the attack was blocked, interrupted, or somehow aborted.

Murder victims generally tend to be family members and intimates rather than strangers (Dawson & Langan, 1994). This is probably because there is more provocation and more at stake within the family. Fairly good statistics exist about homicide among intimates (Bachman, 1994; Dawson & Langan, 1994), but much of the physical violence that ends short of homicide is not reported, whether due to fear of humiliation, retaliation, or other factors.

A small study by Rosenbaum and Bennett (1986) found that homicidal depressed patients are more likely to have a personality disorder, to have been physically abused as a child, to abuse alcohol or drugs, and to be suicidal than are non-homicidal depressed patients. The event precipitating the depression is more likely to be sexual infidelity, either real or fantasized, which is more a narcissistic injury than an object loss.

Another study, by Rasche (1993), looks at the reasons given by those who murdered their mate. She notes that most homicides, including those of a mate are reactive, unplanned assaults. "It is clear . . . that the single greatest motive in this sample of mate homicides was the offender's refusal to accept the termination of the relationship" (p. 82). When jealousy, infidelity, and rivalry were added to concerns about termination (categorized as possessiveness), such concerns about the relationship accounted for 49% of the killings. In contrast to those with other motivations for killing their spouse, half of the possessive offenders accosted their victims outside in the street, in places of employment, in bars or other establishments, in secluded areas and cars, and even in the hospital. In 58% of these cases there was no victim provocation at all. Instead, possessiveness lingered beyond the situation in which it was engendered. Revenge did not seem to be at work as a major motive.

In many affair-related situations no prior violence had occurred. That, however, is no guarantee that it won't happen. As therapists, we tend to overlook the potential for violence among those who have so far kept it together. The primary focus has been on battering as a pattern of behavior, and on couples where there has been a history of physical abuse. Reasons for overlooking the potential for affair-related violence include:

- the expectation that there won't be violence because there hasn't been in the past;
- our denial because of our discomfort with anger or the idea of violence;
- the view that a single episode of violence might be deserved punishment; and
- violent behavior or a tendency toward it is hidden by clients because of shame about it.

Overlooked or hidden, the violence can be just as deadly.

Pattern of Affair-Related Violence

Johnston and Campbell (1993) have identified a pattern of divorce-specific violence. Their findings are relevant for those whose marriage ends with an Exit Affair, and a similar pattern may occur in other types of affairs. Components of the divorce-specific pattern of violence described in their research include:

1. Violence may be sudden and unexpected, or erupt from verbal conflict.
2. The initiator of violence may be male or female.
3. The violent partner is most likely to be one who has been left or who loses in court,
4. The violence is uncharacteristic, usually only one or two incidents,
5. The violence is not repetitive, as with battering.
6. The violent spouse experiences shame and embarrassment. Violent behavior does not fit with the sense of self.
7. Violence ranges from shoving to homicide.

When affair-related violence occurs it is usually among the Exiters, Intimacy Avoiders, and to a much lesser degree, the Conflict Avoiders. If you think of a continuum of functioning within each type of affair, those who might become violent would fall at the dysfunctional end of the continuum and carry the most unresolved baggage. Conflict Avoiders would never intend to become violent, but those who bottle up their emotions too severely and for too long may explode with the provocation of an affair. The Intimacy Avoiders are battlers to begin with, and their battles escalate easily. Some Intimacy Avoiders are borderline personalities, with poor impulse control, inadequate boundaries, and extremes of emotion. Here, the violence is not likely to be affair-specific but part of a continuing pattern with the affair exacerbating the pattern. With an Exit Affair, the loss of the marriage compounds the betrayal, and the legal process of divorce may further aggravate the situation. Violence is possible with Sexual Addicts but the spouses of addicts are more likely to take on a victim identity and put up with the situation. Split Selves are usually not violent because they tend to be so over-responsible.

☐ Issues that Increase the Violence Potential

Despite the visual and verbal fantasies of doing harm, most betrayed spouses do not become violent. Instead they obsess, argue, withdraw, or otherwise express their unhappiness. When combined with certain situational and personality factors, an affair can be the final straw that leads to violence in a small number of cases. The difference between those who act out their rage and those who don't is linked primarily to the depth of unresolved ego wounds from the past, whether a support system exists, use of alcohol or drugs, the presence of weapons, and how this wound—the abandonment and humiliation stemming from the affair—is handled. Individual, couple, and systemic issues all play a part in setting the stage for potential violence.

The essence of affair-related violence is rage at being betrayed, the core of which is feeling abandoned, humiliated, and powerless. Research indicates that abandonment and powerlessness are linked to extreme violence (Eckhardt & Deffenbacher, 1995; Meloy, 1992; Tsytsarev & Grodnitzky, 1995). What better than a partner's affair to make one feel abandoned and powerless? Violence is an attempt to counter and defend against these feelings. The pain and rage of being betrayed are not lessened by separation. In fact, separation is likely to exaggerate such feelings because it is experienced as another abandonment.

Some people who become physically violent in the wake of an affair have a history of spouse abuse or other violent behavior. Others have never been physical, and it is these people I focus on in this chapter. When they do explode it is because they have reached their breaking point. A sudden ego wound can precipitate violence, such as stumbling upon the partner's affair, or discovering that one's spouse has moved out and moved in with the third party. When discovery of the affair is coupled with separation the wound goes even deeper.

Another precipitant can be losing a custody battle—court battles over children are seldom about the best interests of the children. Most often they are a way of defending against further loss. Other recent losses, such as the death of a parent or the loss of a job, may set the stage for experiencing an affair as the final straw. The most severe violence is usually linked to the availability of a weapon. It is often fueled by alcohol or drugs. Research studies indicate that 40–80% of violence-related emergency room visits are associated with alcohol or drug abuse (Brady, 2000). In my research with mediators, nasty remarks and alcohol are cited as the two biggest catalysts for physical violence among clients with actions taken relative to the divorce process (i.e., filing charges, going off with assets) coming next (Brown, 1997).

Individual Issues: Emotional Dynamics Underlying All Physical Violence

Underneath any instance of physical violence are feelings of helplessness and powerlessness, combined with distress at not having control. The anger that propels the violence is a defense against these powerless feelings. The anger and the violence are ways of trying to regain control by exercising control over another person. Those who are emotionally fragile are unlikely to see their own contribution to the situation.

Life hands everyone situations where feelings of powerlessness are paramount. Not everyone develops the ability to cope appropriately with these feelings. Coping skills can be viewed on a continuum, ranging from little or no ability to tolerate feelings of powerlessness to the ability to tolerate such feelings in any situation. Depression and personality disorders are strongly associated with impulsive aggression and anger attacks (Brady, 2000).

Another critical element is the degree of stress that leads to feeling powerless. An individual who encounters fewer stressors, and ones of less severity can get by with weaker coping skills. Many people deliberately avoid situations where they might feel powerless. Other individuals are flattened, or flatten others, when the stress they experience outruns their ability to handle their own powerlessness.

Those at risk of engaging in affair-specific violence are generally better put together emotionally than those who react with physical violence on a regular basis, but they are "brittle." Often they are not consciously aware that they feel powerless, because being aware of their powerlessness threatens their very sense of self. They have a low tolerance for stress because it increases their sense of powerlessness. The low tolerance for stress and the explosive force of bottled emotions, combine to make the threshold for violence lower. In other words, the last straw comes sooner.

When these individuals are no longer able to deny their anger, they express it in a way designed to regain control. They may yell, criticize, bully, or become physical so as not to feel powerless. Usually they do so with the persons they perceive as having wounded them. If alcohol or drugs are involved, the risk of violence escalates as self-control lessens and misperceptions increase. Because so much has been kept inside, when these people do explode, the explosion can be extreme, even homicidal.

We know from the literature on child development that the origins of this "brittle" personality go back to childhood. These often were the kids who were criticized and bullied by their parents. Generally no one cared how these children felt or what they needed. When children are neglected, bullied, or abused they feel powerless, and in fact, they are. It is so threatening for a child to feel powerless in a bad situation that the child develops whatever ways of coping are possible in that situation. A broadly used way of coping is to tune out the pain and the powerless feelings. Some people become pleasers, suppressing their anger as well. Others cope by exercising control over someone who is weaker. Meanwhile, the unresolved pain and anger from childhood sits inside, embers burning, and continually requires immense energy to contain the fire.

Couple Issues: Stress Resulting From Changes in the Relationship

Individuals with serious issues from their childhood enter marriage with the idea that this partner or this marriage will make up for the neglect and pain of the past. They choose a partner who represents their own unfinished business.

When the honeymoon period is over, and it becomes clear that there are differences and conflicts, these spouses experience a sense of betrayal and disappointment. Instead of tuning in to their emotions and expressing their hurt or disappointment, these people suppress their feelings or express them inappropriately through attempts to control. The spouse is seen as the problem—the spouse is not fitting the script. Efforts to work on the marriage are more often efforts to change the spouse. Each desperately but unwittingly tries to get the other to make up for the past, and each feels increasingly powerless as these efforts fail, as they are bound to. One or both spouses may become agitated, or depressed.

Even in good marriages, once children arrive the marriage relationship experiences additional stress. When spouses are immature or bear childhood wounds, the normal stresses of parenting are compounded. The spouse is blamed for not disciplining the kids, for working late, and so on, but the underlying issue is the powerlessness experienced when the marriage is not working like it "should."

One or both spouses may turn to an affair. When discovered, it can ignite the rage that is a defense against feeling powerless. If the affair is an Exit Affair, the sense of powerlessness is even greater. The partner being left may try to forcefully prevent the other partner from leaving. Efforts to control are often countered with threats to take the kids away or to empty the bank account. The secrets kept and lies told as the marriage deteriorates add fuel to the fire. The fear of being abandoned escalates, triggering fight or flight reactions. One spouse's flight may provoke the other's fight. Without effective methods for handling these intense and difficult emotions, the situation can easily deteriorate into physical violence.

In affairs other than the Exit Affair, separation is often used as a threat after the disclosure of an affair. The intent is to regain control but the threat often backfires if the other spouse retaliates by separating. Separating in the midst of a crisis usually compounds the crisis. Separation itself encompasses so many changes that the stress level increases dramatically, the physical self as well as the emotional self is negatively affected. The sense of powerlessness and abandonment are increased by an impulsive separation.

Systemic Issues

Influences outside the immediate family also play a part in whether violence occurs. Most likely to influence the situation, for better or worse, are the extended family, friends and community, and the legal system.

Voices from outside, those of the extended family, may be soothing or may escalate the sense of powerlessness. Spouses who have the potential to become violent are less likely to have families who are helpful. Family members may involve themselves directly in the couple's problems, such as taking sides, criticizing or giving advice ("I wouldn't put up with it if my wife had an affair"), and spreading the word throughout the family about what is going on. Alternatively, the extended family may wash their hands of one or both spouses, thus adding another layer of abandonment. Sometimes there is no extended family due to death, desertion, or estrangement.

The spouses may feel shame and humiliation as they anticipate how their friends will react. Some friends are bound to back away, acting in judgment of the straying partner, recoiling from the obsession of the betrayed spouse, or not wanting to be contaminated by the "mess."

Others act much like family, taking sides, judging, and giving advice. Fortunate couples have at least one friend who continues to be a true friend to both.

When the participants in an affair are members of the same community, whether that be church, PTA, or the condo association, that community also experiences a betrayal of trust. This usually results in divided loyalties and disruption of the group. Some communities are able to be caring and even-handed toward their members; many are not. For example, some churches will shun those involved in an affair.

Our legal system also plays a role in setting the stage for violence. The very fact that litigation is seen as appropriate to settle family issues such as parenting arrangements and affairs sends the message that fighting is the route to take. When an affair is revealed, the betrayed spouse often talks of divorce, is advised by friends and relatives to head for divorce, and often turns to a lawyer for help. The appeal of the legal system is its promise of exerting control over the spouse and winning all the spoils. Yet the reality is that the adversarial nature of the legal process fuels the fear of losing everything that is important, thus adding to the feelings of powerlessness.

☐ Violence Prevention

Affair-related violence is most likely to occur at the time of disclosure or shortly thereafter. This is the point at which feelings of powerlessness and abandonment are the greatest. Another prime time for violence is when an additional emotional injury occurs, such as an abrupt move-out by the spouse, loss of custody, or encountering the spouse with the third party. In those extreme cases where affair-related homicide occurs, emotional fragility, impulsivity, and the availability of a weapon are significant contributing factors.

For the therapist, the first step toward preventing violence is making a multi-faceted assessment of the situation. A solid assessment provides the basis for making decisions about how to intervene. While we can't know for sure whether a particular person will become violent, we can assess the potential for violence and when the potential is present, we can approach those involved in a way to minimize violence.

Assessing Risk Factors for Violence

Since the potential for violence has some correlation with certain behavior and personality patterns and with certain points in the process of an affair, I have developed two tools to use in assessing the situation. The first assessment tool (Figure 14.1) is used to describe elements present in the couple's situation that might contribute to violence. In assessing the risk of violence, it's useful to identify the nature and context of the couple's problems. The relevant facts can be indicated in the worksheet presented in Figure 14.1. The second (Figure 14.2) is used to develop a profile of risk factors having to do with the person. These are not definitive but are to be used to help clarify your thinking about the level of risk that is present.

Probably the most important screening tool you have is your gut response to the situation. If you are feeling anxious or afraid, you may have good reason, so pay attention to those feelings and choose your actions accordingly.

In Betty Broderick's case, her ex-husband had told friends that, "if Betty was determined to kill him—and was willing to pay the consequences—nothing would stop her" (Wallace, 1990, p. 14). Nothing did stop her. However both had acted foolishly. Betty retaliated with the best of them for being dumped. Dan Broderick, a prominent malpractice attorney, used the legal system and money manipulations to harass and control Betty. She countered. And on it went until Betty killed Dan and his wife, who had been the third party. Neither they nor anyone else seems to have tried to put a stop to the deadly escalation.

Individual Issues—Identity, ability to connect with others, prior trauma and loss; alcohol or drug use.

Couple Issues—Changes in power; loss and pain; fear; secrets and lies; provocative behavior.

Family and Friends—Estrangement, negative judgments, taking sides, deaths, severe illness, etc.

Systemic Issues—Legal and court requirements; support system; expectations of friends and community; overload.

Triggering Issue—"Last straw"; ego wounds; shame and rage; powerlessness.

FIGURE 14.1. Framework for assessment. (©1995 Emily M. Brown)

Rate the following items for each spouse:

	1 not true	2	3	4	5 extremely true

Has history of acting-out behavior

Is rigid or controlling

Lacks friends

Currently perceives self as having
  been betrayed

Has difficulty managing helpless or
  powerless feelings

Currently feels humiliated

Feels he or she is losing everything

Had difficulty coping with past crisis

Has history of physical violence,
  explosive temper, or rages

Has history of acquiescing and
  bottling up feelings

Has history of severe mental illness,
  such as paranoia

Has made threats

Parent or sibling committed suicide
  or homicide

Is an alcoholic or drug addict

Owns a gun

What is your gut reaction to this person?

Based on your ratings of the above factors, what is your assessment of
the risk of violence?

FIGURE 14.2. Assessing the risk of violence. ©1995 Emily M. Brown.

Managing the Situation to Prevent Violence

If your assessment indicates that violent behavior is a possibility, preventive actions are in order. Your actions will vary depending on what
type of violence is brewing. If you are working with both spouses,
either individually or together, you will have a greater awareness of
what is happening between the spouses, and thus a greater ability to
confront incipient problems quickly. The down side is that safety may
be a greater problem—each knows when and where the other will be
seeing you. In addition there is a risk that either spouse may become
possessive of you and distrustful of your work with the other. On the
other hand, the potentially violent spouse may feel abandoned by you
if you stop seeing one or both of them, thus adding another stressor to
a risky situation. You might consider referring each to separate therapists for individual work. If there is any possibility of a physical explosion or homicide, couples work is out of the question for now. If you
see either one individually you will need to ensure safety. You will
need to decide what treatment format will be safe.

   If you decide to see them as a couple, talk directly about your concerns for their safety, using "I" messages. Help them develop a plan to
de-escalate and defuse situations outside the therapy session, such as
deciding who will leave when an argument starts, where that person
will go, and who each person will turn to for support. Keep in mind
that we are talking here about people who have never been violent
before, but who are stressed beyond their capacity and are close to
their breaking point.

   Stay connected emotionally with your clients, validating their pain,
fear, and powerless feelings. It's fighting *against* the powerlessness
that is dangerous. Use calming strategies and encourage your clients
to use them whenever they start experiencing any sort of upset. Deep
breathing, stretching, and running are useful in disrupting obsessive
thinking. Sometimes space is needed, but not isolation.

   If you are working with only one spouse, your approach will depend on whether your client is the potentially violent person or the
other spouse. When working with the spouse who could be the recipient of an attack, help that person realistically assess the potential danger, including their gut sense, and plan accordingly for safety. When
working with the potentially violent person, talk directly about the
potential, what would trigger violence, and what needs to happen for
the person to manage his or her anger and refrain from violence. Do
so in a manner that is calm, caring, and direct but non-threatening.
Find out what motivations your client has that could lead in a positive
direction, and stress your concern for your client's well-being. If your

client is unwilling or unable to take the necessary actions, involuntary hospitalization may be necessary.

The focus with either spouse is on learning how to avoid escalating the situation, maintaining control of their own behavior, and taking actions to ensure their own safety. Helping them make use of their support system is important. If they lack a support system, refer them to an appropriate support group.

Working with Those at High Risk of Violence

When your assessment indicates potential violence, the following actions can be taken to reduce that potential:

- Listen to both spouses and accept and acknowledge the feelings of each.
- When the emotion expressed (verbally or non-verbally) is anger, help the person get beneath the anger to the underlying emotion which is probably hurt, fear, or powerlessness. Acknowledge and connect with that feeling. Keep in mind that anger is a secondary emotion that defends against the primary emotion. Encouraging the expression of anger in this situation is inflammatory. Getting to the core feeling can be grounding, but because it exposes vulnerability, it is sometimes best done without the partner in the room.
- Consider the extent to which individual therapy with each spouse should replace couples work for the time being.
- Avoid strategies that increase the individual's sense of powerlessness or loss of control. This is not the time to discuss differences.
- Refer the angry spouse to an anger management course.
- Recommend that both spouses read *Men and Anger*, by Murray Cullen and Robert Freeman-Longo (1996).
- Be active and positive. Help the individual utilize the healthy aspects of the self.
- Maintain control of the process. You are responsible for who is in the therapy room, who talks and when, and for setting boundaries on what is and is not permissible. Nip in the bud any verbal attacks on the other spouse.
- Be cautious, ensure no surprises, attacks, humiliation, or shaming.
- Be aware of danger points and choose the timing of your interventions accordingly.
- Develop specific plans with each spouse for avoiding potentially violent situations.

- Be on the alert for suicidal ideation as well as violence directed toward the spouse or others
- Refer a potentially violent person to a psychiatrist for a medication consult. SSRIs and other medications are showing promise for decreasing aggressive behavior (Brady, 2000).
- Arrange for safekeeping of any weapons. Help the spouse who owns the weapon decide on someone else who can remove the weapon and keep it in a safe place. If that is not appropriate, help the other spouse plan how to remove the weapon in a safe manner.

Professional Teamwork

Think about professional teamwork when the situation is potentially violent. If you are seeing the couple and they don't have individual therapists, refer each spouse to a therapist who is knowledgeable about violence (plus substance abuse if appropriate). This provides each spouse with individual support and an emotional outlet. Depending on the volatility of the situation, you may see them as a couple less frequently or not at all for a period of time. Get releases from your clients so that you can team up with their individual therapists and any other professionals with whom they are involved. That way there are several of you staying on top of the situation and working together to defuse it. If you are seeing only one of the spouses it is just as important to be in touch with the other professionals involved with the couple or the family.

Occasionally one of the professionals involved is worse than no help. This might be an inexperienced therapist who is taken in by the client's story, or someone who encourages a client to get all their anger out when what they need is a calming situation. Work with those professionals to see if you can get them on board.

When you are working with tough situations like these, you need someone to talk to, whether it be a supervisor, consultant, or peer support group. You also need to make sure that you balance your life so that you have time to unwind.

If the Situation Becomes Violent

If violence occurs despite all efforts to prevent it, stay calm so that you can decide how best to ensure everyone's safety. Get help—call the police, arrange for hospitalization, call for back-up, or do whatever is needed.

If you are physically present, keep in mind the phases of the aggressive cycle. The cycle begins with a trigger incident that is followed by escalation. During these phases the person is able to talk and you may be able to help them back away so that they don't reach the crisis phase. Acknowledge the person's emotions and ask what he or she needs right now. Be respectful. Set whatever limits are needed in a calm but no-nonsense manner.

If escalation continues, the crisis phase is next. Here the person loses the ability to talk and judgment is at its worst. The professional needs to stay neutral, calm, and genuinely supportive, making suggestions such as, "Take a deep breath," or "I want to keep you safe." Don't argue about anything—instead "yes" them to death. After the crisis phase comes the recovery phase in which the person calms down but still can't talk. Stay silent, just being present. In the post-crisis phase the person can talk again. This is when you can say, "That behavior is not safe. Tell me what I can do so that it doesn't happen again" (Torpey, 1996).

Duty to Warn

The Tarasoff case (Tarasoff v. Regents of the University of California, 1976), in which the court decided that psychotherapists have a duty to warn potential victims of dangerous clients, has implications for our work. If assessment indicates risk *and* the person is making threats or clearly intends to do harm to specific persons, we have a duty to warn. At the same time, Tarasoff (1976) does not encourage indiscriminate warning.

In writing on Tarasoff, VandeCreek and Knapp (1993) state that, "When working with life-endangering patients, the psychotherapist changes roles, from an ally trying to activate the healthy aspects of the person to an agent of social control who determines that an intended victim must be warned, or that the patient must submit to an evaluation for an involuntary commitment" (p. 1).

Judge Mosk, of the California Supreme Court that handed down the Tarasoff decision, wrote a separate decision in which he said that instead of adhering to the standards of the profession, "I would restructure the rule designed by the majority to eliminate all reference to conformity to standards of the profession in predicting violence. If a psychiatrist does in fact predict violence, then a duty to warn arises." (VandeCreek & Knapp, 1993, p. 7). Mental health professionals might want to consider whether to adhere to Mosk's proposal as well as Tarasoff.

Similar issues arise relative to affairs and AIDS. Is the therapist obligated to warn the sexual partners of the client who has AIDS? Some states have laws prohibiting professionals from warning a sexual partner of a client with AIDS. Others don't. Check out the situation in your state. VandeCreek and Knapp's (1993) book on Tarasoff provides a detailed discussion of this issue. Schlossberger and Hecker (1996) pose the issue as the need for therapists to determine whether the danger posed by the person with AIDS falls within the scope of the legal duty to warn, and when it does, the countervailing legal and therapeutic need to protect client confidences. The primary point of their discussion is that there is a duty to warn when clients are engaging in illegal behavior, but no duty to warn when the dangerous behavior is legal. That means the therapist needs to know whether state law requires seropositive clients to inform their partners.

However you decide to handle duty to warn situations, make sure you document it. Also document your consultations and collaborations on the case.

☐ Summary

It is only the situations where violence gets out of hand that you hear about. When you've done a good job preventing violence you may hear nothing. Think through how you would choose to proceed, so that if you are faced with a high-risk situation you are ready to intervene in an effective manner. Although you won't know exactly what you have prevented, working in a way that prevents the escalation of violence is valuable for all our clients. It is respectful, fair, and helps people move through a difficult process in a way that works for them. It is also good practice.

III

LEGACIES: OUR CLIENT'S AND OUR OWN

Personal legacies come together in the therapy session, coloring the nature of the treatment process, for better or worse. We are similar to our clients in many ways. We too know the tyranny of family secrets and the pain of family conflict. For most therapists, it is no accident that we have been drawn to the field of marital and family work. Our personal experience leads us to believe that change is possible, and that personal relationships can work. Our clients certainly hope that this is true.

Our clients bring to the therapy process the pain of the affair and their underlying issues, many of which tie into to the family of origin. We bring our skills and our personal histories. The outcome depends on our clients' commitment to exploring and confronting their issues, and our ability to conduct a process that is unimpeded by our own issues.

For our clients, affairs can be a catalyst for major change, or another step in a process of deterioration. Some marriages survive in good health, others survive, and a number end. The relationship that began as an affair may flourish or die. A "successful" outcome has more to do with the quality of life than marital status. Whatever the outcome, there are gains and losses.

For the therapist, affairs touch us where we live. They tap into our own fears and experience with betrayal. If we help our clients face an affair, we may have to face the betrayals in our own life. Not facing issues means forever being on the run and living in fear of betrayal. We can learn much from each other—about courage, about love and betrayal, and about the ingredients of intimacy. For our clients and ourselves, honest self-examination and emotional connection with our partners is an essential component, whether in a life partnership with a spouse or in a limited partnership with a therapy client.

Affairs have always been with us, and that is not likely to change. Whether they continue to be as frequent remains to be seen. Although the sexual freedom of previous decades is damping down a bit, our society is not doing well in teaching children the skills necessary for an intimate relationship. Our society emphasizes rationality and didactic learning, a method that is ineffective for addressing emotional issues. As individuals and as a culture we pass on to the next generation the issues we have not been able to resolve.

Recent research by Lewis, Amini, and Lannon (2000) suggests that the connection between two limbic brains (the part that deals with emotions) is the conduit that makes change and healing possible in the emotional self. By becoming emotionally attuned to each other mammals "alter the structure of one another's nervous systems. Psychotherapy's transformative power comes from engaging and directing these ancient mechanisms" (2000, p. 168).

If we can learn to connect emotionally, both personally and professionally, and help our clients do the same, not only will our lives be enriched, but the legacy we pass on to future generations will change.

CHAPTER

Affairs, Divorce, and Remarriage

An affair forever changes the marriage, whether or not the affair is revealed or addressed. The first affair is a critical juncture in the marriage, and speaks of innocence lost and an alteration of trust. Subsequent affairs signal that the underlying issues remain unresolved. In the long run, how affairs are handled makes all the difference.

Many outcomes are possible and any one of them can be positive or negative. Approximately 50% of marriages that experience an affair continue (Lawson, 1988), some for better and some for worse. Sometimes the affair continues as well. Among the 50% whose marriages end, the affair usually concludes some time later. Remarriage to new partners is likely for approximately two-thirds of those who divorce (Norton & Miller, 1992). However, only a small number of these remarriages are between the straying partner and the third party.

☐ The Aftermath of the Affair

What makes the outcome of an affair positive or negative? How does remarriage fare when the relationship began as an affair? What are the lasting effects of an affair for family and friends? Will the family patterns that led to the affair carry over into the next generation?

Important, though painful, lessons can be learned from an affair, whatever the outcome. Often this is first time that those involved have been faced with examining themselves and their feelings and behavior patterns. Although most would choose never to go through

315

the experience again, many feel the cost was worth it because of the growth forged through pain and hard work. Others however, are not ready to confront their own issues, and deny their pain as well as the significance of the affair.

Issues to be Resolved by Type of Affair

The issues to be resolved vary with the type of affair. Conflict Avoiders need to learn how to address differences and conflicts. Otherwise they are likely to repeat the same behavior in this marriage or a subsequent one, or proceed toward a Split Self or an Exit Affair. Intimacy Avoiders who do not learn how to tolerate and enjoy closeness, will continue to feel puzzled and disheartened by the conflict they stir up. Sexual addicts must learn how to satisfy their needs in healthy ways, or forever be caught in the empty cycle of pursuit and disappointment, sometimes with life-threatening results. Split Selves need to give up the fantasy of replacing their defective family of origin with the perfect family, and learn to attend to their own feelings. Exiters must learn to deal with their losses or be destined to carry past losses with them. Everyone needs to forgive and be forgiven for their past betrayals.

Old patterns can be changed, but change requires commitment and hard work. Pain is the usual incentive for change, but hope is a necessary partner. A childhood of abuse or dishonesty makes it difficult to trust, to believe that relationships can be better, or that one is entitled to anything good, thus diminishing hope. Committing to self-examination and change is a courageous step in the struggle toward intimacy. According to Lewis, Amini, and Lannon (2000), emotional change occurs only in a relationship in which there is an emotional connection. Emotional relationships are perceived as especially risky by those who did not have secure emotional attachments in early childhood. The authors point out that people need to pick their therapist carefully because it is the emotional connection in the therapy relationship that will influence change—for both client and therapist.

Important Factors in the Outcome of an Affair

The outcome of an affair can be viewed along many dimensions. A common approach asks whether specific criteria are met, such as: Is the marriage continuing? Has the capacity of one or both spouses to be honest and intimate increased? Are the spouses able to forgive each other? Has the affair developed into an intimate relationship?

Are affairs recurring? Another approach assesses the participants' satisfaction with the outcome.

Continuing the marriage is not by itself a sign that the affair is resolved. Nor does ending the marriage resolve the underlying issues as so many hope it will. In some cases, the affair can be regarded as an indirect but effective step toward problem solving. Although based on a faulty or incomplete definition of the problem, the strong emotional response to the affair has the potential to generate a more accurate definition. Once the nature of the problem is clear, it is possible to work on solving it. In other cases, the problem being addressed is never identified, and the affair creates additional problems without leading to significant change. One measure of a successful affair then, is whether the participants come to understand the message embedded in the affair.

Learning to Resolve Issues

Clinical experience suggests that the single most significant factor in the outcome of an affair is whether or not the individuals involved faced and resolved their issues. This is true whether the marriage continues or ends, and applies to life after marriage and to remarriage as well. Has the affair been used as a step in learning to be intimate or is it a way to avoid intimacy? Since avoidance underlies all affairs, facing one's own issues as the result of an affair constitutes a major change. For most people, resolving issues of this magnitude requires therapy.

Alice and Eric provide an example of what is possible when previously avoided issues are addressed:

> "I never experienced that kind of pain before in my life! I was disoriented emotionally and spiritually. It was chaotic! But gradually, out of that long emotional journey, maturity came about. I'm so much better grounded as a person—which of course is part of why I'm happier," remarked Eric.
>
> Alice, first his lover and now his wife, said, "I would do it again for myself—my own pain is okay, and in terms of the life we have and the wife that I am, it was personally worth it. But it was the pain I caused for other people—I'm too sensitive and too aware to ever put anyone through that again. But back then, especially at first, we got into a lot of denial about the people we were hurting. We wanted the relationship so badly that we justified it with all kinds of reasons."
>
> Explained Eric, "I felt guilty for a long time, but as I became more realistic about what was possible in my first marriage, that helped. I realize now that I wouldn't have stayed in the marriage anyway—I may actually have stayed longer because I felt guilty about our affair . . . . It

got resolved by confessing to God, by sharing with others, and being forgiven. It took about ten years."

Alice underscored Eric's comments: "We've spent years working on our personal issues as well as on our relationship. If we hadn't dealt with our own personal issues, there's not a chance in the world it could have worked." Alice and Eric are discussing their marriage of 14 years, which began as a friendship and became a Split Self Affair. "We have a strong emotional bond between us, and we like and respect each other. We have similar values. Our love is not just physical but has a wholeness to it."

David and Becky's experience is different:

David and Becky's relationship started in a similar way. They met at work, and were friends for over a year before they became lovers. David was something of a mentor to Becky, being 22 years older than she. Theirs was a passionate affair, and each felt understood and nurtured, despite (or because of) the secretive environment of the affair.

Two years after they began their affair, David left his wife and moved in with Becky, who was single. Fifteen months later when David's divorce was final, they married. Within seven years the bloom was gone. Becky's career had taken off, and she no longer needed David's reassurance. She wanted David to share her excitement, but over the years he had gradually become somewhat distant. Since his retirement a year earlier, he was getting stodgy. Becky decided to see a therapist, something neither of them had done earlier, but it was too late for the marriage. Sadly, what had started off with love and affection, ended with a whimper.

Alice and Eric's enduring and loving remarriage is the result of hard work by each of them on personal and relationship issues. David and Becky, not understanding that they had work to do, fell into old and ineffective behavior patterns when they encountered new problems.

Survival of the Marriage

Marriages can survive an affair and be stronger for the experience, or they can limp along, with issues unexamined and intimacy nowhere to be found. The marriage is more likely to survive when the straying partner is male, and the affair was primarily a sexual rather than an emotional attachment (Glass & Wright, 1985).

The Emotional Bond

Couples whose relationship started with a strong emotional bond—a deep and genuine liking for the other person, a chemistry if you will—

are those who are most likely to resolve the affair and derive satisfaction from staying together. Those marriages without this emotional glue seem less able to work out a satisfying relationship no matter how much effort they expend on communicating or sharing feelings.

Couples who rebuild trust are not looking for easy answers or fantasy solutions. They are willing to work hard, and to confront painful or frightening issues, and to share their feelings with their partner. Trust is rebuilt on the basis of behavior, not promises. The happiest marriages are those which are equitable. Over- and under-benefitted spouses are less satisfied (Glass & Wright, 1988). Although marriages without emotional glue may continue for other reasons, many of them end.

Reibstein and Richards (1993) question the emphasis on society's expectation of a strong and exclusive emotional bond between spouses in noting the "parallels between the exclusiveness of mother–baby attachments and the ideal for adult heterosexual relationships" (p. 203). They suggest that, "People may have strong needs for an exclusive, all-embracing relationship as a result of their early experiences with their mothers. Are there ways in which these needs can be modified so that patterns of marriage are less demanding? If we expected less of marriage, perhaps some of its contradictions could be reduced" (1993, p. 206).

Many couples enter marriage expecting that the other person will make them feel whole, as their mother once did or as they believe she should have. When they discover that this is never going to happen, some accept the challenge and work toward feeling complete enough themselves. Others feel needy and distraught and devote their efforts to all sorts of maneuvers to get their spouse to assuage their neediness. This is dependency, not an emotional bond.

Individuals who are more emotionally mature are less emotionally needy. Thus their emotional bond with the spouse is not based on neediness but on genuine attachment to the other person. The work of rebuilding, individually or together, almost always leads to some increase in maturity. However many couples are unaware or choose not to face the issues that account for their neediness.

Honesty and Fidelity

Fidelity is an issue for couples who stay together, although less so for those who have examined and resolved their issues. Hunt (1969) found that those who return to fidelity for internal reasons are more likely to remain faithful. "Those who gave up their affairs primarily because of fear, inconvenience, threats, or penalties are more likely to steal cautiously back into the forbidden territory of infidelity" (Hunt, 1969, p. 258).

Among those couples who seek help with an affair, those most likely to create a healthy relationship are the Conflict Avoiders and the Intimacy Avoiders, particularly those who had a strong emotional bond in the early days of the marriage. No statistics are available to tell us whether those who seek professional help with an affair are more likely to stay together than those who do not, although clinical experience suggests that this is true. Possibly those couples who use therapy already have a stronger emotional commitment to the marriage.

Therapy may be most effective in helping people learn to deal honestly with themselves and with others. In some cases this honesty leads to an admission that the marriage is dead or dying, and subsequently to divorce, whereas continuing the past pretense might have allowed the marriage to continue in form if not in spirit.

Couples who stay together after an affair without exploring personal and relationship issues may find themselves becoming lonely and more resentful. These spouses often develop parallel but increasingly separate lives to insulate against the marital atrophy. As the marriage deteriorates further, other affairs may follow. Exit Affairs are common. Conflict Avoiders who continue in the marriage risk progressing to a Split Self Affair.

When the Marriage and the Affair Continue

Some marriages continue in form only, with the affair(s) continuing parallel to the marriage, over the course of many years. These may be Split Self or Sexual Addiction Affairs. Although the marriage is little but an empty shell, its structure provides some of the necessities of life and may provide some satisfactions. In these situations the husband is usually the straying partner. The wives of these men lack self-esteem or have doubts about their ability to survive on their own. In therapy, a daughter described her mother's discovery of her father's affair as "the day mother opened her eyes, and the day she closed them."

Letters to Ann Landers (1989b, p. F5) tell why some wives continue in their marriage despite their husband's affairs:

- I have Bob's name, his children, the respect of the community, and more than enough sex. One of these years Bob will decide he has had enough outside activity and that will be the end of it. All I have to do is wait. (21 year marriage)
- It's easier to keep it going than to break it up. My husband and I are good friends. Period. (25 year marriage)

- He left the priesthood to marry me. The humiliation of a failed marriage would be extremely painful for him. Also . . . I have a great deal of guilt and I don't think I could handle more.
- Why do I want him? Because even though I may have only half of the old goat, it's better than nothing. (21 year marriage)

When the Marriage Ends

In Hunt's (1969) study of affairs, one third of his interviewees were eventually divorced as a direct result of the affair, although not necessarily to marry the third party. In Lawson's (1988) more recent study, the marriage ended for almost half of those having affairs. The more affairs, the more likely the marriage is to end. Many of these are likely to be Exit Affairs in which the affair is a means of ending the marriage and not the reason for the divorce.

Among the marriages that end with an affair, most of the affairs end as well. Of all those in Lawson's (1988) study who divorced, only about 10% married their lover (this is about 5% of those who had affairs). When the wife is the straying partner, the marriage is more likely to end (Lawson, 1988). Reasons for this include women's greater tendency to be emotionally as well as sexually involved in the affair (Glass & Wright, 1985; Reibstein & Richards, 1993), the continuing double standard that regards a woman's affair as a greater breach of trust, and the woman's greater dissatisfaction with the marriage (Glass & Wright, 1988). Interestingly, separation was not more frequent among those who hold traditional sexual values, but was more common among those whose values had changed from permissive to traditional or vice versa (Lawson, 1988).

For those who do not remarry, the quality of life varies. Some former spouses maintain their emotional ties, calling each other daily and participating together in family functions, never quite risking entrance into the larger world. Others make a new life for themselves, with friendships or enduring love relationships. Some prefer not to remarry while others do not have the option to marry again. (Beginning at about the age of 30, women outnumber men, and increasingly so each year (U.S. Bureau of the Census, 2001.) When compounded by the tendency of men, especially as they get older, to marry younger women, it becomes clear that older women have fewer options to remarry than do younger women or men).

Those who cling to their obsession and bitterness about the affair have the most difficult time putting their life in order again. Usually these are Split Self or Exit Affair spouses who refuse to give up on their investment in the perfect, or even not-so-perfect family. Years later they are still trying to extract what they feel is due them from their children as well as from their former husbands.

Remarriage and Affairs: Examined and Unexamined

Of the two-thirds of individuals who remarry following divorce (Norton & Miller, 1992), most hope to find the intimacy that was lacking in the first marriage. However remarriages are more fragile than first marriages, and have a somewhat higher rate of divorce. The prognosis for the second marriage depends to a large degree, on what was learned in the first.

The unexamined affair, along with the unexamined self, creates problems in the next marriage. When the former spouses move on to new partners and new marriages, taking with them the old patterns of interacting, the same old problems are likely to develop. New problems arise as well. Moreover, the new spouse and the old are usually similar in important ways. What is lacking are effective approaches to solving the problems that arise. When affairs were part of the picture in the first marriage and were unexamined, they are a likely response to problems in the next marriage as well. Occasionally these affairs are with the former spouse. Sometimes it takes a second pass at the same problem to realize the problem is one's own, and not solely that of the partner.

Although the average time between separation and remarriage is three years, one in every six divorced persons remarries almost as soon as the divorce is final (Lobsenz, 1985). The quicker the remarriage, the more likely it is that the lessons have not been learned, and that the situation is one of trying to exchange the "wrong" spouse for the "right" one. An old saying warns that one should stand alone before standing with another; otherwise the other is in danger of being knocked down.

> George's mother (see Chapter 8) remarried several times, always right after her most recent divorce. She looked to the men around her to take care of her, and never addressed her issues. When the current man failed to meet her expectations, she moved on. With increasing age, and the toll exacted by alcohol and disappointment, she became unable to function adequately.

Premature remarriage happens because of loneliness, patterns of accommodation, the need to prove something, the desire to be taken care of, or wishful thinking. Second marriages that begin for these reasons have a poor prognosis.

Jeff agreed to Midge's urgings to get married, despite knowing he had unfinished business with his former wife as well as his mother. He had doubts but overrode them in pursuit of his fantasy that Midge would make him happy. In actuality he was still doing what the women in his life wanted, and suppressing his own feelings.

The factors that help in working out the marital issues are similar to those that make a difference in remarriage. A willingness on the part of both spouses to examine their personal issues is crucial as is exploring and changing the ways in which they interact with each other. What is most important is not the resolution of any particular issue, but the development of effective ways for solving problems.

Self-Examination Before Remarriage

Allowing time for grieving and for taking stock of one's self after the marriage ends is important before committing to a new partner. Time also is required to identify and resolve the issues underlying the affair. Learning to be emotionally honest, first with one's self and then with one's partner, helps guard against future betrayals.

The first relationships after separation are best considered as transitional—that is, they are people to learn from, but probably not to marry. The likelihood is high that old issues will surface, although at first the new partner may appear to be just the opposite of the former spouse. Taking time before remarrying allows issues to surface and be addressed. Critical questions to answer before remarrying include: What are my issues that contributed to the affair and to the end of the marriage? To what degree have I examined my behavior in those areas? Am I still getting tangled up in the same old ways, such as avoiding conflict, finding ways to distance from intimacy, or picking someone who is not available?

It is crucial to be emotionally divorced before making a commitment to remarry. Becoming emotionally divorced means understanding one's own contribution to the marital breakup and rebuilding and living one's own life (See Chapter 9, Figure 9.1). This takes a minimum of two years and usually considerably longer. When each partner has developed the ability to be both self-sufficient and intimate, the outlook for the new marriage is good.

Moira and Al have been married for nine years, and are looking forward to being alone with each other when the last child leaves home. They met several years after each was divorced. They were attracted by the ease with which they could talk to each other, not just about light subjects, but about the pain of the past, about family issues, and about themselves. They could be playful and they could confront each other. This was a big change from the past.

During his first marriage, Al had been involved in a Conflict Avoidance Affair. Even with therapy, he and his wife were unable to resolve their issues and decided to end the marriage. Since then Al has worked on confronting issues, rather than avoiding them. Moira's Exit Affair was related to her difficulties with loss. Three years after separating, and encouraged by her therapist, Moira talked at length with her former husband. They reviewed their life together, and discussed the pain and loneliness each experienced at the end of the marriage and their inability to talk about it at the time. Moira reached closure in a way she had never been able to do before.

Al and Moira told each other about the ways in which they were tempted to avoid taking responsibility for themselves, so as to lessen the chance of getting away with it. As the relationship grew more serious, they began to discuss Moira's children, and discovered they had somewhat different views on child-rearing. They discussed their differences at length, and tried several approaches to see how they worked. About a year after meeting, they began living together. At this point, Moira's daughter's resentment of Al became apparent. A consultation with a therapist specializing in stepfamily issues helped them think clearly about how to approach the problem.

By hassling through their issues Moira and Al learned that they had the ability to solve the problems that arose in their relationship. In addition to learning how to resolve differences, they expanded their resources by drawing on outside expertise. Their ability to face issues gave them the courage to marry two years after moving in together.

When the Affair Becomes the Marriage

Affairs with an emotional as well as a sexual attachment are the most likely to lead to marriage. Generally these are the Exit and Split Self Affairs. Successful remarriage depends on resolution of the hidden issues that led to the affair. Building a marriage is hard enough, but these couples face additional challenges in regard to trust, relationships with children, guilt, and the lack of time between relationships. Some couples may have lost important emotional supports if the affair created a scandal in the family or the community. For some couples, remarriage is a great success; others find they have jumped from the frying pan into the fire.

The love and the excitement of being together help initially, but tremendous effort is required to build an intimate and secure relationship. The same self-examination and hard work that are important for any remarriage are important here. If the partners do not understand the meaning of the affair, and the issues that led to the affair are unresolved, chances are good that this marriage is likely to end in much the same way the first marriage ended—with an affair.

One of the problem areas when the affair becomes the marriage is the lack of time between the first marriage and the new relationship. The period for settling in and stabilizing the new relationship is abbreviated. The couple may not have time to develop effective problem-solving techniques. The children's need for time to absorb the changes in the family is often overlooked. When children are plunged into the new relationship before they have grieved for the ending of their parents' marriage, they often become resentful or over-responsible. Most problematic, the new relationship can obscure the need to examine one's own issues. Of course, this does not have to occur, and some couples move gradually toward remarriage, addressing these issues as they go.

The Examined Affair and Remarriage to the Third Party

Prior to remarriage, the affair needs to be tested against the dailiness of the real world. Outside the womb of the secret, how will the couple cope with his need for romance and her need for separate space? What about the kids, and homework, and sitters that cancel at the last minute? Is this relationship, in which the two adults have led a sheltered existence, strong enough to open its arms to his or her children? Can this couple work through the problems that arise any better than the original couple?

> Diane and Ed have made it work. Married for ten years now, their relationship began as an Exit Affair when Ed met Diane, who was divorced, during a business trip. Ed's heart attack a year earlier had resulted in a decision to make major changes in his life: stop smoking and drinking, eat right, and exercise. Without the anesthesia of alcohol, Ed became aware that his marriage consisted of a lot of drinking, a lot of arguing and, until recently, a lot of activities focused on the kids. It was pretty much like the other marriages he saw.
>
> Ed was intrigued by Diane because she was different than Ed's wife and the other women he knew. He could talk to her and she listened, and understood. At first Ed did not talk to Diane much about the problems in his marriage, because he felt disloyal to his wife and children. Later he talked occasionally about divorce, trying to sort out for himself how he felt about it.
>
> Diane's life was busy, and for a year she saw Ed only on those occasions when he came to town every couple of months. She liked Ed, but she thought the relationship had a 5% chance of making it, and did not

want to get too involved. Diane was flabbergasted when Ed called to tell her he had told his wife about their affair and that he was leaving his marriage.

Ed says now, "The initiative to go forth and do something about my bad marriage was the relationship with Diane. It was an incentive. Until I got involved with her I hadn't done a lot of thinking about my marriage. I wasn't aware that a relationship like this was possible. I went through a fairly long period of guilt—a couple of years. I come from a family that had never had a single divorce, and here was an affair on top of that. Time helped with the guilt, but so did acknowledging that it was a bad marriage and that it was only partly my fault."

Diane was uneasy because Ed was not used to talking about his feelings. Ed, however, responded to Diane's encouragement and began to share more. Ed believes now that Diane taught him how to talk, and their communication is one of the things they feel best about.

Diane also was concerned that Ed might have an affair with someone else in the future, since he had done so with her. This fear gradually went away as Diane learned more about what had gone wrong in Ed's marriage. Diane commented, "When he became clearer about what a really awful situation it had been, it helped me feel secure because I was amazed at his tenacity at hanging in there for so long. Of course I had to look at what he got by staying in a bad marriage for so long." As they talked more and felt more solid in the relationship, sufficient trust built up to alleviate Diane's concern about fidelity. They suggest to others that it is important to understand and share what went wrong in the first marriage, particularly their own contributions.

Diane and Ed agree that their marriage has worked because of their efforts to communicate, and the resulting growth of intimacy. Diane says, "We've been extremely vigilant in terms of when there's a problem or a glitch, to get it on the table, and if that doesn't work, go get help right away." She adds, "It's been absolutely beyond my wildest imagination that it could be this good."

Unsuccessful Remarriage to the Third Party

When couples try to transfer the emotions of the affair into a marital relationship without understanding their own issues, they encounter problems. Not only is it impossible to maintain the early romance in a settled relationship, but all the unresolved issues are lurking close by.

Bev, who pursued a married executive in her company and eventually married him, has regrets. Her husband now blames her for the loss of his children and grandchildren, and for manipulating him into marriage. She thinks he will probably leave her in the near future, and guesses that he is already involved with another woman. She is deeply disappointed with their life together, but is not ready to take any action. She will wait until he moves out before deciding what she wants to do. Although depressed, she sees no need for therapy. She believes that once her husband leaves, her life will be better.

☐ The Legacy

Not only are the participants affected by the affair, but family and friends also may experience lasting consequences. How the affair is handled is as important as the affair itself. Families are greatly affected by whether the affair is treated as a family secret that no one can discuss, or whether the betrayal has been talked about sufficiently to gain a sense of closure.

> In Alexandra's family (see Chapter 13), none of the siblings talk openly about family issues, especially their father's affair and the woman he has been living with for the past 12 years. "So much goes unsaid, but it is all assumed. . . . There's no way to have an intimate connection in my family."
>
> Ever since Dad left, one of the siblings has always managed to be at home with Mom, even when that has meant leaving spouse and children to do so. Even so, Mom continues to be bitter, and complains that she is not supported by her children since they have a relationship with their father. Of her father Alexandra says, "I don't trust him, he's good at deceiving. About his affair, I could never trust what I heard. There was a seed of deception from the beginning."
>
> In high school, a teacher gave Alexandra her first bit of hope that she could leave home emotionally. Therapy provided her with what her parents did not. In college she knew she wanted to understand families. Like many others who want to face emotional issues rather than hide from them as did the family of origin, she has become a therapist.

Legacies for Children

When the marriage ends with an affair, children's reactions are influenced by whether they have been asked to take sides and whether they still feel betrayed themselves. The tragedy is when parents involve the children in their fight, poisoning them against the other parent and the third party. By handing off their own burdens in this manner, they interfere with the child's emotional development. Enduring family rifts are a frequent result. Pretending that everything is normal when everyone knows a crisis is occurring is another way that some parents hand off their problems to the next generation.

Remarriage to the third party elicits strong feelings from the children, especially when loyalty battles continue between parents. Children of all ages resent the parent who introduces them to the third party without an honest discussion of the situation. However with time and with work, children can grow to love the step-parent and feel comfortable with the new marriage, while still feeling sad for the parent who was left. Eric's daughter felt badly that her mother was hurt, but told Alice, her stepmother to whom she is now close, "If it hadn't happened, I wouldn't have you."

Legacies for the Family

Knowing about a relative's affair is problematic when the spouse does not know. This comes up most often for siblings and in-laws who usually believe the old adage that "blood is thicker than water." It is not always clear however, whether "blood" is expected to expose or keep the secret. Relatives who do not tell feel upset and helpless at watching the betrayal, and often decide to pull back from the relationship. The spouse who discovers that close relatives knew for years but did not tell, may feel a double betrayal. Those relatives who disclose the secret to the spouse are often afraid of causing more pain or making the situation worse. Siblings are sometimes resented for exposing the secret, particularly when the sibling relationship is competitive.

A particularly difficult issue is the child who is born of an affair. Most spouses are unable to tolerate the physical reminder of the affair, whether the mother is the straying partner or the third party. Therefore, shortly after the pregnancy or birth of the child is revealed, the spouse usually ends the marriage. The child may or may not be told the truth about who his parents are. Lawson (1988) reports that a British study on the formation of blood antibodies indicated that 30% of the men tested could not be the biological fathers of their children. Thus children born of affairs may be more common than is realized. It seems likely that in many, if not most of these cases, the child's parentage is not known to the spouse or to the child.

The potential harm comes from the damage caused by family secrets. In some families, everyone but the child knows the child's parentage. The child who is excluded from such important information becomes the outsider in the family. In attempting to make sense out of the confusion, the child usually blames himself for being bad. The child whose parentage remains a secret is also denied accurate information about heredity and genetic makeup.

Karpel (1980) describes the reaction 20 years later of a man told at age 15 of his illegitimacy and adoption: "It was *my* background. I had a right to know" (p. 300). It was as if the man was saying, "How could you let me live a lie?" Karpel goes on to remark that, "This might just as easily be said by the man whose wife has spared him the *feelings* of having been betrayed but not the betrayal itself" (p. 300).

Legacies for the Therapist

Any therapeutic relationship that succeeds in making desired changes has a strong emotional component because real change occurs at the emotional and not the rational level. What does his mean for the therapist? It means that the important factor in therapy is not whether the marriage continues but whether the clients can learn to use their emotional selves in new ways. This requires that the therapist be attuned to the client's basic emotions, an exciting and an exhausting process. According to Lewis, Amini, and Lannon (2000), tuning in emotionally changes the therapist as well as the client through a process of emotional give and take. Each has different things to offer and to receive. We may become more courageous in our own emotional journey as we venture into the wilds with a client. Or we may be moved by their profound expression of strong emotions. For us the ability to be present is a privilege and one that contributes to our own growth.

☐ What Happens to the Affair

When the affair ends, can there be a friendship between the straying partner and the third party afterwards? Certainly not immediately. Later, with issues resolved and relationships rebuilt, possibly. When the marriage is continuing, renegotiating the friendship is not likely because it is experienced by the spouse as a threat. The loss of the friendship between the straying partner and the third party is one of the many costs of the affair. If the marriage ends, and the affair was built on an emotional attachment, a new friendship can sometimes be worked out.

☐ Factors in Successful Resolution of the Affair

Betraying partners and spouses with the best prognosis are those who take the warning in the affair seriously and set to work on themselves, and when appropriate, on the relationship. Factors that contribute to a successful resolution of the affair include:

- Reclaiming one's own feelings;
- Sharing emotions with others;
- Understanding the marital issues and the meaning of the affair;
- Grieving, rebuilding, and forgiving;
- Changing dysfunctional behavior;
- Developing and committing to a process for resolving problems; and
- Replacing fantasies with realistic expectations of oneself, one's partner, and the marriage.

Years later, participants in affairs have mixed feelings about the experience. Would they do it over again? From those whose lives change for the better, a resounding yes. They also say that given where they were and who they were, they probably could not have done it differently, although they would have liked to. They do not intend to do it over again.

Intimate relationships provide the best opportunities to learn and to grow emotionally. They are filled with events that bring joy and sorrow, excitement and disappointment, pain and delight. Some partners, however, are stuck—they are unable to feel, to accept, or to share. When opportunities in the marriage have not been used and issues are not understood, an affair can be the catalyst for change. The affair offers an opportunity to become honest, to reclaim one's self and separate one's life from the legacy of the past, and to learn how to connect emotionally with another human being, whether or not that is the spouse. The greatest sin is wasting the opportunity.

16

Family Therapists, Family Patterns, Family Secrets, and Affairs

Our clients are not the only ones who struggle with secrecy and avoidance. These are the most difficult issues for many therapists. Some of us collude to keep the affair a secret in an attempt to decrease the spouse's pain, or because we believe that not all secrets should be shared. Or, we find ourselves mired down with a couple because we are afraid to confront the issue for fear it will result in divorce. We mistake exploring the true nature of the situation with creating pain; we confuse helping them with alleviating their pain. While help may mean increased pain in the short term, our clients need to experience and move through their pain before it can dissipate.

Karpel (1980) writes, "Therapists suddenly find themselves thinking that they cannot reveal the secret for fear of precipitating the disintegration of the family or precipitating suicide or murder. Such fears may in some cases be justified; often they are not" (p. 301).

A therapist talks about her struggle:

> I recognize my own tendency to collude with avoidance. That's my way of dealing and I have history around that and so I can be aware that I will shy off in a family situation, particularly when that isn't my contract. Despite the fact I think systemically, I will shy away unless I have explicit permission to go into marital stuff. And part of that I think comes from a position of respect when I work with a family. But I think part of it is fed by my own tendency to step back more than might be necessary—or helpful."

Many of us come from families that kept secrets, or abhorred anger, or were dysfunctional in other ways. Is our desire to protect the spouse from the secret really a desire that we ourselves be protected? If so, we need to identify what our need for protection is about. What is our need to believe that a marriage can flourish after an extramarital affair without the affair being addressed? Who is it we are protecting?

The following comments were made by therapists as they explored their own issues regarding affairs:

> When it comes too close I become cautious. I'm not really sure how to deal with it because I'm so aware that it's hitting so near the bones for myself. So that makes it hard sometimes—I can feel myself getting more hesitant, where I wouldn't if it wasn't so close. At that point I either talk about it, think about it, or do something to ground myself so I can just sort of distance—can recognize that this is another situation.

> I don't find affairs a moral issue at this point in my life. I think I would have earlier. My ex-husband was a Sexual Addict. And I played my own part in whatever was going on, if I had been able to see that. He used to tell me that these things didn't mean that much to him. If I could have known, if I could have believed that—at this point I can believe that. At that point I couldn't.

> My framework is psychoanalytic—this is all very foreign to me.

> I get a pain right here (putting her hand over her heart) when I find out I'm working with an affair. I don't know what the right thing is to do—that's where the pain is—but I feel a moral responsibility to do the right thing. It's the same depth of fear about doing the right thing as I have with suicide gestures.

If your practice is with couples and you are not seeing a high proportion of affairs among your clients, you may be obstructing the view. Probably your clients are perceiving your reluctance or aversion to dealing with affairs, and are saving you (and themselves) from the discomfort.

The Over-Responsible Therapist

Our goals for the client are sometimes unrealistic. We may want the issues resolved and the marriage rebuilt more than do they, perhaps as a talisman for our own marriage. Alternatively, we may assume that an affair means the marriage is over and prematurely focus on divorce.

We sometimes take excessive responsibility for our client's marriage. Until recent years therapists generally believed that their role was to help the couple save the marriage. Lucy, for example, was told, "We don't talk about divorce here," when she sought help in thinking about divorce. Therapists have broadened their approach, but the inclination persists toward saving marriages. This is appropriate when it is what the couple wants. It is not useful when it stems from the therapist's need to maintain hope about his or her own marriage or about marriage in general, or when it is based on the therapist's belief that divorce is wrong. The current buzzword is family reunification. The concept is that a bond exists that shouldn't be broken. Most often this is applied to parents and their children, but it also is being applied to spouses. It assumes that the choice of the marriage partner has innate integrity, regardless of how ill-founded or destructive the choice has proven to be.

It is as important to focus on the issues that could, conceivably, lead to divorce, as it is to focus on making positive changes in the relationship. Excluding part of the dialogue needed between spouses shortchanges them. Particularly when one spouse is considering or has already made a decision to leave, it is important to surface that decision. An emphasis on saving the marriage that restricts the couple's exploration of the realities of their situation is not helpful.

In some cases, doing too much for our clients stems from our own codependency. We need them to need us, in order for us to have value. We may feel basically undeserving, so we work hard to redeem ourselves through helping our clients. We do not deserve to pursue our own lives (and are afraid to as well). We may sublimate our needs by living through our clients' needs, their successes and failures becoming merged with our own. Instead, we need to learn how to help our clients help themselves, rather than help them avoid their issues by trying to rescue them. When the issues are our own, we need to work on them directly.

Intolerance of Affairs

Some therapists are intolerant of certain types of affairs—usually Sexual Addiction. Anne remarked, "I understand having a moment of weakness, and I understand falling in love with someone, but sustained promiscuity for its own sake! That's where my values come in—'You mean you're just screwing around?' That makes my blood boil."

Others are intolerant of one member of the triangle. Often this relates to affairs in one's own family. Katrina was aware that she usually sided with the spouse who is obsessively angry at the third party. She justified her anger: "That woman doesn't have any right to break up someone else's marriage." Further exploration disclosed that Katrina's anger was really at her father and his affair. The affair was a family secret that everyone knew about but no one was allowed to discuss, so Katrina had coped by blaming her father's lover. This displacement carried over into the therapy process.

Norm, who had been the straying partner in several Conflict Avoidance Affairs remarked:

> The hardest thing I've had to do in a group leadership role was to try to be really patient with the spouses, and to really understand. I always understood the betrayers, could understand their humanness, could understand where their morals were, where my morals were. But I have a hard time with the aggrieved victimized spouse who can't get off dead center, and I find myself having a lot of trouble with males and females who just couldn't see that they were a contributing factor to the whole shmear. I think oftentimes I showed a good deal of impatience. I'm learning that I have to be patient and equally understanding of the difficulties they're having recognizing the role they play in this syndrome.

Others are intolerant of all affairs. Ministers and pastoral counselors in particular, often feel a bigger obligation regarding issues of fidelity than do other therapists. This is especially true when they went into the ministry to gain control over issues regarding their own sexuality. Holding a strong moral position against infidelity is often an attempt to keep one's self from succumbing to temptation, or even acknowledging one's own temptation. When Jimmy Carter admitted to "lust in his heart," a huge cry went up from those who want to see the world in terms of good and bad, and do not want any reminders of their own ambivalence.

Taibbi (1983) remarks that, "It is difficult to remain objective: the topic is one that can easily rub into the therapist's own skin. The therapist needs to be clear about his or her own values and to be alert for identification, vicarious support, projections, reaction formations" (p. 204).

Morality and Judgment

One area of confusion for many therapists relates to the judgments we must make. We are continually assessing, making decisions about how to proceed, and intervening on the basis of those decisions. Ideally we do so using our professional knowledge and our skills. Sometimes however, the therapist imposes moral rather than professional judgments. Moral judgments focus on the right and the wrong way to behave, the good person and the bad. They oversimplify the situation and interfere with understanding how the affair developed and with making professional judgments about how to proceed toward resolving the issues. Moral judgments are a way of distancing from a situation we find threatening.

I am differentiating moral judgment from larger issues of morality. For me, morality centers on issues such as honesty, integrity, and concerns about the impact of one's actions on another. These are certainly issues in an affair and they account for most of the extremely painful emotions associated with affairs. Straying partners often describe their behavior as wrong and experience guilt because of it. Their spouses agree and we often agree too. The distinction for us needs to be on exploring these concerns rather than stopping with judgment. Betsy Mandel-Carley (2000), a therapist in Memphis, comments, "It is not our job to pass judgment, but it is our job to help clients name and understand all the implications of their behaviors, psychological as well as modeling for kids, etc., and thus I feel we need to not pretend there aren't moral issues involved. It's how to handle the repercussions once the process is understood. . . . It's that difficult ability to go back and forth from process to content that allows couples to heal. If the perpetrator doesn't have some moral regret, and the injured party doesn't understand the underlying issues involved in the process, healing won't happen" (Mandel-Carley, personal communication, June 2000).

Fear of the Intensity of the Feelings

Intense feelings are part of the turf when working with affairs. Can we tolerate, even encourage, the expression of rage by the spouse who has just learned of the affair? If we cannot, the spouse will know that we are afraid of anger, and will hold back, sacrificing her needs to ours. Can we manage our anxiety and pain as we help the couple face the true nature of their situation? We shortchange our clients if we keep them from feeling their pain in order to protect us from ours. Can we keep from rescuing them when the intent is really to rescue our selves?

Our own feelings signal us in many ways when we encounter emotionally difficult territory. We may become physically tense or develop a headache or upset stomach. Our pacing may be off as we rush through an uncomfortable issue, delay getting to it, or become distracted by a side issue. We may obsess about an upcoming session, avoid scheduling it, or even forget the session. Monitoring our own reactions and identifying what is ours is an important aspect of therapy, and allows us to get the help we need rather than passing our issues on to our clients. Self-monitoring also is of use diagnostically. For example, we may be able to quickly spot evasive behavior by our own level of anxiety.

The intense emotional connection with a spouse in pain may feel overwhelming. Some therapists resist this empathic intensity for fear of drowning in it. Joan reported that her prior therapist told her to "get over it," by the fifth session.

We may find the level of dishonesty and denial disconcerting, or be unsure that we are strong enough to confront it effectively. Many of us find it hard to be confrontive, and fear that being tough means we are not the caring, nurturing people we would like to be. It is not surprising that at times we may feel angry or want to push away the client who presents us with our own issues. Instead, we have to separate our issues so we can help them with theirs.

Sandra, an experienced marriage and family therapist comments:

> I'm very aware when I'm working with clients when it really touches, particularly if there's anything that they're touching that's fresh. That is very, very difficult. Talking about it in supervision or with another therapist, is a blessing.

It can be appropriate to expose our feelings in response to our clients, provided it is therapeutic for them. For example, "I feel sad" to a couple who is grieving, acknowledges their pain. Such a statement also can take care of us, but needs to be the result of a conscious decision about what is therapeutic.

The Impaired Therapist

A few of us lose control and cross professional boundaries, engaging in an affair with a client. Professional codes of ethics are explicit that this is unethical behavior. Lincoln Stanley (personal communication, June 23, 2000), Ethics Case Manager of the American Association for Marriage and Family Therapy, says that almost 11% of all ethics cases involve allegations of sexual or romantic dual relationships, and two-thirds of the cases charged under the specific sections prohibiting dual relationships with clients, students, and supervisees involve similar allegations. Somewhere between 6–15% of therapists, mostly men, admit to having sex with clients (Boodman, 1989). Among psychiatrists, the profile is, "Males over 40 in solo practice who are depressed, unhappily married, 'burned out' professionally and abusing drugs or alcohol" (Boodman, 1989, p. H10).

An affair is one of most destructive acts in which a therapist can engage with a client. In therapy, clients reveal their most vulnerable selves. Taking advantage of their vulnerabilities is a breach of the therapeutic contract and a devastating abuse of the trust given by the client to the therapist.

The clients who are most likely to be sexualized by a therapist are those who have experienced abuse in the past, often of a sexual nature, that results in confusion about what is appropriate behavior for themselves and for authority figures. They tend to be fragile and depressed, with a history of self-blame. The therapist usually insists that the sexual relationship is good therapy, that it will help, and the client feels too needy and dependent to question the authority of the therapist. It is those clients who are least able to protect themselves from boundary violations who are most vulnerable to victimization by the therapist.

On a lighter note, Frieda Fromm-Reichmann, a psychiatrist and teacher, is said to have cautioned her students, "Don't have sex with your patients. They'll be so disappointed!"

☐ Helping Ourselves

What can we do to enhance our ability to separate our own issues from our client's? The big danger is in not being aware of our issues. If you have not already done so, make a list of those issues which increase your discomfort when working with affairs. Identify whether your issues relate to your own affair, affairs within your family or among friends, avoidance of certain feelings or of strong emotions, over-responsibility, over-identification, intolerance, secrecy, problems in your own relationship, or fears about your ability to control your own reactions or behavior. Some of these categories overlap.

With an awareness of your own issues around affairs and a willingness to explore them, you can probably resolve them. Some issues lend themselves to supervision. Other issues, such as unfinished business around your own affair, require therapy. Refrain from working with those clients who set off your issues, until you can separate your client's issues from your own.

Learning Experiences

In addition to supervision and possibly therapy, you can draw up your own plan for learning experiences that can fill gaps in your training and experience. Peer supervision groups that discuss the ways in which it is easy to get tangled up with an affair can be very useful. These groups are most helpful when we feel free to bring up those personal issues that are spilling over into our work with clients.

> Rob reviewed with his peer group three cases in which couples came in after disclosure of an affair, but soon dropped out of therapy. Rob had felt very uncomfortable in each of these cases. With the group's help, Rob looked at how frightened he was as a child when his father had an affair and no one in the family talked about it. Rob realized he had been walking around his clients' affairs, just as he had tiptoed around his father's affair.

Role play is an excellent way to explore threatening aspects of an affair.

> Barb remarked, "I think playing the male straying partner helped me understand some of his feelings. I've had a lot of—not just impatience, but some intolerance—indignation. I don't know, there's a part of me that still feels it's an uncaring thing to do. I still would probably identify more with being a spouse than I would with being a straying partner, but I don't feel so angry. I can be open to listening to him."

You might embark on a self-designed reading program to learn more about a particular aspect of affairs. You could focus on family secrets if they are part of your heritage, on compulsive sexual behavior, adult children of affairs, or on any one of numerous other issues. The references at the end of this book provide many excellent resources for therapists. You also can seek out therapists who work with a facet of affairs that interests you, and talk with them or attend their lectures or workshops.

Keeping Our Personal Lives in Order

Just as an epidemic of breast cancer makes us anxious about our health, a rash of affairs may make us anxious about our own relationship. When we get too much of an issue, we need to talk about it with our partner, or with close friends or colleagues. Humor, even black humor, also helps.

Safety for children flows from parents being there for the children. Safety for parents can emanate from the therapist being there. Who provides safety for the therapist? Keeping our own relationships in order, and dealing honestly with our selves and our partners provides the best protection. We need to ensure balance in our lives—a balance between work and home, friends and family, partner and self. When we do this we do not need our clients to take care of us.

Our Sense of Effectiveness

Where does our sense of competence come from, and how do we measure that when we're working with affairs? Some of us are tempted still, to measure our success by whether the client's marriage survives. Since survival of the marriage is our client's choice and responsibility, we need to use other means of assessing our work. Our responsibility is for the process of therapy so our measures of effectiveness need also to relate to the process. Elements of the process include facilitating communication, exploration, and honesty on behalf of intimacy.

Following is a self-assessment checklist that relates to the process of therapy. Use it to review your most recently completed case involving an affair, and as a guide in reviewing future cases. Your answers will help you identify your progress as well as your problem areas.

- Was the process one that facilitated the client's exploration and understanding of themselves and of their relationships?
- Was I honest throughout the process, not just about the secret? Did I adhere to my standards of honesty throughout the process?
- Did the process facilitate honesty between the spouses?
- Was I able to work with the intense feelings, including the pain and the fear, and help the client give appropriate expression to those feelings? If not, what were the feelings I had difficulty with?
- Was I able to tolerate and acknowledge the spouse's intense rage without reinforcing it?
- Did the process facilitate examining the issues underneath the affair?
- Did I refrain from taking responsibility for the client's decisions about his or her life?
- Did I stay within my boundaries, including how I dealt with secrets, as well as within my professional code of ethics?
- Was I able to separate my issues from their issues? If not, what are my issues that need to be addressed?
- Was I truly unbiased toward each person involved in the affair? If not, who did I have difficulty with and why?
- Do I have any leftovers from this case? If so what are they and what do they mean?

Our Shared Quest for Intimacy

Our own life experience can enhance, rather than distort the process of therapy if we learn how to use it appropriately. We know how betrayal feels, whether or not it is the betrayal of an affair. We know how we have contributed to problems in our own relationships, and how easy it is to overlook or rationalize our own behavior. We know how hard it is to face our own issues and to express ourselves honestly. We also know the exhilaration when we break through to another person. Hopefully we know too the experience of forgiving and being forgiven.

The degree to which we are aware of and have resolved our own issues is the degree to which we will be able to help our clients resolve theirs. Our own struggle for intimacy allows us to understand the depths of our clients' struggles, and to empathize with them. We know where many of the pitfalls are located, and can post warning lights. We can guide them in exploring their deepest feelings. Our resolution of our own issues enables us to believe that they too can resolve their issues, and thus we offer hope. When our clients are courageous in their own journey, we cheer for them and wish them well. As human beings, we have in common the struggle for intimacy, and what a powerful life quest it is!

Short of life and death, the quest for love and intimacy is the greatest drama in each of our lives. As therapists we are privileged to share in our clients' drama.

RESOURCES FOR THERAPISTS AND THEIR CLIENTS

☐ Finding Help on the Internet about Affairs

The Internet holds trash and treasure. These are some of the better sites on affairs. Also search using keywords such as "extramarital affairs" or "infidelity."

www.affairs-help.com (Emily Brown's site)
www.pages.prodigy.com/divorceplus/div00.htm
www.itstessie.com (Religious)
www.vaughan-vaughan.com
http://hometown.aol.com/affairlady/affair.html
http://divorcesupport.miningco.com/people/divorcesupport/msub10.htm

☐ Information and Treatment for Sexual Addiction

American Foundation for Addiction Research	www.addictionresearch.com
Sex Addicts Anonymous	(713) 869-4902
Sex and Love Addicts Anonymous	(617) 332-1845
Sexaholics Anonymous	(615) 331-6230; saico@sa.org
The Meadows Wickenburg, AZ 85390	1-800-MEADOWS; www.themeadows.org or info@themeadows.org

☐ Information and Training about Separation and Divorce

www.pages.prodigy.com/divorceplus/div00.htm

http://divorcesupport.com

Association for Conflict Resolution Washington, DC (formerly Academy of Family Mediators, Society for Professionals in Dispute Resolution, and CREnet)	(202) 667-9700; www.mediate.com
AFCC—An Association of Family, Court, and Community Professionals	(608) 664-3750; afcc@afccnet.org
Centers for Families, Children, and the Courts Judicial Council of California	(414) 865-7579 or (414) 865-7741 www.courtinfo.ca.gov/ programs/cfcc

☐ Information about Research

University of Texas, Department of Human Ecology, Pair Project.

www.utexas.edu/research/pair

☐ Books for Your Clients

Brown, E. M. (1999). *Affairs: A guide to working through the repercussions of infidelity.* San Francisco: Jossey-Bass.

DeAngelis, B. (1992). *Are you the one for me?* New York: Dell.

Gottman, J. M. (1994). *Why marriages succeed or fail.* New York: Simon and Schuster.

Lerner, H. G. (1993). *The dance of deception.* New York: HarperCollins.

Lerner, H. G. (1989). *The dance of intimacy.* New York: Harper and Row.

Spring, J. A. (1996). *After the affair.* New York: HarperCollins.

Vaughan, P. (1998). *The monogamy myth: A personal handbook for recovering from affairs* (Rev. ed.). Newmarket.

REFERENCES

Amato, P. R., Loomis, L. S., & Booth, A. (1995). Parental divorce, marital conflict, and offspring well-being during early adulthood. *Social Forces, 73*(3), 895–915.

American Association for Marriage and Family Therapy (AAMFT). *AAMFT Code of Ethics.* Washington, DC.

Atwater, L (1982). *The extramarital connection.* New York: Irvington.

Bachman, R. (1994, January). *Violence against women: A national crime victimization report.* Washington, DC: Bureau of Justice Statistics, U.S. Department of Justice.

Bakker Aides Sentenced to 17 Years. (1989, September 9). *The Washington Post,* pp. C1, C11.

Baris, M. A., & Garrity, C. B. (1988). *Children of divorce: A developmental approach to residence and visitation.* DeKalb, IL: Psytec.

Beattie, M. (1999, June 3). Honour killings continue to punish Pakistani women. *The Globe and Mail,* p. A13.

Berne, E. (1966). *Principles of group treatment.* New York: Grove Press.

Boodman, S. G. (1989). Sex during therapy. *The Washington Post,* p. H10.

Botwin, C. (1988). *Men who can't be faithful.* New York: Warner.

Bowlby, J. (1979). *The making and breaking of affectional bonds.* London: Tavistock.

Bradshaw, J. (1988). *Healing the shame that binds you.* Deerfield Beach, FL: Health Communications.

Brady, K. (2000, May 15). The treatment and prevention of violence. Paper presented at the 153rd Annual Meeting of the American Psychiatric Association. Chicago, IL.

Branden, N. (1989). *Judgment day: My years with Ayn Rand.* Boston: Houghton-Mifflin/ Marc Jaffe.

Brown, E. M. (1976). A model of the divorce process. *Conciliation Courts Review, 14*(2), 1–11.

Brown, E. M. (1995). Framework for assessment of the situation. Handout for the training programs, *Flashpoints: Identifying and preventing affair specific violence* and *Flashpoints: Identifying and preventing violence in separation and divorce.*

Brown, E. M. (1995). Assessing the risk of violence. Handout for the training programs, *Flashpoints: Identifying and preventing affair specific violence* and *Flashpoints: Identifying and preventing violence in separation and divorce.*

Brown, E. M. (1997, July 19). *Flashpoints: Identifying and preventing violence in separation and divorce.* Presented at Academy of Family Mediators Annual Conference, Falmouth, MA.

Brown, E. M. (1999). *Affairs: A guide to working through the repercussions of infidelity.* San Francisco: Jossey-Bass.

Brown, E. M. (2000). Sequence of steps in treating affairs. Handout for the training program, *Affairs: Getting the message.*

Buss, D. A. (1989). Conflict between the sexes: Strategic interference and the evocation of anger and upset. *Journal of Personality and Social Psychology, 56,* 735–747.

Buss, D. A. (2000). *The dangerous passion: Why jealousy is as necessary as love and sex.* New York: Free Press.

Carnes, P. (1983). *Out of the shadows.* Minneapolis, MN: CompCare.

Carnes, P. (1985). *Counseling the sexual addict.* Minneapolis, MN: CompCare.

Carnes, P. J. (1988b, November 13). Sexual addiction and the family. Paper presented at the National Council on Family Relations, Philadelphia, PA.

Carnes, P. J. (2000). *Sex addiction treatment at The Meadows.* Wickenburg, AZ: The Meadows.

Carnes, P. J. (1989b, October 26). Contrary to love: The sex addict. Paper presented at the Conference of the American Association for Marriage and Family Therapy, San Francisco, CA.

Carnes, P. J. (1989a). Sexually addicted families: Clinical use of the circumplex model. In D. Olson (Ed.), *The circumplex model* (pp. 113–140). Binghamton, NY: Haworth.

Carter, E. (1988). *The changing family life cycle.* New York: Gardner.

Charny, I. (1992, April 1). The impact of extra-marital relationships on the continuation of marriages. Paper presented at the International Congress on Family Therapy, Jerusalem, Israel.

Cullen, M., & Freeman-Longo, R. E. (1996). *Men and anger.* Holyoke, MA: NEARI.

Dawson, J. M., & Langan, P. A. (1994, July). *Murder in families.* Bureau of Justice Statistics Special Report, Washington, DC: U.S. Department of Justice.

DeAngelis, B. (1992). *Are you the one for me?* New York: Dell.

Depner, C. E., Leino, E. V., & Chun, A. (1992). Interparental conflict and child adjustment: A decade review and meta-analysis. *Family and Conciliation Courts Review, 3,* 323–341.

Department of Defense. (1998). Uniform Code of Military Justice. Washington, DC: Author.

Eckhardt, C. I., & Deffenbacher, J. L. (1995). Diagnosis of anger disorders. In H. Kassinove (Ed.), *Anger disorders: definition, diagnosis, and treatment* (pp. 27–47). Washington, DC: Taylor & Francis.

Emery, R. (1988). *Marriage, divorce, and children's adjustment.* Newbury Park, CA: Sage.

Emery, R. (1982). Interparental conflict and the children of discord and divorce. *Psychological Bulletin, 92,* 309–330.

Fein, E., & Schneider, S. (1996). *The rules: Time tested secrets for capturing the heart of Mr. Right.* New York: Warner.

Frank, L. (1999, September). The intimate Hillary. *Talk, 1,* 166–174, 248, 250–251.

Furstenberg, F. F., & Cherlin, A. J. (1991). *Divided families.* Cambridge, MA: Harvard University Press.

Gerson, R. (1989). Genograms, family patterns, and computer graphics. Paper presented at the conference of the American Association for Marriage and Family Therapy, San Francisco, CA.

Glass, S. P., & Wright, T. L. (1985). Sex differences in type of extramarital involvement and marital dissatisfaction. *Sex Roles, 12*(9/10), 1101–1120.

Glass, S. P., & Wright, T. L. (1988). Clinical implications of research on extramarital involvement. In R. A. Brown & J. R. Field (Eds.), *Treatment of sexual problems in individual and couples therapy* (pp. 301–346). New York: PMA.

Glass, S. P., & Wright, T. L. (1989). Therapist bias vs research: Extramarital treatment issues. Paper presented at the conference of the American Association for Marriage and Family Therapy, San Francisco, CA.

Glass, S. P., & Wright, T. L. (1992). Justifications for extramarital relationships: The association between Attitudes, behaviors, and gender. *Journal of Sex Research, 29,* 361–387.

Goodman, E. (1988, March 1). Can Jimmy Swaggart be saved? *The Washington Post,* p. A19.

Goodman, E. (1998, August 20). Hillary's next—and most difficult—role. *Boston Globe,* p. A19.

Goodwin, D. K. (1987). *The Fitzgeralds and the Kennedys: An American saga.* New York: Simon and Schuster.

Gottman, J. M., & Krokoff, L. J. (1989). Marital interaction and satisfaction: A longitudinal view. *Journal of Consulting and Clinical Psychology, 57*(1), 47–52.

Gottman, J. M. (1994a). *What predicts divorce?* Hillsdale, NJ: Lawrence Erlbaum.

Gottman, J. M. (1994b). *Why marriages succeed or fail.* New York: Simon and Schuster.

Greenhut, R. (Prod.), & Allen, W. (Dir.). (1986). *Hannah and Her Sisters* [film]. Orion.

Guerin, P. J., Jr., Fay, L. F., Burden, S. L., & Kautto, J. G. (1987). *The evaluation and treatment of marital conflict.* New York: Basic Books.

Heavey, B. (1998, July 19). Under the veil. *The Washington Post,* p. E10.

Hite, S. (1987). *Women and love: A Cultural revolution in progress.* New York: Knopf.

Hoagland, J. (1999, January 14). Infidelity, lies and national security. *The Washington Post.*

Humphrey, F. G. (1987). Treating extramarital relationships in sex and couples therapy. In G. R. Weeks & L. Hof (Eds.), *Integrating sex and marital therapy: A clinical guide.* New York: Brunner/Mazel.

Hunt, M. (1969). *The affair.* New York: World Publishing.

Hunter, M. (1989). *The first step: For people in relationships with sex addicts.* Minneapolis, MN: CompCare.

Huston, T. L., Caughlin, J. P., Houts, R. M., Smith, S. E., & George, L. J. (2001). The connubial crucible: Newlywed years as predictors of marital delight, distress, and divorce. *Journal of Personality and Social Psychology, 80,* 1–16.

Johnson, R. E. (1970). Some correlates of extramarital coitus. *Journal of Marriage and the Family, 32,* 449–456.

Johnston, J. R., & Campbell, L. E. G. (1988). *Impasses of divorce: The dynamics and resolution of family conflict.* New York: Free Press.

Johnston, J. R., & Campbell, L. E. G. (1993). Parent-child relationships in domestic violence families disputing custody. *Family and Conciliation Courts Review, 31*(3), 282–298.

Kalter, N. (1987). Long-term effects of divorce on children: A developmental vulnerability model. *American Journal of Orthopsychiatry, 57,* 587–600.

Karpel, M. (1980). Family secrets: I. Conceptual and ethical issues in the relational context; II. Ethical and practical considerations in therapeutic management. *Family Process, 19,* 295–306.

Kasl, C. D. (1989). *Women, sex, and addiction.* New York: Ticknor & Fields.

Kayser, K. (1993). *When love dies.* New York: Guilford.

Kinsey, A. C., Pomeroy, W. B., & Martin, C. E. (1948). *Sexual behavior in the human male.* Philadelphia: W. B. Saunders.

Kinsey, A. C., Pomeroy, W. B., Martin, C. E., & Gebbhard, P. H. (1953). *Sexual behavior in the human female.* Philadelphia: W. B. Saunders.

Lake, T. (1979). *Affairs: The anatomy of extra-marital relationships.* London: Open Books.

Landers, A. (1989a, November 1). *The Washington Post,* p. D9.

Landers, A. (1989b, September 3). *The Washington Post,* p. F5.

Laumann, E. O., Gagnon, J. H., Michael, R. T., & Michaels, S. (1994). *The social organization of sexuality.* Chicago: University of Chicago Press.

Lawson, A. (1988). *Adultery: An analysis of love and betrayal.* New York: Basic.

Lehman, E. (Prod.), & Nichols, M. (Dir.). (1966). *Who's Afraid of Virginia Wolf?* [film]. Warner Bros.

Lerner, H. G. (1993). *The dance of deception.* New York: HarperCollins.

Lerner, H. G. (1989). *The dance of intimacy.* New York: Harper and Row.

Lewis, T., Amini, F., & Lannon, R. (2000). *A general theory of love.* New York: Random House.

Lobsenz, N. (1985, September 1). How to make a second marriage work. *Parade,* p. 12.

Lyne, A. (Dir.), Jaffe, S., & Lansing, S. (Prods.). (1987). *Fatal Attraction* [film]. Paramount.

Mace, D., & Mace, V. (1959). *Marriage east and west.* Garden City, NY: Dolphin Books.

Mann, J. (1986, June 27). Children coping with divorce. *The Washington Post,* p. B3.

Mann, J. (1998, August 26). What has Clinton wrought? 4 women reflect. *The Washington Post,* p. D14.

Mantegazza, P. (1935). *The sexual relations of mankind.* New York: Eugenics.

McGoldrick, M., Gerson, R., & Shellenberger, S. (1999). *Genograms: Assessment and interventions* (2nd ed.). New York: Norton.

Meloy, J. R. (1992). *Violent attachments.* Northvale, NJ: Jason Aronson.

Morin, R. (1994, March 6). How to lie with statistics: Adultery. *The Washington Post.*

Murstein, B. I. (1974). *Love, sex, and marriage through the ages.* New York: Springer.

Nichols, M. (Dir. and Prod.). (1986). *Heartburn* [film]. Paramount.

Norton, A. J., & Miller, L. F. (1992). *Marriage, divorce and remarriage in the 1990's.* Current Population Reports #P23-180. Bureau of the Census, U.S. Department of Commerce.

Orford, J. (1985). *Excessive appetites.* Chichester, NY: John Wiley & Sons.

Peck, B. B. (1975). Therapeutic handling of marital infidelity, *Journal of Family Counseling, 3,* 52–58.

Pittman, F. (1989). *Private lies.* New York: Norton.

Quinn, S. (1987, May 10). The wife. *The Washington Post,* pp. B1, B4.

Raffel, L. (1999). *Should I stay or go?* Lincolnwood, IL: Contemporary Books.

Rasche, C. E. (1993). "Given" reasons for violence in intimate relationships. In A. Wilson (Ed.), *Homicide: The victim/offender connection* (pp. 75–100). Cincinnatti, OH: Anderson.

Reibstein, J. (1990) Parental affairs and the adolescent child: A structural, life-cycle issue. Unpublished manuscript.

Reibstein, J., & Richards, M. (1993). *Sexual arrangements: Marriage and the temptation of infidelity.* New York: Charles Scribner's Sons.

Ricci, I. (1997). *Mom's house, dad's house: Making two homes for your child* (2nd ed.). New York: Fireside.

Richardson, L. (1985). *The new other woman.* New York: Free Press.

Richardson, L. (1986). Another world. *Psychology Today, 20*(2), 23–27.

Richardson, L. (1988). Secrecy and status: the social construction of forbidden relationships. *American Sociological Review, 53,* 209–219.

Rosenbaum, M., & Bennett, B. (1986). Homicide and depression. *American Journal of Psychiatry, 143,* 357–370.

Ross, S. (1988). *Fall from grace.* New York: Ballantine.

Salovey, P., & Rodin, J. (1985). The heart of jealousy. *Psychology Today, 19*(9), 22–25, 29–29.

Scarf, M. 1987. *Intimate partners.* New York: Random House.

Schlossberger, E., & Hecker, L. (1996). HIV and family therapists' duty to warn: A legal and ethical analysis *Journal of Marital and Family Therapy, 22*(1), 27–40.

Schneider, J. P. (1988). *Back from betrayal: Recovering from his affairs.* San Francisco: Harper/Hazelden.

Shearer, L. (1987, December 6). Intelligence report. *Parade,* 19.

Sheehy, G. (1987, September). The Road to Bimini. *Vanity Fair,* 131–139, 188–194.

Sheehy, G. (1999, November 7). Hillary's choice. *Parade,* 4–6.

Simmel, G. (1950). *Sociology of Georg Simmel.* New York: Free Press. (Original work published 1902–1903)

Smedes, L. B. (1996). *The art of forgiving.* New York: Ballantine.

Specter, M. (1990, February 25). What's America doing in bed? *The Washington Post,* p. B1.

Spring, J. A. (1996). *After the affair.* New York: HarperCollins.

Stapen, C. H. (1989, August 31). To tell the truth. *The Washington Post,* p. D5.

Strean, H. S. (1980). *The extramarital affair.* New York: Free Press.

Streitfeld, D. (1987, November 10). Shere Hite and the trouble with numbers. *The Washington Post,* pp. B1, B4.

Sullivan, K. (1997, December 22). Japanese director commits suicide. *The Washington Post,* p. C1.

Taibbi, R. (1983). Handling extramarital affairs in clinical treatment. *Social Casework, 64,* 200–204.

Tarasoff v. Regents of the University of California. (1976). 17 Cal. 3d 425, 551 p. 2d 334.

Thompson, A. P. (1983). Extramarital sex: A review of the research literature. *The Journal of Sex Research, 19*(1), 1–22.

Thompson, A. P. (1984). Emotional and sexual components of extramarital relations. *Journal of Marriage and the Family, 46,* 35–42.

Torpey, R. (1996, October 18). Managing aggression. Presentation sponsored by Central Maryland Catholic Charities, Emmitsburg, MD.

Trueheart, C. (1989, September 5). The man who up and left. *The Washington Post,* pp. C1–C2.

Tsytsarev, S. V., & Grodnitzky, G. R. (1995). Anger and criminality. In Howard Kassinove (Ed.), *Anger disorders: definition, diagnosis, and treatment* (pp. 91–108). Washington, DC: Taylor & Francis.

U.S. Bureau of the Census. (1998, March). Marital Status and Living Arrangements (update). Current Population Reports, p. iv. Author.

U.S. Bureau of the Census. (2001). National estimates: Annual population estimates by age group and sex, selected years 1990 to 2000.

VandeCreek, L., & Knapp, S. (1989, 1993). *Tarasoff and beyond: Legal and clinical considerations in the treatment of life-endangering patients* (Rev. ed.). Sarasota, FL: Professional Resource.

Vaughan, P. (1998). *The monogamy myth* (Rev. ed.). New York: Newmarket.

Wallace, A. (1990, June 3). Till murder do us part. *LA Times Magazine,* p.14.

Squires, S. (1985, May 15). Divorce after a decade. *The Washington Post,* Health, p. 10.

Wallerstein, J. S., & Kelly, J. B. (1980). *Surviving the breakup.* New York: Basic.

Welter-Enderlin, R. (1993). Secrets of couples and couples' therapy. In E. Imber-Black (Ed.), *Secrets in family and family therapy* (pp. 47–65). New York: W. W. Norton.

Westfall, A. (1989). Extramarital sex: The treatment of the couple. In G. R. Weeks (Ed.), *Treating Couples* (pp. 163–190). New York: Brunner/Mazel.

Williams, P. (1988, June 1). A double life on the road. *The Washington Post,* pp. C1–C3.

Yalom, I. D. (1975). *The theory and practice of group psychotherapy.* New York: Basic.

Yardley, J. (1988, October 31). The coverage is a scandal!. *The Washington Post,* p. D2.

Yen, M. (1989, April 10). Refusal to jail immigrant who killed wife stirs outrage. *The Washington Post.*

Yen, M. (1989, September 9). Bakker aides sentenced to 17 years. *The Washington Post,* pp. C1, C11.

INDEX

ABOUT THE AUTHOR

Emily M. Brown, LCSW, is Director of Key Bridge Therapy & Mediation Center in Arlington, Virginia. She works with couples, individuals, and families regarding the underlying issues in marriage, divorce, and betrayal. Throughout the United States and in Europe she offers workshops for professionals on treating the issues associated with extramarital affairs and other relationship issues. Her recent book, *Affairs: Working Through the Repercussions of Infidelity,* is written for the general public. She has also written a variety of articles for professionals on affairs, divorce, and divorce mediation and has appeared on a variety of radio and television programs on those subjects.

LINCOLN CHRISTIAN UNIVERSITY

126068